John Zinkin and Christopher Bennett

The Principles and Practice of Effective Leadership

John Zinkin and Christopher Bennett

The Principles and Practice of Effective Leadership

—

DE GRUYTER

ISBN 978-3-11-070780-9
e-ISBN (PDF) 978-3-11-070787-8
e-ISBN (EPUB) 978-3-11-070806-6

Library of Congress Control Number: 2021937382

Bibliographic information published by the Deutsche Nationalbibliothek
The Deutsche Nationalbibliothek lists this publication in the Deutsche Nationalbibliografie;
detailed bibliographic data are available on the Internet at http://dnb.dnb.de.

© 2021 Walter de Gruyter GmbH, Berlin/Boston
Cover image: Gettyimages/Photos.com
Typesetting: Integra Software Services Pvt. Ltd.
Printing and binding: CPI books GmbH, Leck

www.degruyter.com

Advance Praise for *The Principles and Practice of Effective Leadership*

"This book should be read by all aspiring leaders, and those already in a leadership position.

For middle managers it offers a seminal document upon which other books and courses can build, and for those already in positions of leadership it will provide a context through which 'good leadership', or 'leadership for good' may be challenged and re-evaluated.

The book contextualizes leadership through the evaluation of three historic leaders: Elizabeth Tudor, Napoleon Bonaparte and Mustafa Kemal Atatürk. It is an inspired approach and allows for the analysis to be distilled to its essence without any concession or overlay of contemporary politics, management trends and fashions, or the impact of current communications and technology. John Zinkin and Chris Bennett have done a brilliant job of condensing centuries of history through the filter of leadership whilst remaining valid and coherent.

The book concludes with the essential templates of an actionable leadership development structure. None of which should be omitted from any organisation's portfolio of leadership development tools. I found myself challenging my pre-conceptions of political and business leaders I have worked with or around as well as my more modest personal experience in leadership. In that respect it is an exceptional document and should be essential reading for all existing and aspiring leaders."

Tony Heneberry, *Founder, CEO Solutions*

"The distinction and interplay between management and leadership is a critical one for academics and practitioners in the real world. How these two concepts can work together or are possibly the same thing can make all the difference to organizations and their performance and the individual's productivity, effectiveness and self-esteem. John Zinkin and Chris Bennett have explored this and other important concepts in this book which can be used for teaching and a provocative series of discussions in the classroom and the boardroom. They are to be congratulated."

John H. C. Colvin *FAICD, Director of the BoardWalk Consultancy,*
Chief Executive Officer and Managing Director of the
Australian Institute of Company Directors (2008–2015).

"There is often a confusion about the role of managerial and leadership roles in the running of organisations which can lead to suboptimal corporate governance. John Zinkin and Chris Bennett explore the relationship between the two concepts using examples from history in this new book that challenges conventional assumptions. The book will be of interest to practitioners and academics and provides a good

https://doi.org/10.1515/9783110707878-202

starting point for serious conversations about how effective corporate governance can be achieved."
Dr Roger Barker, *Director of Policy and Corporate Governance at*
The Institute of Directors (UK)

"The central propositions in the book are striking and original – that leadership is morally neutral, that leadership is managerial, that leadership techniques can be learnt and that leadership and management as well as strategy and tactics exist on a continuum. These propositions are often markedly different from much of what is set out in the business literature. In upholding the proposition that effective leadership is a morally neutral activity that can be learned, the authors are in sync with some of the world's great thinkers such as Machiavelli and Bertrand Russell.

I recommend this provocative and stimulating book unreservedly as a must read for all executives and decision makers, both in the private and public sector."
Dato Dr. R. Thillainathan, *Member of the Board of*
Directors of Genting Berhad, Public Investment Bank Berhad,
and IDEAS Policy Research Berhad

"Taking the long view gives a very different perspective from close-up examination of a topic. This book includes a fresh analysis comparing the leadership impacts of three people who lived 400, 200 and 100 years ago – sufficient time to understand their legacies. Each of them initiated long-lasting changes in their respective countries – Elizabeth I launching Britain on its path to a global empire, Napoleon Bonaparte changing the structure of French society – and indeed of many other countries in and beyond Europe – and Mustafa Kemal Atatürk who founded modern Turkey.

This book gives a unique, century-spanning perspective, but also drills down to specific incidents, actions and outcomes. Importantly, the book also considers the ethical and unethical aspects of their leadership styles. This book helps us to grapple with the question of leadership legacy within the context of both ethical and unethical behaviour – a key topic in the current, highly transparent 2020s world where unethical behaviours are called out and amplified instantaneously, whereas the outcomes of wise leadership decisions often take years, decades or centuries to be revealed."
Edward Clayton, *Lead Advisory Partner, Capital Projects &*
Infrastructure, PwC Malaysia & Vietnam

"Books on leadership tend to fall into three broad categories – biographies that put the leader in the context of their time and reports on the choices they made, analytical deconstructions of the forms of leadership and experiential syntheses of being a leader. While all are insightful ways to think about leaders and leadership, these genres leave readers to make what they can of how these perspectives merge to create a leader.

In *The Principles and Practice of Effective Leadership* John Zinkin and Chris Bennett provide that much needed synthesis. Through the lived experiences of three of history's most famous leaders Zinkin and Bennett show us how they understood the challenges of their time and led their people as individuals with great strengths and real weaknesses. They then lead us through a detailed deconstruction of their leadership that contrasts the decisions they made and why they made them. In a time when uncertainty and complexity are the norm, this is a synthesis that helps us to better understand how people from very different times and very different circumstances build their leadership to navigate uncertainty and complexity."

Dr Gary Dirks, *Senior Director of the Julie Ann Wrigley Global Futures Laboratory and Lightworks®, Arizona State University*

"John Zinkin and Chris Bennett are authorities in the field of leadership. In their *The Principles and Practice of Effective Leadership*, they have taken on the important subject of leadership, integrated it with the field of ethics, and put it in a powerful framework of principles for effective leadership that are easy to understand and ready to apply. Of the many books on leadership I have read, John Zinkin's and Chris Bennett's book is by far the most comprehensive, interesting, insightful and inspiring text. Their detailed applications of ethical leadership principles and theories are very well analyzed, carefully proposed and, in my view, totally relevant. The need for such a review of leadership was long overdue and long awaited.

The Principles and Practice of Effective Leadership will be one of the key readings for all my future students, and I recommend it to be used widely by educators and executives to have better chances to succeed in today's highly competitive global business environment."

Cosimo Faiello, *Associate Professor, Department of Electrical, Electronic and Computer Engineering, The University of Western Australia*

"This is a modern, innovative and refreshing contribution to management and leadership literature. It's a must read for those interested in these important and central topics."

John Rudd, *Professor of Marketing and Head of Marketing Group, Warwick Business School*

Acknowledgments

We are grateful to a number of people whose guidance helped us articulate and develop our thinking in writing this book. We are especially grateful to Dr Gary Dirks for his discussions on the role of collectives, neuroscience, and the focus of the book as we developed it, to Professor John Rudd for keeping us on the straight and narrow of logic and to Professor Sander Van Der Leeuw for his anthropological insights, to Edward Clayton and Dr Dato Thillainathan for their input on effective and ethical decision-making, to John Colvin and Dr Roger Barker for their practical insights, to Tony Heneberry for his help in clarifying our thinking about our target audience, and to Associate Professor Cosimo Faiello and Kate Addison for their different generational perspectives. If we have misunderstood or misrepresented their ideas, the fault is entirely ours.

We are grateful to Mary Sudul, our copy editor, whose meticulous attention to detail and care in improving the text, as always, has made the book better. We would like to thank Jaya Dalal for her excellent coordination of production, as always, and Nijandhanraj for final production.

John Zinkin and Christopher Bennett
Kuala Lumpur
May 2021

https://doi.org/10.1515/9783110707878-203

Contents

Introduction

We believe the dichotomy between *leaders* and *managers* described in much business literature fails to recognize how the two roles overlap. "Leadership" is mainly considered to be the ability of an individual to create a superordinate goal for a group and communicate it in a compelling way to "followers." "Management" is seen as the organization and control of resources to achieve a particular goal. They are both skills needed by those in charge of running organizations effectively. Leaders make things happen through other people. So do managers. Leaders must be able to define the vision, mission, and values of their organizations and communicate these compellingly to their followers. Managers must do the same in their areas of responsibility – itself an act of leadership. Thus, leadership and management belong on a continuum of skills.

The view that leaders "do the right thing," whereas managers "do things right"[1] emphasizes that leaders concern themselves with strategy, while managers deal with the resulting tactics and that these are in some way separate. However, feasible strategies are determined by tactical considerations; and appropriate tactics are determined by strategic objectives. Strategy and tactics exist on a continuum; separated only by the time span over which they operate. Their separation is a convenience for analysts and facilitates the allocation of responsibilities. Consequently, we believe the usual distinction is misleading and that effective leadership inevitably incorporates effective management, and vice versa.

Our central proposition is that leadership techniques are morally neutral. We recognize that history has more bad people than good as great leaders. It is unfortunate, but true. The great morally uplifting leaders are so few they probably can be counted on the fingers of two hands. Moreover, *they succeeded because their ideas were powerful;* their teachings were memes – "ideological viruses" that spread independently of the survival of their hosts, mutating just like biological ones do. For example, Jesus' teachings bear little resemblance to what became of Christianity and Christianity's internecine warfare over which version was the truth (or the Buddha's to Buddhism). The same is true of Islam with its Sunni-Shia, Sunni-Ahmadiyya splits; and the different murderous interpretations of Sunni thinking reflected in Al-Qaeda, Daesh (Islamic State), and Al Shabab.

We explain what effective leadership "is" and that there are techniques that can be learned to make leaders more effective. Like all techniques, they are morally neutral. What matters is how they are applied. This means that what matters for effectiveness is not the same as what matters for moral goodness in leadership. The distinction comes from the objectives and the way in which leaders make their decisions.

We conclude that effective leadership depends on the application of morally neutral techniques, but show that leaders who had morally good objectives created longer lasting legacies. The deployment of leadership techniques for "evil" ends can be effective in the short term; but longer-term lack of good moral content undermines

https://doi.org/10.1515/9783110707878-205

achievements. That is why the most important chapter in our book is the last one: how to make right-good decisions applying six ethical approaches, while making use of all the morally neutral techniques we discuss in earlier chapters.

Like Bertrand Russell, we believe effective leadership is a morally neutral activity that can be learned:

> If there is a science of [leadership] success, it can be studied just as well in the successes of the wicked as in those of the good – indeed better, since the examples of successful sinners are more numerous than those of successful saints. But the science, once established will be just as useful to the saint as to the sinner. *For the saint, if he concerns himself with politics, must wish, just as the sinner does, to achieve success.*[2]   [Emphasis ours]

We hope to demonstrate this in the book, which is divided into three parts.

Part 1: Lessons from History

In Part 1, we suggest there are universal but morally neutral techniques for effective leadership. We show that the effectiveness of particular leadership techniques depends on the context in which they are practiced. We argue that correct context identification, and selection of leadership techniques deployed in response, determine the effectiveness of leaders. We reconcile the two apparently contradictory positions of Machiavelli, and illustrate our proposition, by briefly examining the careers of three great historical leaders. We chose leaders from history rather than current leaders because we believe distance from events is important to be able to assess the lasting lessons to be learned from their successes and failures and their remarkable understanding of complexity, intellectual curiosity, and mastery of detail. They were not guilty of oversimplification in the face of complicated circumstances, but were able to adhere to a long-term vision of the kind of society they wanted to create. We chose Elizabeth Tudor, Napoleon, and Atatürk.

Chapter 1, Leadership is Morally Neutral, makes the case that leadership is morally neutral and contextual; distinguishes between purpose, power and personality; and explores why leaders have followers and compares different styles of leadership. The chapter revisits Machiavelli's ideas in *The Prince* and *The Discourses on Livy* to reconcile the apparent contradictions between the two books. We conclude that the apparent disagreement between the two books is the result of differences in context, purpose and result.

Chapter 2, Elizabeth Tudor, briefly covers the career of a remarkable woman and her success in turning England from an impoverished, divided, and second-tier nation in the affairs of Europe into a wealthy, successful, and confident nation overcoming the threats posed by France, Spain, and Scotland to become a leading European power at the dawn of its global adventure, and changing global geopolitics as a result.

Chapter 3, Napoleon Bonaparte, briefly discusses the career of a Corsican outsider who saved the French Revolution and laid the foundations of modern France out of the ruins of its "Ancien Regime." Despite his ultimate downfall, caused by excessive ambition and lust for glory, he left a lasting legacy that changed Europe and the US as a result of his courage, military genius, and ability to establish institutions needed for modern nation states.

Chapter 4, Mustafa Kemal Atatürk, briefly examines the career of Mustafa Kemal who played a critical part in the ANZAC defeat at Gallipoli. As commander in chief of the Turkish Nationalist forces defending Turkey from dismemberment by the victorious Allies after World War I, he beat them decisively and negotiated a favorable peace. He created a modern Turkish nation out of the ruins of the Ottoman Empire, turning it into a secular, western-facing country with its own Turkish identity where none had existed before.

Chapter 5, Leadership Lessons from History, compares the performances of Elizabeth Tudor, Napoleon, and Atatürk to see what can be learned based on the characteristics of ethical/unethical and effective/ineffective leaders and how they compare with Machiavelli's definition of effective leadership discussed in Chapter 1. It concludes that the most important factor in being an admired leader is operational effectiveness (competence).

Part 2: Leadership *Is* Managerial

In **Chapter 6, Managerial Leadership**, we explain why leadership cannot be separated from effective management and conclude that leadership is managerial, and best encapsulated in the concept of "wayfinding." We look at the role of leaders in setting strategy and the relationship with tactics, using sailing as a metaphor for what we can learn from Polynesian "wayfinding." We then discuss the role of leadership in dealing with the distinct external and internal constraints organizations face.

Part 3: Leadership Techniques

In Part 3, we discuss the techniques "wayfinders" can learn to be both effective and ethical.

Chapter 7, Dealing with Volatility, Uncertainty, Complexity, and Ambiguity, explores how "wayfinders" need to recognize that a reactive approach to volatility, uncertainty, complexity, and ambiguity (VUCA 1.0) affects decision-making and why they need to adopt a proactive approach (VUCA 2.0).

Chapter 8, Reconciling VUCA with the Need for Simplicity, explores the role of evolution and neuroscience in the ways people process information, make decisions, and communicate; and shows how "wayfinders" can harness them to increase their effectiveness, as both leaders and managers, by reconciling approaches to VUCA with the need to keep things simple.

Chapter 9, Combining Two Leadership Models with Managerial Skills, explains why leadership effectiveness depends on "wayfinders" reconciling the dominance and prestige models of leadership; and having the appropriate suite of managerial skills to ensure that their imagined futures are translated into reality.

Chapter 10, Communicating Effectively, discusses effective communication by understanding the importance of "Three As" (audience, angle, and attitude); how "Three Rs" (reviewing, recognizing, and rewarding performance) signal behavioral expectations; and how "Four Cs" (clarity, consistency, coherence, and codes of conduct) clarify organizational purpose, values, and expected behavior.

Chapter 11, Ethical and Effective Decision-Making, explores the impact of duty-based and consequential ethics on decision-making; and develops a simple and practical framework for making right-good decisions by combining virtue ethics, effectiveness, mutuality, predictability, utility, and personalistic ethics to provide a six-stage decision making process. It shows how the "Five P" performance framework helps to cross-check that ethical considerations are used when deciding strategy.

References

1 Pascale, R. (1990), *Managing on the Edge* (New York: Simon and Schuster).
2 Russell, B. (1947), *A History of Western Philosophy* (London: George Allen and Unwin), p. 531.

Part 1: **Lessons from History**

Universal but morally neutral techniques exist for effective leadership, but the effectiveness of particular leadership techniques depends on the context in which they are practiced. The correct context identification, and selection of leadership techniques deployed in response, determine the effectiveness of leaders.

In order to reconcile the two apparently contradictory positions of Machiavelli, and illustrate this proposition, we briefly examine the careers of three great historical leaders: Elizabeth Tudor, Napoleon Bonaparte, and Atatürk.

We chose these leaders from history rather than current leaders because we believe temporal distance from events is important to be able to assess the lasting lessons from their successes and failures and their remarkable understanding of complexity, intellectual curiosity, and mastery of detail. They were not guilty of oversimplification in the face of complicated circumstances, but were able to adhere to a long-term vision of the kind of society each wanted to create.

https://doi.org/10.1515/9783110707878-001

Chapter 1
Leadership is Morally Neutral

Throughout history, followers of certain leaders have been prepared to die to achieve what was asked of them. Effective leaders persuade their followers to change the world or to resist change through good timing, a strong sense of purpose, exceptional ability, communicating their vision, and influencing their followers' values.

Some modern literature on leadership defines "leadership" as "morally good leadership" and redefines leadership to achieve immoral or amoral ends as "power wielding" instead.

> Leaders are individuals who exercise authority and exert power. They get other people to go along, to follow. Inspiration is part of the appeal to others, *but, as Freud insisted, so are fear, coercion, and conformity.* To pretend leaders are not power wielders – a pretence which Barbara Kellerman argued was embraced by a "tacit alliance" among theoreticians, practitioners, researchers, educators, consultants, and trainers – was to "whistle in the dark" . . . *Freud, not Carlyle, speaks to our contemporary awareness of . . . the "dark side" of leadership.*[1]   [Emphases ours]

Only considering leadership deployed for good purposes as "leadership" is problematic; it confuses, misleads, and is a barrier to understanding:[2]

1. **Confusing:** For most people, "leader" refers to "any individual who uses power, authority and influence to get others to go along."[3] Hitler, Stalin, and Mao are commonly called "leaders" and not "power wielders."

2. **Misleading:** The distinction is false because:

> Leadership can be considered the exercise of influence, or a power relation, or an instrument of goal achievement, or a differentiated role . . . Those definitions are value-free and there is no good reason to distinguish "leaders" and "power-wielders"; to compare them is not to compare apples and oranges, but apples and apples.[4]

3. **Barrier to understanding:** "We need to learn about good leadership by studying both what makes good leaders and what makes bad leaders so that we can avoid their mistakes . . ."[5]

Conflating three ingredients of leadership: *Power* (how they acquire and maintain their positions); *personality* (how they energize followers), and *purpose* (what leaders try to achieve); makes understanding the whole process difficult.

Leaders can be divided into those with morally "good" purposes and those with "bad" purposes. The ways they achieved, maintained, and used their power can be characterized as morally "good" or "bad"; and as having "positive" or "negative" impacts depending on subjective judgments. Different individuals reach different conclusions about the "goodness" or "wickedness" of the purposes of leaders, based on their own values and beliefs.

https://doi.org/10.1515/9783110707878-002

Historically, many leaders regarded as being great and effective were considered to have "evil" purposes; while some whose purposes are considered to have been "good," achieved and maintained power in morally unacceptable ways – or were not good people to be around.

> Historically, political theorists have been far more interested in the question of how to control the proclivities of bad leaders than in the question of how to promote the virtues of good ones. Influenced by religious traditions that focused on good and evil, and often personally scarred by war and disorder, the best political thinkers have had a rather jaundiced view of human nature.[6]

We suggest that effective leadership tools and techniques are morally neutral and are best considered separately from assessing morality – which involves subjective judgments about the ends sought. This is discussed further in the concluding chapter of this book.

Advice from the Ancients

The conflation of leadership techniques with "morally good" leadership has a long history. Many ancient philosophers believed leaders should be "virtuous" in what they aspired to achieve and did not see the tools and techniques of leadership as distinct from the purposes to which they were directed.

Confucius[i] advised rulers to be "benevolent" and "virtuous":

> He who rules by virtue is like the polestar, which remains unmoving in its mansion while all the others revolve respectfully around it.[7]

When asked how rulers should rule, Confucius replied:

> Approach them with dignity and they will be respectful. Be yourself a good son and a kind father and they will be loyal. Raise the good and train the incompetent, and they will be zealous.[8]

Lao Tzu,[ii] Confucius' contemporary, recognized there were bad leaders as well as good ones, but still did not separate the means and ends of leadership. He said:

> A leader is best when people barely know he exists, not so good when people obey and acclaim him, worst when they despise him. But of a good leader, who talks little, when his work is done, his aim fulfilled, they will say, "We did this ourselves."[9]

---

i Confucius (551 BCE–479 BCE).
ii Lao Tzu (6th century BCE).

Plato[iii] writing in *The Republic*, 100 years after Confucius and Lao Tzu, also conflated "morally good" and "effective" leadership but partially addressed the context of leadership. He set out four leadership contexts, each driven by a different virtue, shown in Table 1.1.

Table 1.1: Plato's Four Leadership Contexts.

Leadership Context	Aspect of the Soul Involved	Driving Force	Virtues Needed
Philosopher Kings	Logos (Reason)	Philosophy: Love of learning	Wisdom: Knowledge of what is best for each part as well as the whole
Guardians	Thymos (Emotion)	Love of honor, victory, and reputation	Courage: Preservation of true beliefs about pain, pleasure, and fear
Harmony between philosopher kings, guardians, and producers	Eros (Material Desires) and Thymos working in harmony with Logos	Love of money and all the things it buys to satisfy appetites	Temperance: All agree to follow the better part over the interest of the worse part
The entire soul follows the philosophic part, with each doing its own part and enjoying its own pleasures	Each of the three groups working on achieving their own ends, without meddling	Subordination to Logos: All parts doing their own work and not overthrowing Logos	Justice: The power of each part doing its own specialized work

Source: Based on Bauman, D. C. (2018), "Plato on Virtuous Leadership: An Ancient Model for Modern Business," *Business Ethics Quarterly*, Volume 28, Issue 3, pp. 251–274, https://www.cambridge.org/core/journals/business-ethics-quarterly/article/plato-on-virtuous-leadership-an-ancient-model-for-modern-business/06C603D9B188138E321BE8249AA55A08/core-reader, accessed on April 24, 2020.

Plato went on to describe five types of leader, shown in Table 1.2.

Plato conflates "effective" and "morally good"; but differs from Confucius and Lao Tzu by recognizing five types of ruler, *suitable for different political contexts, with different purposes and virtues.*

Kautilya,[iv] a hundred years after Plato, author of the *Arthashastra*, a manual on government for India's Mauryan Dynasty (contemporaries of Alexander the Great) also

---

iii Plato (428/7 BCE–348/7 BCE).
iv Kautilya (375 BCE–283 BCE).

Table 1.2: Plato's Five Types of Leader.

Type of Leader	Dominant Soul Part	Dominant Virtues	Ultimate Purpose
Philosopher	Logos (Reason)	Wisdom	Seeking truth/living a good and fine life
Timocratic	Thymos (Emotion)	Courage	Honor and victory
Oligarchic	Eros (Material Desires) with some Thymos	Temperance limited by courage	Wealth and making money
Democratic	Eros with limits on lawless desires	Limited temperance	Freedom with few limits
Tyrant	Eros without limits on lawless desires	None	Power and satisfying lusts

Source: Based on Bauman, D. C. (2018), "Plato on Virtuous Leadership: An Ancient Model for Modern Business," *Business Ethics Quarterly*, Volume 28, Issue 3, pp.251–274, https://www.cambridge.org/core/journals/business-ethics-quarterly/article/plato-on-virtuous-leadership-an-ancient-model-for-modern-business/06C603D9B188138E321BE8249AA55A08/core-reader, accessed on April 24, 2020.

recognized the contextual nature of leadership and, while still being concerned with morality, advised:

> None can hide their weakness from relatives. Relatives can also be a source of weakness. He who is with limitations searches for other's limitations.
> Politics is a place where there are neither enemies nor friends – for long . . . You've no great friend, but yourself . . . You are your worst enemy, too.[10]

Marcus Aurelius,[v] Roman Emperor in the 2nd century CE, advised against idealism, and recommended a rational, contextualist approach:

> That men of a certain type should behave as they do is inevitable. To wish it otherwise were to wish the fig-tree would not yield its juice. In any case, remember that in a very little while both you and he will be dead, and your very names will quickly be forgotten.[11]

> If anyone can show me, and prove to me, that I am wrong in thought or deed, I will gladly change. I seek the truth, which never yet hurt anybody. It is only persistence in self-delusion and ignorance which does harm.[12]

> Adapt yourself to the environment in which your lot has been cast, and show true love to the fellow-mortals with whom destiny has surrounded you.[13]

---

v Marcus Aurelius (CE 121–180).

We shrink from change; yet is there anything that can come into being without it? What does Nature hold dearer or more proper to herself? Could you have a hot bath unless the firewood underwent some change? Could you be nourished if the food suffered no change? Is it possible for any useful thing to be achieved without change? Do you not see, then, that change in yourself is of the same order, and no less necessary to Nature?[14]

Sejong the Great,[vi] of the Korean Joseon dynasty, recognizing that policy should be dictated by real world contextual factors, instructed his subjects in 1425 CE to "speak truth to power":

I am neither virtuous, nor skilful at governing. There will definitely be times when I do not act upon the heavens' wishes. So, look hard for my flaws and make me answer to their reprimands.[15]

Machiavelli's Insight

In the 16th century CE, Machiavelli, perhaps influenced by the beginning of the scientific revolution, approached leadership differently from preceding writers. He was not a philosopher advocating an ideal. Instead, he attempted a sociological analysis of leadership behavior,[16] examining how leaders behaved in practice; what they had tried to achieve; and why they failed or succeeded. His priority was not how a leader "ought" to behave but, rather, what was effective in different contexts.

In *The Discourses*[17] he focused on what effective leaders had done in the past and why they had done it. In *The Prince*[18] he contrasted the behavior of past leaders with that of leaders of contemporary states in Italy. He concluded that the techniques of effective leadership were morally neutral; to be assessed by results rather than intentions. He analyzed the contextual conditions under which rulers acquired power, and did not impose a utopian, "one size fits all" description. His disdain for "morally pure" leaders, like the Florentine monk Savonarola[vii] who was overthrown because he was unwilling to make the compromises necessary for staying in power,[19] was a novel concept.

For Machiavelli, understanding the context in which the political leader operated was essential, in contrast to Aristotle's normative approach to virtuous leadership.

---

vi Sejong the Great (1397–1450), fourth king of the Joseon dynasty and inventor of the Korean alphabet.
vii Girolamo Savonarola (1452–1498) was a Dominican monk and Puritan fanatic who became the moral dictator of Florence in 1494 when the Medici were temporarily exiled. "A visionary, prophet and formidably effective hellfire preacher, obsessed with human wickedness and convinced that the wrath of God was about to fall upon the earth, he detested practically every form of pleasure and relaxation . . ."
Cavendish, R. (1998), "Execution of Girolamo Savonarola," *History Today,* Volume 48, Issue 5, May 1998, https://www.historytoday.com/archive/months-past/execution-girolamo-savonarola, accessed on May 17, 2020.

Machiavelli distinguished between six types of government in a cycle of renewal and decline (perhaps drawing on the ideas of the Greek historian Polybius[viii]); and on whether the ruler was acquiring power in an insecure environment or was an established ruler in a secure polity. The context and conditions determined what the ruler could aspire to do and how to achieve it.

Six Types of Government

In *The Discourses*, Machiavelli described six governmental types[ix] – three effective and three ineffective:

> Others – and with better judgment many think – say that there are six types of government, of which three are very bad, and three good in themselves but easily become corrupt, so that they too must be classed as pernicious . . . For Principality easily becomes Tyranny. From Aristocracy the transition to Oligarchy is an easy one. Democracy is without difficulty converted into Anarchy. So that if anyone who is organizing a commonwealth sets up one of the first three forms of government, he sets up what will last but for a while . . .[20]

He described an original state of nature, though he did not use the term, that is similar to that described by Hobbes in *Leviathan*:[21]

> For in the beginning of the world, when its inhabitants were few, they lived for a while scattered like the beasts. Then with the multiplication of their offspring they drew together and, in order the better to be able to defend themselves, began to look about for a man stronger and more courageous than the rest, made him their head, and obeyed him.[22]

In such conditions, the ruler needed to be a warrior, braver and stronger than the rest to justify his following. As stability was established, the polity needed to have laws and a justice system. This led to a different way of choosing rulers and the qualities they needed:

> When later on they had to choose a prince, they did not have recourse to the boldest as formerly, but to one who excelled in prudence and justice.[23]

Arguing from the establishment of Rome with its rise of hereditary kings, who began to abuse their power, Machiavelli continued:

> . . . [hereditary princes] considered that princes have nought else to do but to surpass other men in extravagance, lasciviousness, and every other form of licentiousness. With the result the prince came to be hated, and, since he was hated, came to be afraid, and from fear soon passed to offensive action, which quickly brought about a tyranny.[24]

---

viii Polybius (c200–118 BCE).

ix   The cycle comprises Principality (monarchy) – rule by one; Aristocracy – rule by the best; Oligarchy – rule by the few; Tyranny – rule by a tyrant; Democracy – rule by the people; and Anarchy – rule by none, leading back to monarchy.

Machiavelli agreed with Aristotle that *tyranny* is nearly the worst sort of government (other than anarchy) because of its ineffectiveness and that tyrants should be resisted. The paranoia of tyrants led to unjustified purges of the tyrants' supporters; in turn leading to plots backed by the masses and the formation of *aristocracies* to replace tyrants (e.g., Rome's ejection of Tarquin) because the rebels were perceived as noble and generous:

> . . . conspicuous for their liberality, magnanimity, wealth and ability, for such men could not stand the dishonourable life the prince was leading.[25]

Over time, the descendants of the original aristocrats reverted to avarice to become an *oligarchy*.[26] Again, excesses led to the masses overthrowing them and replacing them with *democracy*. In time democracy declined into *anarchy*, to be finally replaced by a *principality* to bring order to chaos[27] – restarting the cycle.

Machiavelli's solution to the problem of the cycle was to create a system, incorporating the three good types of government in the same state to ensure that principality (king), aristocracy (barons), and democracy (bourgeoisie) kept each other in check. This was developed by Lycurgus[x] for Sparta where it endured for 800 years.[28] Rome did the same with the two consuls (replacing the king), the Senate (representing the aristocracy), and the tribunes (representing the people);[29] and this approach was deployed by France in Machiavelli's time, which he admired.[xi] In the case of Rome, he wrote:

> And so favoured was it by fortune that, though the transition from Monarchy to Aristocracy and thence to Democracy, took place by the very stages and for the very reasons laid down earlier . . . none the less the granting of authority to the aristocracy did not abolish altogether the royal estate [the consuls, and in exceptional conditions the dictators], nor was the authority of the aristocracy wholly removed when the populace was granted a share in it. *On the contrary, the blending of these estates made a perfect commonwealth; and . . . it was friction between the plebs and the senate that brought this perfection about . . .*[30]   [Emphasis ours]

---

x Lycurgus (800–730 BCE) "After creating the senate, Lycurgus addressed the question of land ownership. At this time there was an extreme inequality among the Spartans, with most of the wealth and land in the control of only a few. Most of the people felt poor and unhappy. Arrogance and envy, luxury and crime, resulted from this unequal distribution of property. Lycurgus divided the land equally, so that merit – not money – became the only measure of a man's worth. Lycurgus intended to remove any inequalities in ownership of personal property as well as real property, but he realized that it would be too difficult to proceed openly. Therefore, he took an indirect approach. His solution was to ban ownership of any gold or silver, and to allow only money made of iron. The iron coins of Sparta were dipped in vinegar to make the metal brittle and worthless. Merchants laughed at this money because it had no intrinsic value, so imports of luxuries stopped. Robbery and bribery vanished from Sparta instantly." Plutarch, "Lycurgus, The Father of Sparta," https://www.ahistoryofgreece.com/biography/lycurgus.htm, accessed on May 17, 2020.

xi There are important similarities with the American Constitution and the British Parliamentary system.

Machiavelli recognized that states sometimes have to make difficult decisions quickly. He argued that the Roman Republic's unique solution to this problem, the invention of temporary dictatorship, was a key reason for its early success:

> Of Rome's various institutions this [dictator] is one that deserves to be considered . . . *For without such an institution, cities will with difficulty find a way out of abnormal situations. For the institutions normally used by republics are slow in functioning.* No assembly nor magistrate can do everything alone. In many cases they have to consult one another, and to reconcile their diverse views takes time. Where there is question of remedying a situation which will not brook delay, such procedure is most dangerous.[31] [Emphasis ours]

Unlike most commentators who believed the tension between the aristocrats in the Senate and the people was the cause of the end of the Roman republic, Machiavelli argued the opposite,[32] showing that, as is suggested in *The Prince*, he did not think that autocracy was the most effective governmental form:

> . . . in every republic there are two different dispositions, that of the populace and that of the upper class and that *all legislation favourable to liberty is brought about by the clash between them.*[33] [Emphasis ours]

Two Types of Republic

Machiavelli believed that the appropriate type of government is determined by the type of republics the framers of their constitutions wanted to establish, in other words *it depended on context*. He described two types of republic: small and static, exemplified by Sparta and Venice; and large empire-building types, represented by Rome. The former could be ruled effectively by an aristocracy (Sparta) or oligarchy (Venice), while the latter could only be ruled effectively by a tripartite power structure combining prince, aristocrats, and people. *This difference in governance was an inevitable consequence of the long-term ambitions of the respective states.*

Sparta chose to stay small and did so by refusing to admit foreigners. Lycurgus' laws were egalitarian, prescribing equality of property rather than equality of rank. Poverty was shared, the plebeians were not that interested in acquiring power as there were few positions available and nobles did not mistreat the plebeians (the *helots*[xii] did not count). Venice used foreign mercenaries to expand, and did not need a large population to provide soldiers.

> . . . it was necessary for Rome's legislators to do one of two things if Rome was to remain tranquil like the aforesaid states: either to emulate the Venetians and not employ its plebs in wars, or, like the Spartans, not to admit foreigners. Rome did both these things, and by doing so,

---

xii Helots were slaves owned by the Spartan state. They came from the groups of people that the Spartans subjugated.

gave the plebs alike strength, increase and endless opportunities for commotion. On the other hand, had the governments of Rome been such as to bring greater tranquillity, there would have ensued this inconvenience, that it would have been weaker, owing to its having cut off the source of supply [of its own soldiers] which enabled it to acquire the greatness at which it arrived, so that, in seeking to remove the cause of the tumults, Rome would have removed also the cause of expansion . . .

. . . *If then, you want to have a large population and to provide it with arms so as to establish a great empire, you will have made your population such that you cannot now handle it as you please. While, if you keep it either small or unarmed so as to be able to manage it, and then ac-quire dominions, either you will lose your hold on it or it will become so debased that you will be at the mercy of anyone who attacks you* . . . Rome might have indeed emulated Sparta, have appointed a prince for life, and have made its senate small; but it would not in that case have been able to avoid increasing its population with a view to establishing a great empire; nor would the appointment of a king for life and of a small number of senators have been of much help in the matter of unity.[34]   [Emphasis ours]

Expected Behavior of a Ruler

Machiavelli understood that context determines how rulers behave. He used what he called the five good Roman emperors (Titus, Nerva, Trajan, Hadrian, and Marcus Aurelius) [35] as examples in *The Discourses*. His analysis did not differ materially from what would be expected from earlier writers on political governance:

What he will find *when good princes were ruling, is a prince securely reigning among subjects no less secure, a world replete with peace and justice. He will see the senate's authority respected, the magistrates honoured, rich citizens enjoying their wealth, nobility and virtue held in the high-est esteem, and everything working smoothly and going well.* He will notice on the other hand, the absence of any rancour, any licentiousness, corruption or ambition, and that in this golden age everyone is free to hold and defend his own opinion. He will behold, in short, the world triumphant, its prince glorious and respected by all, the people fond of him and secure under his rule.[36]   [Emphasis ours]

Apparently contradicting what he wrote in *The Prince*, Machiavelli argued in *The Dis-courses* that cruelty is not a solution for a successful prince:

He then who sets out to govern the masses, whether in a free state or in a principality, and does not secure himself against those who are hostile to the new order, is setting up a form of government that will but be short-lived. True, I look upon those rulers as unhappy who, to make their government secure have to adopt abnormal methods because they find the masses hostile; for he who has but the few as his enemies, can easily and without much scandal make himself secure, but *he who has the public as a whole for his enemy can never make himself se-cure; and the greater his cruelty, the weaker does his regime become. In such a case the best remedy he can adopt is to make the populace his friend.*[37]   [Emphasis ours]

Finally, Machiavelli considered that rule of law was an essential factor in a stable, successfully governed state:

> . . . no well-ordered republic allows the demerits of its citizens to be cancelled out by their merits; but, having prescribed rewards for a good deed and punishments for a bad one, and having rewarded someone for doing well, if that same person afterwards does wrong, it punishes him, regardless of any of the good deeds he has done . . . *if a citizen who has rendered some signal service to the state, acquire thereby not merely the repute which the affair has brought him, but is emboldened to expect that he can do wrong with impunity, he will soon become so insolent that civic life in such a state will disappear.*[38]   [Emphasis ours]

Machiavelli's apparent contradictions can be understood by realizing that in *The Discourses* Machiavelli reviewed how to run an established state; whereas in *The Prince* he was offering advice to a new ruler of Florence who still had to establish his position, with examples from antiquity and contemporary states. The *advice is contextually dependent* based on observation of rulers who *gained* power in ancient Rome or Greece, or in the recent past in Italy's unstable states. Machiavelli focused on what works, rather than what is "morally defensible." Thus, for a prince who was trying to establish or consolidate power, Machiavelli advised:

> *Cruelties can be called well used (if it is permissible to speak well of evil) that are done at a stroke, out of the necessity to secure oneself and then are not persisted in but are turned to as much utility for the subjects as one can. Those cruelties are badly used which, though few in the beginning, rather grow with time.*[39]   [Emphases ours]

The Mongols adopted this policy as they expanded westward across Central Asia into the Middle East; slaughtering the inhabitants of cities that resisted their advance and treating well those that surrendered without fighting.[40] President Truman justified dropping two atomic bombs on Japan to end World War II on similar grounds.[xiii]

Machiavelli accepted brutality when expanding an empire or crushing a revolt, and explained that new rulers or usurpers need to remember to do things differently from the previous government; that innovations will be resisted by interests that benefit from the status quo ante (the previously existing state of affairs):

> *The innovator makes enemies of all those who prospered under the old order, and only lukewarm support is forthcoming from those who would prosper under the new. Their support is lukewarm partly from fear of their adversaries, who have existing laws on their side, and partly because men are generally incredulous, never really trusting new things unless they have tested them by experience. In consequence, whenever those who oppose changes can do so, they attack vigorously, and the defence made by the others is only lukewarm.* But to discuss this subject thoroughly we must distinguish between innovators who stand alone and those who depend on

---

xiii "Truman stated that his decision to drop the bomb was purely military. A Normandy-type amphibious landing would have cost an estimated million casualties. Truman believed that the bombs saved Japanese lives as well." "51g. The Decision to Drop the Bomb," *USHistory.org*, https://www.ushistory.org/us/51g.asp, accessed on May 19, 2020.

others, that is between those who to achieve their purposes can force the issue and those who must use persuasion. In the second case, they always come to grief, having achieved nothing; when, however, they depend on their own resources and can force the issue, then they are seldom endangered. That is why all armed prophets have conquered, and unarmed prophets have come to grief.[41]   [Emphasis ours]

Given the need or desire of a new ruler to do things differently, Machiavelli counseled the ruler to replace beneficiaries of the status quo ante *immediately* to minimize dissent, the possibility of resistance, and to encourage interest in maintaining a new governing coalition:

> *When he seizes a new state, the new ruler must determine all the injuries that he will need to inflict. He must inflict them once for all, and not have to renew them every day, and in that way, he will be able to set men's minds at rest and win them over when he confers benefits.* Whoever acts otherwise . . . is always forced to have the knife ready in his hand and he can never depend on his subjects because they, suffering fresh and continuous violence, can never feel secure with regard to him. *Violence must be inflicted once for all; people will then forget what it tastes like and so be less resentful.*[42]   [Emphases ours]

He warned princes who wanted to take over cities or states with the help of insiders that they needed to understand their supporters' motives for inviting a foreigner into their state:

> Princes who have recently seized a state for themselves through support given from within, that they should carefully reflect on the motives of those who helped them. *If these were not based on a natural affection for the new prince, but rather on discontent with the existing government, he will retain their friendship only with considerable difficulty and exertion, because it will be impossible for him in his turn to satisfy them.*[43]   [Emphasis ours]

Machiavelli qualified his warning by identifying the difficulties a prince could experience if he had relied upon nobles rather than the populace to establish his position:

> A man who becomes prince with the help of the nobles finds it more difficult to maintain his position than one who does so with the help of the people. *As prince, he finds himself surrounded by many who believe they are his equals, and because of that he cannot command or manage them the way he wants.* A man who becomes prince by favour of the people finds himself standing alone, and he has near him either no one or very few not prepared to take orders.[44]   [Emphasis ours]

He noted that a prince could consolidate his position and improve the conditions of the state by developing a Renaissance equivalent of talent management, combined with reasonable taxation so that people could go about their business and not worry that the wealth they created would be taken from them arbitrarily:

> A prince should also show his esteem for talent, actively encouraging able men, and honouring those who excel in their profession. Then he must encourage his citizens so that they go peaceably about their business . . . One man should not be afraid of improving his possessions, lest they be taken away from him, or another deterred by high taxes from starting a new business. *Rather, the prince should be ready to reward men who want to do these things and anyone who endeavours in any way to increase the prosperity of his city or his state.*[45]   [Emphasis ours]

Machiavelli knew that a prince never lacked advice; but believed it should be given only when sought, and counsel considered carefully, with an open mind. Advisers should be encouraged to "speak truth to power." But he did not believe that advisers would give disinterested advice and thought that the onus was on the prince to ask good questions, instead of relying on the wisdom of the adviser, lest he be unduly influenced by the counselor:

> A Prince must, therefore, never lack advice. But he must take it when he wants to, not when others want him to; indeed, he must discourage everyone from tendering advice about anything unless it is asked for. All the same, he should be a constant questioner, and he must listen patiently to the truth regarding what he has inquired about. *Moreover, if he finds that anyone for some reason holds the truth back, he must show his wrath . . . a prince who is not himself wise cannot be well advised, unless he happens to put himself in the hands of one individual who looks after all his affairs and is an extremely shrewd man. In this case, he may well be given good advice, but he would not last long because the man who governs for him would soon deprive him of his state.* But when seeking advice of more than one person, a prince who is not himself wise will never get unanimity in his councils or be able to reconcile their views. Each councillor will consult his own interests; and the prince will not know how to correct or understand them. Things cannot be otherwise, since men will always do badly by you unless they are forced to be virtuous. So the conclusion is that *good advice, whomever it comes from, depends on the shrewdness of the prince who seeks it, and not the shrewdness of the prince on good advice.*[46]   [Emphases ours]

Virtù and Fortuna

When Machiavelli wrote about virtù, he associated it with the leaders' ability to deal with fortuna. In ancient Rome, fortuna was the bringer of good luck and abundance, but fickle and unreliable. In Machiavelli's time, fortuna was associated with the darker side of risk and the dashing of hopes. In essence, he was writing about dealing with Volatility, Uncertainty, Complexity, and Ambiguity of modern theorists and consultants:

> Her symbol was the turning wheel, which people rode to the top, only to be thrown to the bottom at the next turning. Fortuna embodied the tawdry and transitory glory of the world that the thoughtful Christian must seek to transcend by focusing on the unchangeable goods of virtue and faith, which had eternal glory in Heaven . . .
>
> . . . Machiavelli uses fortuna to refer to all of those circumstances which human beings cannot control, and in particular, to the character of the times, which has direct bearing on a prince's success or failure . . .[47]

Machiavelli goes further in his representation of fortuna as being the "dark side" of the force that drives human affairs:

> Where conventional representations treated Fortuna as a mostly benign, if fickle, goddess, who is the source of human goods as well as evils, *Machiavelli's fortune is a malevolent and uncompromising fount of human misery, affliction, and disaster.* While human Fortuna may be

responsible for such success as human beings achieve, *no man can act effectively when directly opposed by the goddess.*[48]   [Emphases ours]

However, leaders can tackle fortuna through the force of virtù; and as long as fortuna and virtù are aligned, as long as the prince demonstrated flexibility to deal with changing contexts, adapted accordingly, and took decisive action, he could mitigate fortuna's effects:

> Virtù is the human energy or action that stands in opposition to fortune. While Machiavelli's use of the word does not exclude the idea of goodness or virtuous behavior, it does not necessarily include it, either. *Virtù is drive, talent, or ability directed toward the achievement of certain goals, and it is the most vital quality for a prince.* Even criminals like Agathocles[xiv] or extremely cruel rulers like Severus[xv] can possess virtù. Machiavelli sometimes seems to say that virtù could defeat fortuna if it was properly applied. If a prince could always adapt his virtù to the present circumstances, he would always be successful . . . *It may not be possible to completely cancel out the effects of changing fortune, but by decisive action, it is possible to prepare for changes and to mitigate their bad effects.*[49]   [Emphases ours]

Machiavelli employed virtù to refer to the range of personal qualities the effective prince must possess to "maintain his state" and to "achieve great things":

> This makes it brutally clear there can be no equivalence between the conventional virtues and Machiavellian virtù. Machiavelli's sense of what it is to be a person of virtù can thus be summarized by his recommendation that the prince above all else must possess a "flexible disposition." *That ruler is best suited for office, on Machiavelli's account, who is capable of varying her/his conduct from good to evil and back again "as fortune and circumstances dictate."*

> Machiavelli sees politics to be a sort of a battlefield on a different scale. Hence, the prince just like the general needs to be in possession of virtù, that is, to know which strategies and techniques are appropriate to what particular circumstances. Thus, virtù winds up being closely connected to Machiavelli's notion of the power. *The ruler of virtù is bound to be competent in the application of power; to possess virtù is indeed to have mastered all the rules connected with the effective application of power. Virtù is to power politics what conventional virtue is to those thinkers who suppose that moral goodness is sufficient to be a legitimate ruler*: it is the touchstone of political success.[50]   [Emphases ours]

Machiavelli, like Napoleon, believed that successful leaders made their own luck:

---

xiv "Agathocles of Syracuse (361–289 BCE) ruled as tyrant of the Sicilian city for over 25 years. Ambitious, unprincipled, and seeing himself as a new Alexander, he attacked Carthage and made conquests in southern Italy, but ultimately his quest for a lasting Sicilian-Italian empire failed." Cartwright, M. (2016), "Agathocles of Syracuse," *Ancient History Encyclopedia*, June 3, 2016, https://www.ancient.eu/Agathocles_of_Syracuse/, accessed on May 19, 2020.

xv "Lucius Septimius Severus was Roman emperor from April 193 to February 211 CE." Hurley, P. (2011), "Septimius Severus," *Ancient History Encyclopedia*, April 11, 2011, https://www.ancient.eu/Septimius_Severus/, accessed on May 19, 2020.

> . . . when we come to examine their actions and lives [Cyrus, Romulus, Theseus and others like them,] they do not seem to have had from fortune anything other than opportunity. *Fortune, as it were, provided the matter but they gave it its form; without such prowess the opportunity would have come in vain.*[51]   [Emphasis ours]

Perhaps a more balanced view on the role of luck is that of Duc de La Rochefoucauld:

> However great may be the advantages she bestows, it is not nature alone, but nature helped by luck that makes heroes.[52]

> Nature provides the merit; chance calls it into play.[53]

Machiavelli believed that effective leaders must "seize the day" to deal with fortuna:

> As fortune is changeable whereas men are obstinate in their ways, *men prosper so long as fortune and policy are in accord, and when there is a clash they fail.* I hold strongly to this: *it is better to be impetuous than circumspect;* because fortune is a woman and if she is to be submissive it is necessary to beat and coerce her. Experience shows that she is more often subdued by men who do this than by men who act coldly.[54]   [Emphases ours]

Reconciling Machiavelli's Two Approaches

The apparent contradiction between Machiavelli's advice in *The Discourses* and *The Prince* is resolved when we consider the contexts in which the two books were written. *The Prince* was supposed to help Machiavelli regain an administrative position in the government of the newly returned Medici ruler of Florence.[55] One can therefore expect that he would speak well of princely regimes in that volume. Comparing what he had to say about republics in the Discourses, it would appear that he preferred the republican model of government to the princely model. He noted one important caveat, the greater difficulty republics have in taking timely executive decisions in times of national emergency. He pointed out Republican Rome's ingenious solution – the creation of the temporary, time-bound dictatorship:

> Furthermore, *a dictator was appointed for a limited time, and for the purpose of dealing solely with such matters as had led to the appointment.* He had authority to make what decisions he thought fit in order to meet a definite and urgent danger, and to do this without consultation; and anyone he punished had no right of appeal. But *he could do nothing to diminish the constitutional position of the government, as would have been the case if he could have taken away the authority vested in the senate or in the people, or have abolished the ancient institutions of the city and made new ones.* Wherefore, in view of the short duration of the dictatorship, of the limited authority which the dictator possessed, and of the fact that the Roman people were not corrupt, it was impossible for the dictator to overstep his terms of reference and to do the state harm. On the contrary, *experience has shown that the dictatorship was always useful.*[56]   [Emphases ours]

The time limit on dictatorship was so rigid that should a dictator exceed the time agreed, he was likely to be assassinated:

He interpreted the Roman dictatorship as a constitutional office: one or two men were voted absolute power by the senate solely for the duration of the emergency (if they went on beyond that they were, constitutional theory had it, ipso facto outlaws, marked for the knife of the patriotic assassin).[57]

Machiavelli saw that the appropriate behavior of a ruler was contextually dependent. If the ruler was part of a well-established and secure polity, if the people were not corrupt and loved liberty, if the ambitions of the state were limited so that tranquility was more important than empire-building, then the best way for the ruler to work with his people was to combine a top-down and bottom-up process. Alternatively, an oligarchic system of republican government like that of Venice made sense, except that it relied on mercenaries who had no patriotic stake in defending it.

The advantage of the republican over princely forms of government was adaptability and the ability to meet changing circumstances by calling on a variety of talented people. Machiavelli illustrated this using the example of Rome's different strategies during its sixteen-year war with Hannibal. After the disasters of Lake Trasimene and Cannae, Rome appointed a dictator (Fabius) who understood the need for asymmetrical warfare with cautious, delaying guerrilla tactics to turn Hannibal's effective attacking force into an ineffective army of occupation.[xvi] Fabius' tactics gave Rome time to recover and wear down the Carthaginians who were far from home. When the time came to take the war to Carthage, Fabius was not the right commander, being temperamentally unsuited to conduct an aggressive war of pitched battles. Rome chose Scipio in his place who defeated Hannibal in North Africa, ending Carthage's threat to Rome. Machiavelli's contention was that a ruler who had been successful with one long-range strategy would not have been able to make the change and if Fabius had led the Roman legions to Africa, they would have lost. In other words, *the most important quality in a ruler was adaptability and an understanding of the changes in context as fortuna decided to deal him a different hand.*

The other factor leading to differences between the approaches to leadership in the two books is whether the ruler is trying to establish his rule or take over another state (*The Prince*) or whether the ruler is already established and secure (*The Discourses*).

If the ruler is trying to take over another state or still has to establish his rule, then he must do whatever it takes to achieve power and authority; for *without power and authority, the ruler is unable to do anything.* Machiavelli was very clear that in these circumstances the prospective ruler should act "immorally" to achieve power. He could destroy existing institutions; move populations to new places; appoint new governors; make the rich poor and the poor rich;[58] and inflict the pain all at once so that resistance was broken and the survivors had time to forget the cruelty and get on with their lives, rather than having to look over their shoulders in fear of the next purge. Duc de La Rochefoucauld supported this approach:

---

xvi The parallels with the US military experience in Iraq or Afghanistan are striking.

Some crimes are become innocent even glorious by their sheer impudence, number, and enormity. This is why public thefts become skilful moves, and annexing provinces without justification is called making conquests.[59]

In *The Prince*, Machiavelli repudiated the received wisdom that "morality" always led to effectiveness, at least as far as the "means" of achieving power were concerned. He argued that a ruler will fail if he is always "good" and that effective rulers adapt to their circumstances:

So, as a prince is forced to act like a beast, he must learn from the fox and the lion: because the lion is defenceless against traps and a fox is defenceless against wolves. Therefore, one must be a fox in order to recognize traps, and a lion to frighten off wolves. Those who simply act like lions are stupid. So, it follows that a prudent ruler cannot, and must not, honour his word when it places him at a disadvantage and when the reasons for which he made his promise no longer exist.[60]

He went further citing the example of Pope Alexander VI's faithlessness:[xvii]

But it is necessary to be able to disguise this character well, and to be a great feigner and dissembler; and men are so simple and so ready to obey present necessities, that one who deceives will always find those who allow themselves to be deceived. I will mention only one modern instance. Alexander VI did nothing else but deceive men, he thought of nothing else, and found the occasion for it; no man was ever more able to give assurances, or affirmed things with stronger oaths, and no man observed them less; however, he always succeeded in his deceptions, as he knew well this aspect of things. It is not necessary therefore for a prince to have all of the above-named qualities, but it is very necessary to seem to have them.[61]

Machiavelli thought the immoral or amoral phase of leadership was only effective when a ruler was establishing control over the state. Once that was achieved, Machiavelli urged the ruler to behave benevolently and that acting tyrannically would not maintain his rule.

In this view, *The Prince* was not a justification for tyranny and must be read in conjunction with *The Discourses*. Machiavelli made it clear that a prince should appoint people based on merit; encourage business, and allow individuals to retain the fruits of their labor by taxing them lightly; and encourage his courtiers to tell the truth so that he could make better decisions. *The Prince* was an explanation that at certain times in a ruler's rise to power the "ends justify the means" – once power was acquired, Machiavelli expected the ruler to be benevolent to maintain his rule.

The Discourses reads differently because Machiavelli was not writing for a prince who had just returned from exile; but instead was examining how the Roman Republic had achieved success in a way that neither Sparta nor Venice had. He described

---

xvii The parallels with Lenin, Hitler, and Stalin in the 20th century are striking, as is the similarity with the rise of populist leaders in the 21st century who trade in "fake news" on social media to undermine belief in the truth in the post-truth world since 2016. Their ways of achieving power would have met with approval from Machiavelli, at least from a technical perspective.

rulers who governed only in the ways suggested in *The Prince* as bad rulers; or else were exculpated, like Romulus for killing Remus, his own twin brother, because they were the founders of the polity, forced by circumstance and fortuna to behave cruelly.[62]

Machiavelli was clear that for any ruler to be successful, he had to have virtù, by which he meant:

> . . . capable of varying her/his conduct from good to evil and back again "as fortune and cir-
> cumstances dictate" . . . just like the general needs to be in possession of virtù, that is, to
> know which strategies and techniques are appropriate to what particular circumstances . . .
> The ruler of virtù is bound to be competent in the application of power; to possess virtù is in-
> deed to have mastered all the rules connected with the effective application of power. Virtù is
> to power politics what conventional virtue is to those thinkers who suppose that moral good-
> ness is sufficient to be a legitimate ruler: it is the touchstone of political success.[63]

Bertrand Russell pointed out in *A History of Western Philosophy*,[64] the "moral and immoral" parts of Machiavelli's approaches can be reconciled by seeing them as ob-servations of what he believed about effective "means" to achieve "ends" that de-pended on values and beliefs.

Machiavelli identified three (in his view) desirable political "ends": national in-dependence; security; and a well-ordered constitution. In *The Discourses*, it is clear that Machiavelli considered the best constitution to be one that divided legal rights between princes, nobles, and the people. The "amoral" aspects of Machiavelli's doc-trine were concerned with how to achieve power and how to choose means that were fit for this sole purpose – namely getting into a position of power and authority that allowed the prince to attain the desired ends.

Machiavelli's originality lies in his treatment of "means" in a scientific manner, without regard to whether the desired ends were "good" or "evil." *Success* means achieving the prince's purpose, whatever it might be, with his greatest contribution to discussions on leadership being his insistence on understanding the context with which rulers or leaders deal and the separation of "means" and "ends." *This appre-ciation led him to conclude that effective leaders act on the basis that "the ends justify the means" because without achieving the power and authority needed to act, they could not be effective, no matter how morally justified they were.*

What is Leadership?

In her book *Bad Leadership: What It Is, How It Happens, Why It Matters*, Barbara Kellerman noted the assumption that *leadership is considered a form of behavior, which gives followers the choice whether to be led or not*. This is an innovation origi-nating with Burns' *Transformational Leadership*,[65] published in 1978 and *Authentic Leadership*,[66] published in 1989. Both attempted to redefine leadership as *exercising power over others based on mutual advantage*:

> . . . leaders engage others by creating shared meaning, speaking in a distinctive voice, demonstrating the capacity to adapt and having integrity . . .[67]

Leaders who coerced their followers, were not leaders – Burns redefined them as "power wielders."[68] This morally uplifting redefinition ignores the reality of leadership's and followership's dark side:

> That leaders engage others by creating shared meaning, speaking in a distinctive voice, demonstrating the capacity to adapt and having integrity.[69]

It is true, however, that there were five characteristics that appeared to be timeless (no change in the ranking between 1987 and 2007) and universally accepted[xviii] when we consider what makes leaders *admired* according to Kouzes and Posner. In the 2020 review of the five top characteristics of most *admired* leaders, there appears to have been a change, shown in Table 1.3.

Table 1.3: Top Five Characteristics of Admired Leaders.

2007 Survey of 75,000 Respondents	2020 Survey of 20,000 Respondents
1. Honest (89%)	1. Honesty and Integrity
2. Forward-looking (71%)	2. Inspiration
3. Inspiring (69%)	3. Competence
4. Competent (68%)	4. Fairness
5. Intelligent (48%)	5. Supportive

Source: Kouzes, J. M., and Posner, B. Z. (2007), *The Leadership Challenge, 4th Edition* (San Francisco: John Wiley & Sons), pp. 30, 31; Kouzes and Posner 2020 Survey cited in "5 Traits of Admired Leaders," *Foundations of Management,* University of Notre Dame, October 9, 2020, https://www.notredameonline.com/re sources/leadership-and-management/5-traits-of-admired-leaders/, accessed on December 5, 2020.

"Honesty and integrity" were explained as:

> The most frequently mentioned characteristic in the survey was honesty. Someone viewed as an honest person who manages with integrity and ethics is considered a leader who can be trusted. People are more willing to follow this person.

---

xviii The cut-off point in 2007 was set at more than 50% of the 75,000 surveyed respondents agreeing in the following countries: Australia, Canada, Denmark, Japan, Korea, Malaysia, Mexico, New Zealand, Singapore, Sweden, and the US. The fifth characteristic, Intelligent, received 48%. Kouzes, J. M., and Posner, B. Z., *The Leadership Challenge* (San Francisco: John Wiley & Sons, 2007), p. 31.

Integrity and honesty go hand in hand. Employees know if someone follows through with actions they say they will take, they are someone who can be trusted for their honesty and leadership . . .[70]

"Inspiration" was explained as:

Employees are much more likely to respond to a leader that has passion and a positive attitude. Leaders who are truly engaged and who have energy are the leaders who will gain more followers . . .[71]

"Competence" was explained as:

Your team wants to believe you have technical skills and the solid judgment to make decisions for the company . . .[72]

"Fairness" was defined as:

Fairness goes far in motivating employees and volunteers. If people feel they are being treated unfairly, they have less motivation. Being just and being consistent earns people's trust and respect . . .[73]

"Supportive" was explained as:

By focusing on followers, leaders put their employees or volunteers in a position to succeed. The leader removes hurdles, gathers resources and information and draws on contacts to make that happen.

Great managers emphasize the development of their employees' strengths to help them further their talent, while seeking ways to support their weaknesses . . .[74]

Why do Leaders Lead, and Followers Follow?

Hobbes,[75] Locke,[76] and Hegel[77] all saw that leaders and followers engage in a compact to protect all against the anxieties caused by disorder and death. Hobbes and Locke saw social contracts based on satisfying two of Plato's elements of the soul: *Logos* (the rational part) and *Eros* (the biological part with its desire and appetite for material things).[78] Hegel added Plato's third element, *Thymos* (the emotional part of being human: the need for honor, recognition, and respect). What differentiated Hegel's position was his emphasis on the obligations and risks to life he believed leaders must accept if they are to maintain legitimacy in the eyes of their followers:

We left off our account of the Hegelian dialectic . . . at the conclusion of the beginning period of human history, when man first risked his life in a battle for pure prestige. The state of war that prevailed in Hegel's "state of nature" (although Hegel never used such a term) did not lead directly to the establishment of civil society based on a social contract, as it did for Locke. *Rather it led to the relationship of lordship and bondage, when one of the primordial combatants, fearing for his life, "recognized" the other and agreed to be his slave.*[79]   [Emphasis ours]

The disaster of Munich in 1938 was unavoidable because the British Prime Minister, Neville Chamberlain, sought a rational and materially beneficial outcome (Logos and Eros), and could not understand Hitler was driven by overwhelming emotion (Thymos), reflecting Hegelian worldviews:

> *The alternative for him was never anything but world power or doom in the most literal sense.* "Every being strives for expansion . . . and every nation strives for world dominion." *That proposition derived, he thought, straight from the aristocratic principle of Nature, which everywhere desired the victory of the stronger and annihilation or unconditional subjugation of the weak.* From this point of view, he was entirely consistent at the end, when he saw the whole game lost and doom impending, and remarked to Albert Speer, who found the sentiment profoundly shocking: "If the war is lost, the people will be lost also. *It is not necessary to worry about what the German people will need for elemental survival . . . For the nation has proved to be the weaker, and the future belongs solely to the stronger eastern nation"* . . . For the last time he bowed to the law of Nature, "this cruel queen of all wisdom" which had imperiously ruled his life and thought.[80]   [Emphases ours]

Stark evidence of Hitler's attitude is a conversation with a foreign dignitary when the German advance stalled outside Moscow:

> If the German people are no longer so strong and ready for sacrifice that they will stake their own blood on their existence, *they deserve to pass away and be annihilated by another, stronger power . . . If that is the case, I would not shed a tear for the German people."*[81]   [Emphasis ours]

Hobbes agreed with Hegel, when he discussed the state of nature:

> . . . No Knowledge of the face of the Earth; no account of Time; no Arts; no Letters; no Society; and which is worst of all, continuall feare, and danger of violent death; And the life of man, solitary, poore, nasty brutish and short.[82]

Instead of idealizing the thymotic focus as being the desirable aristocratic principle of nature, where the strong dominate the weak (as Hegel did), Hobbes explained why and how humanity found an alternative to aristocratic contest in a bourgeois solution:

> To this warre of every man against every man 'tis also is consequent; that nothing can be Unjust. The notion of Right and Wrong, Justice and Injustice have there not place. Where there is no common Power, there is no Law: where no Law, no Injustice. Force, and Fraud, are in warre the two Cardinall vertues. Justice, and Injustice . . . are Qualities, that relate to men in Society, not in Solitude. It is consequent also to the same condition that there be no Propriety, no Dominion, no Mine and Thine distinct; but onely that to be every mans that he can get; and for so long as he can keep it. And thus much for the ill condition which man by meer Nature is actually placed in; though with a possibility to come out of it, consisting partly in the Passions,[xix] partly in his Reason.[xx]

---

xix Plato's *Thymos* discussed earlier in the chapter.
xx Plato's *Logos* discussed earlier in the chapter.

> The Passions that encline men to Peace, are Feare of Death; Desire of such things as are necessary to commodious living;[xxi] and a Hope by their Industry to obtain them. And Reason suggesteth convenient Articles of peace, upon which men may be drawn to agreement.[83]   [Emphases ours]

Followers of toxic leaders can be best understood by appreciating leadership as an interaction between leaders and led; not as something leaders do to followers.[84] Toxic leaders succeed initially because their followers enable them but often eventually fail, leaving their countries or businesses wrecked.

Followers crave authority, order, security and a sense of belonging; and all leaders, including toxic ones, understand this:

> Illusions are the umbilical cord linking leaders and followers. Leaders understand their followers needs for illusions . . . Too often, historians define leadership as something imposed by the leader upon the masses. *The true story is more complex. Hitler could carry out his plan to exterminate Jews and dominate the world only with the help of millions of German voters, workers, and soldiers.*[85]   [Emphasis ours]

For individuals, leaders satisfy needs for certainty, simplicity, and security. Freud went further in explaining why people seek strong father figures as leaders:

> "For Freud, on the other hand, *dependency inevitably led to a marked reduction in intellectual engagement on the part of group members.* Part of this dynamic, what would later come to be known as *"groupthink"* . . . *involved placing a higher value on group membership than on individual autonomy.* But Freud added that the presence of a strong, attractive individual leader exacerbated the tendency to submerge the individual into the group. Group members provided the leader with love and expected that love to be reciprocated equally to the members. This was Freud, so, yes, that attraction was in part sexual; a libidinous attraction to the father-figure/leader.

> In Freud's view, the great man is "the father that lives in each of us from his childhood days for the same father whom the hero of legend boosts of having overcome." The "picture of the father," then, includes the "decisiveness of thought, the strength of will, the self-reliance and independence of the great man [and] his divine conviction of doing the right thing which may pass into ruthlessness." *The great man will be admired, trusted, and followed.*

> However, "one cannot help but being afraid of him"   (Freud, 1937/1967: 140)

> . . . And Freud did not stop with that warning. By admiring a leader unconditionally, followers were submitting to authority. In so doing, followers rendered themselves vulnerable. *Submission enabled an authority figure who "dominates and sometimes even ill-treats them."*[86]
> (Freud, 1937/1967: 111) [Emphases ours]

We follow leaders because the emotional or economic rewards are implied *and/or* costs of not following are high. Resistance creates confusion and uncertainty; the states most followers want to avoid – resistance is doubly hard.

---

xxi Plato's *Eros* discussed earlier in the chapter.

Toxic leaders exploit four basic emotional needs and two primal fears:

1. *Need for authority*: From childhood, we are acculturated into followership – doing what our parents, elders, and authority figures tell us to. "Getting along by going along" is an important social lesson learned early. Such behavior is usually evolutionarily advantageous in immature individuals but can be disadvantageous in adults.

2. *Need for security*: Security is a basic human need:[87]

> The security of the family structure is gone, and [they] seek replacements for parental authority, often finding leaders who promise security. After the September 11, 2001, terror attacks, for instance, Americans traded the freedom of hassle-free travel for the security of baggage searches and long delays at airport X-ray machines.[88]

3. *Need to feel special*: People follow leaders who make them feel part of something bigger and more important or beautiful than they are.

4. *Need to belong*: People conform and accept norms of behavior that may be anything but normal; vide the "Milgram experiment"[89] which showed how the behavior of "normal" individuals can be distorted by the desire to conform. Although individuals want to be valued for themselves and recognized as special, they need to be part of community finding meaning in their approval.

Leaders (whether benevolent or toxic) play on people's fears; the fear of excommunication or ostracization, and the fear of powerlessness. The fear of "social death" inhibits followers speaking truth to power:

> Toxic leaders demand more fealty than benign leaders require, and they do not tolerate dissent or questions about their decisions. The psychological pressure makes it especially difficult for whistle-blowers . . . [to] alert leaders and outside authorities about problems within a company.[90]

All leaders behave badly or irrationally at times; and toxic leaders typically exhibit the following behavior:[91,92]

1. Lacking integrity and honesty, lying to bolster a compelling vision
2. Putting their personal glory above the well-being of others
3. Narcissism and arrogance fostering incompetence and corruption
4. Intimidating, demoralizing, demeaning, and marginalizing others
5. Violating opponents' and followers' basic human rights; stifling criticism
6. Retaining power by undermining potential successors and failing to nurture other leaders
7. Feeding followers' illusions, misleading through untruths and misdiagnoses based on fear
8. Stifling constructive criticism, "shooting the messenger," encouraging compliance
9. Setting constituents against one another, encouraging division
10. Subverting institutions, structures, and processes intended to generate truth, justice, and excellence

Such traits ought to be obvious to all; so how do such leaders stay in power? Whether they are national leaders, like Stalin, Mao, or Hitler; or the CEO of a company, like Al Dunlap[xxii] – the answer lies in the feeling of powerlessness of followers, who do not realize others feel the same way because toxic leaders stifle dissent.[93]

We accept leaders' interpretations of the world because we do not accept that the world is random.[94],[95] We need plausible causal explanations; however improbable. It is the way our brains are hardwired[96] (discussed further in Chapter 9). Leaders satisfy those needs, even when they lie or are mistaken.[xxiii]

In an increasingly uncertain world, leaders are assumed to know what they are doing.[97] The angst we experience when we do not understand what is happening makes us more likely to turn to those who give the appearance of being strong and certain.[98]

At the group level, decision-making is complex. It is difficult for ten people to reach consensus – think of ten people agreeing on what to eat for dinner! We need hierarchies to enable decision making in large groups. Leaders do a great deal of demanding work: engaging stakeholders, understanding different perspectives, and comprehending time horizons.[99] The outcome of such work is highly uncertain and ambiguous. Most people do not want to deal with ambiguity, or the anxiety caused by the fear of failure. They defer to those who have no such qualms, who may turn out to be good, bad, or toxic leaders. This behavior creates the "Iron Law of Oligarchy," that we divide ourselves into leaders and led.[100] This division of labor means that leaders get better at tolerating ambiguity; and followers demand ever greater certainty.

Morally bad (evil) leaders make a compact with their followers who, in turn, reinforce the behavior of these leaders by allowing them to behave in increasingly arbitrary and autocratic ways over time. To explain why, Barbara Kellerman divided followers into three groups – each rational in how it accommodates evil leadership:[101]

1. *The silent majority.* These are the bystanders – going along with what is being done because it is too much effort or too risky to disagree, but they do not believe in what is being proposed. They neither participate in, nor oppose it.
2. *The doers of evil.* They follow orders because that is what they are supposed to do – as efficiently and effectively as possible, because they are being measured and rewarded accordingly, or because the personal costs of not complying are too great.
3. *The acolytes.* These are the true believers who support the evil vision – because they believe it is the right thing to do, or because they will obtain social, psychological, or emotional benefits from enthusiastic alignment:

---

xxii Former CEO of Sunbeam Corporation.
xxiii As of December 16, 2019, President Trump had made 15,413 false claims since becoming president. "Trump has made over 15,000 false or misleading statements since becoming President, report says," *The Independent*, December 16, 2019. He continues to assert that he did not lose the 2020 Presidential election, despite all the evidence to the contrary.

Members of the entourage derive their status and raison d'être from their relationship to the leader. So, they are always dedicated to keeping their leader in power.[102]

In discussing whether leaders are "effective" or "ineffective," "good," "bad," or "toxic," we must define what we mean. The words "good" and "bad" have two distinct usages: a subjective moral judgment and an objective assessment based on meeting specified criteria.

The first criterion by which we can define whether a leader is "good" or "bad" in common parlance is whether the leader is "ethical" (shown in Table 1.4).

Table 1.4: Ethical and Unethical Leaders Compared.

Ethical Leaders	Unethical Leaders
Ethical leaders are more likely to be effective in the long-term because their decisions reflect:	Unethical leaders often end up being ineffective because their decisions are undermined by their:
1. *Benevolence:* Being magnanimous, having empathy, being able to connect to individuals and nature, affirming the value of the universe and the ecology (Confucius' test).[103]	1. *Callousness:* The leader and some followers are unkind or uncaring, ignoring the needs and wants of most members of the group for which they are responsible.
2. *Fairness:* Decisions taken are seen to be just and fair because they do not favor cronies or friends at the expense of others who equally or more qualified.	2. *Corruption:* The leader and followers lie, cheat, or steal; and put self-interest ahead of public interest cloaking their actions with hypocrisy.
3. *Open-mindedness:* A willingness to think "out of the box" to reflect changed contexts.	3. *Insularity:* Minimization or disregard of the impact of actions on the health and welfare of the "other" – that is, the people outside their organization who are affected by its actions.
4. *Mercy:* Compassion and forgiveness toward followers and enemies whom he/she has the power to punish.	4. *Ruthlessness:* Disregard to pain caused to others when deciding what to do.[104]

Source: Based on Kellerman, B. (2004), *Bad Leadership: What It Is, How It Happens, Why It Matters* (Boston: Harvard Business School Press); Guo, Q. et al. (2012), "The Values of Confucian Benevolence and the Universality of the Confucian Way of Extending Love," *Frontiers of Philosophy in China*, Vol. 7, No. 1 (March 2012), pp. 20–54, https://www.jstor.org/stable/44259370?seq=1, accessed on April 24, 2020.

The second criterion used to define whether a leader is "good" or "bad" compares "effective" and "ineffective" leadership, with success in achieving desired outcomes as the yardstick. Table 1.5 compares effective and ineffective leaders.

Note that the dimensions are not mutually exclusive. Leaders can be both ineffective and unethical.

Table 1.5: Effective and Ineffective Leaders Compared.

Effective leaders	Ineffective leaders
Effective leaders succeed because of:	Ineffective leaders fail because of:
1. *Competence:* Leaders and followers exercise an appropriate balance of skill/will to achieve desired outcomes.	1. *Incompetence:* Leaders and followers lack the skill/will to sustain effective action aimed at achieving the desired outcomes.
2. *Flexibility:* The ability to adapt to changing strategic contexts, tactical situations, and operational needs.	2. *Rigidity:* Leaders and followers are unable to adapt to new ideas and circumstances.
3. *Self-control:* The ability to remain calm and make rational decisions under pressure.	3. *Intemperance:* The leader lacks self-control and makes irrational decisions abetted by followers.

Source: Based on Kellerman, B. (2004), *Bad Leadership: What It Is, How It Happens, Why It Matters* (Boston: Harvard Business School Press); Guo, Q. et al. (2012), "The Values of Confucian Benevolence and the Universality of the Confucian Way of Extending Love," *Frontiers of Philosophy in China*, Vol. 7, No. 1 (March 2012), pp. 20–54, https://www.jstor.org/stable/44259370?seq=1, accessed on April 24, 2020.

The defining characteristic of "great leaders" lies in their legacy and governance – great leaders build or create institutions that outlast them. We do not argue that "great leaders" are necessarily "good."

The issues of leadership are similar seen through the historian's, politician's, or businessperson's lens. There is one consequential difference between the tools available to business leaders, politicians, and military leaders. Leaders of legitimate businesses cannot apply brute force to staff or commercial rivals, whereas political and military leaders, and criminal groups can and do.

The cycle of change and creative destruction is faster in business than in politics because the ability of any enterprise to impose stability on the competitive environment is limited. In commerce, customers demand ever better products and competition provides them with what they want. Businesses that fail to adapt to innovation and competition are ultimately taken over or fail.[105] Successful companies adapt to changing contexts. Effective business leaders pay continual attention to their operational context, adapting accordingly (incrementally where possible). Only monopolies and cartels can enforce environmental stability for any length of time.

Political leaders, once in power, make great efforts to preserve the status quo, promoting the value of order and stability. They rarely innovate because they can resist incremental change, using the authority of the state to control information and coerce populations. They are not faced (except in democracies at elections) with the twin pressures of changing customer demands and competitive offers. The absence of incremental political change leads to pressures that can lead to dramatic upsets. President Kennedy summarized this idea when he said, "Those who make peaceful revolution impossible will make violent revolution inevitable . . ."[106] Examples abound: the American, French, Russian revolutions, and decolonization after World War II.

Summary

Leaders have followers. Great leaders maintain their followers regardless of whether their purpose is moral or immoral, suggesting that the effectiveness of leadership is independent of morality. Defining leadership as "morally good leadership" is unhelpful to students and practitioners of leadership.

What matters is what leaders are trying to achieve, how they achieve it, how power is acquired, and how they interact with their followers. The effectiveness of leadership techniques depends on the context in which they are practiced and, consequently, correct identification of context determines the effectiveness of leaders.

Ancient philosophers in China, Greece, India, and Rome exhorted leaders to be benevolent and moral. Plato proposed four leadership contexts, each with its own virtues, leading to five types of leader: philosopher kings; property owning aristocrats, oligarchs, democrats, and tyrants.

Machiavelli was an early social scientist interested in what worked as a separate issue from what he wished would happen. To get a correct understanding of his thinking, it is essential to reconcile his writings in *The Discourses* with his writings in *The Prince*.

There are two views of what leaders offer their followers:

1. *Hobbes and Locke suggested it was economic well-being and safety from violent death.* This view is expressed in the American *Declaration of Independence*'s "pursuit of happiness."

2. *Hegel espoused the need for respect, self-esteem, and honor* for those who feel left behind, disadvantaged, and resentful that they are not respected. Such people are natural followers. Their craving for authority and security, and their need to be made to feel special and to belong to something bigger than themselves, combined with their fear of exclusion and their feeling of powerlessness, leaves them vulnerable to the charisma and illusions created by toxic leaders. The angst they experience when they do not understand what is happening makes them turn to an individual who gives the appearance of being strong and certain. Such followers divide into the "silent majority" who go along with what is happening; "doers of evil" who execute policies because they are following orders; and "acolytes" – true believers.

It is important to unpack the elements that make leaders effective or ineffective instead of contrasting them. "Good" and "bad" have two meanings:

1. *Subjectively:* "Ethical" leaders are judged to be benevolent, fair, open-minded, and merciful. "Unethical" leaders are callous, corrupt, insular, and ruthless.
2. *Objectively:* "Effective" leaders are competent, flexible, and self-controlled. "Ineffective" leaders are incompetent, rigid, and intemperate. Toxic leaders are both unethical and ineffective.

Effective leaders pay continual attention to the context in which they operate and adapt accordingly and incrementally wherever possible. Political leaders strive to preserve the status quo by promoting the value of order and stability. They rarely innovate because they can resist incremental change by using state power to control information and coerce populations. However, reluctance to change peacefully can lead to violent revolution, or business catastrophe.

References

1 Spector, B. A. (2016), "Carlyle, Freud, and the Great Man Theory more fully considered," *Leadership*, 2016, Vol. 12, No. 2, p. 258.
2 Kellerman, B. (2004), *Bad Leadership: What It Is, How It Happens, Why It Matters* (Boston: Harvard Business School Press), p. 13.
3 Ibid.
4 Ibid.
5 Ibid.
6 Ibid., p. 5.
7 Confucius (479 BCE), *Analects of Confucius* (New York: Norton, 1997), p. 6.
8 Ibid., p. 8.
9 Lao Tzu, https://www.brainyquote.com/quotes/lao_tzu_121709, accessed on October 22, 2020.
10 Prabhu, U. M. (2019), "Kautilya on Overcoming Limitations in Leadership," *The Kautilya Project, Vedic Management Center,* April 21, 2019, https://www.vedic-management.com/kautilya-on-mindful-leadership-overcoming-limitations-in-leadership/ accessed on April 24, 2020.
11 Marcus Aurelius (1964), ed., Staniforth, M., *Meditations* (Harmondsworth: Penguin Books), Book 4.6, p. 65.
12 Ibid., Book 6.21, p. 96.
13 Ibid., Book 6.39, p. 100.
14 Ibid., Book 7.18, p. 108.
15 Quoted by Banyan (2020), "South Korea's liberal rulers unleash their inner authoritarians," *The Economist,* August 20, 2020, https://www.economist.com/asia/2020/08/20/south-koreas-liberal-rulers-unleash-their-inner-authoritarians, accessed on August 21, 2020.
16 Nederman, C. (2019), "Niccolò Machiavelli," Zalta, E. N. (ed.), *The Stanford Encyclopedia of Philosophy* (Summer 2019 Edition), May 28, 2019, https://plato.stanford.edu/archives/sum2019/entries/machiavelli/, accessed on May 17, 2020.
17 Machiavelli, N. (1531), *The Discourses on Livy* (Harmondsworth: Pelican Classics, 1970).
18 Machiavelli, N. (1513), *The Prince* (Harmondsworth: Penguin Books, 1999).
19 Ibid., p. 19.

20 Machiavelli (1531), op. cit., Book 1, Discourse 2, p. 106.

21 Hobbes, T. (1651), *Leviathan* (London: Andrew Crooke), Chapter 13, 62, quoted in (London: Penguin Classics, 1985), p. 188.

22 Machiavelli (1531), op. cit., Book 1, Discourse 2, p. 107.

23 Ibid.

24 Ibid.

25 Ibid.

26 Ibid., p. 108.

27 Ibid., p. 109.

28 Ibid.

29 Ibid., pp. 110–111.

30 Ibid., p. 111.

31 Ibid., Book 1, Discourse 34, p. 195.

32 Nederman (2019), op. cit.

33 Machiavelli (1531), Book 1, Discourse 4, p. 113.

34 Ibid., Book 1, Discourse 6, pp. 121–122.

35 Ibid., Book 1, Discourse 10, p. 136.

36 Ibid., Book 1, Discourse 9, p. 132.

37 Ibid., Book 1, Discourse 16, p. 155.

38 Ibid., Book 1, Discourse 24, p. 173.

39 Machiavelli (1513), *The Prince* (London: Penguin Classics, 1999), Chapter VIII, p. 30.

40 Keegan, J. (1993) *A History of Warfare* (London: Pimlico), p. 210.

41 Machiavelli (1513), op. cit., Chapter VI, p. 19.

42 Ibid., Chapter VIII, pp. 30–31.

43 Ibid., Chapter XX, p. 70.

44 Ibid., Chapter IX, p. 32.

45 Ibid., Chapter XXI, p. 74.

46 Ibid., Chapter XXIII, p. 77.

47 Nederman, C. (2019), "Critical Essays Virtù, Fortuna, and Free Will," *Cliffs Notes*, https://www.cliffs notes.com/literature/p/the-prince/critical-essays/virtxf9-fortuna-and-free-will, accessed on March 7, 2020.

48 Ibid.

49 Ibid.

50 Nederman (2019), op. cit.

51 Machiavelli (1513), op. cit., Chapter VI, p. 18.

52 La Rochefoucauld (1678), *Maxims* (Harmondsworth: Penguin Classics, 1979), Maxim 53, p. 44.

53 Ibid., Maxim 153, p. 56.

54 Ibid., p. 82.

55 Crick, B. (1970), *Introduction to Discourses* (Harmondsworth: Penguin Classics), p. 18.

56 Machiavelli (1531), 34, pp. 194–195.

57 Crick (1970), op. cit., p. 30.

58 Ibid., Discourse 26, p. 176.

59 La Rochefoucauld (1678), op. cit., Maxim 608, p. 120.

60 Machiavelli (1513), op. cit., Chapter XVIII, p.56.

61 Ibid., Chapter XVIII, p. 57.

62 Machiavelli (1531), op. cit., Discourse 18, p. 164.

63 Nederman (2019), op. cit.

64 Russell, B. (1947), *A History of Western Philosophy* (London: George Allen and Unwin), pp. 530–531.

65 McGregor Burns, J. (1978), *Leadership* (New York: HarperCollins).

66 Warren Bennis, W. (1989), *On Becoming a Leader* (New York: Basic Books).

67 Kellerman (2004), op. cit., p. 9.

68 Ibid., p. 8.

69 Ibid., p. 9.

70 Ibid.

71 Ibid.

72 Ibid.

73 Ibid.

74 Ibid.

75 Hobbes, T. (1651), *Leviathan* (London: Penguin Classics, 1985).

76 Locke, J. (1690), *Second Treatise on Civil Government.*

77 Hegel, G. W. F. (1807), "The Phenomenology of Mind," cited in Fukuyama, F. (1992), *The End of History and the Last Man* (London: Penguin Books), pp. 192–193.

78 Plato, *The Republic, Part V, Book IV,* Lee, H. D. P. translated (London: Penguin Classics, 1987), pp. 139–149; Plato, *Phaedrus and Letters VII AND VIII* (London: Penguin Books, 1973), pp. 61–63.

79 Fukuyama (1992), op. cit., p. 192.

80 Fest, J. C. (1974), *Hitler* (London: Weidenfeld & Nicholson), p. 218.

81 Ibid., p. 655.

82 Hobbes, T. (1651), *Leviathan* (London: Andrew Crooke), Chapter 13, 62, quoted in (London: Penguin Classics, 1985), p. 186.

83 Ibid., p. 188.

84 Lipman-Blumen, J. (2004), *The Allure of Toxic Leaders: Why We Follow Destructive Bosses and Corrupt Politicians – and How We Can Survive Them* (Oxford: Oxford University Press), reviewed in *Get Abstract, Compressed Knowledge*, p. 2, https://www.getabstract.com/en/summary/the-allure-of-toxic-leaders/4368, accessed on March 30, 2020.

85 Ibid., p. 3.

86 Spector (2016), op. cit., pp. 257–258.

87 Maslow, A. H. (1943), "A Theory of Human Motivation," *Psychological Review*, 50 (4), pp. 370–396, http://psychclassics.yorku.ca/Maslow/motivation.htm, accessed on April 23, 2020.

88 Lipman-Blumen (2004), op. cit., p. 3.

89 "Milgram Experiment – Obedience to Authority," *Explorable*, https://explorable.com/stanley-milgram-experiment#:~:text=Conclusion%20%2D%20Obedience%20to%20Authority,65%20%25%20never%20stopped%20giving%20shocks. Accessed on July 16, 2020.

90 Lipman-Blumen (2004), op. cit., p. 4.

91 Ibid., p. 3.

92 Burns, W. A. (2017), "A descriptive literature review of harmful leadership styles: Definitions, commonalities, measurements, negative impacts, and ways to improve these harmful leadership styles," *Creighton Journal of Interdisciplinary Leadership*, Vol. 3, No 1, July 2017, p. 40, https://www.researchgate.net/publication/319030964_A_Descriptive_Literature_Review_of_Harmful_Leadership_Styles_Definitions_Commonalities_Measurements_Negative_Impacts_and_Ways_to_Improve_These_Harmful_leadership_Styles, accessed on April 24, 2020.

93 Lipman-Blumen (2004), op. cit., p. 4.

94 Taleb, N. (2001), *Fooled by Randomness: The Hidden Role of Chance in the Markets and Life* (New York: W. W. Norton).

95 Taleb, N. (2010), *The Black Swan: The Impact of the Highly Improbable* (New York: Random House).

96 Kahneman, D. (2011), *Thinking, Fast and Slow* (London: Allen Lane).

97 Milgram, S. (1974), *Obedience to Authority: An Experimental View* (New York: Harper & Row).

98 Lipman-Blumen, J. (2001), "Why Do We Tolerate Bad Leaders – Magnificent Uncertitude, Anxiety and Meaning," in *The Future of Leadership*, eds. Warren Bennis et al. (San Francisco: Jossey-Bass).

99 Jacques, E. (1990), "In Praise of Hierarchy," *Harvard Business Review*, January 1990.

100 Michels, R. (1962), *Political Parties* (New York; Free Press), p. 66.

101 Kellerman (2004), op. cit., pp. 25–27.

102 Lipman-Blumen (2004), op. cit., p. 3.

103 Guo, Q. et al. (2012), "The Values of Confucian Benevolence and the Universality of the Confucian Way of Extending Love," *Frontiers of Philosophy in China*, Vol. 7, No. 1 (March 2012), pp. 20–54, https://www.jstor.org/stable/44259370?seq=1, accessed on April 24, 2020.

104 "Ruthlessness," *Cambridge English Dictionary*, https://dictionary.cambridge.org/dictionary/english/ruthlessness, accessed on May 4, 2020.

105 Grove, A. (1999), *Only the Paranoid Survive: How to Exploit the Crisis Points that Challenge Every Company* (New York: Penguin Random House).

106 Kennedy, J. F. (1962) *Remarks on the first anniversary of the Alliance for Progress*, 13 March 1962, https://www.brainyquote.com/quotes/john_f_kennedy_101159, accessed on April 24, 2020.

Chapter 2
Elizabeth Tudor

Machiavelli's description of a successful state could have been written about Queen Elizabeth I's reign at its height.

> . . . a prince securely reigning among subjects no less secure, a world replete with peace and justice . . . its prince glorious and respected by all, the people fond of him and secure under his rule.

After the defeat of the Spanish Armada in 1588, Pope Sixtus V declared:

> She certainly is a great queen and were she only a Catholic, she would be our dearly beloved daughter. Just look how well she governs! She is only a woman, only mistress of half an island, and yet she makes herself feared by Spain, by France, by the Empire, by all![1]

The England Elizabeth inherited was in a parlous state. Elizabeth achieved a remarkable turnaround in her personal fortunes, and those of England,[2] in large part because of her mastery of detail, noted by the French ambassador in 1601:

> It is not unusual to behold princes form great designs, but to regulate the conduct of them, to foresee and guard against all obstacles in such a manner that, when they happen, nothing more will be necessary than to apply the remedies prepared long before – this is what few princes are capable of.[3]

Machiavelli's advice in *The Prince*, a book Elizabeth would have read, might have been designed for an insecure, potential ruler of questionable legitimacy, and whose right to rule was disputed by foreign powers. She mastered deception, dissimulation, prevarication, and circumvention. Circumstances dictated that she did not follow Machiavelli's advice in two critical areas.

Unlike her sister Mary, and her half-brother Edward VI who persecuted Protestants and Catholics respectively, Elizabeth realized that England was too evenly split in its religious affiliations for her to immediately replace beneficiaries of the old regime.[4] Instead, she sought to find a balance between Catholic nobles and extreme Protestants, gaining time to manage supporters of Mary, Queen of Scots. She eliminated her rival without provoking a civil war or wars with Scotland or France.[5] That Elizabeth should take an accommodating attitude to doctrinal differences was unsurprising. She believed:

> There is only one Jesus Christ. The rest is a dispute over trifles.[6]

Fulminations against female monarchs were typical of the age, compounding Elizabeth's difficulties.[7] Elizabeth never accepted the supremacy of men and made that clear.[8] An assessment four hundred years after her death summarized her contribution:

https://doi.org/10.1515/9783110707878-003

> For forty-five years . . . Elizabeth had given her country peace and stable government . . . During that time England had risen from an impoverished nation to become one of the greatest powers in Europe . . .[9]

There were failures. She died £400,000 in debt, £266,000 of that was inherited from her sister, Mary.[10] She lent money to Essex, and funded wars in France. She gave financial support to the Dutch revolt against Spain, costing more than £250,000.[11] The war in Ireland was expensive. The combined total was £5,000,000.[12] Her revenues were much less (in 1588 she only received £392,000). Calais remained in French hands, Ireland was only partially subdued, and England had not established a successful colony in the New World. She avoided dealing with the problems of the royal finances through her investments in privateering, delayed the rise of Puritanism, and avoided Parliament's attempts to limit the powers of the Crown.[13]

Elizabeth Before Accession

Declared a bastard in infancy, Elizabeth was still royal and a piece in the dynastic political game. At age 10, Elizabeth was brought to court by Katherine Parr, Henry VIII's final wife, who ensured she had the best education possible. She had a natural talent for learning, and mastered[14] Latin, Greek, French, and Italian.[15] Throughout her life, Elizabeth set aside three hours a day to read historical books.[16] Her linguistic facility allowed her to deal with ambassadors without intermediaries.

Elizabeth learned to survive in a complex and dangerous dynastic and political environment. Her life had been difficult while her father was alive and became more so after his death. During her half-brother Edward VI's reign, Thomas Seymour, the brother of the Lord Protector (regent) sought to marry Elizabeth without seeking permission from the Privy Council and the King; revelations of earlier dalliances with Seymour damaged her reputation and she was placed under house arrest. The next threat came from John Dudley, Earl of Warwick who sought to use her as a dynastic pawn and marry her to his brother or his son to protect the Protestant succession. Elizabeth was carefully circumspect in conversation and correspondence. When ordered by Dudley to come to London to be at dying Edward's bedside, she prevaricated, sending word that she was too ill to travel. Edward died on July 6, 1553, and four days later Lady Jane Grey was proclaimed Queen.[17] Dudley's plot failed; the people supported Mary's claim and the succession devised by Henry VIII took its course.[i] Lady Jane Grey reigned for nine days only. She and Dudley were executed.

Queen Mary (Elizabeth's half-sister) was a serious threat to Elizabeth's life because Elizabeth was the unwilling figurehead for those seeking to replace her. Once

---

i Edward VI, followed by Mary, and then Elizabeth.

Mary's accession was secured, Elizabeth sought to establish a good relationship by seeking permission to come to Court. Mary aggressively promoted Catholicism and sought Elizabeth's conversion. Elizabeth conformed in form only (for example, she promised to attend Mass but when the time came, she pretended to be ill and made a memorable fuss). Mary's affection cooled quickly. The Imperial ambassador advised Mary that Elizabeth would create trouble and should be excluded from the succession. Mary agreed[18] but lacked evidence to send Elizabeth to the Tower of London. Elizabeth obtained leave of absence from court and left in December. During the winter, conspiracies with the aim of using Elizabeth as a dynastic pawn began, resulting from resistance to Mary's proposed marriage to Philip II of Spain. Whether Elizabeth was involved or not, the ringleaders used her name. She was ordered to the Tower, sent by river rather than through the streets of London where there would be too many well-wishers. Elizabeth was terrified and feared for her life. She wrote to Mary, protesting innocence.[19] Mary remained suspicious, but after three months Elizabeth was sent from London to Woodstock under house arrest.

In 1555, Mary began persecuting Protestants. This time Elizabeth went to confession and received the sacrament at the altar, but required her chaplain to read the litany and many prayers in English. When Mary found out, she told Elizabeth she must use the Latin service used at court; Elizabeth promised to obey.

Elizabeth and Mary were reconciled in 1555 at a face-to-face meeting.[20] Elizabeth's position was strong enough for her to no longer worry about her life; in part because Philip II realized that Parliament would not ratify his marriage to Mary if Elizabeth were imprisoned or banished. There was another failed rebellion, but this time Mary wrote to Elizabeth refusing to believe that she was involved. Mary came to depend on Elizabeth's company after Philip II returned to Spain. Mary experienced another phantom pregnancy and rumors of her impending death spread. Sir Nicholas Throckmorton wrote to Elizabeth advising her that, on taking Mary's place, she should adopt a temperate approach:

> It shall not be meet that either the old [Mary's] or the new [Elizabeth's council] should wholly understand what you mean, but to use them as instruments to serve yourself with.[21]

Elizabeth's early life taught her how to survive; that she needed to be independent of domestic or foreign factions if she was to achieve her objectives; and that marriage was a dangerous estate. Her actions as Queen reflected these lessons:

> All her training and experience, her self-discipline and abnegation, her loneliness and sorrows endured had been for this 'crown imperial,' which was hers of right. She was determined never to give it up and for the rest of her life self-preservation became her first care.[22]

Elizabeth as Queen

Elizabeth avoided making irrevocable commitments wherever possible.[23],[ii] She faced five strategic challenges: (1) finding a compromise on religion; (2) settling the succession; (3) the threat presented by Mary, Queen of Scots; (4) the threat posed by Spain; and (5) managing the changing economic environment.

Finding a Compromise on Religion

Elizabeth's early decision to celebrate Mary's death with a Catholic Mass on December 14, 1558 (because that is what Mary would have wanted),[24] signaled her wish to compromise. All she required from subjects was loyalty to herself, the state, and outward conformity to laws covering religion.[25]

Four religious issues needed to be resolved: (1) deciding whether the Pope or Monarch headed the English church, (2) reconciling differing Catholic and Protestant beliefs about the nature of the sacrament, (3) establishing a uniform way of worshipping, and (4) protecting the role of bishops. Elizabeth set about dealing with them as a matter of urgency:

1. **Supremacy:** There had always been tension between the Monarch and the Pope over authority and wealth. In England, these tensions had come to a head under Elizabeth's father who, by declaring himself head of the church, acquired religious as well as secular authority and control of the church's wealth. Elizabeth aimed to reassert the supremacy of the Monarch over the Church in England. She emphasized the continuity of Anglicanism with the English medieval Church and introduced an act to re-establish the Monarch as the "supreme head"[26] of the Church, which encountered some resistance on grounds of her gender,[iii],[27] and she accepted the title of "Supreme Governor" instead. In practice, she wielded the same authority as her father. From her supreme governorship flowed a divine right of kingship.[28] All clergy were required to swear an oath of loyalty to the Queen.[29]

2. **Communion:** Elizabeth was not fanatical about religion. However, her faith mattered to her and her belief in the Last Judgment guided her behavior.[30]

3. **Uniformity:** She was not a Protestant radical, she loved ritual and music. She kept the clergy's caps, copes, and capes; and candles and crucifixes in her private chapels; but got rid of miracles, indulgences, incense, and the veneration

---

ii Following a brief, disastrous, military adventure in France, Elizabeth avoided making irrevocable commitments wherever possible. Mattingly, G. (1959), *The Defeat of the Spanish Armada* (London: Jonathan Cape), p. 143.

iii St. Paul had stated that no woman was permitted to act as apostle, shepherd, or preacher, rendering Elizabeth unfit. Weir, A. (1998), op. cit., p. 59.

of the Virgin Mary. She also insisted that the service be conducted in the proper form and in English.[31] Passage of the Act of Uniformity in 1559 was a compromise to maintain the continuity of the Church, provide stability, and gain assent, if not full support.[32] Her policy was to frame the issues of religion as inclusively as possible.

Once the Thirty-Nine Articles were formulated, Elizabeth decreed there should be no further research into theological matters. Too many preachers "prophesying" and sermonizing would lead to presbyters, elders, and religious communities thinking they had the divine right to run the country. It could lead to the destruction of a "big tent" church, end episcopacy, and ultimately bring about the end of monarchy.[33]

There were disputes in Parliament about the proposals, however the peace signed with France on March 19, 1559, gave Elizabeth room to maneuver. She delayed – adjourning Parliament until after Easter when it passed the Royal Supremacy Act and the Act of Uniformity which made Anglicanism England's official faith, set down rules of religious practice and worship,[34] and enforced a new prayer book (which compromised between radical Protestant and more conservative views). Elizabeth kept the reformed church catholic. The formulation was as wide as possible; consequently, it was essential that there should be one liturgy to avoid endlessly differing interpretations.

There was broad support for the settlement and few refused to take the oath of loyalty to the Queen. Elizabeth's tolerant approach worked, but did not keep everyone happy. She faced numerous threats following Pope Pius V's excommunication of her in 1570. Catholics were torn between loyalty to the Queen many of them respected, if not loved, and loyalty to the Pope who they believed was God's representative on Earth. Many Catholics compartmentalized their spiritual and secular allegiances. From the time of the excommunication onward, Catholics were seen as a threat to the Queen and the realm.[35]

4. **Episcopacy:** Radical Protestants in Parliament wanted to abolish the episcopacy and allow marriage for the clergy. Elizabeth was opposed to the former policy and disliked the latter. She was able to insist on maintaining the episcopal structure as representing continuity with the medieval church and the "laying on of hands" that dated back to the time of St. Peter, increasing the legitimacy of the hierarchy in the Church. It allowed her to control the appointment of bishops, limit "prophesying" from the pulpit, and redirect some church income to help fill budgetary shortfalls. Above all, she felt that successful attack on the bishops and the stripping away of ritual would ultimately lead to an attack on the monarchy itself.[36]

Marriage, Alliances, and Succession

Marriage has always been an important tool of diplomacy; between 1534 and 1572 Elizabeth had more than twenty suitors.[37] None were successful, despite the pressure Parliament and the Privy Council put on her to marry. In considering a marriage, Elizabeth had to choose between Spain, France, the Holy Roman Empire, important English suitors, and remaining unmarried.[38]

Playing one suitor off against another could be advantageous. She kept Philip II of Spain interested just long enough, at a time when peace had not yet been achieved with France. After France dropped its backing of Mary, Queen of Scots' claim to the English throne and Philip II married the Valois Elisabeth, Elizabeth hoped to maintain friendly relations,[39] but Philip II became obsessed with regaining England for the Catholic Church. As relations with Spain deteriorated, Elizabeth used marriage discussions with the Austrian branch of the Hapsburg family to maintain good relations with the Holy Roman Emperor – Philip II's uncle,[40] but Elizabeth's affection for Robert Dudley, Earl of Leicester, worried the Emperor.

The Imperial ambassador was disappointed when she turned the Emperor's son down, claiming that she had no wish to get married.[41] In his opinion, the obstacle was the tainted Robert Dudley, Earl of Leicester,[42] whose wife was found dead with a broken neck at the bottom of the stairs in her home in 1560. He was cleared of her alleged murder, but it became obvious to Elizabeth that she could not marry him and retain the loyalty of her subjects.

During early 1565, Elizabeth was under pressure to either marry Charles IX, the very young king of France, or to marry an Englishman (a topic that created serious division in her council). Elizabeth again prevaricated, suggesting to the Imperial ambassador that she might still marry Dudley. Again, the deal breaker was religion. Just when Elizabeth seemed to be willing to marry Charles, the Imperial ambassador discovered that Philip II was now objecting to Charles marrying a heretic Queen. This change in the political context ushered in a realignment where Spain and Portugal (England's oldest ally) became England's mortal enemies. And France (England's hereditary enemy since the time of Henry II) became England's ally.[43] The universal view was that, as long as Elizabeth remained unmarried, Catholic Mary, Queen of Scots presented an existential threat.[44]

Elizabeth became interested in the Duc D'Anjou when English and French interests converged over the need to help the Dutch in their revolt against Spain, and "frenzied wooing" began. Religious issues intervened again, and Elizabeth came to understand that if she was to keep the love of her subjects, she could never marry Anjou, or Leicester. She used the objections of Parliament to explain why she had to amicably break off negotiations.[45]

Her decision not to marry allowed Elizabeth to create a uniquely successful public relations persona, but left the question of the succession unanswered.

Neutralizing the Threat of Mary, Queen of Scots

The threat to Elizabeth posed by Mary, Queen of Scots was threefold: (1) her claim to the English throne; (2) being Queen of Scotland when Scotland and England were not on friendly terms; and (3) being the only viable Catholic alternative to Elizabeth.

1. **Claim to the throne:** Mary, Queen of Scots was the only child of James V of Scotland and Mary of Guise of Lorraine. Mary grew up French and married Francis, the son of the French king. Her Tudor antecedents put her next in line to the English throne after Elizabeth. Moreover, she was legitimate. Some Catholics regarded her claim to the throne as better than Elizabeth's.[46] Elizabeth saw Mary as her successor for some years but, in the end, Elizabeth appointed Mary's son, James, as successor.

2. **Sovereign of a potential enemy:** When Elizabeth became Queen, there were French troops in Scotland. Elizabeth was concerned that England could find itself between a hostile France in the South, and Franco-Scottish troops in the North. In June 1560, Elizabeth negotiated a treaty with the Scots whereby the French agreed in the name of Mary, Queen of Scots to recognize Elizabeth as Queen of England; Mary would no longer quarter the royal arms of England with her own. The French would leave Scotland and the government of Scotland would be in the hands of the Scottish council – neither England nor France would interfere in Scottish matters.[47]

Mary delayed signing the treaty despite statements of friendship and loyalty and Elizabeth's urgings.[48] In 1561, after the death of her husband Francis II, Mary went to Scotland, still not accepting that she had no claim on the English throne.

Mary sent her advisor William Maitland to ask Elizabeth if she would be willing to revise the terms of the Treaty of Edinburgh and recognize her as the heir presumptive. Elizabeth was disappointed, but admitting she knew of no better claim than Mary's, she had no objection to naming her if Henry VIII's will and the Act of Succession did not prevent her from so doing. She advised Maitland that it would be better if Mary showed herself a good friend of England – the English would then be well-disposed to accept her as the rightful heiress. She also admitted her concern at the danger to her person of endorsing Mary. It was Mary's turn to be disappointed. At a second audience with Elizabeth, Maitland warned that Mary might resort to force to take the crown, if she was not named.[49]

Elizabeth and Mary agreed to meet in the north of England despite the outbreak of civil war in France between Catholics and Protestant Huguenots. The first time that fighting broke out in France, Elizabeth insisted on going ahead with the meeting. However, the second time, Elizabeth realized she could not appear to abandon the Protestant cause. Elizabeth decided to postpone the meeting for a year.[50]

Mary's ambition to marry a leading Catholic prince worried Elizabeth. If she were to marry a prince of the royal houses of Spain, Austria, or France, Elizabeth would once again be facing a Catholic threat with Scotland as a springboard for invasion. She warned Mary not to marry the heir to the Spanish throne saying that if she did so, she would be regarded as an enemy for life.[51]

Elizabeth's near-death encounter with small pox in 1562 created pressure once again to resolve the succession question. Although Parliament opposed Mary's claim, Elizabeth wrote affectionate letters to her and punished those who had written a pamphlet deriding her claim.

Elizabeth wanted Mary to marry Dudley and proposed it to Maitland, whose initial private reaction was that it was inappropriate given that Dudley was Elizabeth's discarded lover, a commoner suspected of treason, and the possible murderer of his wife. Few believed Elizabeth could be serious.[52]

Mary needed an heir and, unlike Elizabeth, she needed the companionship of a husband.[53] She was not enthusiastic about marrying Dudley, nor were the Scots. They were also not enthusiastic about Mary's eventual choice, Lord Darnley,[54] who she married in 1565,[55] giving birth to a son, James, the future James VI, king of Scotland and later James I, king of England.

Mary's promotion of Catholicism provoked a failed revolt in Scotland[56] but her victory was short-lived. Her marriage to Darnley was a disaster and she turned to David Rizzio, her corrupt Italian secretary, for comfort.[57] Rizzio was murdered in front of Mary.[58] For a short while, Elizabeth, who had been genuinely horrified by events, and Mary were once more on friendly terms. However, Mary was still working to establish her claim to succeed Elizabeth. She actively sought to undermine her cousin's position in England[59] even though Elizabeth promised to block any legislation that harmed Mary's claim in return for an undertaking that she would not press her claim as long as Elizabeth lived.[60]

On February 8, 1567, Mary announced that she was willing to sign the Treaty of Edinburgh, seven years late. On February 10, 1567, Darnley was murdered.[61] Many were suspect: Catholic kings and the Pope did not want Catholicism tarnished by association with Darnley; the Scottish lords associated with Darnley in the murder of Rizzio who had been betrayed by him wanted him dead; Elizabeth was suspected because Darnley was opposed to the rise of Protestantism led by Mary's half-brother, the Earl of Moray. The evidence began to point to Mary and the Earl of Bothwell.[62]

After a travesty of a trial on April 12th, Bothwell was acquitted. On April 24th, he abducted Mary and "ravished" her, making it impossible for her to refuse to marry him. On June 3rd, the Church of Scotland granted Bothwell a divorce for adultery with one of his wife's maids. Now free, he married Mary on May 15th. The Scottish nobles found the marriage intolerable. Bothwell fled and ended his life in Denmark. Mary was imprisoned at Lochleven. The incriminating "Casket Letters" between Mary and Bothwell became known. The Scottish lords offered her a choice between divorcing Bothwell, abdicating, or being put on trial. She rejected the three options, asking to sail away. The Pope refused to have any more to do with her. She abdicated under duress on July 24th and James was crowned king on July 29, 1567.

Elizabeth was outraged at the deposition of a monarch[63] and initially refused to recognize Moray's appointment as head of the regency council or James' coronation as King of Scots.[64]

Mary escaped from Lochleven, was defeated, and crossed the border into England on May 16th, placing herself under Elizabeth's protection. Restoring her to the Scottish throne was impractical, sending her to France or Spain dangerous, and she could not be left at liberty in England as a focus for Catholic rebels. Mary was held in custody, and informed that she could not meet Elizabeth or come to court unless and until she was cleared of the charge of murder.[65,66] A commission of inquiry found that nothing could be proved against her, but *not* that she was not guilty.[67]

Mary was no longer a threat as sovereign of a hostile power.

3. **Leader of Catholic revolt:** In England, Mary seemed more interested in her claim to the English throne rather than in regaining her Scottish crown. She began to plot against Elizabeth. Although Philip II was strictly neutral toward Elizabeth at this time, his ambassador de Spes disobeyed orders and plotted with disaffected northern nobles to liberate Mary and make her Queen of England – encouraging the Duke of Norfolk to marry her. Elizabeth suspected treason and was angered by the thought of Mary's involvement. Elizabeth knew that Norfolk had considered marrying Mary and gave him the chance to tell her, but he did not.

Elizabeth, furious, confronted Norfolk and made him swear to have nothing further to do with the Scottish cause. Terrified, Norfolk made light of his interest in Mary. Elizabeth was unimpressed and showed disfavor so clearly that Norfolk was shunned at court. He retreated to his stronghold pleading illness, too afraid to go to Windsor, despite Mary's urging that he should deal boldly with her cousin and be brave.[68]

Additionally, a rebellion was brewing in the north of England resulting from resentment at royal interference in the region; a desire to restore Catholicism, and resentment of Protestant councilors; and anger at Elizabeth's failure to settle the succession on Mary. Catholics in the rest of England were loyal, but the North, under the Earls of Northumberland and Westmorland, had never reconciled to Elizabeth.

The plan was to murder all northern royal officials and liberate Mary with whom they had been in touch since the spring of 1569. The King of France was involved and the Florentine banker Roberto Ridolfi funded the revolt. Cecil and Elizabeth knew from the start about the preparations, but could not risk Norfolk joining them and bringing the eastern counties with him. If he were to do that, it had been decided to put Mary to death. Elizabeth neutralized Norfolk but the northern earls went ahead and marched south with 2,500 men, sacking Durham Cathedral on their way to Tutbury where Mary was held. Elizabeth ordered Mary moved to the Protestant Midlands; Windsor was prepared for a siege and the royal army 28,000 strong was sent to deal with the rebels under the leadership of Earl of Sussex. He pursued Northumberland and Westmorland to the Scottish border where they escaped to Scotland.

Elizabeth decided to make an example of the defeated rebels, instructing the Earl of Sussex to spare no one. By February 1570, between 600 and 750 commoners had been hanged; two hundred gentry had forfeited their estates and goods. Elizabeth thought it unfair that the planners of the revolt had escaped while ordinary people had lost their lives. Norfolk was demoted. Westmorland and the Countess of Northumberland fled to Flanders. Northumberland was captured by the Scots, handed over to the English, and executed in York in August 1570. The plan to execute Mary was shelved.[69] Another revolt in the north, led by Lord Dacre was ferociously suppressed by Lord Hunsdon, the Queen's cousin.

Matters became more complicated when Moray was assassinated in Scotland and the Kings of France and Spain pressed Elizabeth to restore Mary to the Scottish throne. Given Mary's unpopularity in Scotland and her involvement in plots in England, Elizabeth was only prepared to offer support if Mary ratified the Treaty of Edinburgh.

On February 15, 1570, the Pope excommunicated Elizabeth, depriving her of her kingdom; absolving Catholics from allegiance to her; extending the anathema to all who supported her; and inciting her subjects and foreign princes to rise up against her in a holy crusade. The Pope's encouragement of Mary's supporters to replace Elizabeth made every Catholic in England a potential traitor and was a serious papal mistake, changing the issue from a religious argument to a political one which, as a result, broke the power of the northern nobles.[70] Catholics condemned to death were now viewed as traitors, not martyrs for their faith. Protestants attitudes hardened becoming more patriotic and protective of the Queen.

In 1571, Mary plotted again to overthrow Elizabeth using the service of Roberto Ridolfi, the Florentine banker, who could move freely across countries. Ridolfi believed, incorrectly, that half of the English were Catholic and reckoned that thirty-three peers of the realm with as many as 39,000 troops would support Mary. He wrote to the Pope, the Duke of Alva, Spain's military commander in the Low Countries, and Philip II to get their support for the holy cause of ridding England of Elizabeth. Alva was supposed to provide 6,000 crack troops to invade England at Harwich, merge with Norfolk's men, rescue Mary, capture Elizabeth, and take London.

Alva's army, tied down by the Dutch revolt, had neither the money nor the men to devote to the project. Moreover, he thought the enterprise foolhardy, would make the plight of English Catholics worse, and provoke Elizabeth into executing Mary. He wrote to Philip II to warn him off the scheme. Ridolfi's cipher was not foolproof and members of his team were careless.[71] Elizabeth was still trying to negotiate with Mary through Bishop Ross, proposing that James would be sent to England to be educated away from the influence of Presbyterians. Mary appeared ready to renounce her claim to England in favor of Elizabeth and her issue. When the Scottish delegates came to negotiate, stalemate was soon reached and they returned to Edinburgh because they could not sign a treaty without first calling a Parliament.

It was at this point a messenger of Bishop Ross was searched and found to be carrying secret letters from Ridolfi. Under weeks of cross-examination, the messenger broke down and revealed the plot and the names of the thirty to forty peers of the realm Ridolfi was relying on. Ross was interrogated and placed under house arrest. Elizabeth's agents in Europe reported a widespread plot involving foreign troops to depose Elizabeth, and enthrone Mary.

Another messenger was stopped and his bag was found to contain gold from France and a letter in cipher to Mary's supporters. Norfolk's secretaries were interrogated and on September 7th, Norfolk was arrested and taken to the Tower. This investigation led to the death of Norfolk in 1572; along with the incrimination of Arundel, Lumley, Southampton, Cobham, and the Spanish ambassador.

Bishop Ross said he was relieved when he freely confessed that Mary was not fit to have another husband having poisoned her first (Francis II), consented to the murder of the second (Darnley), married Darnley's murderer (Bothwell), and then led him to battle so that he would be killed.[72] His confession astounded his interrogator, Dr Wilson who wrote:

> Lord, what a people are these; what a Queen, and what an ambassador![73]

When Mary was confronted with the evidence, she denied it; claiming never to have dealt with Ridolfi; and as for Norfolk, he was Elizabeth's subject and no business of hers.

The French king, Charles IX, formerly his sister-in-law's champion, now decided to abandon Mary, observing:

> Alas, the poor fool will never cease until she loses her head. They will put her to death. It is her own fault and folly.[74]

Elizabeth resisted pressure from a unanimous Parliament to have Mary tried for treason and executed immediately.[75] Parliament drew up a Bill of Mary's offenses, depriving her of her claim to the throne; and making it an offense for anyone to proclaim or assert it. To everyone's surprise, Elizabeth vetoed it, causing her councilors to despair, given their intelligence from abroad that the Pope and Philip II were now set upon overthrowing her. Sparing Mary forced Elizabeth to execute Norfolk instead, having delayed his execution for nearly a year. The St. Bartholomew's Day massacre on August 24th[iv] increased pressure on Elizabeth to have Mary executed, but Elizabeth was unwilling to provoke the Pope and Philip II. On September 10th, she requested the Earl of Mar demand Mary's return to Scotland to be tried for the murder of Darnley. Mar would only agree if English soldiers were present at the scaffold. This would implicate Elizabeth who then abandoned the idea.[76]

By 1575, it was clear to Mary that all that was left for her was her claim to the English throne. She saw herself as a champion of Catholicism, whose mission was to overthrow Elizabeth, and restore England to the true faith. Elizabeth's spymaster, Walsingham, had intercepted enough of her letters to know that Mary was only waiting for the time when she could replace her cousin.[77]

In 1580, when Pope Sixtus V once more encouraged all Catholics to assassinate Elizabeth,[78] Parliament repeatedly asked Elizabeth to take tough measures against recusants and missionaries. In 1581, the Recusancy Act was passed, raising the fine for non-attendance at Anglican services to a severe £20 per month; imposing a penalty of a year in prison for participating in a Mass; and classifying anyone who converted to Catholicism as a traitor. Anyone defaming the Queen would be pilloried, have both ears cut off, and be fined £200. For a second offense, the punishment was death. Even so, there was no widespread persecution and over the next twenty years only 250 Catholics would be executed or die in prison.[79] Mary's reinvigorated plotting led to Philip II threatening war, which he withdrew as Elizabeth's relations with the Duc d'Anjou became closer.[80] In May 1582, the Guises, the Pope, Philip II, and Mary, supported by the Jesuits began to plot to replace Elizabeth. By early 1583, they had put together a seriously flawed plan envisaging reinstating Mary as Scottish co-ruler with her son James VI.

Walsingham kept a watch on Francis Throckmorton, who he believed was Mary's agent.[81] In November 1583, Throckmorton was arrested. Under torture, he revealed Philip II's plan for the "Enterprise of England," designed to put Mary on the throne. It was clear the Pope and the Jesuits were involved; there were to be four invasions of Scotland, Ireland, Sussex, and Norfolk, coordinated by Catholics at home and abroad. All that was needed was to provoke rebellion. Mary and Mendoza, the Spanish ambassador, were deeply implicated. Walsingham was in possession of several of Mary's letters.[82] Elizabeth refused to bring Mary to justice, but had Throckmorton executed and Mendoza expelled. Spain never sent a replacement.

The situation on the Continent became more threatening. Anjou died of a fever in June 1584; in July, William of Orange, the leader of the Dutch Protestants, was assassinated on the orders of Philip II; Parma was capturing city after city in the Netherlands. Elizabeth was sure that the next target would be England. She now had to curb the activities of Mary.

---

iv The massacre on the 23rd–24th August 1572 of up to 30,000 French Huguenots ordered by the French King, Charles IX.

Mary was still treated as a queen – Elizabeth paid her costs of food, fuel, and hunting. In 1584, Elizabeth decided security should be tightened. Meanwhile the Privy Council formalized a Bond of Association, whereby a league of Protestant gentlemen swore to take up arms and destroy Mary should anything happen to Elizabeth. Parliament agreed that the terms of the Bond needed modifying before it became law. In the future, any person suspected of plotting treason would have to be tried first before being executed.[83] Upon being shown the Bond to warn her to desist, Mary protested her innocence and signed it. Two days later, she wrote to Philip II urging him to proceed with the Enterprise, regardless of any danger to herself.

In an attempt to avoid bringing Mary to trial, Elizabeth tried but failed to persuade James VI to share the throne with his mother. He refused, not wishing to have his mother in Scotland to create trouble. Elizabeth kept his refusal secret. Mary became aware that her son was not going to support her, and had signed the Treaty of Berwick with Elizabeth on July 5th;[84] so she became desperate.

Gilbert Gifford, a trainee Catholic priest, was arrested and was turned. He was instructed to pass on all the letters from the French embassy to Mary; replies were to be passed to Walsingham, whose secretary, an expert in codes and ciphers, would decipher, copy, and reseal the letters before sending them to their intended destinations. Elizabeth followed developments closely.[85]

In March 1586, Philip II obtained the blessing of Pope Sixtus V, and financial support for the planned invasion that was to be a crusade – a holy war to be fought on a grand scale. On May 20th, Mary wrote to Mendoza declaring her intent to:

> . . . cede and give, by will, my right to the succession of [the English] crown to your King your master, considering the obstinacy and perseverance of my son in heresy.[86]

Philip II decided to pass his claim to his daughter. Mary wrote to Mendoza assuring Spain of her support for the invasion and promising to get her son's help. She also wrote to Paget saying it was now urgent to proceed. Walsingham had both letters on his desk. The letter to Paget explained the role of Father Ballard in inciting a rebellion to coincide with the invasion due in the summer. Walsingham was able to track Ballard's contact with Anthony Babington (a zealous twenty-five-year-old who had been involved in a hare-brained plot to assassinate the entire Council at a Star Chamber meeting). Walsingham decided to turn this latest plot to the government's advantage.

On June 25th, Mary wrote to Babington, who replied on July 6th with the outline of his plot, seeking approval and guidance. Mary replied briefly on July 9th. The letter Walsingham was waiting for came on July 17th where Mary endorsed the plot and Elizabeth's murder; allowing Walsingham to deal with Mary under the new 1585 Act of Association. He added a forged postscript to request the names of his co-conspirators before forwarding it to Babington on July 29th.

On August 9th, Mary's guardian, Sir Amyas Paulet, searched Mary's belongings when she was out hunting and impounded three chests full of letters, jewelry, and money which he sent to Walsingham. He arrested her, and her two secretaries. Elizabeth wrote to thank him.[87]

Babington confessed he had plotted to kill the Queen and made seven statements, incriminating Mary and his collaborators. The Council demanded that Elizabeth call Parliament to deal with Mary. Elizabeth tried to delay. She knew Parliament would insist on a trial and execution. On September 9th, Elizabeth summoned Parliament. The verdict was a foregone conclusion. On the 20th, Babington and his five co-conspirators were condemned to a traitor's death – hanged, disemboweled at Burghley's insistence while still alive, and then drawn and quartered.[v,88]

Soon the general public knew about the plot and wanted Mary executed as its chief. Elizabeth wanted to spare Mary because she was an anointed monarch, but realized that her subjects wanted more. The Council made the case for Mary's execution: there was evidence to prove Mary's guilt that could be brought to court, James VI would not object as he would benefit from Mary's death, her death would clear the way for a Protestant successor, France had long abandoned Mary, and Philip II was already committed to overthrowing Elizabeth.

Elizabeth had to consider that Mary was a foreigner not subject to English law; and an anointed sovereign answerable only to God, even though her lawyers concluded that Elizabeth was within her rights to prosecute Mary under the new 1585 statute.

Mary refused to acknowledge the competence of the court of thirty-six appointed commissioners. Only when Elizabeth's chief advisor, Lord Burghley, warned her that she would be tried in her absence, did Mary agree to attend the trial. Just as the trial was about to conclude with a verdict of guilty, given the weight of evidence against Mary, Elizabeth sent a message to order the court to reconvene in ten days' time in London. The delay did not change the verdict. Mary was found guilty of being an accessory to the conspiracy and of imagining and compassing Elizabeth's destruction. The punishment for which under the new 1585 statute was death and disinheritance. The sentence would be left for Elizabeth and Parliament who had to ratify the verdict.[89]

Elizabeth was inclined to pardon Mary as a result of intense pressure from the French and Scottish ambassadors and offered to do so, if Mary truly repented and confessed. However, Mary refused to admit guilt. Elizabeth prevaricated and procrastinated.[90] Her hesitations lasted from October 29th until December 4th when the proclamation was read out, confirming the verdict. When Parliament sent another deputation to her on November 24th, she prevaricated again.[91] Finally, on February 1st, Elizabeth signed Mary's death warrant. The next day, Elizabeth sent a message

---

v The public were appalled at the cruelty. The next day Elizabeth ordered that the remaining seven conspirators be drawn and quartered *only after they were dead.*

to her secretary, Davison, instructing him not to lay the warrant before the Lord Chancellor until she spoke to him once more. When he told her it had already been sealed, she was alarmed. The Lord Chancellor and Davison went to see Burghley, who called a meeting of the Council where the ten councillors took it upon themselves on February 4th to draft an order for the warrant to be executed, without telling the Queen; and it was sent to Fotheringhay, where Mary was held.[92]

On February 8th, Mary was executed and Londoners celebrated wildly. Elizabeth, however, was furious, remorseful, and in real grief. She feared God's reaction and the damage to her international reputation. Elizabeth exaggerated her grief and anger at her councilors to maximize plausible deniability. The courts in Europe were not deceived by attempts to avoid blame. The French king was furious but too busy with his own problems to do anything about it. James VI needed to remain on good terms with Elizabeth if his succession to the English throne was to be guaranteed, and only offered token protests. Only the Pope and Philip II were willing to act, and the execution confirmed what they had intended all along.[93]

The reason why Elizabeth hesitated so long before deciding to execute Mary may have been what she had written to the Scots when they wanted to put Mary to death, namely that there was no law in Scotland whereby subjects could try an anointed monarch and put such a monarch to death. It violated the concept of the "divine right" of kings.

From a Machiavellian perspective, Elizabeth's tolerance of Mary, Queen of Scots' plotting may have seemed unwise, but Elizabeth needed time to manage the threat of support from France; and in the end, she was successful in getting rid of her rival without provoking civil war, or war with Scotland, or France, having made it clear to all that she was against the killing of an anointed monarch, however much that person had intrigued against her.

Neutralizing the Threat Posed by Spain

It is not surprising that Spain should have become an existential enemy given Philip II's obsession with recapturing England for the Roman Catholic Church, the beginning of a global commercial rivalry, and the asymmetrical warfare adopted by Elizabeth in response.

Elizabeth neutralized the Spanish threat through policies of plausible deniability in naval skirmishes, the use of proxies in France and the Netherlands, and by building a navy superior to Spain's. Elizabeth's direct military involvements in France, the Low Countries, and Ireland proved less successful, however, because she appointed poor commanders.

1. **Commercial rivalry:** During the 16th century, two large oceanic trades developed: one to the Americas as a national private monopoly for Spain, the other to India as a national public monopoly for Portugal. Spanish settlers in the Americas imported the goods they needed and paid for imports through the products of plantations, ranching, and mining dependent on slaves to work them. This created a new trade flow with West Africa. In the middle of the century, the settlers discovered silver mines in Peru, encouraging a dramatic increase in trans-Atlantic trade with sugar, hides, and bullion traveling east to pay for the rise in manufactured goods going west to serve the growing Spanish populations in the Americas.[94] By 1580, exports from Seville were more than 20,000 tons (twenty percent of Spain's shipping capacity). Ships using well-known routes across the Caribbean and Atlantic risked shipwreck and being boarded by pirates or privateers, mainly French. The Spanish adopted a convoy system to protect their ships.[95]

The Slave Trade was dominated by the Portuguese who supplied the Brazilian plantations, and the Mexican and Peruvian mines. Portuguese contractors were licensed by the Spanish government to sail directly from Lisbon to Spanish America. Many slavers sailed, unlicensed, from Guinea and smuggled goods along with slaves.

Sir John Hawkins, after a first profitable legal voyage, planned a second on a bigger scale with Elizabeth and several of her Privy Councilors as secret investors. The second voyage went well, but Spanish authorities were now reducing foreign participation; and Elizabeth forbade his return to the West Indies. A third voyage was undertaken but it fared poorly. In 1567, Hawkins persuaded the Queen to let him go one last time. This voyage ended in disaster in San Juan de Ulua,[96] making it clear that there was no possibility of compromise on trade. Sir Francis Drake took revenge through an intermittent privateering war from 1570 to 1585 that proved profitable for the Queen who was still a hidden shareholder.[97]

In 1577, Elizabeth approved Drake's circumnavigation of the globe demonstrating to Spain and the rest of Europe that Spain could not monopolize the trans-Atlantic or the East Indies trades. The expedition found opportunities for English merchants and distracted Philip II.[98] The venture was extremely profitable. When Drake returned to England, he had amassed three million ducats or over £1,500,000[99] (worth £5,992,905,000 today[vi]). Elizabeth's share enabled her to pay the national debt and still leave her with £42,000, (worth £159,810,800 today) that she invested in the Levant Trading Company.[100] In 1580, Elizabeth knighted Drake on board the *Golden Hind*, justifying Drake's actions as reparations for putting down the northern rebellions aided by Spain.[101] Philip II continued to deny

---

vi According to the Bank of England calculator, £1 in 1577, would have been worth £3,995.27 in 2019.

trading rights to the English; but privateers, encouraged by Elizabeth, continued to defy his authority to do so.[102]

2. **Asymmetrical warfare:** When Elizabeth came to the throne, she had little revenue to finance her policies[103] and could not secure additional funding from Parliament. Necessity was the mother of invention as far as building a navy capable of protecting England:

> Alongside diplomacy, Elizabeth supported and licensed men who had previously been pirates in English waters, turning them into state-sponsored privateers practicing legal piracy against England's enemies. These men gained valuable experience on the seas and, when needed, used their military skills to strengthen the diminutive Royal Navy.[104]

For example, Drake's Caribbean unprofitable raids in 1572–1573 to avenge the events of 1568 yielded invaluable experience in seamanship, supply, and siege tactics.[105] Hawkins and Drake were important actors in the defeat of the Spanish Armada in 1588.

Fundamental to Elizabeth's policy was the fine legal distinction between pirate and privateer. In the 1560s, there were nearly 10,000 pirates in England. Elizabeth created a fleet of more than 16,000 privateers by issuing letters of reprisal and commission. They waged undeclared war against Spain at little cost to the Crown,[106] which contributed to Spain's bankruptcy in 1575 by raising the cost of defending their trade across the Atlantic and making it harder to supply their troops in the Netherlands.[107]

A policy of using the pirates/privateers to weaken Spain emerged over time. It allowed England to build naval capability to fight Spain economically. It also diverted the energies of the pirates away from the Channel to long-range piracy against the enemies of England.[108]

Elizabeth was sympathetic to Dutch rebels opposed to Spain: they were co-religionists – Philip II was now married to Elisabeth of Valois, sister of the French King, who, actively persecuting Protestants, raised the threat of a Catholic Franco-Spanish anti-Protestant axis; and England's commercial interests were not served by Spanish domination of the Netherlands, demonstrated by the embargo on all English trade imposed by the Dutch regent (Philip's half-sister) in 1563. She justified her actions on grounds of English protection of heretics and piracy against Spanish ships in the Channel.[109]

By 1563, there were more than 400 known English pirates operating in the four seas around England.[110] Yet Elizabeth had only a small navy when she became Queen; with only twenty-one of the original thirty 300-ton ships Edward VI inherited from Henry VIII, and six smaller vessels. As late as 1603, the Royal Navy only consisted of twenty-nine vessels.[111]

Elizabeth needed money to rebuild and repair the fleet and pay the £7,000 debt to the Admiralty owed by Queen Mary. Instead of raising taxes to pay for these needs, she rented out ships to private adventurers for trading, exploration, and privateering activities. She had in effect inherited a fleet with a permanent organization to maintain and administer its ships – something no other ruler had. However, as a result of the incompetence in Mary's reign, Elizabeth had limited resources for the navy. The naval defense of England relied on a core of ships that would be supplemented by the merchant marine and private owners in the event of a national emergency.[112]

Elizabeth had invented a public-private partnership model for her naval needs. Even though she employed her own shipwrights, the sailors who hired her ships were expected to repair and outfit the ships. The opportunity for them to make use of naval warships made privateering a more successful joint venture enterprise, increasing the amount of privateering against Spanish ships in the Atlantic and those supplying the Spanish army in the Netherlands. Elizabeth almost created a self-financed navy.[113]

The manpower costs were small. Twenty years into her reign only 3,760 sailors and 1,900 soldiers served the state.[114] She chose not to have a large standing navy, unlike the Spanish and Portuguese – yet there were enough seamen to be called upon in case of a national emergency. Sailors preferred her approach because they got a share of the ship's profits; and discipline was lighter.[115]

3. **Plausible deniability:** Whenever the Spanish complained about the activities of English privateers, Elizabeth increased the punishments for seamen found guilty of less significant types of piracy while denouncing attacks on Spanish property publicly.[116] As late as 1587, Elizabeth was still following this policy. When Drake was ordered to sail to Cadiz to "singe the King of Spain's beard," she sent a countermanding order just late enough for it to miss him, to allow her ministers to maintain that England and Spain were not at war, and at the same time reassuring Parma in the Netherlands that negotiations were still ongoing.[117]

Her proposed solutions to Spain's problems in the Low Countries were reasonable from her perspective: no centralized government (which Philip had already conceded) and the adoption of "Cujus regio, ejus religio"[vii] – officially the Netherlands would be Catholic, but liberty of conscience would be allowed – a formula that was to be adopted later at the end of the Thirty Years War in 1648 – but which proved unacceptable to Philip II who would not tolerate heresy.[118]

In addition, Parma was no longer interested in peace. He was instructed by Philip II to lure Elizabeth into negotiations and keep her off balance, as the invasion of England had been decided upon. England, however, did not drop its guard and prepared for war.[119]

---

vii The principle that the religion of the monarch determines the official religion of a nation.

4. **Investing in a superior navy:** Elizabeth's navy was the most powerful in Europe and had fighting-ships ("galleons"), fitted with broadside guns as ship destroyers; rather than acting as rams, or floating troop carriers.[120] Elizabeth made sure that her ships and crews were in top condition for the spring of 1588.[121]

Philip II decided to go to war with England to regain control over the Netherlands and began to build his Armada of 130 vessels, 31,000 men, and 2,431 cannons. The objective was to control the Channel and allow the Duke of Parma and his Dunkirk-based army to cross to England.

In 1587, Drake was sent to attack the Spanish fleet at Cadiz.[122] The raid led to a crucial delay because Philip II's admiral, the Marques of Santa Cruz, died; to be replaced by the inexperienced Duke of Medina-Sidonia, who, by his own admission, knew more about gardening than war. The Armada failed spectacularly

> Of the 130 ships that had left Spain, perhaps 85 crept home; 10 were captured, sunk, or driven aground by English guns, 23 were sacrificed to wind and storm, and 12 others were "lost, fate unknown."[123]

Dealing with Socio-Economic Change

Elizabeth inherited an economic crisis resulting from Henry VIII's and Edward VI's currency debasement. She dealt with it swiftly, and profitably.[124] However, despite the glory of the court, power was shifting from the Monarch and Lords to the Commons in Parliament; and, once the Spanish threat receded, the rise of Puritanism became a threat to the religious-social contract of 1559.

1. **Increased poverty:** There were three causes of the increase in poverty. The first was growth in population from three to four million. The second was displacement from the countryside to the cities as a result of the dissolution of the monasteries and the enclosures of the land. The third was bad harvests, soaring prices, and high taxes in the 1590s.

    Elizabeth's prompt and efficient replacement of the debased currency helped combat inflation in the early years of her reign. However, government-introduced price controls in 1563 and wage ceilings for skilled workers led to a drop in living standards.[125]

    Enclosures[viii] aggressively adopted as the wool trade became more important, forced people off the land. As a result, those living in the countryside found themselves without employment and nowhere to live. The traditional charitable approaches of leaving money to alms-houses to house the poor was no longer sufficient, forcing the government to categorize the poor. Broader

---

viii Legally consolidating (enclosing) small landholdings into larger farms, used from the 13th century CE.

measures were needed to prevent the vagrants and beggars from becoming a threat to law and order.[126]

Poor laws were passed in 1563, 1572, 1576, 1597, and 1601, indicating the seriousness of the problem. This was exacerbated by the dissolution of the monasteries that reduced rural employment and care of the poor. The 1572 law represented a major shift in thinking, recognizing society's responsibility for the poor for the first time. Citizens were taxed to pay for the poor. The 1576 Act gave the poor work to do, supplying wool as a raw material for them to work with. The 1597 Act appointed an official in each parish responsible for looking after the poor, creating a national framework implemented at local level. It is, however, a tribute to their lasting success that two of the Acts, from 1597 and 1601, endured until well into the nineteenth century.[127]

2. **Shift in power:** In medieval political theory, Parliament's role was to petition, not to initiate or command. Three trends undermined the theory: First, the Crown's dependence on the Commons for finance inevitably led to Parliament wanting to call the tune. Second, Parliament was frequently called to legislate on crucial matters of Church and State – legitimizing monarchs; breaking with Rome; proclaiming the monarch as supreme head of the Church, or in Elizabeth's case as governor; and establishing the succession. Such consultation led Parliamentarians to consider that if they had power to grant authority; did they not also have the power to take it away? Third, was the rise of the gentry – politically conscious and economically dominant, in opposition to established aristocrats.[128]

3. **Rise of Puritanism:** By the end of Elizabeth's reign, the rising Puritan gentry and merchant classes controlled the economy. Puritans regarded themselves as apart from other Protestants. Their beliefs challenged the aristocratic establishment structure of society and the role of the Church. As early as 1573, the threat they presented to the Tudor concept of monarchy had been recognized by Elizabeth.[129]

Mastery of Image Management

Elizabeth understood that from the moment she woke to the time she went to bed, she was on show. As late as 1597, when she was 64, the French ambassador noted how impressive it was "to see how lively she is in body and mind, and nimble in everything she does."[130] Another foreign visitor to her court in the autumn of 1602, not long before she died, saw her outside "walking as freely as if she had been only eighteen years old."[131] Elizabeth had a well-earned reputation as an outstanding dancer and in February 1600 when she was 67, she was persuaded by the cousin of the French queen to dance "to show that she is not so old as one would have her."[132] She was so vigorous in old age that James VI, king of Scotland began to worry about succeeding her, believing that she "would endure as long as the sun and moon."[133]

Aware of the importance of appearances, she controlled her image throughout her reign – paying close attention to costume, hairstyles, and jewelry.[134] She encouraged the public association of her with female biblical heroes who had saved the Israelites from their enemies.[ix] It played well with the spirit of her times. She paralleled herself with Judith in a book of prayers that she wrote, published In English, French, Italian, Spanish, Latin, and Greek.[135] Presenting herself as the Virgin Queen[136] allowed her to become a semi-divine object of veneration by her subjects who needed a replacement for Catholic worship of the Virgin Mary. It allowed her to claim that she was married to her kingdom, concentrating on the greatest good for her people. It allowed her to reject Parliament's pressure in 1559 to get married:

> *Nothing, no worldy [sic] thing under the sun, is so dear to me as the love and goodwill of my subjects.* In the end this shall be for me sufficient, that a marble stone shall declare that a queen, having reigned such a time, lived and died a virgin.[137]   [Emphasis ours]

November 17th, the date of her accession was a national holiday, celebrated with festivities and church bells. The frontispiece of the Bishops' Bible printed from 1569, showed Elizabeth crowned by the four Virtues: Fortitude, Justice, Mercy, and Prudence. Paintings of her success after the defeat of the Armada were hung in churches that were now devoid of their Catholic ornaments. Her image appeared in woodcuts, brooches, badges, medals, and coins. Miniatures were worn like icons by both sexes to demonstrate loyalty and deference to their Queen.[138]

The physical and spiritual boundaries created allowed her to reframe rulership, reinforced by an extensive literature associating her with literary heroines of antiquity.[x] Her many references and those of writers of her time comparing her with Judith, the slayer of Holofernes, reinforced the belief that she was a bulwark against Catholic enemies and that Knox was wrong in fulminating against female rulers. The ultimate tribute to her was Spenser's *The Faerie Queen.*

Elizabeth did not just dominate her court with her collection of dresses and jewelry, her exuberant dancing and virtuosity in Latin; she *more than any English sovereign showed herself to her subjects.* Her coronation was one of the most expensive

---

ix "Queen Elizabeth I of England was the subject of the greatest number of biblical analogies drawn in the early modern period. Analogies were drawn both by apologists and by Elizabeth herself throughout the entire span of the queen's reign, and for almost a century after her death. Elizabeth's comparisons with Deborah the Judge, Queen Esther, Daniel the Prophet, King Solomon, and King David [and to Judith, the chaste widow of the Apocrypha]." Norrie, A. (2016), "Elizabeth I as Judith: reassessing the apocryphal widow's appearance in Elizabethan royal iconography," *Renaissance Studies,* Vol. 31 No. 5, p. 707.

x Comparing her to the virgin Astraea of Virgil's *Eclogues* returned to earth to usher in a golden age where there was eternal peace and to the virgin Diana, the huntress.

ever seen, preceded by a round of speeches, pageants, and processions at which she participated.[139] She took care to appear before commoners as well as courtiers; touring the country 25 times a year, traveling in great style with a retinue of 300 wagons and 200 horses. Elizabeth justified the expense and discomfort of these "progresses":

> We come for the hearts and allegiance of our subjects.[140]

Locals were treated to free display of pageants and fireworks. She never missed an opportunity to make great speeches, emphasizing how special she was. Just before her coronation, as she was about to mount her chariot, she prayed loudly and spontaneously so all could hear her:

> O Lord Almighty and Everlasting God, I give thee most hearty thanks that thou hast been so merciful unto me to spare me to behold this joyful day. And I acknowledge that thou hast dealt as wonderfully and as mercifully with me as thou didst with thy true and faithful servant Daniel, thy prophet whom thou delivered out of the den from the cruelty of the greedy and raging lions. Even so was I overwhelmed and only by thee delivered. To thee therefore only be thanks honor and praise forever. Amen.[141]

This was a clear claim to her subjects that she had been saved by God to lead them out of religious error that would be understood by all who heard it.

At the same time, she maintained the common touch, silencing the crowd to listen to the words of welcome by a child whose task was to greet her in verse. Eyewitnesses noted how attentively she listened and how moved she was by what she heard.[142] As she walked from Westminster Abbey to Westminster Hall after being crowned, she had a smile for everyone. She knew how to work the crowd and never forgot her responsibility for the well-being of her subjects. When a deputation of judges came to pay their respects after her coronation, she commanded them:

> Have a care over my people . . . They are my people. Every man oppresseth them and [de]spoileth them without mercy. They cannot revenge their quarrel nor help themselves. See unto them, see unto them, for they are my charge.[143]

When she arrived in Cambridge, she was invited to address the university. Spontaneously, she addressed them in excellent Latin, impressing the audience:

> Although that womanly shamefacedness, most celebrated university and most faithful subjects, might well determine me from delivering this my unlaboured speech and oration before so great an assembly of the learned, yet the intercession of my nobles and my own good will towards the university have prevailed with me to say something. And I am persuaded to the thing by two motives; the first is the increase of good letters, which I much desire and with the most earnest wish pray for; the other is as I shall hear your expectation.[144]

She succeeded in breaking the taboo against women at the university, she indicated her support for what the university was doing and that it was of national importance, she indicated[145] she was there to listen, and she bonded by speaking in learned Latin. The audience was astonished and roared their love, crying "Vivat Regina!"

The most important speech she gave to establish her special place in the hearts of her subjects was at the Tilbury military encampment during the naval battles with the Armada in 1588, where against the advice of her councilors, given the real threat of assassination, she went wearing the armor of a cavalry officer, looking resplendent on her horse:

> My loving people, we have been persuaded by some that are careful for our safety, to take heed how we commit ourselves to armed multitudes, for fear of treachery. *But I assure you, I do not desire to live to distrust my faithful and loving people. Let tyrants fear. I have always so behaved myself that, under God, I have placed my chiefest strength safeguard in the loyal hearts and goodwill of my subjects; and therefore I am come amongst you as you see, at this time, not for my recreation and disport, being resolved, in the midst of heat and battle, to live or die amongst you all,* and to lay for my God and for my kingdom and for my people, my honour and my blood, even in the dust. *I know I have the body of a weak and feeble woman, but I have the heart and stomach of a king, and of a king of England too,* and think foul scorn that Parma or Spain, or any prince of Europe should dare to invade the borders of my realm; to which rather than any dishonour shall grow by me, *I myself will take up arms, I myself will be your general, judge, and rewarder of every one of your virtues in the field. I know already for your forwardness you deserve rewards and crowns; and we do assure you, in the word of a prince, they shall be duly paid you.* [Emphases ours]

Perhaps the best description of the special relationship Elizabeth had with her subjects is captured in her last address to Parliament in 1601, known as "The Golden Speech":

> I do assure you there is no prince that loves his subjects better, or whose love can countervail our love. There is no jewel, be it of never so rich a price, which I set before this jewel: I mean your love. For I do esteem it more than any treasure in riches; for that we know how to prize, but love and thanks I count invaluable. And though God hath raised me high, yet this I count the glory of my crown, that I have reigned with your loves.[146]

References

1 Sixtus V. (1588), quoted in Weir. A. (1988), *Elizabeth the Queen* (London: Jonathan Cape), p. 399.
2 Mattingly, G. (1959), *The Defeat of the Spanish Armada* (London: Jonathan Cape), p. 30.
3 Duc de Sully (1601), quoted in Weir (1988), op. cit., p. 471.
4 Machiavelli, N., (1513), *The Prince*, (Harmondsworth: Penguin Books, 1999), Chapter VIII, pp.30–31.
5 Williams, N. (1972), *Elizabeth I, Queen of England* (London: Sphere Books), p. 82.
6 Weir (1988), op. cit., p. 54.
7 Knox, J. (1558), *First Blast of the Trumpet Against the Monstrous Regiment of Women*, quoted in Weir (1988), op. cit., p. 222.
8 Ibid., p. 166.
9 Weir (1988), op. cit., p. 487.
10 Ibid., p. 3.
11 Mattingly (1959), op. cit., p. 42.

12 "Elizabeth I (r.1558–1603)," *Royal Encyclopaedia*, https://www.royal.uk/elizabeth-i, accessed on October 4, 2020.

13 Weir (1988), op. cit., p. 487.

14 Williams (1972), op. cit., pp. 8–10.

15 Ibid., p. 9.

16 Weir (1988), op. cit. p. 14.

17 Ibid., pp. 22–23.

18 Ibid., p. 26.

19 Elizabeth I (1554), quoted in ibid., pp. 31–33.

20 Elizabeth I and Mary I (1555), quoted in ibid., p. 41.

21 Throckmorton, N. (1558), quoted in ibid., p. 47.

22 Ibid., p. 49.

23 Ibid., p. 40.

24 Axelrod, A. (2000), *Elizabeth I, CEO: Strategic Lessons from the Leader Who Built an Empire* (Paramus, New Jersey: Prentiss Hall Press), pp. 94–95.

25 Weir (1988), op. cit., p. 59.

26 Williams (1972), op. cit., p. 70.

27 Berlatsky, J. (2003) "A Reformation Survivor: The Case of Archbishop Nicholas Heath, Lord Chancellor of England, and the Rule of Women," *The Historian*, Vol. 65, No. 5 (FALL 2003), p. 1, https://www.jstor.org/stable/24452489?seq=1, accessed on October 7, 2020.

28 Ibid., p. 71.

29 "Queen Elizabeth I: Religious Settlement," *Elizabethi.org 1998–2020*, https://www.elizabethi.org/contents/elizabethanchurch/settlement.html, accessed on October 7, 2020.

30 Ibid., p. 55.

31 Weir (1988), op. cit., p. 58.

32 Williams (1972), op. cit., p. 64.

33 Ibid., p. 68.

34 "An Acte of Uniformitie of Common Praier, And Service in the Church, And The Administration of The Sacraments 1559," http://justus.anglican.org/resources/bcp/1559/front_matter_1559.htm, accessed on October 7, 2020.

35 "Queen Elizabeth I And Catholics," https://www.elizabethi.org/contents/elizabethanchurch/catholics.html, accessed on October 7, 2020.

36 Axelrod (2000), op. cit., pp. 91–92.

37 Overview of Elizabeth I, *Historical Association*.

38 "Queen Elizabeth I: Marriage and Succession," *Elizabeth.org 1998–2020*, https://www.elizabethi.org/contents/marriage/, accessed on October 12, 2020.

39 Weir (1988), op. cit., p. 62.

40 Count von Helfenstein (1559), quoted in Weir (1988), op. cit., pp. 60–61.

41 Elizabeth I, quoted in ibid., p. 73.

42 Baron Breuner (1559), quoted in ibid., p. 87.

43 Ibid., p. 278.

44 Conversation between Catherine de Medici and Sir Thomas Smith (1572), quoted in ibid., pp. 284–285.

45 Elizabeth I (1579), quoted in ibid., pp. 329–330.

46 Axelrod (2000), op. cit., pp. 188–189.

47 Weir (1988), op. cit., p. 91.

48 Axelrod (2000), op. cit., p. 189.

49 Weir (1988), op. cit., pp. 127–128.

50 Ibid., p. 132.

51 Ibid., p. 133.

52 Ibid., p. 143.

53 Ibid., p. 145.

54 Ibid., pp. 148–150.

55 Ibid., p. 163.

56 Elizabeth I, quoted in ibid., p. 167.

57 Weir (1988), op. cit., p. 168.

58 Ibid., p. 174.

59 Ibid., p. 177.

60 Ibid., p. 183.

61 Ibid., p. 185.

62 Elizabeth I (1567), quoted in ibid., p. 186.

63 Ibid., p. 189.

64 Ibid., p. 191.

65 Ibid., pp. 194–195.

66 Elizabeth I (1568), quoted in ibid., p. 197.

67 Weir (1988), op. cit., pp. 200–201.

68 Ibid., pp. 207–208.

69 Ibid., pp. 210–212.

70 Weir (1988), pp. 212–214.

71 Williams (1972), op. cit., p. 174.

72 Ibid., p. 175.

73 Wilson (1572), quoted in ibid., p. 175.

74 Charles IX (1572), quoted in ibid., p. 277.

75 Weir (1988), op. cit., p. 281–283.

76 Ibid., p. 289.

77 Ibid., p. 295.

78 Ibid., pp. 334–335.

79 Ibid., p. 335.

80 Ibid., p. 340.

81 Ibid., p. 347.

82 Ibid., pp. 349–350.

83 Ibid., pp. 350–353.

84 Ibid., p. 365.

85 Elizabeth I (1585), quoted in ibid., p. 361.

86 Mary, Queen of Scots (1586), quoted in ibid., p. 363.

87 Elizabeth 1 (1586), quoted in ibid., p. 366.

88 Weir (1988), op. cit., p. 367.

89 Ibid., pp. 368–370.

90 Elizabeth I (1586), quoted in ibid., p. 372.

91 Ibid., p. 373.

92 Ibid., p. 376–378.

93 Ibid., pp. 380–381.

94 Parry, J. H. (1963), *The Age of Reconnaissance* (London: Weidenfeld and Nicholson), pp. 177–178.

95 Ibid., p. 181.

96 Thomas, H. (1977), *The Slave Trade: The History of the Atlantic Slave Trade 1440–1870* (London: Picador), p. 158.

97 Parry (1963), op. cit., pp. 183–185.

98 Ibid., pp. 75–76.

99 Andrews, K. (1984), *Trade, Plunder, and Settlement: Maritime Enterprise and the Genesis of the British Empire* (Cambridge: Cambridge University Press), p. 53, cited in ibid., p. 76.
100 Cummins, J. (1995), *Francis Drake, Lives of a Hero* (New York: St Martin's Press), p. 125, cited in ibid., p. 76.
101 Ibid.
102 Snyder, A. J. (2006), "The Politics of Piracy: Pirates, Privateers, and the Government of Elizabeth I, 1558–1588," *Department of History, University of North Carolina, Wilmington,* p. 51, https://libres.uncg.edu/ir/uncw/f/snydera2006-1.pdf, accessed on October 19, 2020.
103 Ibid., p. 2.
104 Ibid., p. 3.
105 Ibid., p. 73.
106 Ibid., p. 4.
107 Ibid., p. 74.
108 Ibid., pp. 4–5.
109 Doran, S. (2000), *Elizabeth I and Foreign Policy, 1558–1603* (London: Routledge), p. 15, cited in ibid., p. 12.
110 Oppenheim, M. (1891), "The Royal and Merchant Navy Under Elizabeth," *The English Historical Review,* Vol. 6, No. 23, (July 1891), p. 473, cited in ibid., p. 23.
111 Ibid., pp. 465–466, cited in Snyder (2006), op. cit., p. 24.
112 Snyder (2006), op. cit., p. 25.
113 Ibid., p. 25.
114 Swinburne, H. L. (1907), *The Royal Navy* (London: Adam and Charles Black), p. 29, cited in ibid., p. 26.
115 Snyder (2006), op. cit., p. 26.
116 Ibid., p. 5.
117 Mattingly (1959), op. cit., pp. 93–94.
118 Ibid., pp. 171–172.
119 Ibid., pp. 173–174.
120 Ibid., pp. 175–176.
121 Ibid., pp. 176–177.
122 Spencer, U., Prestwich, M. et al. (2020), "Elizabethan Society," *Encyclopaedia Britannica, Inc.,* September 6, 2020, https://www.britannica.com/place/United-Kingdom/Elizabethan-society, accessed on September 8, 2020.
123 Ibid.
124 "Restoring England's currency," *Royal Museums Greenwich,* https://www.rmg.co.uk/discover/explore/restoring-englands-currency, accessed on October 25, 2020.
125 Briscoe, A. (2011), "Poverty in Elizabethan England," *BBC,* February 17, 2011, http://www.bbc.co.uk/history/british/tudors/poverty_01.shtml#:~:text=Elizabethan%20England%20faced%20a%20mounting,series%20of%20strict%20Poor%20Law, accessed on September 8, 2020.
126 Ibid.
127 Ibid.
128 Spencer and Prestwich et al. (2020), op. cit.
129 Ibid.
130 French ambassador (1597), quoted in Axelrod (2000), op. cit., p. 60.
131 Ibid., p. 60.
132 Ibid., p. 61.
133 Ibid.

134 Cartwright, M. (2020), "Elizabeth I and the Power of Image," *Ancient History Encyclopedia Foundation,* May 29, 2020, https://www.ancient.eu/article/1562/elizabeth-i–the-power-of-image/, accessed on October 26, 2020.

135 Marcus, L. S., Mueller, J., and Rose, M-B. (2000) (eds.), *Elizabeth I: Collected Works* (Chicago, IL: University of Chicago Press), p. 157, quoted in ibid., p. 710.

136 Ibid.

137 Elizabeth I (1559), quoted in Cartwright (2020), op. cit.

138 Cartwright (2020), op. cit.

139 Axelrod (2000), op. cit., p. 52.

140 Elizabeth I, quoted in ibid, p. 74.

141 Elizabeth I (1558), quoted in ibid., p. 53.

142 Axelrod (2000), op. cit., p. 69.

143 Elizabeth I (1558), quoted in ibid., p. 72.

144 Elizabeth I (1564), in ibid., p. 75.

145 Mattingly (1959). op. cit., p. 296.

146 Elizabeth I (1601), quoted in Axelrod (2000), op. cit., p. 147.

Chapter 3
Napoleon Bonaparte

Born in Corsica of an impoverished noble family and without backers, Napoleon Bonaparte chose an army career after rejection by the navy, coming to prominence at the siege of Toulon. His interests were wider than war. He used military victories to introduce enduring reforms and laid the foundations of much of modern Europe and the US. His career divides·into three phases: Rising Star; Reformer; and Warrior-Emperor.

Rising Star

Apprenticeship

Napoleon, a Corsican Italian speaker, was sent to boarding school at age nine and was taught French, a belief in French greatness, and the importance of military service and honor. His mother had strong religious beliefs, but his father was an agnostic. He was not a Christian and adopted a cult of honor, patriotism being the first duty, and courage its chief virtue. To die for one's country rendered one immortal:[1]

> Mourir pour le pays n'est pas un triste sort:
> C'est s'immortaliser par une belle mort.[2,i]

He felt that to die in bed was shameful.

In 1783, England and France ended their naval war.[ii] He applied for a cadetship in the British navy. Serving under a foreign flag was not unusual at that time, but he was not accepted and, at age 15, entered the École Militaire in Paris instead. He did well in exams and graduated after one year instead of the normal two. Napoleon became an officer at age 16.[3]

His political readings led him to believe that France needed reform to constrain the power of the monarch. In 1786, he wrote:

> We are members of a powerful monarchy, but today we feel only the vices of its constitution.[4]

---

i To die for one's country is not a sad fate;
  It is to render oneself immortal through a beautiful death.

ii The "Anglo-French War" lasted between 1778 and 1783 when France and Britain fought in the English Channel, the Mediterranean, the Indian Ocean and the West Indies. The eventual French victory helped cement the United States' independence from Britain.

https://doi.org/10.1515/9783110707878-004

A history of England[5] seems to have influenced his thinking about the nature of kingship.[iii] He wrote:

> The principal advantage of the English Constitution consists in the fact that the national spirit is always in full vitality. For a long spell of years, the King can doubtless arrogate to himself more authority than he ought to have, may even use his great power to commit great injustice, but the cries of the nation soon change to thunder, and sooner or later the King yields.[6]

Napoleon was interested in the English constitutional monarchical system. He described his approach to governing in his early career:

> I have ensured the happiness of a hundred families. What pleasure to die surrounded by one's children and able to say: 'I have had a hard life, but the state will benefit from it; through my worries my fellow citizens lie calmly, through my perplexities they are happy, through my sorrows they are gay.[7]

He rejected Christianity on utilitarian, nationalistic grounds:

> . . . declares that its kingdom is not of this world; how then can it stimulate affection for one's native land, how can it inspire any feelings but scepticism, indifference and coldness for human affairs and government?[8]

On July 14, 1791, he swore an oath of loyalty to the revolutionary Constitution.[9]

> Napoleon, at twenty-one, was a contented man, burning with enthusiasm for a popular movement which embodied many of his aspirations . . . bringing justice to France, an end to oppression, and possibly also to Corsica.[10]

The Revolution did not turn out as he hoped. Between August 10th and September 7th, power passed to the Jacobins. Mobs broke into Paris prisons and killed more than a thousand men and women. By the end of the month, King Louis was jailed and declared France a Republic.[11] Napoleon returned to Corsica in October 1792 to escape the Paris bloodbath.[12]

Other European powers attacked the Republic, which defeated the Austro-Prussian army at Valmy, invaded Belgium (an Austrian possession), threatened Holland, and seized Nice and Savoy from King Victor Amadeus of Piedmont.

"Saving the Revolution"

France was not only fighting other European nations who sought to restore the monarchy, but itself as parts of France resisted Robespierre's Terror. Napoleon settled his family in Marseille, and took part in the successful attack on rebel National Guardsmen

---

iii "What was wrong with France, Napoleon decided, was that the power of the King and the King's men had grown excessive; the reform Napoleon wanted – and the point is important in view of his future career – was a constitution which, by setting out the people's rights, would ensure that the King acted in the interest of France as a whole." Cronin, V. (1979), *Napoleon* (London: Collins), pp. 48–49.

from Marseille who had seized Avignon on July 24th.[13] Unwilling to kill more French-men, Napoleon pleaded to be allowed to go and fight the enemies of France. He was granted temporary command of the artillery at Toulon. He formulated and executed a plan to retake the city. He showed great bravery, continuing the attack on foot after his horse was shot from under him; he was badly wounded in the thigh. Promoted to Brig-adier General on December 22nd, his rapid rise was resented. His friendship with Ro-bespierre's brother was an embarrassment when Robespierre was executed. He was accused of spying for the Genoese and placed under house arrest. Cleared but demoted by Aubry (the radical War Minister),[14] he bided his time until he was asked by Paul Barras, "Will you serve under me? You have three minutes to decide." Napoleon unhes-itatingly answered "Yes."

On October 4th, Napoleon defended the Tuileries, the seat of government, from a rebel attack by 30,000 men; with only 5,000 troops and 3,000 militiamen he broke the attack, saving the Revolution.[15]

The Italian Campaign

Napoleon was promoted to full general and assumed command of the Army of the Interior.[16] He was given command of the rag-tag Army of Italy:

> In thirteen months, Napoleon had scored a series of victories which outshone all the combined victories in Italy during the past 300 years. With an army of never more than 44,000 Napoleon had defeated forces totalling four times that number: he had won a dozen major battles, he had killed, wounded or taken prisoner 43,000 Austrians, he had captured 170 flags and 1,100 cannon. [17]

Napoleon achieved success in Italy through:[18]
1. **Discipline:** He insisted on officers providing receipts for everything requisitioned. He compensated for damage and theft by his troops. Looting was severely pun-ished. He was ruthless with suppliers who provided sub-standard merchandise or stole supplies. When one supplier tried to bribe Napoleon to ignore his embez-zling, Napoleon exclaimed:

> Have him arrested. Imprison him for six months. He owes us 500,000 ecus in taxes.[19]

2. **Incentives for bravery:** He rewarded bravery at both the regimental and indi-vidual level. The braver individuals rose faster in the ranks. He was the first to commemorate the fallen brave – using part of Milan Cathedral's building fund to build eight pyramids with the names of the fallen French, grouped accord-ing to demi-brigade.[20] In 1805, he commissioned the Arc de Triomphe in Paris to celebrate the "unknown warrior" after his victory at Austerlitz.[21]

3. **Unity of command:** Allowing use of his troops as part of a single battle plan coordinating activities despite geographical separation.
4. **Surprise:** Napoleon attacked wherever he spotted a weak point in enemy defenses, achieved by feints and flanking attacks. In his campaign against the Piedmontese, Napoleon marched his army almost non-stop for ninety-six hours through the steep foothills of the Alps and threw his men into four battles, running circles around the enemy.[22]
5. **Speed:** As he put it in a letter to the Directory:

> If I have won successes over forces very much superior to my own . . . it is because, confident that you trusted me, my troops have moved as rapidly as my thoughts.[23]

6. **Concentration of forces:** He massed infantry firepower: bringing it to bear on a single point and after taking it, moving them quickly to the next task.[24]

Napoleon's success, independence of action, and moderation in the treaty he signed with the Piedmontese worried Paris and they considered arresting him. General Henri Clarke observed Napoleon for nine days; based on his favorable report, Paris promised Napoleon support.

Reformer

Napoleon's reforming instincts were apparent in Italy, Egypt, and when he was chosen as First Consul.

Italy

At the end of the Italian campaign, Napoleon introduced reforms to bring Republican benefits to the conquered. He allowed the traditional form of government, but replaced pro-Austrian officials. He abolished feudal obligations, encouraged Italians to start their own newspapers, and promoted equal rights regardless of religion, or ethnicity.[25] He treated Italian scholars and intellectuals with respect and won the admiration of the people for the way he treated them, however, he stole works of art which he sent to Paris to become property of the French people.[26]

The Directorate in Paris saw no advantage in helping Italians under French control. Napoleon believed otherwise, he thought it essential Milan should become a republic to ensure loyalty to the Revolution. In October 1796, he called for volunteers to fight Austria and 3,700 enrolled in a "Lombard legion" to fight alongside the French. He presented them with their own red, white, and green tricolor flag (which became the Italian national flag). He persuaded Paris to let him establish a republic in Milan, modeling its constitution on that of France. On June 29, 1797, the

Cisalpine Republic was born. In his address to the people, Napoleon declared his purpose:

> In order to consolidate liberty and with the sole aim of your happiness, I have carried out a task such as hitherto had been undertaken only from ambition and love of power . . . Divided and bowed under tyranny for so long, you could not have won your own freedom; left to yourself for a few years, there will be no power on earth strong enough to take it from you.[27]

The new republic was successful. The former Papal States, led by Bologna asked to join. Genoa's aristocratic government crumbled. In mid-1797, Napoleon replaced it with the Ligurian Republic. In doing this, he emphasized the positive elements of republicanism and preached moderation in the transition:

> To exclude all the nobles from public functions would be a shocking piece of injustice: you would be doing what they did themselves, in the past . . . *whenever the people of any state, but particularly of a small state, accustom themselves to condemn without hearing, and to applaud speeches merely because they are passionate: when they call exaggeration and fury, virtue; equity and moderation, crimes; the ruin of the state is at hand.*[28]   [Emphasis ours]

At the treaty of Campo Formio on October 17, 1797, Napoleon secured Austria's recognition of the two new Italian republics. France's chief diplomat and Napoleon's future foreign minister, Talleyrand, was disappointed by Napoleon's decision to sacrifice Venice to gain Holland for France against his advice;[iv] he wrote, "We are not in Italy to become traffickers in nations." Talleyrand believed this action yielded the Republic's moral high ground as a liberator, making it no different from autocratic states like Russia and Prussia that "trafficked in nations."[29] Napoleon thought otherwise:

> Religion, the feudal system, and monarchy have in turn governed Europe for twenty centuries, but from the peace you have just concluded dates the era of representative governments.[30]

Egypt

The expedition to Egypt presented to the Directorate by Talleyrand on March 5, 1798, had three objectives: The first was to defeat the Mamelukes and make Egypt a French colony; the second was to provide a stepping stone to attack British India (continuing the Anglo-French war of 1778–1783); and the third (entirely Napoleon's idea), to teach and to learn. Napoleon believed France had a civilizing mission and his instructions as commander-in-chief, which he drafted, stated:

> He will use all the means in his power to improve the lot of the natives of Egypt.[31]

---

iv This divergence in views was to become more serious over the years, leading to a parting of the ways that ultimately brought about Napoleon's downfall.

The Directors were happy to have Napoleon and his dangerously Jacobin soldiers far away in Egypt. They hoped that he would fill the Republic's coffers, as he had done in 1796 and 1797 with the booty stolen from Italy.[32] Talleyrand himself had mixed motives in suggesting the expedition, as the Prussian ambassador, Sandoz Rollin, reported to Berlin after a conversation with Talleyrand that the real reason for the expedition was:

> to distract the [French] government and its military forces from those revolutionary ideas which are creating such an uproar in Europe. *For the concept of a universal republic is as much an impossibility as was that of a universal monarchy.*[33] [Emphasis ours]

The expedition was to be both a military conquest and a scientific discovery. To this end, Napoleon took with him scholars, scientists and artists. In mid-May, Napoleon sailed with 50,000 men.[34]

On June 9, 1798, Napoleon reached Malta, which belonged to Order of the Knights of St. John of Jerusalem. Its capital, Valletta, was defended by ten-foot-thick walls, a thousand guns, and 332 knights. Napoleon bribed the 200 French knights who resented their German Grand Master to stir up support for the Republic. Napoleon believed that it was essential to take Malta, as well as Egypt, to control the route to India, as part of France's long-running global war with England.[35] On June 12th, Malta was ceded to France. In six days, he abolished slavery, Jews were given equal rights and allowed to build a synagogue, he freed 2,000 Turks and Moors, and decreed nobody could take religious vows before they were thirty. Finally, he established fifteen primary schools for the population of 10,000, whose purpose was to inculcate "the principles of morality and the French Constitution," and provided scholarships for sixty Maltese boys to be educated in Paris as Frenchmen for free. On the seventh day, he left for Egypt.[36]

He captured Alexandria, and marched south the next day, meeting the Turkish-Egyptian army at the Great Pyramids. The enemy comprised 8,000 Mameluke cavalry (with antiquated ideas of chivalric warfare and outmoded equipment), and 16,000 Egyptian infantry. After two hours the battle was over: for a loss of 200 men, Napoleon destroyed or captured the enemy army of 24,000 and was the master of lower Egypt.[37]

All did not to go according to plan strategically. Nelson raided Aboukir Bay in the Battle of the Nile, crippled the French fleet, and ended the threat to India. Napoleon's army was cut off – unable to receive supplies, reinforcements, and letters. Napoleon's apparent lack of concern over Nelson's victory was his first failure to appreciate the critical strategic importance of naval power.

Napoleon ruled Egypt by decree and established a consultative council of 189 prominent Egyptians to "accustom the Egyptian notables to the ideas of assembly and government." In Egypt's fourteen provinces he set up councils of nine Egyptians, advised by a French civilian to deal with policing, food supplies, and sanitation. He created the first postal service, stagecoach service between Cairo and Alexandria, and a mint. He built windmills to pump water and grind corn, and street lamps in Cairo; started work on a 300-bed hospital for the poor; and set up four quarantine stations to deal with the plague. Using a set of Arabic typefaces that he had brought with him from France, he printed a definition of ophthalmia and manuals on how to treat the plague and smallpox.[38] Napoleon tried to persuade the muftis that he and his men were Muslims at heart, but realized that asking his troops to become circumcised and give up wine to prove it was unachievable.

The muftis proclaimed that Napoleon was God's messenger and a friend of the Prophet. He was able to govern Egypt peacefully. Egyptians saw a man who cared about justice. For example, when Napoleon learned that some Arabs of the Osnades tribe had murdered a peasant and stolen the village's sheep, Napoleon ordered a staff officer to take 300 horsemen and 200 camels to catch the criminals and punish them.

The surprised sheik asked:

Was the fellah your cousin that you are in such a rage at his death?

Napoleon replied:

He was more. He was one whose safety Providence had entrusted to my care.

The sheik responded:

Wonderful! You speak like one inspired by the Almighty.[39]

Napoleon's discovery program yielded new insights into ancient Egypt and Nubia.[40]

Meanwhile, Talleyrand's failure to negotiate a treaty with the Ottomans had serious consequences. Under pressure from England, the Turks declared war on France. Napoleon unreasonably regarded Talleyrand's failure as a betrayal:

It had been agreed with the Directors and Talleyrand that immediately after the departure of the expedition to Egypt, negotiations should be opened with the sultan concerning the object of this expedition. Talleyrand himself was to be the negotiator and *was to start for Constantinople twenty-four hours after the expeditionary corps to Egypt had left the port of Toulon.* This promise, expressly requested and positively given, was forgotten. Not only did Talleyrand remain in Paris, but no negotiation took place.[41]

Talleyrand could not keep his promise for two reasons. First, the ship that was supposed to take him to Turkey was captured by the British on its way to fetch him. Second, given the threat of a new war with England, Russia, and Austria, the Directors had more important things for him to do than to go to Turkey and he was not allowed to leave.

To prevent a Turkish army entering Egypt, Napoleon took 13,000 men, 900 cavalry, and forty-nine guns to Gaza which he captured on February 23rd. He took 2,000 Turks prisoner whom he freed on the condition they did not fight again, as he did not have enough food for both his troops and prisoners. On March 7th, he stormed Jaffa, where he captured 4,000 Turks, some of whom he had released in Gaza. Once again, he did not have enough food and had to choose between releasing them to fight again or to shoot them. He called a council of war and after two days of discussion, on March 10th, Napoleon had them shot.

Napoleon attempted to capture Acre but, on May 7th, abandoned the siege – in his third setback since Corsica and Aboukir Bay – and returned to Egypt. When he reached Jaffa, several hundred of his soldiers contracted the bubonic plague. For the sick who could travel, Napoleon issued the following order:

> All horses, mules and camels will be given to the wounded, the sick and plague-stricken who show any signs of life. Everyone not sick goes on foot, starting with me.[42]

On July 25th, Napoleon, now back in Egypt, attacked the Turks who had disembarked at Aboukir two weeks earlier. His 8,000 men beat the 9,000 Janissaries, driving them into the sea where 5,000 drowned, 2,000 were killed, and 2,000 were captured.[43] Napoleon and his army were now safe.

Shortly after the battle, Napoleon received a packet of newspapers from France. Reading them, he discovered France's critical situation. France faced England, Turkey, Naples, and Russia, in addition to Austria. An Anglo-Russian army had landed in Holland; an Austro-Russian army had captured Zurich; a Turco-Russian army had captured Corfu; and an Austro-Russian army had invaded Italy, defeated the French at Cassano, and dismantled the Cisalpine Republic. France was in a state of economic collapse. Everything Napoleon believed in was failing. He returned to France in secret, handing his command over to General Kléber on August 23, 1799, and landed in France on October 9th. The army he left behind was defeated by the Turks and English and repatriated in 1801.

First Consul

Napoleon developed a close working relationship with Talleyrand, who was instrumental in the first coup d'état of September 4, 1797, and with the triumvirs of the Directory. Napoleon explained his political program to Talleyrand and made it clear that he was unhappy with the temporary nature of the Directory in a letter to him:

> Despite our good opinion of ourselves, we Frenchmen are amateurs in the political arena. We do not even understand, as yet, the difference between the executive, legislative, and judiciary functions. *In a state such as ours, where all authority issues from the nation – where the people are sovereign – the power of the government must be regarded as representative of the people, who rule in accordance with the Constitution.*[44]   [Emphasis ours]

A week later, Napoleon wrote again:

> Our actions must be guided by sound policy, and such a policy is nothing more than that which results from the calculation of combinations and chances. If we adopt such a policy, then, for a long time to come, we shall both be the greatest nation, and the arbiter, of Europe.[45]

Talleyrand was clear that the Directory was incapable of re-establishing France as the dominant power in Europe, but the combination of Napoleon and himself would bring sufficient energy and genius to find a middle way between the *ancien regime* and the Jacobin left.[46] They were totally different personalities with different ideas about power and its purpose, but at this time their temperaments were complementary for the immediate future:

> [For Talleyrand] power was nothing more than a means, a tool to be wielded for the good of France and the peace of Europe, but also for his own benefit, as the means to pleasure. From that perspective, politics became pre-eminently the 'science of the possible' – the art of attaining, with the least possible expenditure of effort, the best possible result. *Bonaparte, however, conceived of power and glory as the purpose of his being, and the pursuit of those qualities as overriding all considerations, political as well as moral . . . This final divergence of views alone would one day bring Talleyrand and Bonaparte to a parting of the ways.* At this stage in their relationship, however, each was what the other needed . . . Bonaparte had military fame. *At the age of twenty-eight, he had conquered Italy and brought Austria to its knees. For this, his sword alone had been sufficient. But he also had political ambitions, and for the realization of these he had need of Talleyrand, a statesman and politician of proven ability and discretion. And Talleyrand, for his part saw in Bonaparte the soldier who had both the means and the will to impose order in France and make peace in Europe.* The encounter of Talleyrand and Bonaparte in history was that rare event, the confluence of complementary forces at the moment of perfect opportunity. Both recognized it as such, and both were determined to take advantage of it.[47]   [Emphases ours]

The coup was successful; but Napoleon and Talleyrand failed to be elected to the Directory.[48]

Napoleon began to work with Sieyès on drawing up a new constitution, his reason being:

> We have no government because we have no constitution, at least not the kind we need. It is for your genius to produce one. Once that is done, nothing will be easier than to govern.[49]

Sieyès was willing to work with Napoleon because, as he confided to a friend:

> I intend to work with General Bonaparte because of all the soldiers he is the nearest to being a civilian.[50]

He also believed that:

> . . . the political parties of France saw in Bonaparte not a man who could be called to account for his actions, but one whom circumstances made indispensable and whose favor it was essential to win.[51]

Talleyrand explained to Barras that Bonaparte wanted to reform the Directory by reducing the number of Directors from five to three, with Barras as lead director ruling France. A week later Talleyrand called on Barras again, accompanied by Napoleon's brother, Lucien Bonaparte, president of the Council of Five Hundred, and Fouché, Minister of Police. Talleyrand repeated Bonaparte's plan, *but without mentioning the name of who would be First Consul*. Barras did not realize that he was about to be removed from his position on November 9th, still thinking that he would be the First Consul. When Talleyrand and Admiral Bruix came to Barras' house to explain what was going to happen, appealing to his love of country, pointing to the troops outside his window, and to his love of money, Barras signed his letter of resignation, couched in the loftiest language of principle, written by Talleyrand, and took the 3,000,000 francs, promising to go quietly.[52]

Napoleon made a badly judged speech to the Council of Five Hundred but Murat and his armed men dissolved the recalcitrant Council ensuring the success of the coup. The amenable Council of the Ancients then decreed that they now represented the entire nation and that:

> . . . four of the Directors having resigned, and the fifth being under surveillance, a temporary executive body of three members will be appointed.[53]

It then voted

> . . . temporarily to create a consular executive committee composed of Citizens Sieyès and Roger Ducos, former Directors, and General Bonaparte. They will bear the titles of Consuls of the Republic.[54]

A few days later, Talleyrand, once again Foreign Minister, proposed to Napoleon that he should be *primus inter pares*:

> It is necessary that you be first among the Consuls and that the first among the Consuls have all the responsibility for anything relating directly to policy – that is, to the Ministry of the Interior and the Ministry of Police for internal affairs and to my ministry for external affairs, as well as the two principal means of implementing policy: the army and the navy . . . Thus you will have control of the essential branches of government and will thereby be enabled to attain a noble end: the reconstruction of France.[55]

On December 13, 1799, the new Constitution was promulgated and Napoleon was named First Consul, to hold office for ten years, invested with *constitutional* monarchical powers.[56]

The new constitution was voted on by the French people with Napoleon, Cambacérès, and Lebrun as Consuls and passed with a vote of 3,011,007 in favor and 1,562 against.[57]

Napoleon was a workaholic, working on average eight to ten hours a day during his four-and-a-half-year term as Consul. The remaining third of the day, he spent attending the Council of State that met every day in the early months, and later several days a week.

Napoleon inherited a bankrupt France with 167,000 francs in cash in the exchequer and debts of 474 million francs. The civil service had not been paid for ten months; the army was not paid, fed, or clothed; and hundreds of children in foundling homes had died of starvation. Napoleon needed cash and raised two million francs in Genoa, three million from French bankers, and nine million from a lottery.

He introduced a new system of tax collection yielding 660 million from direct taxes annually. Instead of increasing income taxes, he taxed wine, cards, and carriages in 1805, salt in 1806, and tobacco in 1811.[58] To ensure the money was spent wisely, he created two ministries, the Ministry of Finance and the Treasury.[59] The bankers charged France 16 percent on the loans; Napoleon believed that anything above 6 percent was usury. Unhappy with the bankers, he created the Bank of France with capital of 30 million francs, with the power to issue notes to the extent of its gold reserves. It was a success.[60]

Centralization was key in Napoleon's thinking. The Revolution abolished unions, and introduced standardized weights and measures. He attached great importance to national unity. His justification for creating a single Legion d'Honneur in May 1802, rewarding both military and civilian excellence, was that doing otherwise would split France into two camps.[61] His desire to preserve the unity of the French nation led him to grant an amnesty to Royalists, inviting them to return as Frenchmen to serve their country – and some 40,000 took up the offer[62] – and to emancipate Protestants and Jews.[63]

A grave political problem was what to do about the Roman Catholic Church. What was left of the French Church had been split into two by the Revolution: those priests who swore loyalty to the Revolution and the majority who remained loyal to the Pope. It was theoretically possible to have two churches side by side, except it went against the idea of centralization. Napoleon recognized the political importance of religion and projected whatever religious affiliation suited his purposes at particular times.[64] To put an end to division and to avoid religious war, Napoleon agreed to a compromise, giving the Pope power to depose bishops; in return, Napoleon had a clean sweep of bishops. The number of bishops was reduced to sixty; they would be appointed by Napoleon, and the Pope would invest them. The State would pay the salaries of bishops and priests and place at their disposal all the unnationalized churches. Under pressure from the Council of State, which regarded the new deal as insufficiently Gallican[v] seventy "organic articles" were added to the Concordat (the agreement with the Pope), including the one that asserted that the Pope must abide by the decisions of an ecumenical council.[65]

In April 1802, Napoleon reopened the churches of France – the most popular act of his rule.[66] The Concordat remained in force till 1905 and was the model for thirty similar treaties between the Vatican and foreign governments. As the Pope himself said, "The Concordat was a healing act, Christian and heroic."[67] Talleyrand was complimentary:

> When Napoleon re-established religion in France, he performed an act not only of justice, but of great cleverness. The Napoleon of the Concordat is truly the great Napoleon, the man enlightened and guided by his genius.[68]

---

[v] Holding a doctrine (reaching its peak in the 17th century) which asserted the freedom of the Roman Catholic Church in France and elsewhere from the ecclesiastical authority of the Papacy.

Napoleon is remembered for his success as a reformer. He rationalized routine government activities, reorganizing France into the ninety-eight administrative Departments it still has today, each with its own Prefect, with delegated powers from Paris to decide what was best for his Prefecture, applying the new Civil Code or Code Napoleon as it became known. The Code Napoleon of 1807 is still the law of France, Belgium, and Luxembourg. It has left its imprint on the civil laws of Germany, Holland, Italy, and Switzerland, as well as carrying its ideas of political equality and the importance of strong families as far afield as Bolivia and Japan.[69]

Napoleon shaped and encouraged nationalism in Europe: Belgium and Holland were the result of his political administration; he resurrected a dismembered Poland by creating the Grand Duchy of Warsaw; he provided the administrative basis for the Italians[vi] and Germans to think of themselves as nations rather than petty principalities. In order to put France on a better financial footing and reduce his exposure to attack from the British in the Americas, in 1803 Napoleon sold France's 828,000 square miles of land[vii] in North America to Thomas Jefferson for $11,250,000 in cash plus $3.7 million in forgiven debts in the Louisiana Purchase; reconfiguring the United States to help it become the leading power in the world.

He subsidized education, revolutionizing France's secondary education system with the introduction of the lycée,[viii] and the baccalaureate exams.[70] He wanted to ensure that teaching was uniform, while recognizing the need to compromise with the religious schools. To this end, he created the Imperial University, which did not

---

vi Napoleon succeeded at Campo Formio in getting the Austrians to recognise his fledgling republics, but had to capture Venice and trade it to the Austrians to get them to agree to give up Milan. These actions laid the foundations for the reunification of Italy in 1871.

vii The land that was bought enclosed all of Arkansas, Missouri, Iowa, Oklahoma, Kansas, Nebraska, and parts of Minnesota, North Dakota, South Dakota, New Mexico, Texas, Montana, Wyoming, Colorado, and of course Louisiana. The land purchased also included parts of what is now Alberta and Saskatchewan in Canada. The Louisiana Purchase now makes up about 23% of the territory of the United States. http://www.surfnetkids.com/go/66/ten-facts-about-the-louisiana-purchase/, accessed on January 3, 2021.

viii The key was the establishment of thirty *lycées*, which provided educational opportunities beyond the secondary schools and replaced the *écoles centrales*. Every appeal court district was to have a *lycée*, and they were to be completely supported and controlled, by the state. Scholarships were provided, with about one-third going to sons of the military and government, and the rest for the best pupils from the secondary schools. Bernard, H. (1969), *Education and the French Revolution* (Cambridge: Cambridge University Press), cited by http://www.napoleon-series.org/research/soci ety/c_education.html#19, accessed on January 3, 2021.

The *lycées* had a six-year term of study, building on the work of the secondary schools. The curriculum included languages, modern literature, science, and all other studies necessary for a "liberal" education. Each *lycée* was to have at least eight teachers, as well as three masters (a headmaster, an academic dean, and a bursar). The government provided a fixed salary for teachers, as well as bonuses for successful teachers who also received a pension. Teachers were chosen by Napoleon from a list of recommendations provided by inspectors and the Institute. The inspectors were given overall responsibility for inspecting the schools on a regular basis.

last, though the concept of a centralized, standardized curriculum, taught by qualified professionals controlled by the state did.

Upon achieving a balanced budget,[71] Napoleon set about building three great canals,[xi] three great ports,[x] and three great roads across the Alps.[xi] Within France, Napoleon spent 277 million Francs between 1804 and 1813 on roads, lined with trees to protect their users from the sun, changing the look of France forever. He was the first to pave a road in Paris and established its first professional fire brigade. He founded the Bourse (Stock Exchange), and the Administration des Eaux et Forêts to protect the rivers and forests.[72]

France enjoyed a prosperity unknown for 130 years. Agriculture prospered: people who were eating meat once a week in 1799 were eating it three times a week in 1805. Instead of having to import butter, cheese, and vegetable oils – as had been the case before the Revolution – by 1812, France was exporting all three. Industry did well too: exports rose from 365 million francs in 1788 to 383 million in 1812 while imports fell from 290 million francs to 257 million. In 1789, France exported silks worth 26 million francs, rising to 64 million francs in 1812. It imported 24 million francs of cotton in 1789 and by 1812 it was exporting 17 million francs worth. When times were difficult as in the winter of 1806–1807, Napoleon personally spent money from his privy purse to keep the silk industry in Lyon going and bought cloth from Rouen; and in 1811 he secretly advanced enough money to the weavers of Amiens to pay their workers.[73] Napoleon never forgot that he had an economic contract with the people of France, and if he failed to deliver, he would be overthrown:

> I fear insurrection caused by a shortage of bread – more than a battle against 200,000 men.[74]

Warrior-Emperor

Evaluating Napoleon once he became Emperor requires understanding why he set out to establish a dynasty, his role as an exceptional battlefield commander, and his strategic failure.

---

xi The Saint-Quentin, the canal from Nantes to Brest, and the canal linking the Rhone to the Rhine, allowing him to ship goods from Amsterdam to Marseille, from Lyon to Brest without their being exposed to the guns of the Royal Navy.

x Cherbourg, Brest, and Antwerp.

xi Napoleon had roads blasted through the Great St. Bernard, the Little St. Bernard, and the Col de Tende. They were so well built that it became possible to travel freely between Italy, France, and Switzerland for the first time – even in winter.

Establishing a Dynasty

Although initially guided by his republican instincts, by 1804, Napoleon had become a dynast; making himself Emperor, putting his brothers into positions of power in Italy, Spain, and Holland in an attempt to create a dynasty to replace the exiled Bourbons.

What had begun as an attempt to protect his legacy, became an overweening dynastic ambition – replacing rulers, and alienating the other European powers. By 1811, when his empire was at its peak (including Illyria, Tuscany, some of the Papal States, Holland, and the German states bordering the North Sea) and he had a son and heir, he felt the dynasty had been secured. The Swiss Confederation, the Confederation of the Rhine, and the Grand Duchy of Warsaw were bound to France by treaties. Even Austria was tied to France by Napoleon's marriage to Marie-Louise.

His family and in-laws ruled vassal states surrounding the empire: the Kingdoms of Westphalia (Jerome Bonaparte); Spain (Joseph Bonaparte); Italy (Eugene de Beauharnais, Josephine's son as viceroy); Naples (Joachim Murat, Napoleon's brother-in-law); and the Principality of Lucca and Piombino in Italy (Felix Bacciochi, another brother-in-law).[75]

He justified this on three counts: first, there had been attempts on his life, and so he needed to create a succession mechanism to protect the gains of the Revolution; second, the monarchs of Europe were unwilling to accept him and so he needed to build alliances through marriage where possible – hence his marriage to Marie Louise of Austria; third his ex-post justification after he was exiled for the second and last time to St. Helena:

> In establishing a hereditary nobility Napoleon had three aims, (1) to reconcile France with Europe, (2) to reconcile the old France with the new, (3) to wipe out in Europe the remnants of feudalism by associating the idea of nobility with that of public service and disassociating it from any feudal concept.[76]

Exceptional Battlefield Commander

Napoleon's capability as a field commander was first demonstrated by his achievements in Italy:

> In September 1796, he had defeated the Austrians at Bassano; in November at Arcola; in January 1797, at Rivoli; in February at Mantua. In less than a year, Bonaparte had disposed of five Austrian armies and captured the stronghold of the Hapsburgs in Italy. Finally, in April, he had advanced to within a short distance of Vienna, and Austria asked for peace, offering to cede the Netherlands and Lombardy to France.[77]

The years 1805–1807 were to see an astonishing series of victories for the Grand Army. The week before Trafalgar, Napoleon beat the Austrians at Ulm and on

November 13th, Napoleon entered Vienna. On December 2nd, he had his greatest victory against the combined Austrian and Russian armies at Austerlitz. In September 1806, Prussia declared war on France, only to be beaten on October 14th at Jena and Auerstädt. In February 1807, the Russians were defeated at Eylau and routed at Friedland in June.[78]

As a battlefield commander, he was always prepared for integrated action, always planned for the worst outcome, left nothing to chance, recognized that plans had sell-by dates:

> I calculate on the basis of the worst possible case.[79]
> My habit is to leave nothing to chance.[80]
> The plan which was adopted and which was good for the month of June counts for nothing at the end of September.[81]

He made his troops feel they mattered at a unit and individual level. Napoleon emphasized the importance of the individual soldier and took great care to make sure he knew what was happening down to the level of the individual:

> Take good care of the soldier and look after him in detail.[82]
>
> Write to Corporal Bernaudet of the 13th of the Line and tell him not to drink so much and to behave better. He has been given the Cross [of the Legion of Honor] because he is a brave man. One must not take it away from him because he is a bit fond of wine. Make him understand, however, that he is wrong to get into a state which brings shame on the decoration he wears.[83]
>
> In war men are nothing; one man is everything.[84]

He entered into a personal contract with them that brought them victories:

> Soldiers, you are ill-clothed, poorly fed; the government owes you much, it has given you nothing. I will lead you to the richest plains in the world. Rich provinces and great cities will be in your power; you will find there honor, glory and riches . . . You will be able to say with pride: 'I serve with the army that conquered Italy.'[85]

Perhaps because his artillery background required mathematical facility, or because of his upbringing in a family of lawyers he realized the importance of detail, of accurate first-hand information, and fact-based analysis:

> He will be accompanied by some Bavarian engineers but he will take care to see everything for himself.[86]

Napoleon's ability to see the big picture combined with an almost obsessive emphasis on detail, and hypothesis testing was unusual. His attention to detail meant he rejected executive summaries, asking for the full report instead:

> I expected several pages and I get only two lines . . . Your letter tells me nothing . . . [Napoleon wanted the names of the enemy regiments, the names of their commanding generals and] a hundred things, all very important, [including the morale of the enemy, how they are fed,

the strength of the various units and] what is known from conversations with colonels and officers of the corps . . . Redeem all that by writing me in great detail.[87]

He asked for specifics:

> Give the length, width, and quality . . . rivers . . . traced and measured . . . bridges and fords marked . . . number of houses and inhabitants . . . indicated . . . measure the heights of the hills and mountains.[88]

He went so far as to read the muster rolls for an hour every day to know exactly where his forces where deployed:

> I get more pleasure from this kind of reading than a young girl gets from reading a novel.[89]

Napoleon believed in the importance of good information from all sources:

> I must have precise information to adjust my movement and formulate my plan.[90]

> The qualities which distinguish a good general of advanced posts are to reconnoiter accurately defiles and fords of every description; to provide guides that may be depended on; to interrogate the curé[xii] and postmaster; to establish rapidly a good understanding with the inhabitants; to send out spies; to intercept [translate, and analyze] letters; in a word, to be able to answer every question of the general-in-chief when he arrives with the whole army.[91]

He knew it was important to consider the source carefully:

> All the information obtained from prisoners should be received with caution . . . . A soldier seldom sees anything beyond his company; and an officer can afford intelligence of little more than the position and movements of the division to which his regiment belongs. On this account the general of an army should never depend upon the information derived from prisoners, unless it agrees with the reports received from the advanced guard.[92]

Napoleon's mathematical abilities facilitated his effective logistics and deployment of materiel. He looked for optimum performance, abandoning conventional thinking about how many men were needed to execute a plan and what the best infantry firing position was. When his experiments demonstrated that the traditional three ranks firing in turn were less effective than two ranks firing at will, he wrote to General Marmont on October 13, 1813; "We believed . . . but experience has shown . . . " and abandoned the practice.[93]

Perhaps the two most important factors setting Napoleon's military thinking apart were first, his understanding of the importance of bravery, and what could be achieved against impossible odds when troops had no alternative:

> A central authority [should devote] its full powers . . . by profound insight [to give] direction to courage and [thereby make] our success substantial, decisive, and less bloody.[94]

---

xii Vicar.

> Great extremities require extraordinary resolution. The more obstinate the resistance of an army, the greater the chances of assistance or of success . . . *How many seeming impossibilities have been accomplished by men whose only resolve was death!*[95]　　　　　　[Emphasis ours]

He recognized just how dangerous retreat can be:

> In a retreat, besides the honor of the army, the loss of life is often greater than in two battles. For this reason, we should never despair while brave men are to be found with their colors. It is by this means we obtain victory, and deserve to obtain it.[96]

He held no councils of war before battle because of his view that they lead to consensus-based second-best solutions

> The same consequences which have uniformly attended long discussions and councils of war will follow at all times. *They will terminate in the adoption of the worst course, which in war is always the most timid*, or, if you will, the most prudent. The only true wisdom in a general is determined courage.[97]　　　　　　[Emphasis ours]

His unwillingness to hold councils of war before battle did not mean that he never sought other opinions, as he had in Egypt before executing Turkish prisoners. He listened to diverse views in private:

> Never hold a council of war, but listen to the views of each in private.[98]

Napoleon shared, with other great generals he admired, including Alexander the Great, Hannibal, and Julius Caesar, speed, ferocity, and tenacity in attack. Everything was mobile, even artillery – which he kept on the move to support his infantry.

> It is said that the Roman legions marched twenty-four miles a day; our brigades have marched thirty while also fighting.[99]

> Never forget that in war all the artillery must be with the army and not in the park.[100]

The enemy was often bewildered by his unorthodox use of speed and concentration of forces to achieve an overwhelming local advantage:

> We no longer understand anything; we are dealing with a young general who is sometimes in front of us, sometimes in our rear, sometimes in our flanks; *one never knows how he is going to deploy himself. This kind of warfare is unbearable and violates all customary procedures.*[101]　　　　　　[Emphasis ours]

> The line of operation should not be abandoned; but it is one of the most skilful manoeuvres in war, to know how to change it when circumstances authorize or render this necessary. *An army which changes skilfully its line of operations deceives the enemy, who becomes ignorant where to look for its rear, or upon what weak points it is assailable.*[102]　　　　　　[Emphasis ours]

He remembered a defending army usually has the advantage:

> It is an approved maxim in war, never to do what the enemy wishes you to do, for this reason alone, that he desires it. A field of battle, therefore, which he has previously studied and

reconnoitred, should be avoided and double care should be taken where he has had time to fortify and entrench. One consequence deducible from this principle is, never to attack a position in front which you can gain by turning.[103]

If the enemy occupies a strong position you must occupy a position that will force him to attack you.[104]

His most radical innovation was that

he changed the face of warfare from the sport of kings to the nation at arms, with the whole nation being placed on a war footing, conscription, mass production and truly a nation under arms, the beginning of modern "Total War."[105]

Napoleon's conscript armies were the French people at war, fighting for the glory of their country.

It has been argued that four of Napoleon's own personal peculiarities made a difference:[106] (1) his rapid metabolism allowed him to work very fast as a result of unusually large lungs increasing his rate of oxygenation; (2) he needed little sleep, surviving on half hour naps that allowed him to work eighteen-hour and twenty-four-hour days; (3) he understood the importance of topography in warfare; and (4) he saw the world through the eyes of a gunner.

Despite the war weariness of France and Europe, when Napoleon escaped from Elba and returned to France, the Bourbons could not get their soldiers to arrest him. The army of France was still the army of Napoleon, and for this there were the same four reasons that explained how he had raised the morale of his rag-tag army in the Italian campaign of 1793:

1. **He shared the life, dangers, and fate of his soldiers.** He was always in the battle, not leading it from afar.
2. **He empowered his soldiers by giving them a stake in the outcome of the hardships and hazards they were undertaking.** He told his troops what they had to achieve, why they had to achieve it, and what benefits their achievements would have for their country (which Napoleon expressed in terms of the soldiers' families) and for themselves (a combination of glory and plunder).
3. **He promised his soldiers a better future.** He admitted conditions were bad for them in the present, and he used this fact to motivate them by persuading them that they, and only they, possessed the skill, might, courage, and will to create – under his leadership – that better future.
4. **He produced results.** Until 1812, he led his soldiers to one victory after another and addressed them to ensure that they understood the magnitude of each achievement and the role they played in it.[107]

Ultimate Failure of Strategy

Napoleon never really understood the resistance of other European states to French Republican Imperial ambitions. Upon becoming First Consul, Napoleon wanted peace with England now that France had "natural frontiers" as a result of successful fighting, and so, he sent a Christmas message to George III, proposing peace:

> Why should the two most enlightened nations of Europe . . . go on sacrificing their trade, their prosperity, and their domestic happiness to false ideas of grandeur?[108]

George III refused to deal with "a new impious, self-created aristocracy," instructing Grenville, the Foreign Minister, to communicate on paper, but not a letter, with Talleyrand and not Napoleon. In August 1800, William Wickham, reflecting the views of [Prime Minister William] Pitt's Tory party wrote to Grenville:

> I cannot help considering the keeping France engaged in a continental war as the only *certain* means of safety for us, and as a measure to be brought about by us almost *per fas et nefas* [by any means regardless of legality or ethics], if the pushing of another from the plank to oneself from drowning can in any case be called nefarious.[109]

The most important objection to reconciling with the French Republic was given by Edmund Burke, given that Napoleon was successfully proselytizing Jacobin revolution:

> It is not the enmity but the friendship of France that is truly terrible. Her intercourse, her example, the spread of her doctrines are the most dreadful of her arms.[110]

In England, Pitt was concerned with the loss of Antwerp and its adverse impact on trade. Moreover, Windham, the Secretary at War, had promised to get back the estates and privileges of the aristocrats who had sought sanctuary in England. Finally, neither Pitt nor George III were prepared to lose face by settling with the French Republican Empire, regarding such an act as suffering another Yorktown, in a long enduring *global geopolitical contest between France and England.*

Having failed to make peace with England, Napoleon made peace with Russia, Turkey, and the United States. This left Austria alone to face Napoleon who crossed the Alps into Italy to relieve Genoa under siege by Austria at the battle of Marengo:

> The Battle of Marengo in June gave the French command of the Po valley as far as the Adige, and in December another French army defeated the Austrians in Germany. *Austria was forced to sign the Treaty of Lunéville of February 1801, whereby France's right to the natural frontiers that Julius Caesar had given to Gaul – namely, the Rhine, the Alps, and the Pyrenees – was recognized.*[111]
> [Emphasis ours]

Now only England was left at war with France. When Pitt resigned over an unrelated disagreement with George III, his replacement Addington agreed to the peace of Amiens in March 1802, responding to the popular demand for peace in England. England was to give back all the colonial conquests except for Trinidad and Ceylon, return Alexandria to Turkey and Malta to France. France was to return Taranto to

Naples. It was favorable peace for France. Despite the serious misgivings, Parliament ratified the treaty overwhelmingly.

Talleyrand was of the opinion that Napoleon had made a serious mistake in demanding terms that were so favorable to France in a treaty that was signed by Addington – who was a weak Prime Minister. Talleyrand believed that a strong Britain was essential to the peace of Europe and did not want to see it stripped of all it had won since 1792. It was the first of increasingly serious strategic differences between Talleyrand and Napoleon.[112]

Talleyrand had realized that Napoleon was becoming less receptive to counsels of moderation, when in September 1802, Napoleon annexed Piedmont over Talleyrand's protests. The reason was that in the summer of 1802, Napoleon was voted Consul for life by 3,491,000 French votes for and 9,000 against; and given the authority to name his successor. This was a step toward grander things, as Talleyrand explained:

> In order to rule, and to rule hereditarily, as he aspired to do . . . and in order to justify his pretensions to the title of sovereign, he deemed it necessary to annex to France those countries which he alone had conquered . . . never understanding that he might be called to account for so monstrous a violation of what the law of nations considered to be most sacred. *His illusion, however, was not destined to endure.*[113]   [Emphasis ours]

"His illusion was not destined to endure" because the Treaty of Amiens was regarded by Great Britain as the absolute limit they were prepared to concede, whereas for Napoleon it represented the start of further expansion:

> *Bonaparte's conception of international peace differed from that of the British, for whom the Treaty of Amiens represented an absolute limit beyond which they were under no circumstances prepared to go. The British even hoped to take back some of the concessions they had been forced to make. For Bonaparte, on the other hand, the Treaty of Amiens marked the starting point for a new French ascendancy. He was, first of all, intent on reserving half of Europe as a market for France without lowering customs duties – to the indignation of British merchants.* To revive France's expansion overseas, he also intended to recover Saint-Domingue (Haiti; governed from 1798 by the black leader Toussaint-Louverture), to occupy Louisiana (ceded to France by Spain in 1800), perhaps to reconquer Egypt, and at any rate to extend French influence in the Mediterranean and in the Indian Ocean. In continental Europe he advanced beyond France's natural frontiers, incorporating Piedmont into France, imposing a more centralized government on the Swiss Confederation, and in Germany compensating the princes dispossessed of territory on the Rhine under the Treaty of Lunéville with shares of the secularized ecclesiastical states.
>
> *Great Britain was alarmed by this expansion of France in peacetime and found it scarcely tolerable that one state should command the coastline of the Continent from Genoa to Antwerp.*[114]

The disaffected war party in England persuaded Addington to delay handing Malta back to France, even though France had evacuated Taranto. Between January and May 1803, England continued to make new demands of France, Napoleon was insulted in the press, and was presented with an ultimatum which the ambassador did not deign to put on paper.[115] As Talleyrand noted:

> Here we have, without a doubt, the first verbal ultimatum in the history of modern negotiations.[116]

At every point, Napoleon attempted to show some flexibility, despite having once lost his temper with the British ambassador and in a rage threatened to go to war before storming out of the room, after which he apologized when he next saw the ambassador.[117] His desire to avoid war was obvious to all the courts of Europe who considered England morally as well as technically responsible for the breakdown As the Prussian, Hardenberg, no friend of France, wrote:

> It would have been desirable for England to show as much good will for peace as Bonaparte.[118]

On May 18, 1803, two English frigates seized two French merchantmen in an informal declaration of war. On May 20th, France formally declared war.

Although the recall of the émigrés, the Concordat, and Talleyrand's effort to reconcile the old aristocracy with the parvenus of the new regime had gone a long way to weaken royalist sentiment, there were still those who wanted to overturn the revolution and who saw Napoleon as the enemy of legitimacy and of religion – the double foundation on which every throne was built. These arguments were received sympathetically, and on January 13, 1804, they led to a conspiracy that imperiled Napoleon, financed by Pitt. The leader of the plot, Georges Cadoudal, was caught. Napoleon was convinced that the real leader of the plot was the Duke d'Enghien, living at the time over the border in Germany. Napoleon ordered that he be captured and brought back to France to face trial. At night on March 14th, the Duke was seized on neutral territory and brought back to Paris. He was interrogated, found guilty on circumstantial evidence, and executed. The reaction across Europe was one of shocked horror. Napoleon's justification, dictated in St. Helena was that:

> My ministers urged me to arrest the Duke d'Enghien, even though he was residing in neutral territory. [Talleyrand] twice brought me the order for his arrest, and, with all the eloquence at his command, urged me to sign it . . . It was repeated constantly to me that the new dynasty would never be secure so long as one Bourbon survived. This was Talleyrand's basic principle. It was the foundation, the cornerstone, of his political credo . . . The result of my own observations led me to share this opinion of Talleyrand's.[119]

Napoleon justified his action until his death. Two weeks before he died, he asserted that:

> I had the Duke d'Enghien arrested and tried because it was necessary for the security, tranquillity, and honor of the people of France. It was done at a time when the Count d'Artois, as he himself admitted, had sixty assassins in his pay in Paris. Under similar circumstance, I would do the same thing today.[120]

This action cost Napoleon the moral high ground throughout Europe and gave England a much-needed propaganda victory. Talleyrand's comment was that the execution of the Duke d'Enghien:

> . . . was worse than a crime; it was a blunder.[121]

The execution of the Duke d'Enghien and the plot to kill the first Consul marked the end of the consulate and signalled the end of hopes for peace in Europe. On April 30, 1804, the Tribunate voted the following resolution:

> That Napoleon Bonaparte be named Emperor and that, in this capacity, he become responsible for the government of the French Republic; and that the title of Emperor and the imperial power be made hereditary in his family, from male to male, by primogeniture.[122]

On May 10th, the Senate voted unanimously for Napoleon to assume the title of Emperor; on May 19th, Napoleon accepted.

Although the change appeared to be in response to a spontaneous request from the people, he had been planning the move for some time. He only needed the Cadoudal conspiracy to unite the French people in their support of him; and so great was their sympathy, that the scandal of the Duke d'Enghien's execution only mattered to the aristocrats who were not his friends anyway. More seriously it mattered greatly outside France. In Talleyrand's words:

> Bonaparte took advantage of the royalist plot . . . to wrench the title of Emperor from the Senate. It was a title which, with moderation and wisdom, he would have attained in any case, but not quite so soon. He therefore ascended the throne. *But it was a throne smeared with blood.*[123]
> [Emphasis ours]

France was once more a monarchy, even if Napoleon emphasized that his crown and power came, not from heaven but from the people and his own deeds, symbolized by the fact that he crowned himself. Talleyrand's briefing note to France's representatives abroad made this clear:

> *The anointing and the coronation have, in effect, put an end to the revolution. They have placed France under a government which is both appropriate to the nation's power and in keeping with its traditions*; traditions which France, after fourteen centuries, had abandoned only to lose herself in idealistic byways which had no link with the past and no guarantee for the future. *The emperor . . . has saved the state, established internal peace, and fulfilled the hopes of all the people.*[124]
> [Emphases ours]

Once Napoleon was Emperor, his ambition became clear and diverged dramatically from Talleyrand's position. Talleyrand's aim was:

> . . . to establish such monarchical institutions in France which would guarantee the authority of the sovereign while maintaining it within its proper boundaries and to deal with the European powers in such a way as to induce them to forgive France for its good fortune and its glory.[125]

A war on England would take all of France's resources and Talleyrand believed that it was common sense not to provoke other European powers into fighting France at the same time. Yet that is exactly what Napoleon did in May 1805 as a result of his coronation in Milan as the "King of Italy" rather than the less alarming "King of Lombardy," making matters worse by annexing Genoa to France and appointing his sister Elisa as Princess of Lucca and Piombino.[126]

A furious Tsar Alexander exclaimed:

> The man is insatiable! His ambition knows no bounds. He is the scourge of the world. Well, since he wants war, he will get war. And the sooner the better![127]

Napoleon succumbed to hubris, illustrating Lord Acton's saying that "Power tends to corrupt, and absolute power corrupts absolutely . . . " After victories at Ulm and Austerlitz that crushed Austria, Napoleon was in no mood to listen to Talleyrand about long-term strategic objectives or to be magnanimous to the Austrians, unlike his previous behavior in the Italian campaign where he made his name. Talleyrand did not agree with humiliating Austria after its defeat at Ulm:

> Napoleon explained the terms that he wished to impose upon Austria and what territories he wished to take from it. I immediately replied to him that his real interest was not to enfeeble Austria, but to remove it from the other side and place it on his own, so that it would become France's ally.[128]

Talleyrand's suggestion was to remove Italy as the bone of contention between Austria and France by giving Austria the territories to the east that made up modern Romania in return for France taking Austria's possessions in Italy and making Venice a buffer state between the two empires. Austria's power would be increased which would neutralize any desire for revenge and present Russia with a powerful enemy on her western border. Then Russia would seek to expand eastward and come into conflict with England and thus reduce the long-term dangers posed by these two enemies of France who were currently allies. Instead, the resulting treaty of Pressburg on December 27, 1805, stripped Austria of Venetia, the Tyrol, and Vorarlberg; and removed its hold over Bavaria, Baden, and Wurttemberg by granting them autonomy as kingdoms. Francis II lost 2,500,000 subjects and one-sixth of his revenue and had to pay France a war indemnity of 40 million francs.[129]

Henceforth Talleyrand and Napoleon no longer worked together, with Talleyrand betraying Napoleon at Erfurt in 1808. Talleyrand believed that the sole basis for justifying Napoleon's rule was:

> . . . to restore religion, morals and order in France; to encourage English civilisation while restraining English political ambitions; to fortify France's frontiers by the Confederation of the Rhine; to make Italy a kingdom independent both of Austria and France; and to keep the czar at home . . . There should have been the eternal designs of the emperor, and these should have led every one of the treaties.[130]

The young Napoleon might well have agreed with this approach, but Napoleon the Emperor was intoxicated by the victory at Austerlitz and believed he could impose French Imperial peace on Europe by force.[131]

In 1806, Talleyrand reopened negotiations with England's new Foreign Secretary, Charles Fox, who had always been an opponent of war with France and who had alerted the French of a conspiracy to assassinate Napoleon in February. On March 2nd, Napoleon declared to the legislature:

> I desire to have peace with England, and I am ready to conclude it on the basis of the terms granted in the Peace of Amiens.[132]

Talleyrand made considerable progress but the English insisted that George III's Hanoverian possessions were returned to him. This caused embarrassment as Napoleon had already granted them to Prussia, his reluctant ally. After being pressured by Talleyrand, Napoleon agreed, provided Prussia could be compensated appropriately. A disagreement between Talleyrand and Napoleon arose over Sicily which was in English hands and destroyed the trust Fox had in the negotiations.

Hanover was an unexpected problem. Napoleon agreed it should be returned to England, the English ambassador informed the Prussian minister in Paris of the decision; somehow neglecting to tell him that Napoleon had insisted on Prussia being compensated for the loss. When Frederick William III was told the incomplete story, he was outraged at France's perfidy; while the French were outraged at the apparent perfidy of the English.

To make matters worse, the agreement negotiated between Russia and France was challenged by Fox who pointed out to the Russians that the treaty humiliated them. Tsar Alexander, upon rereading the text, and unwilling to offend his ally, informed Paris that he would not ratify it after all. At this delicate moment in negotiations, Fox died, and with him any hopes of a peace. As Napoleon said:

> The death of Mr. Fox was one of the calamities of my life. If he had but lived, there would have been peace.[133]

Frederick William of Prussia ceased to be an ally and demanded that the French withdraw beyond the Rhine by October 8th, confident in the reputation Prussian armies had gained under Frederick the Great. Napoleon replied:

> Your majesty has set an appointment for October 8 and, since I am a gentleman, I would not dream of disappointing you. I am already in the middle of Saxony . . . Today your forces are intact, and you can still negotiate with me in a manner suitable to your rank. Within a month, however, you will be forced to negotiate in different circumstances.[134]

In a three-week campaign, Napoleon crushed the Prussians at Jena and Auerstädt. Napoleon was not deposing the dynasty, unlike the Bourbons in Naples or Prussia's allies (the Duke of Brunswick and the Elector of Hesse-Kassel) in northern Germany. The territories of the allies were merged to form the new kingdom of Westphalia and given to Jerome Bonaparte, Napoleon's youngest brother. The Elector of Saxony had changed sides and was promoted to King of Saxony. Prussia was stripped of half its population and revenue and had to pay an exorbitant indemnity. As Talleyrand feared, these were not terms of a peace, but a prelude to a new war. Prussia, like Austria before it, was compelled to declare war on England, but would never be an enthusiastic ally, deprived of its self-respect and pride. Napoleon seemed incapable of understanding Talleyrand's point of view. As far as Talleyrand was concerned, Napoleon had introduced a malevolent and dangerous enemy into the empire.[135]

The continental blockade to close all European ports to British shipping made matters worse. Napoleon closed not just France and her dependent states' ports to English shipping, but commanded neutral states to do the same or face invasion by French armies. This "Continental System" failed on three counts – (1) it could not be enforced because of the Royal Navy, (2) it encouraged smuggling, and (3) it adversely impacted the economics of Napoleon's empire.

While Napoleon was in Berlin, he took the fateful decision to destroy at any price the Spanish Bourbons when Spain declared for England.[136] Russia was still at war and rather than fight it in a winter campaign, Napoleon decided to go to Warsaw to get the active support of the Poles. His lasting affair with Marie Walewska helped the cause of Polish patriotism and the creation of the Grand Duchy of Warsaw.[137]

Napoleon left Warsaw in early February 1807 to prosecute the war against Russia. On February 7th, he defeated them at Eylau, but it took till mid-June to defeat them conclusively at Friedland and force Alexander to seek peace. A truce was signed on June 21st and a meeting between the two emperors was set for June 25th at Tilsit on a barge in the middle of the river Niemen. The ruler of the West and the ruler of the East talked alone, without attendants and what they said was unrecorded. Napoleon used the meeting to declare to the King of Prussia, who had been left standing in the rain on the riverbank, that the terms of peace with Prussia were decided by both Alexander and himself; and that out of respect for his friend Alexander, he had agreed to strip Prussia of half its territory and population rather than destroy it.[138]

The King of Prussia begged for mercy and upon receiving none asked his wife to come to Tilsit and intercede. When asked by Napoleon:

How did you dare to make war against me, madame, with such feeble means at your disposal?[139]

The Queen of Prussia replied:

Sire, we were blinded by the glory of the great Frederick. It misled us as to the true state of our power.[140]

The terms of the treaties of Tilsit were generous to France. Alexander agreed to the creation of the Grand Duchy of Warsaw using the lands ceded by Prussia; and agreed it should be ruled by Napoleon's ally the King of Saxony. Russian troops were to withdraw from Dalmatia and the Ionian islands. Alexander was to act as mediator between England and France, and Napoleon between Russia and Turkey. The public treaty was supplemented by a secret one in which, if England refused to make peace with France, Russia would declare war on England and require its client states to do the same; and in return, if Turkey failed to make peace with Russia, France would join the war with the Sultan. In effect, the two emperors had agreed to divide the world between them. The English reaction when they found out was to bombard Copenhagen and capture the Danish fleet, ensuring it would not fall into French hands.

Napoleon appeared to have won everything he sought, except that as Talleyrand pointed out it was a road that led:

> . . . from military dictatorship to universal monarchy and from universal monarchy to Moscow.[141]

On August 7, 1807, Talleyrand resigned on his return from Tilsit because he could no longer support Napoleon's hunger for personal glory at the expense of peace in Europe; and Napoleon never understood why Talleyrand argued for policies that would bring peace and order to Europe rather than "glory" to Napoleon:

> I served Bonaparte while he was emperor as I had served him when he was Consul – that is with devotion as long as I could believe that he himself was devoted to the interests of France. But as soon as I saw him beginning to undertake those radical enterprises which were to lead him to his doom, I resigned my ministry. For this he never forgave me.[142]

Napoleon began to make more strategic errors; first by becoming involved in an internal royal family dispute in Spain, using it as a chance to appoint another brother to the throne. Talleyrand advised against it and denounced it soon after it was done, leading to an uprising that offered the English an entry point into the war with France. European society did not forgive Napoleon depriving the Spanish Bourbons of their throne, not by force, but by deceit, or as Talleyrand had accused him of "cheating at cards" when he explained to Napoleon why dispossessing the Spanish Bourbons in a parable would do him so much harm:

> If a gentleman does foolish things, if he has mistresses or treats his wife and friends shabbily, he will certainly be blamed; but, if he is rich, powerful and clever, society will treat him with indulgence. But if that same man cheats at cards, he will forthwith be banished from decent society, and he will never be forgiven.[143]

Thereafter Napoleon regarded Talleyrand as an enemy; only to understand what was meant when he was in St. Helena and accepted he was to blame:

> I embarked very badly on the Spanish affair. I confess that the immorality of it was too shocking, the injustice too cynical.[144]

The cynical way in which Napoleon had stolen the throne of Spain was used as an argument by Alexander's mother to persuade him to move away from friendship with Napoleon and his alliance just before he and Napoleon were due to meet in

Erfurt. Alexander was already troubled by the economic damage done to Russia by the Continental System banning trade with England. After two defeats and a shameful treaty, he felt like a beggar going to a feast as he could only acquiesce in whatever Napoleon was going to propose.[145]

Napoleon's next error was to rely on Talleyrand to help him persuade Alexander to comply, as an embittered Austria was beginning to see opportunities for revenge in the problems Napoleon was experiencing in Spain. Talleyrand used the time in Erfurt to persuade Alexander that Napoleon's ambitions were not the same as France's interests. There is no question that Talleyrand betrayed Napoleon; whether he betrayed France is another matter.[146]

When Napoleon left Paris for Spain, Talleyrand let it be known that he was opposed to Napoleon's policies. He did this to unite important influencers of public opinion who wanted peace and for Napoleon to moderate his ambitions. He publicly made peace with Fouché, the Minister of Police and this was duly reported to Vienna by Metternich who characterized the situation as being one where there were now two parties in France. The leader of one was the Emperor and the other were the masses with Talleyrand and Fouché at their head.

When Napoleon learned about this, he immediately returned to Paris. On January 27, 1809, Napoleon summoned Fouché and gave him a tongue lashing, which Fouché accepted. The next day he summoned Talleyrand and opened the public dressing down saying officials and Grand Dignitaries of the Empire (Talleyrand) must stop speaking their minds in public; they existed by his will alone and were mere reflections of the one who had created them, that to doubt the emperor was to betray the emperor and to differ was treason. For an hour Napoleon abused Talleyrand, accusing him of being the cause of every mistake that had occurred; calling him a thief, a traitor, a liar, a coward, and an atheist. Talleyrand remained composed throughout. Napoleon incensed at this, taunted Talleyrand with his lameness, his wife's stupidity and her infidelity, and finally called him a "shit in a silk stocking." Talleyrand's only comment as he left was, "What a pity that so great a man should be so ill bred."[147]

Napoleon, having lost his temper, expected the display would be forgotten or forgiven as quickly as by him but should have known that Talleyrand would not forgive and would defend himself. The day after the tantrum, Talleyrand presented himself at Metternich's embassy and announced:

> The time has come. It is my duty to enter into direct contact with Vienna.[148]

Once again Austria went to war, invading Bavaria. Napoleon assembled an army of raw recruits and captured Vienna on May 12, 1809, but the bulk of the Austrian army was camped on the northern bank of the Danube. In attempting to engage them, Napoleon was forced back to Essling where he was defeated for the first time, losing 20,000 men. The Tsar, who was supposed to come to Napoleon's aid, merely moved his troops along the border, following Talleyrand's advice, provoking Napoleon to comment:

> This is not much of an alliance. They are all expecting to have a rendezvous on my grave but I shall disappoint them.[149]

France was panicked by the news that Napoleon had been wounded and that England was preparing to invade. Fouché, backed by Talleyrand, mobilized the National Guard and quickly dispatched 60,000 men to the frontier, commanded by Marshal Bernadotte who had once plotted against Napoleon. These actions proved unnecessary because the bad weather prevented the English from landing and Napoleon inflicted a decisive defeat on the Austrians at Wagram on July 6th.

After the Congress of Erfurt, Alexander distanced himself from Napoleon and his plans. In the spring of 1812, Napoleon gathered his army in Poland attempting to intimidate the Tsar. His attempt at intimidation failed and the Grand Army of 422,000 men, including contingents from Prussia and Austria, crossed the river Niemen. The Russians retreated, adopting a scorched earth policy. At the beginning of September, Napoleon reached the approaches to Moscow with 100,000 men, and on September 7th, Kutuzov, the Russian commander-in-chief engaged the Grand Army at Borodino in a savage but indecisive battle. On the 14th, Napoleon entered Moscow to find it abandoned. That night a huge fire destroyed most of the city. Matters were made more difficult because Alexander in St. Petersburg refused to negotiate and kept Napoleon waiting just long enough for the premature onset of winter to have disastrous results on the withdrawal and retreat from Moscow.

By the time the Grand Army crossed the Berezina river, there were only 10,000 fit-for-combat soldiers left. Most had died from the cold – between November 14 and December 7, 1812, temperatures ranged from −26 °C and −37.5 °C.[150] The disaster encouraged all of Europe to defy Napoleon: Germans demonstrated against France, the Prussians and Austrians withdrew their troops, Italians began to turn their backs on him. In France, discontent was so bad that Napoleon hurried back ahead of his soldiers to regain control.

The forces ranged against France in 1813 were no longer mercenary armies, but armies of nations fighting for their freedom. The French were no longer committed to Napoleon's goals. In May 1813, Napoleon won battles at Lutzen and Bautzen against the Russians and Prussians, but desperately needed reinforcements. Austria mediated, leading Napoleon to accept an armistice and a congress in Prague. Favorable terms were offered. The French Empire was to return to its natural boundaries. The Grand Duchy of Warsaw and the Confederation of the Rhine were to be dissolved and Prussia was to go back to its borders of 1805. Napoleon took too long to decide, and on August 10th, Austria declared war.[151]

German contingents joined the allies. On October 16–19th, the Grand Army was torn to shreds at Leipzig. The French armies in Spain were defeated in June. By October, the English were attacking French defenses north of the Pyrenees. In Italy, the Austrians crossed the Adige river, occupying Romagna. Murat was in negotiations with Vienna. The Dutch and Belgians demonstrated against Napoleon.

By January 1814, France was attacked on all fronts. The allies declared they were not fighting France but only Napoleon because he had rejected the terms offered by Metternich that would have respected France's natural borders. Napoleon was unable to defeat the allies or rouse the French. The Legislative Assembly and the Senate were asking for peace and civil liberties.[152]

The March 1814 treaty of Chaumont bound Austria, England, Prussia, and Russia to work together for twenty years to overthrow Napoleon. Each country expected to contribute 150,000 troops. On March 30th, the allies arrived before Paris and the Paris authorities lost no time in negotiating with them. Talleyrand, the president of the provisional government proclaimed the deposition of the emperor and began negotiating with Louis XVIII. As Napoleon reached Fontainebleau, he was told Paris had surrendered and further resistance was pointless. He abdicated on April 6th.

The allies granted Napoleon the island of Elba with an annual income of two million francs provided by France and a guard of 400 volunteers. He kept the title of emperor and arrived on Elba on May 4th. Napoleon wanted to be with Marie-Louise and his son, accusing Austria of stopping her from joining him (in fact, she had a lover and was not interested). France had failed to pay him his allowance. He was being driven to action and the situation in France was promising:

> In 1814 the majority of the French people were tired of the emperor, [but] they had expressed no wish for the return of the Bourbons. They were strongly attached to the essential achievements of the Revolution, and Louis XVIII had come back "in the baggage train of the foreigners" with the last surviving émigrés who had "learnt nothing and forgotten nothing" and whose influence seemed to threaten most of the Revolution's achievements. The apathy of April 1814 quickly gave way to mistrust. Old hatreds were revived, resistance organized, and conspiracies formed.[153]

Bold as ever, Napoleon returned to France. On March 1, 1815, he landed at Cannes with a detachment of his guard. He crossed the Alps, choosing his route carefully to avoid the Royalist Southeast of France; near Grenoble, he won over the soldiers dispatched to arrest him by standing before them and asking:

> Soldiers of the Fifth, will you fire on your Emperor?

On March 20th, Napoleon returned to power as the embodiment of the revolutionary spirit rather than as the Emperor. He did not dare ally himself with the Jacobins, which would have provoked the bourgeoisie who feared a repeat of the Terror of 1793–94. He only set up a copy of the political regime he was trying to replace; but there was little enthusiasm for this project.[154]

Napoleon mustered an army to fight the allies gathering in Belgium and defeated the Prussians at Ligny on June 16, 1815. However, Napoleon was no longer the same general he was as First Consul. Breaking his cardinal rules, he ignored the topographical advantage held by the Duke of Wellington, delayed his attack by a critical four hours, split his command between Ney and Grouchy causing a lack of coordination, and allowed his generals to attack head-on, instead of his previous tactics of feints and encirclements. Even had he won, Waterloo would not have been decisive, as the allies still had 250,000 Austrians waiting to cross the Rhine into France and a further 250,000 Russians already halfway across Germany seeking to repeat the performance of 1813–14, as was made clear by the Austrian emperor when he was told of Napoleon's escape from Elba:

> Napoleon appears anxious to run great risks; that is his business. Our business is to give the world that repose which he has troubled all these years. Go at once and find the Emperor of Russia and the King of Prussia; tell them that I am prepared to order my armies once again to take the road to France.[155]

Again Napoleon abdicated in favor of his son and was exiled; this time to Saint Helena – far enough away from France to neutralize him as a threat to peace in Europe.[156]

As a "Rising Star," Napoleon achieved the objectives of the Directorate. He was magnanimous to defeated enemies in Italy, potentially turning them from revanchist enemies into neutral admirers. In Egypt, he demonstrated ability in land battles and reforming zeal and tolerance. However, he lost sight of the strategic objective of providing a defensible route to attack India in the long-running global geopolitical conflict between England and France.

As First Consul, he showed extraordinary reforming zeal and created a foundation for the modern French state. As long as he worked closely with Talleyrand, he made no major strategic errors. That phase ended with his execution of the Duke d'Enghien, undermining his moral authority.

Becoming Emperor reflected his changed personality; he became autocratic and did not listen to dissenting views, conflating France's interests with his concept of personal glory:

> What is a throne? – a bit of wood gilded and covered in velvet. I am the state – I alone am here the representative of the people. Even if I had done wrong you should not have reproached me in public – people wash their dirty linen at home. France has more need of me than I of France.[157]

He became obsessed with power for its own sake:

> Power is my mistress. I have worked too hard at her conquest to allow anyone to take her away from me.[158]

Despite Talleyrand's warnings, he adopted a flawed strategy and attempted to impose a French European Empire, presenting both Austria and Prussia with an existential conflict, without paying due attention to importance of English naval power.

He failed because he did not understand English strategic perspectives, the importance of naval strategy, the priorities of other European states, and the impact of his increasingly authoritarian behavior. In a sense, he created the coalition that destroyed him.

Becoming Emperor alienated many of his supporters. Perhaps his most serious error was to gamble desperately in 1814 rather than to accept the generous terms offered to him by Tsar Alexander I. As a result, his Marshals forced him to abdicate.

Napoleon's career ended in personal failure. His own evaluation was:

> *I may have had many projects, but I never was free to carry out any of them.* It did me little good to be holding the helm; no matter how strong my hands, the sudden and numerous waves were stronger still, and I was wise enough to yield to them rather than resist them obstinately and make the ship founder. Thus *I never was truly my own master but was always ruled by circumstances.*[159]

His legacy was the creation of modern France with the Code Napoleon, a unified system of administration and education, the establishment of the central bank and stock exchange and the Paris fire brigade, the building of three canals and the improvement of France's roads. He encouraged nationalist sentiments that led to the creation of modern Germany, Italy, and Poland, and his sale of Louisiana made the modern United States possible.

References

1 Cronin, V. (1979), *Napoleon* (London: Collins), pp. 35–36.
2 Corneille, P. (1637) *Le Cid*, IV, 5, quoted in ibid., p. 36.
3 Ibid., pp. 42–43.
4 Napoleon (1786), quoted in ibid., p. 47.
5 Barrow, J. (1762), *A New and Impartial History of England from the Invasion of Julius Caesar to the Signing of Preliminaries of Peace,* cited in ibid., p. 47.
6 Napoleon, quoted in Cronin, V. (1979), *Napoleon* (London: Collins), op. cit., p. 48.
7 Ibid., p. 53.
8 Ibid.
9 Cronin (1979), op. cit., p. 56.
10 Ibid., p. 57.
11 Ibid., p. 65.
12 Ibid., p. 66.
13 Ibid., p.70.
14 Ibid., pp.79–81.
15 Ibid., p. 85.
16 Ibid., p. 87.
17 Ibid., pp. 126–127.
18 Ibid., pp. 127–128.
19 Ibid., p. 127.
20 Ibid., pp. 127–128.

21 Murray, L. (2020), "Arc de Triomphe," *Encyclopedia Britannica*, July 14, 2020, https://www.bri tannica.com/topic/Arc-de-Triomphe, accessed on November 4, 2020.

22 Cronin (1979), op. cit., p. 116.

23 Ibid., p. 128.

24 Ibid., p. 114.

25 Ibid., p. 136.

26 Arndt, E., quoted in ibid., p. 137.

27 Napoleon (1797), quoted in ibid., p. 140.

28 Ibid., p. 141.

29 Bernard, J. F. (1973), *Talleyrand: A Biography* (London: Collins), p. 197.

30 Ibid., p. 143.

31 Ibid., p. 145.

32 Ibid., p. 202.

33 Rollin, S. (1798), in a diplomatic letter to Berlin, quoted in ibid., p. 202.

34 Bernard (1973), op. cit., p. 203.

35 Napoleon in a letter to Talleyrand, quoted in ibid., p. 201.

36 Cronin (1979), op. cit., p. 148.

37 Ibid., p. 149.

38 Ibid., p. 151.

39 Conversation quoted in ibid., p. 153.

40 Ibid., p. 157.

41 Napoleon, quoted in Bernard (1973), op. cit., p. 203.

42 Napoleon, quoted in ibid., p. 163.

43 Ibid., p. 163.

44 Napoleon (1797), in a letter to Talleyrand, quoted in Bernard (1973), op. cit., p. 194.

45 Ibid., p. 194.

46 Ibid., p. 195.

47 Bernard (1973), op. cit., p. 196.

48 Ibid., pp. 192–194.

49 Napoleon, quoted in ibid., p. 168.

50 Sieyès, quoted in ibid., p. 168.

51 Talleyrand, quoted in ibid., p. 221.

52 Bernard (1973), op. cit., p. 225.

53 Ibid., p. 226.

54 Ibid.

55 Talleyrand in conversation with Napoleon, quoted in ibid., p. 227.

56 Talleyrand, quoted in ibid., p. 228.

57 Cronin (1979), op. cit., p. 177.

58 Ibid., p. 195.

59 Napoleon, quoted in ibid., p. 196.

60 Ibid., p. 196.

61 Cronin (1979), op. cit., p. 206.

62 Bernard (1973), op. cit., p. 235.

63 "The Organic Articles," *Musée protestant*, https://www.museeprotestant.org/en/notice/articles-organiques-en-complement-de-la-loi-du-concordat/, accessed on November 8, 2020.

64 From a speech to the Council of State, quoted in Cronin (1979), op. cit., p. 212.

65 Ibid., p. 216.

66 Ibid., pp. 216–217.

67 Ibid., p. 223.

68 Talleyrand (1801), quoted Bernard (1973), op. cit., p. 236.

69 Ibid., p. 200.

70 Molé, Mathieu Louis, Count (1923), *The Life and Memoirs of Count Molé*, Edited by the Marquis de Noailles. 2v (London), 61. Cited by http://www.napoleon-series.org/research/society/c_educa tion.html#20, accessed on January 3, 2021.

71 http://www.historyhome.co.uk/c-eight/france/napfra.htm, accessed on January 6, 2021.

72 Cronin (1979), op. cit., p. 207.

73 Ibid., pp. 207–208.

74 Quoted in Markham, F. (1963), *Napoleon*, cited in Axelrod, A. (2011), *Napoleon: CEO: 6 Principles to Guide & Inspire Modern Leaders* (New York: Sterling), p. 40.

75 Godechot, J. (2020), "Napoleon I, Emperor of France," August 11, 2020, *Encyclopaedia Britannica*, https://www.britannica.com/biography/Napoleon-I/The-Directory, accessed on November 9, 2020.

76 Napoleon's third person memorandum dictated in St. Helena after 1815.

77 Ibid., p. 176.

78 Godechot (2020), op. cit.

79 Letter to the King of Naples, quoted in Markham, F. (1963), *Napoleon*, cited in Axelrod (2011), op. cit., p. 104.

80 Letter to General Murat, March 14, 1808.

81 Letter to the Directory, September 6, 1796.

82 Letter to General Marmont, March 12, 1804.

83 Letter to the chancellor of the Legion of Honor, May 1807.

84 Notes on the Affairs in Spain, August 30, 1808.

85 Address to troops, April 26, 1796.

86 Instructions to General Bertrand, August 25, 1805.

87 Letter to General Bertrand, March 4, 1807.

88 Letter to General Clarke, December 19, 1809.

89 Letter to Joseph Bonaparte, August 20, 1806.

90 Letter to Prince Eugene, March 24, 1806.

91 Military Maxim LXXVI.

92 Military Maxim LXIII.

93 Axelrod (2011), op. cit., p. 161.

94 *Notes on the Political and Military Position of Our Armies in Piedmont and Spain*, June 1794, quoted in Luvaas, J. (1999), *Napoleon on the Art of War*, cited in Axelrod (2011), op. cit., p. 64.

95 Military Maxim LXVII.

96 Military Maxim XV.

97 Military Maxim LXV.

98 Letter to Joseph Bonaparte, January 12, 1806.

99 Letter to the Directory, January 18, 1797.

100 Letter to General Clarke, January 18, 1814.

101 Hungarian officer captured at the Battle of Lodi speaking to Napoleon, whom he did not recognize.

102 Military Maxim XX.

103 Military Maxim XVI.

104 Quoted in Luvaas, cited in Axelrod (2011), op. cit., p. 163.

105 http://www.historyofwar.org/articles/people_napoleon.html, accessed on January 1, 2021.

106 Ibid., p. 114.

107 Axelrod (2011), op. cit., pp. 185–186.

108 Napoleon (1799), quoted in Cronin (1979), op. cit., p. 225.

109 Wickham, W. (1800), quoted in ibid., p. 226.

110 Burke, E., quoted in ibid., p. 226.

111 Godechot (2020), op. cit.

112 Bernard (1973), op. cit., p. 242.

113 Talleyrand (1802), quoted in Bernard (1973), op. cit., p. 246.

114 Godechot (2020), op. cit.

115 Cronin (1979), op. cit., pp. 230–234.

116 Talleyrand (1803), quoted in ibid., p. 234.

117 Bernard (1973), op. cit., p. 248.

118 Hardenberg (1803), quoted in ibid., p. 235.

119 Napoleon, quoted in Bernard (1973), op. cit., p. 253.

120 Ibid., p. 252.

121 Talleyrand (1804), quoted in ibid., p. 254.

122 Bernard (1973), op. cit., p. 256.

123 Talleyrand (1804), quoted in ibid., pp. 256–257.

124 Ibid., p. 257.

125 Talleyrand (1804), quoted in ibid., p. 258.

126 Ibid., p. 259.

127 Alexander I (1805), quoted in ibid., p. 259.

128 Talleyrand (1805), quoted in ibid., p. 261.

129 Ibid., p. 263.

130 Ibid., p. 264.

131 Bernard (1973), op. cit., pp. 261–263.

132 Napoleon (1806), quoted in ibid., p. 267.

133 Ibid., p. 269.

134 Ibid.

135 Bernard (1973), p. 271.

136 Ibid., p. 272.

137 Ibid., pp. 273–274.

138 Ibid., pp. 275–276.

139 Napoleon (1807), quoted in ibid., p. 276.

140 Louisa, Queen of Prussia (1807), quoted in ibid., p. 276.

141 Talleyrand, quoted in ibid., p. 278.

142 Ibid., p. 278.

143 Talleyrand, quoted in ibid., p. 286.

144 Napoleon, quoted in ibid.

145 Bernard (1973), op. cit., p. 289.

146 Ibid., pp. 293–296.

147 Ibid., pp. 300–301.

148 Talleyrand (1809), quoted in ibid., p. 303.

149 Napoleon (1809), quoted in ibid., p. 304.

150 Minard, C., Graph of Napoleon's Russia Campaign 1812, quoted in Godechot (2020), op. cit.

151 Godechot (2020), op. cit.

152 Ibid.

153 Ibid.

154 Ibid.

155 Francis II (1815), quoted in Mackenzie, N. (1982), *The Escape from Elba: The Fall and Flight of Napoleon 1814–1815* (Oxford: Oxford University Press), p. 238.

156 Godechot (2020), op. cit.

157 Napoleon, quoted in https://www.goodreads.com/author/quotes/210910.Napol_on_Bona parte?page=4, accessed on November 13, 2020.
158 Napoleon, quoted in ibid., accessed on November 13, 2020.
159 Napoleon (1816), in conversation with Comte de Las Cases (11 November 1816), *Mémorial de Sainte Hélène*, v. 4, p. 133, https://en.wikiquote.org/wiki/Napoleon_I_of_France, accessed on November 10, 2020.

Chapter 4
Mustafa Kemal Atatürk

Atatürk's feats as strategist and field commander in both the First World War and Turkey's War of Independence would have sufficed to ensure his place among major world leaders. However, he will probably be remembered even more as the builder and modernizer of the Republic, a role that demanded vision, determination and endless patience.[1]

The Ottoman Empire of 1898, however, was not the France of 1792, though the French had confronted a decaying absolute monarchy. The Reign of Terror and its guillotine shattered their revolution, and in the murderous vortex a military leader took control. Napoleon, ultimately shedding the guise of liberator, crowned himself emperor, then waged war from Egypt to Spain to Moscow, his warpath ending at Waterloo. *Was there another, more just, more permanent, conceivably less destructive path to modernity for a Muslim empire who had no Voltaire? Could a constructive Napoleon exist?*[2]   [Emphasis ours]

Napoleon's career ended in personal failure, Atatürk's ended in triumph. The reason for the difference in outcome lies in their motivations. Atatürk's career can be divided into four phases: "Rising Star," World War I, War of Independence, and "Father of the Nation."

Probably no other twentieth-century leader did more for his country than Mustafa Kemal Atatürk. He brought Turkey independence, changed its alphabet and culture, and created a secular democracy. And probably no twentieth-century general had any better battlefield instincts, skill, or discipline, proving himself under fire at every level of command. And certainly, none so adroitly mixed revolutionary politics with military vision. Yet now, almost a century after his great achievements, he is nearly forgotten in the West, and even in Turkey his legacy is in dispute and his achievements threatened.[3]

"Rising Star"

Atatürk began a military career against the wishes of his religious, widowed mother who wanted him to study religion. His mother allegedly had a dream telling her that if her son became a soldier, he would rise to the top:

Zubayde claimed that in a dream she 'saw her son sitting on a golden tray on the top of a minaret.' Running to the foot of the minaret, she heard a voice intoning. 'If you allow your son to go to military school, he shall remain high up here. If you do not, he shall be thrown down.'[4]

Like Napoleon, Atatürk had a facility for mathematics. In order to distance himself from his stepfather, he chose to go to boarding school in Macedonia, which put him on the front line of the disintegrating Ottoman Empire and exposed him to unorthodox ideas.

His Macedonian contemporaries encouraged him to read writers of the French Enlightenment. At age 18, he graduated second in his class, gaining a place in

https://doi.org/10.1515/9783110707878-005

Constantinople's War College and entering its infantry class. He remained fascinated by French political ideas and participated in the intellectual ferment permeating Istanbul. He came to the attention of reformist senior officers, one of whom said that Atatürk would change his country's destiny:

> You are not going to be an ordinary officer like the rest of us; you are going to change the country's destiny. Don't think I'm flattering you; I see in you the signs of ability and intelligence which great men who are born to rule show even in their youth.[5]

In his third year, Atatürk formed a secret society and started a clandestine political publication. His military career continued to progress and he was promoted to staff captain. By this time, his political activities were being watched by the Sultan's spies, and his group was infiltrated. He was arrested, putting his career and life in jeopardy.[6] Atatürk described his experience:

> Two days after we had decided to help him [the purported soldier], I got a note from him asking me to meet him in a café in Bayazid. When I arrived there he had with him an ADC from the palace. Our friend Ismail Hakki was arrested that day, and I the day after . . . I stayed in solitary confinement for a while, then they took me to the palace . . . we were accused of illegal publication and organization, and of holding meetings and discussions in our flat . . . It is probable I owed my freedom to Riza Pasha, the commandant of the college. He sent for me and told me that he knew everything, that he felt obliged to defend us, but urged us to act more carefully from now on.[7]

Atatürk was worried he would be "banished from the army" and considered fleeing.[8] His activities meant he was posted to Syria (rather than to the Balkan provinces). There he decided there was a difference between being a Muslim and an Ottoman. The Arabs professed loyalty to the Sultan, *but only as the Caliph*; and they resented their Turkish overlords who systematically plundered them. Atatürk displayed for the first time his incorruptibility by making it clear that accepting plundered gold was unacceptable:

> After Ozdes admitted he had been offered plundered gold, Kemal snapped, "Do you want to be today's man or tomorrow's?" "Tomorrow's of course," replied Ozdes. "Then you can't take the gold," said Kemal.[9]

This set him apart from the corrupt administrators of the Ottoman Empire:

> . . . [placing] the incident in the context of the Young Turk movement, noting that "revolutionary officers were sincere in their hatred of official corruption; what they wanted was power not money." Corruption had sapped Ottoman will, damaged administration, and weakened the army. Revolutionary organizations, such as the CUP, argued that power in reformist hands, not gold and silver coins on palms, would renew the Ottomans.[10]

Atatürk continued to be posted to areas outside European Turkey and consequently came late to the Committee for Union and Progress (CUP), where he was resented as an opinionated outsider and not entirely trusted by the leadership. He was sidelined because he:

> ... had no respect for the leaders. He quarreled with them all . . . His brother officers disliked him as a self-opinionated, sneering fellow. His criticisms were always salty and bitter, with no humor to sweeten them.[11]

In 1908 there was a successful revolt against the Sultan's authority resulting from the Reval program designed to settle outstanding Balkan issues between the Great Powers at the expense of the Ottomans:

> In June, 1908, King Edward of England and Czar Nicholas met at Reval and drew up a further program for the pacification of Macedonia. The execution of this program was interrupted by the startling series of events which transpired during the latter half of 1908. On July 24, 1908, the bloodless revolution by which the rule of Abdul Hamid was overturned and the Young Turk régime established in the Ottoman Empire was effected.[12]

Atatürk was despatched alone to Tripolitania to explain the policies and goals of the CUP to a group of frightened sheikhs, religious fanatics, and opportunists not aligned with its objectives. He re-established the authority of the constitutional government. In Tripolitania he demonstrated his ability to combine the elements of effective power: diplomacy, intelligence gathering, and the military and economic levers of power.[13]

The religiously inspired counterrevolution against the CUP in 1909 influenced Atatürk's thinking in two ways: first, he observed the power of the telegraph as a medium of influence; second, he noted the danger that religion-inspired attempts to re-establish a feudal autocracy posed to stifle the creative vitality of a modern state. He realized:

> To question the sultan, no matter how impious the man and his regime, could be portrayed as questioning calculated intent, had used this cultural weapon to stir the violent passions of religious militants. *When employed, the entire world became a war zone for the sultan-caliph's opponents; they were no longer mere political adversaries or enemies, but heretics scorned by God and subject to mortal reprisal by the faithful, anywhere, at any time.*[14]   [Emphasis ours]

Atatürk's battlefield career began with the Turco-Italian War of 1911–12. He understood the power of words, images, symbols, and behavior, insisting that officers be well-prepared, smart, and carry themselves well. He did not want his officers "to give the impression they were average men."[15] Like Napoleon, he was thorough in reconnaissance and logistics; for example, insisting that the men's canteens be filled before operations began.[16]

Atatürk demanded accurate information; he did not allow his subordinates to tell him what they thought he wanted to hear; he imposed discipline; and held individuals accountable, without distinguishing between Turk, Arab, or Berber:

> Wars are made by people. An army's value is determined by the value of its officers. The commander is a person who has creative powers.[17]

Atatürk was critical of the inadequate training of the Turkish forces in the First Balkan War, writing a report to the corps commander in Salonika:

> . . . draw a lesson and avoid the continuation of the deep slumber to which we had surrendered ourselves in the past.[18]

Atatürk also commented on the incompetence of commanders:

> The ignorance of the regimental and division commanders in their inspections and criticism evokes in the officers' feelings of astonishment and surreptitiously, ridicule and distrust . . . It is indubitable and indisputable that these regimental and division commanders, with their current mind-set and limited knowledge, would be able to *neither train the troops as they should be trained, that is, in accordance with the current military developments, nor give them orders; command or lead them when need arises.*
>
> *To witness and keep silent about these truths is to endorse the dysfunction of the army, its continued insignificance and its blindness to the vital tasks necessary for the salvation of the nation during the war; and that could only be called treason* . . . To try and find a solution to this situation is the duty of any honourable and conscientious person.
>
> What those who lack the authorization to command can do regarding this subject is to submit their observations and investigations to those who have executive authority . . .
>
> *The office to which I submitted this report was occupied by the very same people who had presided over the force that, at the time, had handed over my homeland Salonika to the Greek Army without any resistance.*[19]   [Emphases ours]

He highlighted systemic failure in command, incompetence, a culture of "divide and rule," and pointless heroics. He was critical of the regimental commander at Dogan Arslan, highlighting his lack of foresight and analysis and inability to adapt to changes on the ground:

> Binoculars in the hands of a professional commander of conscience leading confident soldiers will always defeat a rabble of swords.[20]

He did not approve of joining the Central Powers in World War I, foreseeing that it was unlikely that they could win:

> *We have declared mobilization without fixing our objective. This is very dangerous . . . Looking at Germany's position from a military point of view, I am by no means certain she will win this war.* True, the Germans have overrun strong fortifications at lightning speed and are advancing towards Paris. But the Russians are pushing to the Carpathians and are pressing hard the Germans' Austrian allies. The Germans will thus have to set aside a part of their forces to aid the Austrians. Seeing this, the French will counter-attack and put pressure on the Germans. The Germans will then have to recall their troops from the Austrian front. *It is because an army*

which zigzags to and fro must come to a sad end that I do not feel certain about the outcome of this war.[21]   [Emphases ours]

Wary of fighting a war on two fronts, he recommended a limited war against Bulgaria to regain losses of the First Balkan war[22] but was overruled by the pro-German leaders of the CUP. Turkey entered World War I on November 11, 1914.

World War I

Atatürk joined the 19th Division in Gallipoli which had only one regiment – the 57th – (the 58th and 59th had been assigned elsewhere). He faced the Allied assault with this depleted force. The Gallipoli campaign was ill-conceived by the Allies and it is not our purpose to discuss its evolution and execution. What is clear, however, is that the presence of Atatürk made a critical difference at a critical moment and was instrumental in defeating the Australian and New Zealand Army Corps (ANZAC) landing.

The first wave of ANZAC troops landed on Ariburnu beach at 4:30 a.m. on April 25, 1915. For two hours Atatürk tried to get orders from the divisional commander and then acted on his own authority, leading his regiment to Chunuk Bair where he met the 9th Division's soldiers in full retreat. Understanding the importance of holding the Sari Bair massif (using binoculars rather than a sword, as he put it), he decided to stand – a decision requiring great personal courage, and significant sacrifices from his troops, shown by the following conversation:

> "Why are you running away?" Kemal asked
> "The enemy, sir . . .," the retreating 9th Division soldiers said.
> "Where?"
> "Over there," they replied, pointing toward Battleship Hill. Sure enough, an enemy line was advancing. The enemy troops were already closer to Kemal than the forward element of his own Fifty-seventh Regiment approaching from the eastern slope. He did not know whether reason or intuition compelled him. He turned to the retreating soldiers and said, "You mustn't run away from the enemy."
> "We've no ammunition left," they replied.
> "If you've got no ammunition, you have your bayonets."[23]

He ordered his soldiers to fix bayonets and lie down. The Australians saw the Turks stop, turn, and lie down. To experienced infantrymen, these acts in sequence signaled an ambush: fixing bayonets indicated offensive esprit, and that bold display sold the ruse. Within minutes, the lead battalion of the 57th Regiment arrived, and the Ottoman retreat was over. Turning toward his regiment, Kamal issued his most famous order:

> "I do not expect you to attack, I order you to die! In the time which passes until we die, other troops and commanders can take our place!"[24]

The Turkish counterattack began at 10:24 a.m. – the First Battalion assaulted the Australians on Battleship Hill, followed by the Second Battalion.[25] Atatürk was later to say:

> The 57th Regiment is a famous regiment . . . because they all died.[26]
> No Turkish regiment since has been allowed to wear its [the 57th's] number.[27]

Atatürk showed he had energy, tenacity, and welcomed responsibility:

> Mustapha Kemal was a leader that delighted in responsibility. On the morning of April 25th, he had attacked with the 19th Division on his own initiative, drove the advancing enemy back to the coast and then remained for three months in the Ariburnu front tenaciously and inflexibly resting all attacks. I had full confidence in his energy.[28]

Liddell Hart recognized Atatürk's impact in his *History of the First World War:*

> *At Anzac, too, a great opportunity went begging, although here the initiative of one opponent, the then unknown Mustapha Kemal, contributed to its unfulfillment.* The surprise landing had placed 4000 men before 5 a.m., and another 4000 before 8 a.m., on a shore guarded by only one Turkish company. The next company was more than a mile to the south, two battalions and a battery in local reserve were four miles inland, and still further away lay the general reserve of eight battalions and three batteries, commanded by Mustapha Kemal. He was out watching a regiment at training, when suddenly a number of gendarmes, bareheaded and weaponless, came running frantically towards him, crying – "They come, they come." *'Who comes?' "Inglis, Inglis." He turned to ask, "Have we ball cartridges?" "Yes." "All right. Forward." Leading a company himself and leaving the rest of the regiment to follow, he raced to the great dividing ridge of Chunuk Bair in time (about 10 a.m.) to cross the crest and check the leading Australians as they were climbing up the steeper slopes to the west.* Until now barely 500 Turks had been available to hold up to 8000 Australians, but henceforth the defenders were to be augmented steadily until by nightfall six battalions (perhaps 5000 men) had been brought up, and from 4 p.m. onwards launched in a series of counterattacks which forced back but failed to break the ragged Australian line.[29]
>
> [Emphases ours]

He had personal courage. In one attack, he and his men were surrounded and he was hit in the chest by shrapnel. The shrapnel hit his pocket watch, smashing it, and bruising his chest badly. When an officer next to him pointed out that Atatürk had been shot, Atatürk told him to be quiet as it would hurt morale if his men knew:

> In one counterattack, Kemal and his aides found themselves surrounded by enemy infantry. Then something struck him in the chest. When . . . asked about the incident in 1918, Kemal replied. "Yes, I saw a bullet hole in the right side of my jacket. The military officer next to me said to me, 'Sir, you've been shot.' I thought that hearing this might have a bad effect on the morale of our soldiers. So I put my hand over his mouth. 'Be quiet,' I told him' . . . 'Liman Pasha took the shattered remains of the watch as a souvenir after this battle, and in return he gave me his own watch, which bore his family's coat of arms."[30]

Did Atatürk make a difference? Yet again, the answer is clear:

> The Kemal-inspired counterattacks of 9 and 20 August had, in reality, settled the fate of the Allies' second offensive.[31]

Gallipoli was the crucible in which the military and political leadership of post-Ottoman Turkey was formed:

> A cadre of seasoned cadres emerged, who would go on to bedevil the British for the next three years in Palestine and Mesopotamia . . . in the Turkish War of Independence (1919–1922) . . . In fact, *in that army led by Mustafa Kemal except for Lieutenant General Nurettin Pasha, every senior army and corps commander had served personally with Kemal at Gallipoli.*[32]
>
> [Emphasis ours]

Atatürk's independence of mind led to a rift with the Ottoman high command. He took medical leave of absence as an excuse to cover his disagreement. He received no recognition in the capital for his role in Gallipoli.

Meanwhile, the Russians had broken through on the Eastern Front in Anatolia. Atatürk was sent to the disorganized Second Army, which was short of supplies, as a newly promoted Brigadier General. He telegraphed Istanbul for arms, reinforcements, and supplies but got no reply. The Russians shattered the Ottoman forces in the Coruh Campaign in early July 1916. Atatürk launched a counter-offensive on August 4th, driving the Russians back across the Murat River. By August 8th, the Russians were retreating along the entire front and Atatürk had captured Mus and Bitlis. A Russian counterattack hammered the Third Corps' 14th Division and pressured the 7th. Faced with this new crisis, the Second Army turned over control of the 7th to Atatürk with the objective of relieving the 14th. Again, Atatürk acted on his own initiative and saved the 14th Division:

> We finally succeeded in clearing the pass of Russians. On one of those good days, near one of the highest mountain peaks [Kemal arrived] . . . I came up to him, clicked my boots together, and saluted him. He said to me, "Welcome, Ali Fuad [the Fourteenth Division commander]. Then he suddenly hugged and kissed me. 'I have noticed,' Kemal said, 'that the Second Army commander left you without supplies. Therefore I asked them to let me come help you. *I could not wait for our commander's official orders so I decided to come and save you myself. And thank God, I have saved you.*"[33]
>
> [Emphasis ours]

Atatürk's were the only successes in that summer campaign. As a result, he was put in command of the Second Army:

> Kemal had performed brilliantly as a divisional and group commander at Gallipoli. His stellar performance in command of the XVI Corps further marked him for high command.[34]

Here he met Colonel Ismet Inönü – his ideal foil. A tough soldier, Inönü would go on to lead Turkish forces in the War of Independence and succeed Atatürk as President of the new republic.

The Eastern front was saved for the Turks by the Russian Revolution; the Tsar's armies dissipated, but Baghdad fell to British and Indian troops on March 11, 1917. Rather than take command of an expedition to secure Mecca and Medina in the Arab heartland, Atatürk agreed to concentrate on the defense of Syria, the barrier to British advances on the Turkish heartland – Anatolia. He took command of the

Yildirim Army Group, which had neither the equipment nor the supplies to do the job. Atatürk's objective in agreeing to take command was to persuade the German General Erich von Falkenhayn "from attacking Baghdad and destroying the Seventh Army in a grandiose gesture."[35] He was successful.

War of Independence

The war destroyed the Ottoman Empire; Turkey was occupied and the Allies were planning to dismember it. Atatürk was in charge of a fully functional military force located in Anatolia:

> Although largely unnoticed by the Allies, and still not well known in his own country, Mustafa Kemal had come out of the war in charge of the longest front held by the Ottoman armed forces. He was only 37 and still a brigadier. But his professional reputation was high among Turkish commanders. True, they knew him as a difficult man to work with. He was ambitious and willful . . . played politics to get his way. He was convinced he knew best. But then he usually did, for he had good sense, a rare quality in a world that had torn itself to pieces.[36]

Atatürk's problem in 1919 is shown in a balance sheet of forces. The Nationalists had the skeleton of an army, no money, and no diplomatic standing. Opposing Atatürk: British, French, and Italian forces occupied the wealthiest parts of Turkey; Armenians were eyeing the eastern border provinces of Anatolia; and the Greeks aimed to annex Smyrna and the Ionian coast. The nationalists had popular support, courage, and patriotic determination – and Turkish communities radicalized by the presence of the Greek army in Smyrna.

Atatürk set two objectives: preserve Anatolia and eastern Thrace as Turkish, and get all the foreign troops to leave. He used the telegraph as a tool of personal influence, making himself into a bold, articulate information and decision-making nexus. He used US President Woodrow Wilson's principles of self-determination to justify mobilizing the Turkish people.

Atatürk also fought the Sultan, who was not prepared to defend Turkish interests against the Greeks. Atatürk resigned his commission. He used his rhetorical skills to make the Sultan's government look bad. He demanded that the delegates at the forthcoming Sèvres peace conference must be "people enjoying the nation's confidence," implying that the people had no confidence in the government.[37]

The war of words ended in late October 1919. French troops replaced British soldiers in Marash in southern Anatolia, accompanied by Armenian troops. Fighting broke out between Turks and Armenians, allowing Atatürk to support Turkish guerrillas in the area. The French feared an alliance between Turks and Arabs, which would undermine their gains of Syria and Lebanon from the Sykes-Picot agreement. Picot met Atatürk and a ceasefire was agreed. However, the Nationalists continued to fight. Atatürk saw that the French could be peeled away from their allies and might be persuaded to support nationalist goals. In late January 1920, serious fighting took place in Marash. By February, the nationalists held both Marash and Urfa.

The British occupied Ottoman government buildings in Istanbul to pressure the Sultan. Atatürk sent telegrams urging Nationalists to protect non-Muslims and avoid ethnic and religious reprisals. He used the British occupation of government buildings to declare an end to "the seven-hundred-year-old Ottoman state."[38] On August 10, 1920, the Treaty of Sèvres was signed by the Sultan and his Grand Vizier. Armenia acquired territory in the East; Greece received the Dodecanese Islands and nearly all of Thrace. After five years, Greece would take over Smyrna and its Ionian hinterland.

The Nationalists attacked the Armenians and by October had driven them back across the Arpacay River, leading to an armistice on December 2nd which fixed the border between the two countries. This showed the Allies that the Treaty of Sèvres was unenforceable without a massive troop commitment. The Greeks, however, were willing to make such a commitment and for several months Prime Minister Venizelos sought permission to attack the Nationalists. In October 1920, the Greek government informed Britain it would seek a military resolution and requested money and materiel, even suggesting that British troops cover the Sakarya River in Anatolia as the Greeks advanced.[39] Venizelos lost the November 1920 elections in Greece, but the new government committed itself to following his policy in early January 1921, as was made clear at the London Conference in February 1921:

> The Greek Army in Asia Minor, 121,000 strong, is in position to scatter the Kemalist forces and to impose the will of the Powers as embodied in the Treaty of Sevres.[40]

Fighting broke out on March 23, 1921, on two fronts. The Nationalists repulsed Greek attacks, losing 5,000 soldiers at the battle of Inönü. Atatürk sent a telegram to Ismet designed to encourage him and Turkish nationalists:

> Few commanders in the whole history of the world have faced a task as difficult as that which you undertook in the pitched battles of Inönü . . . It was not only the enemy you have defeated, but fate itself – the ill-starred fate of our nation.[41]

Atatürk also made it absolutely clear what a successful outcome of the war had to be:

> In order to render possible our national and economic development and to succeed in orderly administration, like all states, we must possess absolute independence and freedom in the achievement of our development. *For this reason, we are opposed to all limitations on our political, judicial, or financial development in the setting of our assessed debts. There shall be no change in this matter.*
>
> *By complete independence we mean, of course, complete economic, financial, judicial, military, cultural independence and freedom in all matters.* Being deprived of independence and freedom in any of these matters is equivalent to the nation's and country's being deprived of all its independence.[42]   [Emphasis ours]

The Allies were no longer united: the French and Italians indicated they would accede to Nationalist territorial demands in return for economic concessions. Atatürk, realizing that concessions would not be needed if he won on the battlefield – and if he lost, they would be irrelevant – did not present them to the Grand National Assembly.

On July 10th, the Greek army launched an offensive targeting Ankara with the aim of destroying the Nationalist army and leadership. They were initially successful. Atatürk ordered the army to retreat, saving Ismet the stigma and taking a serious political and military risk, but extending the Greek lines of supply:

> Kemal had recognized in ordering retreat, the further Greek forces were drawn from their bases, the more difficult and dangerous would be the attempt to annihilate the Turkish army . . . *Mustapha Kemal had staked his political existence on the unpopular policy of controlled withdrawal – a policy which required iron strength and confidence to draw the Greek army into not a trap but a wasteland where it would destroy itself.*[43]   [Emphasis ours]

Atatürk chose carefully where to engage the Greeks and was able, through force of personality, to get his commanders to believe in his strategy:

> The Greek armies were marching on to Ankara . . . With a red pen he drew a broad long line in the rear of Sakarya and pointing to this line he said, "We shall beat the enemy here." *We believed him, why and how we believed, I still don't know.*[44]   [Emphasis ours]

The deputies of the Grand National Assembly gave Atatürk near dictatorial powers with a three-month time limit by passing Law 144 on August 5, 1921, appointing him commander in chief of the Turkish armed forces. By following an unorthodox plan of defense,[45] Atatürk achieved success:

> By his personal effort, he had won a battle, which would have been the absolute end of the Turkish independency, if he had lost it.[46]

He forced the Greeks into positions where they lost the advantage and instead of achieving a breakthrough, they were trapped:

> "There is no line of defense but an area of defense. That area is defense of the motherland." This concept rested on flexibility of response and rapidity of movement, not a rigidity of positional warfare.[47]

The Turkish counter-offensive drove the Greeks back to where they had been a month earlier; the Battle of Sakarya cost the Greeks 20,000 casualties and as they retreated, they destroyed everything of value. France, Britain, and Italy proposed an armistice, which the Greeks accepted, but the Turks rejected. The Turkish claim to Anatolia was recognized, but the issue of what to do with the Greeks of Ionia was left to be decided after the Greek withdrawal.

By August 1922, the Greeks were back where they started in 1921.

The Turks were now well armed. On August 26th, Atatürk directed the assault on Greek positions. His battle orders read: "Soldiers your goal is the Mediterranean." Defeated Greek regiments fled toward Smyrna, which was abandoned by the Greek civil and military authorities by September 13th. On October 11, 1922, Greece and Turkey signed an armistice. Turkey had won a war for the first time in nearly two hundred years.

In 1927, Atatürk said of the war:

> To speak of war means not only two armies but two nations coming face to face and fighting against one another with all their being and all their resources, involving both material and spiritual resources. For this reason, *I had to interest the whole Turkish nation in thought, sentiment, and action in the same way as the army on the front.*[48]   [Emphasis ours]

The historians Arnold Toynbee and Kenneth Kirkwood wrote in 1927:

> And the world had the unprecedented surprise of seeing a defeated and apparently shattered nation rise from its ruins, face the greatest nations of the world on terms of absolute equality, and *win from the humiliated victors of the Great War almost every one of its national demands.*[49]   [Emphasis ours]

This was a remarkable performance.[50]

Like Napoleon, Atatürk understood the needs of total war; unlike Napoleon, Atatürk knew when to stop fighting. He appreciated the value of peace, stating immediately after he had won the War of Independence:

> Peace is the most effective way for nations to attain prosperity and happiness.[51]
>
> *Unless the life of the nation faces peril, war is a crime* . . . If war were to break out, nations would rush to join their armed forces and national resources. The swiftest and most effective measure is to establish an international organization which would prove to the aggressor that its aggression cannot pay.[52]   [Emphasis ours]

His focus on peaceful relations is best shown by the fact that defense expenditures were cut by three-quarters during his period of rule. The reduced expenditures reflected his motto: "Peace at home, peace in the world."

Newly independent Turkey established relations with all her neighbors, including hereditary enemies. Atatürk signed pacts with Greece, Romania, and Yugoslavia, territories where the Ottomans had been imperialists; and with Iran, Iraq, and Afghanistan. Turkey was on friendly terms with the USSR, UK, France, Germany, and Italy (enabling Turkey to remain neutral in World War II, despite its strategic importance). In the 1930s, he and Venizelos, the Greek Prime Minister, signed a treaty of peace and cooperation.

In 1932, the League of Nations invited Turkey to become a member. Many of Atatürk's ideas and ideals reflected principles enshrined in the League of Nations:

> As clearly as I see daybreak, I have the vision of the rise of the oppressed nations to their independence . . . *If lasting peace is sought, it is essential to adopt international measures to*

improve the lot of the masses. Mankind's well-being should take the place of hunger and op-
pression . . . Citizens of the world should be educated in such a way that they shall no longer
feel envy, avarice and vengefulness.[53]   [Emphasis ours]

Father of the Nation

In attempting to create a modern nation from the ruins of a multi-ethnic, multi-
religious, polyglot empire where the Ottoman elite looked down upon their Turkish
origins; Atatürk faced similar problems to those the leaders of Austria after World
War I for the much the same reasons:

> After seven hundred years of absolute, or near absolute, rule, a nation like Austria, one totally
> confused about its own identity, could not develop into a functioning democracy virtually
> overnight. The trappings of democracy were there but the content was missing.[54]

The Turkey that Atatürk aimed to modernize had had a terrible decade:

> During the decade between 1912 and 1922, *almost one-quarter of the Anatolian population died in
> wars, and in some regions this figure increased to 60 percent.* Anatolia lost most of its Greek and
> Armenian population in the first quarter of the twentieth century, during which the non-Muslim
> population dropped from 20 percent to 2 percent. *With the loss of professionals and artisans,
> most of whom were not Muslim, Turkey in 1923 was economically more backward than it had been
> ten years earlier.* In other words, Atatürk took over amid the ruins of a once-great empire.[55]

To make matters worse, entrenched vested interests resisted reform, in particular
the religious institutions and their students. Atatürk's experiences left him a determined secularist and hostile to traditional Islam with its focus on an Arab worldview opposed to his nationalist and modernizing objectives:

> Even before accepting the religion of the Arabs [Islam], the Turks were a great nation. *After
> accepting the religion of the Arabs, this religion, didn't effect to combine the Arabs, the Persians
> and Egyptians with the Turks to constitute a nation.* (This religion) rather, loosened the national
> nexus of Turkish nation, got national excitement numb. This was very natural. Because *the
> purpose of the religion founded by Muhammad, over all nations, was to drag to an including
> Arab national politics.*[56]   [Emphases ours]

> For nearly five hundred years, these rules and theories of an Arab Shaikh and the interpreta-
> tions of generations of lazy and good-for-nothing priests have decided the civil and criminal
> law of Turkey . . . Islam – this theology of an immoral Arab – is a dead thing. *Possibly it might
> have suited tribes in the desert. It is no good for modern, progressive state.* God's revelation!
> There is no God![57]   [Emphasis ours]

> Read and listen our history. You'll see that what ruins, enslaves, and ruins nations have al-
> ways come from the blasphemy and evil under the cover of religion.[58]

He wanted to create a legal system that focused on the everyday needs of people
without a religious element:

The nation has placed its faith in the precept that all *laws should be inspired by actual needs here on earth* as a basic fact of national life.[59]   [Emphasis ours]

Atatürk's hostility thoroughly excluded Islam from daily life, religious orders were suppressed; the separation of state and religion was achieved by ending the Caliphate; religious schools were closed, public education was made secular; and Shariah law was revoked, replaced by secular laws. Despite protests, he conceded nothing to the religious traditionalists. Unlike Elizabeth Tudor or Napoleon, Atatürk did not seek a middle ground.[60]

To secure the newly won independence, Atatürk believed that Turkey had to progress in economics, education, and political rights and, in particular, the emancipation of women.

Creating Modern Turkey

On November 1, 1922, the Sultanate, the secular authority of the Ottoman Empire, was abolished and Mehmet VI exiled. His cousin Crown Prince Abdul Mejid II became caliph, though not for long. In March 1924, parliament passed a bill deposing the caliph, abolishing the Caliphate and exiling all members of the Ottoman dynasty.

In the fifteen years as President, before his death in 1938, Atatürk introduced:

a broad range of rapid and sweeping reforms in the political, social, legal, economic, and cultural spheres virtually unparalleled in any other country.[61]

The challenge this presented differed from other recent European revolutions. Atatürk was deliberately shifting the basis of political legitimization; changing the symbols of the political community; and redefining the boundaries of what it meant to be a Turk; while creating a modern economy; all at the same time:

The redefinition of the political community took place in a unique way: *the society withdrew from the Islamic framework into that of the newly defined Turkish nation*. While this process appears similar to the path followed by the European nation-states, *it in fact involved the negation of a universal framework: Islam . . . The Turkish revolution completely rejected the religious basis of legitimation and attempted instead to develop a secular national one . . .* with very little emphasis on the social components of ideologies. This shift was connected with an *almost total displacement of the former ruling class – political as well as religious – by the members of the secondary (bureaucratic and intellectual) elites*. A parallel development involved the broadening of markets, initially controlled by the new ruling elite, and the opening up of the flow of resources. *Attempts were made to crystallize new economic institutions modelled on the capitalist system but imbued with a strong etatist orientation*.[62]   [Emphases ours]

He was able to do this because of support from the secular, rationalist, nationalist military establishment:

The revolution was undertaken by military officers, among whom autonomous political leadership and autonomous religious and intellectual elements had been relatively weak. Nevertheless, these *officers emerged from a modern educational setting and evinced strong ideological and intellectual tendencies. The ideology they carried was secular, rationalist, nationalist, anti-religious, and etatist, with relatively weak social orientations or themes.* Consequently, they displayed a relatively low level of antagonism towards the upper and middle social classes, as distinct from the former political and religious elites; however, these classes were not allowed any autonomous access to the new center, just as they had been barred from the older one. *The revolutionary groups had relatively little contact with the lower classes and the movements of rebellion that flourished among them.*[63]   [Emphases ours]

Atatürk's fundamental belief was that the future of Turkey was with the West:

The Turks are friends of all civilized nations. On condition that they do us no harm and do not interfere with our liberties, foreigners shall always be welcome in our country. Our goal is rapprochement and re-establishment of bonds with other nations. *There are many nations, but there is only one civilization.* For the advancement of a nation, it must be part of this one civilization. *The downfall of the Ottoman Empire began on the day that it haughtily severed its ties with European nations because of its military victories against them. This was a mistake we shall not repeat.*

In keeping with our policies, our traditions and our interests, we are inclined to the establishment of a European Turkey, or to be more precise, a Turkey inclined toward the West.[64]
                        [Emphases ours]

The adoption of the Latin script was a key component of his reforms to promote a sense of Turkish national identity, independent of Islam, orienting the new country toward Europe rather than the Middle East or Asia:

Atatürk's views on social change gain considerable cohesiveness and credibility when brought into the confines of a much-needed conceptual framework. *His numerous secularizing reforms were highly compatible with his alphabet reform and with those reforms designed to promote nationalism and westernization.* Historically, the adoption of a new script is often associated with religious conversion; *the adoption of the Latin script by Atatürk signified his intent to bring about a radical transformation in Turkish religious attitudes, i.e., the adoption of secularism, a non-indigenous religious philosophy, and the disestablishment of Islam.*[65]   [Emphases ours]

Atatürk introduced additional Western-focused reforms: European hats replaced the fez; women stopped wearing the veil; all citizens took surnames; and the Islamic calendar gave way to the Western calendar.[66]

Atatürk believed the cornerstone of education was an easy system of reading and writing. He believed a new Turkish alphabet based on the Latin script was needed, but achieving such a change was difficult because 80 percent of Ottoman Turkish consisted of Arabic, Persian, and French. He insisted that replacing Arabic script would make reading and writing easier and raise the status of Turkish:

Within the Ottoman Empire, the Turks were merely one of many linguistic and ethnic groups, and the word Turk in fact connoted crudeness and boorishness. Members of the civil, military, and religious elite conversed and conducted their business in Ottoman Turkish, which was a mixture *of Arabic, Persian, and Turkish. Arabic remained the primary language of religion and religious law. Persian was the language of art, refined literature, and diplomacy.* What little Turkish there was usually had to do with the administration of the Ottoman Empire Turkish not only borrowed vocabulary items from Arabic and Persian but also lifted entire expressions and syntactic structures out of these languages and incorporated them into the Ottoman idiom. *Thus, pure Turkish survived primarily as the language of the illiterate and generally was not used in writing. Ottoman Turkish, on the other hand, was the language of writing, as well as the language spoken by the educated elite.*

Its multiple origins caused difficulties in spelling and writing Ottoman Turkish. The constituent parts – Turkish, Persian, and Arabic – belong to three different language families – Ural-Altaic, Indo-European, and Semitic, respectively – and the writing system fits only the last of these. Phonological, grammatical, and etymological principles are quite different among them.[67]

[Emphases ours]

More important, the change in script and language signaled that Turkey was to become European:

As the 1920s came to an end, Turkey had fully and functionally adopted, with its 29 letters (8 vowels and 21 consonants), [a new Turkish alphabet with] none of the complexities of the Arabic script, which was ill-suited to the Turkish language. *The language reform enabled children and adults to read and write within a few months, and to study Western languages with greater effectiveness.*[68]

[Emphasis ours]

He insisted on making the change quickly and was personally deeply involved in the research and development of the new script and returned to sources pre-dating Islam:

Under Atatürk's Leadership, Turkey undertook the modern world's swiftest and most extensive language reform. In 1928, when he decided that the Arabic script, which had been used by the Turks for a thousand years, should be replaced with the Latin alphabet. He asked the experts: *"How long would it take?"* Most of them replied: *"At least five years."* *"We shall do it,"* Atatürk said, *"within five months."*[69]

He believed that Turks must appreciate their cultural roots if they were to build a nationalist Turkey:

We shall make the expansion and rise of Turkish culture in every era the mainstay of the Republic.[70]

Atatürk was not prepared to allow conflict between the left and right. and believed in limits to pluralism; communist, fascist, and religious parties were banned:

The Kemalist Revolution led by Mustafa Kemal hoped to develop and strengthen the idea of freedom and to expose dogmatism. And, as Kemalism is based on rationalism, it will continue to be contemporary and progressive, to foster a continuing process of modernization. *Atatürk foresaw what would happen in Europe, with leftist and rightist ideologies taking advantage of the freedom to destroy democratic regimes.* Thus, instead of a full western type pluralism tolerating all forms of extremist political groups, *he favored a limited pluralism under which fascist, communist, and religious parties are banned.*[71]

[Emphases ours]

Creating a westernized state, the ambition of Atatürk and his supporters, required creation of a new principle of citizenship regulating the relationship between constitutionally limited, elected rulers and the people:

> Starting from the early 1920s when the Turkish state emerged as the Ottoman Empire's successor, the men who led the military campaign against the Greeks were concerned with the creation of a state based upon a different set of principles. Believing that they had "to create a modern, therefore western, state in Turkey," Atatürk and his followers, mainly former military officers, were eager to announce to their people and the world community that the old system of arbitrary relations between the ruling elite (*askeri*) and the *reaya* (the tax-paying subjects of the empire who were excluded from politics) would be abolished. *In its place, the western idea of citizenship would be firmly established as the new principle responsible for regulating the relationship between the elected, constitutionally limited rulers and "the people."*[72] [Emphasis ours]

Atatürk and his group of westernizing modernizers believed that the first priority was to provide an ideological framework to provide a vision for the country. Called "Kemalism," the ideology was based on six fundamental principles: republicanism; secularism; nationalism, statism; and revolutionary reform:

> The evolution of events, however, revealed that *the transformation of the reaya into the people-as-sovereign was not their highest priority.* Aware of Turkey's weak military and financial condition and the limited appeal of its pro-western ideas to the uneducated rural and religious-oriented population, they concentrated their attention on the construction and function of the country's political institutions. *With the formation and implementation of guidelines under which the political game had to be performed, the westernists believed that their control over Turkey's social, political and economic evolution would be firm.* Called Kemalism after its mentor, this set of guidelines made up of the principles of republicanism (cumhuriyetçilik), secularism (laiklik), nationalism (milliyetçilik), populism (halkçilik), statism (dev- letqilik) and revolutionism-reformism (inkilapçi-lik), was presented as the much needed vehicle for society's modernization. *The incorporation of these guidelines into the programme of the Republican People's Party (CHP) in 1931 and its Constitution in 1937 justified the tutelary behaviour of the military-bureaucratic elite to transform society from above . . . the Kemalists had felt that 'a different sort of state was needed in Turkey. Perhaps despite the people but for the people. Perhaps a démocratie dirigée . . . the state had to be the imam and the nation the congregation.'*[73]

Atatürk's authoritarian approach was similar to Lenin's – nation, state, and party were indivisible and the party was the teacher of the people. Even though these ideas might have Marxist-Leninist roots, they suited the conditions in Turkey where the people were accustomed to authoritarian rule:

> However, these values appear to have been in harmony with the existing societal ones. As domestic and foreign observers testify, *Turkish society gives a greater emphasis on collective rather than individual rights and values* and therefore Turkish citizens learn from an early age to respect hierarchical-patriarchical [sic] values and view pluralism as a potential threat to social or national cohesion. For instance, Gareth Jenkins observes that *Turks do not have a tradition of tolerating pluralism on a social level . . . and almost invariably bow to authority than challenge it.* Since 'the state is a proper repository of legitimate authority, and the legitimate wielders of that authority have a responsibility to preserve the public order and promote the general

> welfare,' the *reliance of Kemalist rulers on authoritarian-totalitarian attitudes and policies did not appear as an alien feature. The identification of the party (CHP) with the state and the nation with the party and the state justified their non-democratic, tutelary aim to transform society from above.*[74]   [Emphases ours]

A top-down approach did not necessarily mean a corrupt regime. Rather than giving privilege to certain contractors, all construction was planned by experts.[75]

The principle of republicanism was contained in the constitutional declaration that "sovereignty is vested in the nation" and not in a single ruler. The nation-state supplanted the Ottoman dynasty as the focus of loyalty, and the particulars of Turkish nationalism replaced Ottoman universalism. Kemalism stated that all Turkish citizens were equal and that all of them were Turks. The remnants of the millet system that had guaranteed some communal autonomy to non-Muslim groups were abolished. Etatism, or statism, emphasized the central role reserved for the state in directing the nation's economic activities. An important aim of Atatürk's economic policies was to prevent foreign interests from exercising excessive influence on the Turkish economy.

In 1924, the new Grand National Assembly approved a new constitution (replacing that of 1876); vesting sovereignty in the Grand National Assembly representing the people. The single chamber assembly was elected every four years by universal suffrage with the power to legislate; approve budgets; ratify treaties; and declare war. It had power to alter or defer judicial decisions. The judiciary was not empowered to decide the constitutionality of laws passed by the assembly.

The President of the new republic served a four-year term, appointing as Prime Minister whoever had the confidence of the assembly. Throughout his time as President, Atatürk governed a one-party state. The party he founded and controlled in 1923, the Republican People's Party, ensured that his term of office was repeatedly extended. Atatürk justified authoritarian personal rule to secure his reforms. Only once they were secured, would he entrust the government of Turkey to the democratic process.[76]

Misgivings were created by his personal dominance and the speed at which he was pushing ahead with reform. Atatürk introduced a failed experiment with a multiparty system. In 1924, he dismissed his close friend, Inönü, as Prime Minister, appointing a new Prime Minister to lead the newly formed Progressive Republican Party. The timing of this experiment coincided with a Kurdish uprising led by the leader of the Kurdish Naksibendi dervishes to overthrow Atatürk's "godless government and restore the caliph." In 1925, he recalled Inönü to be Prime Minister, rushed through legislation to provide emergency powers for the government for the next four years, and outlawed the newly formed Progressive Republican Party. The army quickly put down the revolt.

The following year there was a plot to assassinate Atatürk organized by a former deputy who opposed the ending of the caliphate. An investigation brought a large number of his opponents before a tribunal; fifteen were hanged and some of

Atatürk's close associates from before the war were exiled. His rule and the single party state were never openly challenged again. He tried another experiment with multiparty politics in 1930 but this experiment also failed.[77]

Atatürk tried to create a liberal democracy by illiberal means.[78] He succeeded in making religious faith a matter of individual conscience, creating a secular system where the Muslim majority (more than 95% of the population) and the small residual Christian minority (after the expulsion of the Armenians and exchange of the Ionian Greeks), and the Jews were free to practice their faith.[79] He fundamentally changed the social structure of the country to a "nation without classes or special privileges" and made peasants a key element of the nation:

> The true owner and master of Turkey is the peasant who is the real producer.[80]

Economic Progress

> Ottoman history is not a history of events and efforts carried out in fulfilment of the desires and requirements of the nation, but it is a history of events carried out in order to satisfy the personal whims and ambitions of a few despots . . . An offer of a trade agreement with Venice was refused by Sultan Suleiman the Magnificent on the grounds it was incompatible with his honor . . . Conquerors by the sword are in the end to be defeated by conquerors of the plow . . . *No matter how brilliant military victories and diplomatic achievements may have been, if they are not reinforced by economic achievements, they cannot be expected to last long. We have, therefore, to crown our brilliant victories with economic victories.*[81]   [Emphasis ours]

Atatürk sought to make inclusive economic progress by reducing the emphasis on Istanbul as an economic center and establishing more economic activities across the country.[82] Turkish GDP per capita tripled from 1923 to 1939 when the rest of the world was in the grip of the Depression and practicing protectionist policies that hurt Turkey's exports. This is some evidence of the effectiveness of the policies adopted in its first five-year plan moving the country ahead with industrialization, using state-owned enterprises to build an industrial infrastructure.[83]

Anatolian peasants, however, still faced economic problems. Some relief was provided in 1925 when the agricultural tax was lifted; and there was some land reform. Atatürk took over more than 38,680 acres and divided them into productive farms – the most notable being the Ankara Forest Farm, Nation Chopper Farm in Yalova, and Piloğlu Farm in Tarsus, later donated to the Turkish Treasury.[84]

Perhaps his most important contribution to economic development was changing the mindset of vested interests and elites from resisting economic progress from fear that it would diminish their privileges and benefits or topple them from power, as had happened in Russia under the Tsar, who held back the development of railways because he feared they could be used to mobilize hostile forces against him.[85]

Unified Modern Education

Atatürk recognized the importance of education. He made this clear when turning down military volunteers who he believed would be more valuable for what was to come after the war:[86, 87, 88]

> Atatürk regarded education as the force that would galvanize the nation into social and economic development. For this reason, he once said that, after the War of Independence, he would have liked to serve as Minister of Education. As President of the Republic, he spared no effort to stimulate and expand education at all levels and for all segments of the society.[89]

It has been argued that the reason why Atatürk was so focused on education reform was that he understood that if the people were educated and empowered, they would protect national democratic institutions and, consequently, their democratic rights.[90]

The education system Atatürk inherited from the Ottomans was primarily religious and did not reflect the needs of a modernizing nation.[91] This approach blocked scientific endeavors and obstructed creative thinking.[92] He was clear that education should focus on scientific fundamentals and should not be based on "superstition."[93] He believed in the need for a blended learning approach, combining partly active, rational, and experimental methods with passive, mobile, and rote methods.[94] Teaching methods would have to change if Turkey was to become a modern state.[95] In his view, transformed education was to be the foundation of everything:

> Gentlemen, the most realistic guides, the real guiding principles are education, science for everything, for materiality, for morality, for success in the world.[96]

He wanted education to create an information society, appreciating the importance of practical, useful information:

> The keystone of our education is to destroy lack of information. If it is not destroyed, we are in the same place. *If we want to have a real escape, firstly we must destroy this, lack of information with all our strength, all our ambitions.*[97]   [Emphasis ours]

The literacy rate in Turkey was 7% in 1921, 10% for men and 4% for women. Only 15% of the people who knew how to read knew how to write, whereas at the end of the 19th century, the rate of literacy was 15%. The "drop" in literacy rate reflected the expulsion of the Greek and Armenian communities that had high levels of literacy.[98] 90% of the population remaining after the expulsions lived in the villages and in 90% of the villages there were no teachers or schools. In the entire country, there were twenty-three high schools with a total of 1,241 students and there were twenty vocational high schools with a total of 2,558 students.[99] There were 18,000 madrassa students officially, but only 1,800 were studying; the others were doing menial work rather than attending the religious schools.[100]

Educational reform was started once the war was over. Experts evaluated schools, recommending school systems, teacher training, teaching programs, staffing, and the establishment and organization of a new Ministry of Education. Atatürk saw education as a motor of development for the nation:[101]

> It is such an education that makes a nation live as a free, independent, glorious and noble society, or that drives into slavery and poverty.[102]

Turkey embarked on an ambitious secular and co-educational free schooling program for children and adults – from grade school to graduate school. Primary education was compulsory. The armed forces implemented an extensive program of literacy and with his personal hands-on involvement raised literacy levels:

> Atatürk heralded *"The Army of Enlightenment." With pencil or chalk in hand, he personally instructed children and adults in schoolrooms, parks, and other places.* Literacy which had been less than 9 percent in 1923 rose to more than 33 percent by 1938. [Emphasis ours]

Atatürk advocated the establishment of a unified education system with a secular curriculum taught in Turkish. The Law on Unification Education closed the madrassas, replacing them with religious (*imam hatip*) schools. A School of Theology was established in Istanbul Ottoman University, replacing Madrasah Süleymaniye. Military high schools became high schools. Education was mandatory for male and female children. The 1924 Constitution of the Turkish Republic, Article 87, stated: "the primary school in education became obligatory and free in state schools for all Turkish people."[103] The Third Heyet-i İlmiye (Education Committee) meeting held in 1926 made scientific contributions to advance the education of the Republic.[104]

On April 3, 1926, the Law Concerning Educational Organization was passed by the National Assembly, encouraging teaching and classifying it as a profession. The Board of Education and Discipline was created as a board of experts in the Ministry of National Education. The "Public Discipline Bureau" was also established as a provincial public education unit.[105] A 1927 regulation provided learning opportunities for people without any education, who had fallen behind, or lacked basic citizenship information that a Turkish citizen should know, in the form of Public Classes, designed to strengthen their sense of Turkish identity. 64,302 citizens attended 3,304 such classes in the 1927–1928 academic year.[106]

At the beginning of 1928, the National Assembly passed a law mandating the use of international numerals. Atatürk repeatedly emphasized the importance of the Latin script in his speeches. On November 1, 1928, the law requiring the change in script was passed in the National Assembly. This law was welcomed because of the desire for a new, easier way of writing, learning to read and write, and increasing the levels of literacy. People were given until June 1930 to continue using the old Arabic script.[107] National schools were established to teach the new Turkish script and help the majority become literate. During 1927–1928 "Village Teaching" schools were opened with a three-year curriculum, shortened from the normal five years. Those who graduated from "Village Teaching" schools were given housing and a garden near their schools.[108]

In 1929, selected students were sent abroad as part of program designed to raise standards to international best practice levels. Students were sent to Germany, France, and other European countries to be trained as teachers in science, foreign language, history, geography, mathematics, art, music, and physical education, as well as engineering.[109]

Education was mobilized to spread the ideology and ideas of the new regime, the Republican People's Party (Cumhuriyet Halk Partisi or CHP) started the program of Public Houses on February 19, 1932. The programs, the houses, and their managers were chosen and overseen by the CHP. The nine areas covered by these programs covered public classes, courses, libraries, publications, dealing with the peasants, language and writing, history and museums, social help, sports, presentations, games and fine arts.[110] In an effort to promote awareness of the distinctiveness of Turkish history, language, and culture, the Turkish Historical Society and the Turkish Language Society were founded on April 12, 1931, and July 12, 1932, respectively, with remits to do research into both.[111]

In 1934, Atatürk went further, suggesting that intelligent sergeants who had completed their military service be appointed as "educators" in villages after completing short-term courses.[112] This program started in 1936, when eighty young men from the Mürvet Plain villages in Ankara, who had completed their military service, were included in the Course for Educators lasting eight months. The educators trained for villages were controlled by the Minister of Education and their progress was independently audited. The course books and programs were prepared for the Courses for Educators; and on June 11, 1937, the Law of Village Educators was passed. According to this law, educators would be trained for guiding villagers in agricultural work, as well as teaching in villages with small populations. These training courses continued until 1946 and provided courses for 8,675 educators. From 1938 onward girls and women were included in the program to train village educators.[113]

Atatürk's root and branch approach transformation of the Turkish educational system was able to overcome many of the social and economic obstacles the country faced:

> While legal reforms, or the Latinization of the script, could be carried out in a single stroke, *the battle for modern education had to be fought in every single village, often by young and inexperienced teachers isolated in conservative milieus. The weaknesses, bottlenecks and imbalances which we still see in the system derive from economic and social problems familiar to all third world countries.* In comparison with other Muslim and Middle Eastern countries facing such problems, Turkey's educational system has achieved impressive results.[114]   [Emphasis ours]

Emancipation of Women

The new 1926 Civil Code, based on the Swiss Civil Code gave women equal rights and opportunities, including political rights (which the Swiss Civil Code denied at the time), abolished polygamy, and gave equal rights in divorce, custody, and inheritance. Education from high school through university became co-educational. In part this was recognition of the support women had given the Nationalists. By the mid-1930s, eighteen women were elected members of Parliament, and later a woman was the first in the world to be chosen as a Supreme Court Justice. That Atatürk put so much emphasis on improving the situation of women is hardly surprising given his stated beliefs:

> In Turkish society, women have not lagged behind men in science, scholarship, and culture. Perhaps they have even gone further ahead.[115]

> We shall emphasize putting our women's secondary and higher education on an equal footing with men.[116]

> Everything we see in the world is the creative work of women.[117]

> If henceforward the women do not share in the social life of the nation, we shall never attain our full development, incapable of treating on equal terms with the civilizations of the West.[118]

> One of the necessities of today is to ensure the rise of women in every way. Therefore, our women will be scholars and scientists and go through all the degrees the men do . . . *If a social organization is content to meet contemporary requirements with only one of the two sexes, that social organization loses more than half its strength . . . Our women, like us, are intelligent and intellectual human beings* . . . Let them show their faces to the world, and let their eyes look on the world carefully, there is nothing to be feared in this.[119]   [Emphasis ours]

Approach to Achieving Change

Atatürk's philosophy was ethno-nationalist and pro-western, requiring a high level of state control over most aspects of life; and these elements determined the goals he set in Kemalism. These determined what he wanted to achieve. His approach to achieving change was based on three elements: (1) a scientific approach to problem-solving; (2) personal involvement in implementation; and (3) an authoritarian instinct that became a cult of personality.

Scientific Approach

In his 1927 book *The Speech,* Atatürk articulated a multi-stage scientific approach to achieving change. In the first phase, he traveled across Turkey to see for himself what the problems were. From these observations, he developed hypotheses regarding what needed to be done to improve matters. He then looked around the developed world for possible solutions and would try to apply them, using expert help. And if they did not work, he would see how they could be improved.

Personal Involvement

He used the force of his personality to drive the changes through, being personally involved in much of the detailed implementation.

His control was most obvious in the field of education where he became Headmaster of the People's Schools.[120] A typical example of his hands-on involvement in education and language reforms occurred in 1937 when visiting Sivas High School where he demonstrated the problems with using old Turkish to learn mathematics. Afterward, he wrote a geometry textbook to help students understand the concepts:

> He saw the phrase *"Müsellesin zaviyetan-ı dahiletan mecmu'ü yüz seksen derecedir,"* a Turkish sentence written with Arabic terms, in an old geometry book. When he asked what this sentence meant, the students could not explain the meaning. *So, he went to the blackboard and explained the phrase and all other geometric terms in the pure Turkish language.* The sentence simply meant, "The sum of angles inside a triangle is 180 degrees." But when written in unknown Arabic words, there was no other way than memorizing for those students. *According to the students, for the first time they understood a geometry fundamental. To resolve the issue further, Atatürk wrote a book on geometry (1937) using terms derived from Turkish verbs and discarding Arabic and Persian nouns and clauses that the Turkish students could not comprehend.*[i,121]

Authoritarianism

Atatürk has been described as a dictator, stubborn, merciless, temperamental, and fearless.[122] He has also been called a genius dictator who created a roadmap for Turkey's modernization and democratization.[123] Despite his reputation for incorruptibility, it has been claimed that the state became his property during the Early Republic because the media were silenced, foundations were nationalized, civil associations closed, traditional universities eliminated, and opposition parties banned.[124]

In a sense he was a man of his time, applying ideas of government that were common globally in the 1920s and 1930s. Germany, Hungary, Italy, Portugal, Spain, and the USSR were totalitarian regimes in Europe, as were Japan and China in Asia. Turkey's trajectory of political development was different – it had transitioned from a theocratic multi-ethnic, but Ottoman monarchy to a single-party Turkish republic, destined by Atatürk to become a multi-party Turkish democracy. He had made the destination and journey clear in his speeches. Even though he was influenced by the totalitarian regimes around him, his republic was not a police state.[125] Moreover, he was not comfortable with the extraordinary powers he had been granted by the national assembly.[126]

---

i A student in that class, the father of computer engineering professor Cem Say, wrote this story years later on his father's behalf (Say, 2016).

A personality cult was built around him and it was central to Kemalism, the semi-official religion of Turkey; and his charisma had elevated him almost into being "The One" of a near-monotheist cult with his mausoleum in Ankara being treated as a secular Mecca.[127]

He was repressive, though apparently not extremely so by the standards of his time or of the French press. When Atatürk wrote a piece for the French newspaper *Le Temps,* he commented that

> He modernised the country with his sword in its sheath having an unconstrained power and with toughness when necessary.[128]

L'Humanité summarized that his biggest achievements were that "he violently repressed Socialist and Communist movement." *La Republique* asserted:

> Remembering such very ferocious Frenchmen as Louis XI and Richelieu, highlighting the violence of Atatürk is taking the problems from a narrow perspective. Has Atatürk saved the state? Any Turk with integrity would say "yes." And that is enough.[129]

It was argued that he was able to contain his excessive impulses, even though he had narcissistic tendencies.[130] And his peaceful rhetoric was quite different from the warmongering of his Fascist contemporaries. He was much more humane and peace-loving than other autocrats of his time.[131]

References

1 Landau, J. M. (1984), "Introduction: Ataturk's Achievements: Some Considerations," in Landau, J.M. ed. (1984), *Atatürk and the Modernization of Turkey* (New York: Routledge), p. ix.

2 Bay, A. (2011), *Atatürk: Lessons in Leadership from the Greatest General of the Ottoman Empire* (New York: Palgrave Macmillan), pp. 20–21.

3 General Wesley Clark, quoted in ibid., p. xiv.

4 Kinross, P. (1992), *Atatürk: A Biography of Mustafa Kemal, Father of Modern Turkey* (New York: William Morrow/Quill), p. 14, cited in Bay, A. (2011), pp. 17–18.

5 Atay, F. R. (1982), *The Atatürk I Knew* (Istanbul: Yapi ve Kredi), p. 27, cited in Bay, A. (2011), op. cit., p. 27.

6 Bay (2011), op. cit., pp. 20–29.

7 Atay (1982), op. cit., cited in ibid., p. 29.

8 Zurcher, E. J. (1984), *The Unionist Factor: The Role of the Committee of Union and Progress in the Turkish National Movement, 1905–1926* (Leiden, Netherlands: Brill), p. 32, cited in ibid., p. 29.

9 Mango, A. (2002), *Ataturk: The Biography of the Founder of Modern Turkey* (New York: Overlook), p. 58, cited in ibid., p. 35.

10 Bay (2011), op. cit., p. 35.

11 Armstrong, H. C. (1933), *Gray Wolf: Mustafa Kemal, An Intimate Study of a Dictator* (New York: Minton Balch), p. 2, quoted in Bay, A. (2011), op. cit., p. 39.

12 Source: Anderson, F. M., and Hershey, A. S. (1918), *Handbook for the Diplomatic History of Europe, Asia, and Africa 1870–1914* (Washington DC: Government Printing Office).

13 Bay (2011), op. cit., p. 42.

14 Ibid., p. 48.

15 Ertuna, H. (1985), *1911–1912 Osmanli-Italyan Harbi ve Kolgasi Mustafa Kemal* [The Turco-Italian War of 1911–1912 and Major Mustafa Kemal] (Ankara: Kultur ve Turzim Bakanligi Yayinalri), pp. 105–106.

16 Ibid., p. 36.

17 Atatürk, quoted in ibid., p. 101.

18 Bay (2011), op. cit., p. 81.

19 Atatürk, (1918), *Zabit ve Kumandan ile Hasb-I Hal* [Interviews with officer and commander] (Genelkurmay Askeri Tarih ve Stratejik Etut Baskangli Yayinlari) [Turkish General Staff pdf of Minber Matbaasi edition] (Ankara: Genelkurmay Basimevi), pdf and translation courtesy Lieutenant Colonel Mesut Uyar, with translation and summaries by Dr. Yutuk Iyriboz, 2010, pp. 7–9, cited in Bay, A. (2011), op. cit., p. 82.

20 Atatürk, quoted in Bay (2011), op. cit., p. 84.

21 Mango (2002), op. cit., p. 137, cited in Bay (2011), op. cit., p. 89.

22 Kinross (1992), op. cit., pp. 78–79.

23 Quoted in Mango (2002), op. cit., p. 146 from Atatürk's 1917 report to the Turkish General Staff. This was also covered separately in Unaydin's March 1918 interview with Atatürk.

24 Ibid.; see Goncu, G., and Aldogan, S. (2006), *The Canakkale War: The Homeland is beyond the Trenches* (Istanbul: MB Publishing), pp. 41–42.

25 Bay (2011), op. cit., pp. 6–7.

26 Gawrych, "Rock of Gallipoli," *US Army Command and General Staff College Battle Command Studies*, Combat Studies Institute, CGSC Faculty, http://www.cgsc.edu/carl/resources/csi/battles/battles.asp, cited in Bay (2011), op. cit., p. 101.

27 Ibid.

28 General Liman Von Sanders quoted by Erickson, E. J. (2010), *Gallipoli: The Ottoman Campaign* (Barnsley, South Yorkshire: Pen and Sword Books), pp. 85–86, cited in Bay (2011), op. cit., p. 107.

29 Liddell Hart, B. (1973), *Liddell Hart's History of the First World War: Fourth Impression* (London: Cassell), pp. 236–237.

30 Atatürk, quoted in Unaydin, R. U. (1918), *Conversations with Anafartalar Commander Mustafa Kemal,* originally published in *Yeni Mecmua* magazine in Spring 1918, cited in Bay, A. (2011), op. cit., p. 110.

31 Fewster, K., Basarin V., and Basarin, H. H. (1985), *A Turkish View of Gallipoli: Cannakale* (Richmond, Australia: Hodja), p. 105, cited by Bay. A. (2011), op. cit., p. 110.

32 Erickson (2010), op. cit., pp. 182–183, cited in Bay (2011), op. cit., p. 111.

33 Fuad, A., quoted in Erickson, E. J. (2001), *Ordered to Die: A History of the Ottoman Army in the First World War* (Westport, CT: Greenwood Press), p. 137, cited in Bay (2011), op. cit., p. 119.

34 Erickson (2001), op. cit., pp. 135, cited in Bay (2011), p. 121.

35 Volkan, V. D., and Itkowitz, N. (1984), *The Immortal Atatürk* (Chicago: University of Chicago Press), p. 99, cited by Bay (2011), op. cit., p. 123.

36 Mango (2002), op. cit., p. 182, cited by Bay (2011), op. cit., p. 131.

37 Ibid., p. 255, cited by Bay (2011), op. cit., p. 147.

38 Ibid., pp. 270–273, cited in Bay (2011), op. cit., pp. 147–148.

39 Bay (2011), op. cit., p. 149.

40 Ibid., p. 149.

41 Ibid., p. 150.

42 Tomak, E. (1988), "Ataturk's Strategic Approach to the Modernization of Turkey," *US Air Force Base*, p. 4, quoted in Halil, A. (1997), "Strategic Vision of Mustafa Kemal Ataturk," *US Army War College* (Carlisle Barracks, Pennsylvania), pp. 10–11.

43 Smith, M. L. (1973), *Ionian Vision: Greece in Asia Minor, 1919–1922* (New York: St Martin's), pp. 225–227, cited in Bay (2011), op. cit., p. 151.
44 Orbay, R., quoted in *Quotations about Atatürk – Turkey,* Republic of Turkey Ministry of Culture and Tourism, cited in Bay (2011), op. cit., p. 152.
45 For details of the campaign strategy adopted by Atatürk, see Bay (2011), pp. 150–155.
46 Orbay, R., *Quotations about Atatürk – Turkey,* Republic of Turkey Ministry of Culture and Tourism, Orbay cited in Bay (2011), op. cit., p. 153.
47 Gawrych (1988), "Kemal Ataturk's Politico-Military Strategy in the Turkish War of Independence, 1919–1923: From Guerilla Warfare to Decisive Battle," *Journal of Strategic Studies* (September 1988), pp. 333–334, cited in Bay (2011), p. 153.
48 Ibid., p. 157.
49 Toynbee, A., and Kirkwood, K. (1927), *Turkey* (New York: Scribner's), p. 115, cited in Bay (2011), p. 157.
50 Halil (1997), op. cit., p. 11.
51 "Mustafa Kemal Ataturk," kandogan@cs.umd.edu January 12, 1994, http://www.columbia.edu/~sss31/Turkiye/ata/hayati.html, accessed on November 22, 2020.
52 Ibid.
53 Ibid.
54 Clare, G. (1982), *Last Waltz in Vienna: The Destruction of a Family 1842–1942* (London: Pan Books), p. 95.
55 Akgül, A. S. (2019), "The Case of Atatürk Reforms in Early Turkish Republic Between 1923–1946 From an Educational Perspective," Master's Thesis, Harvard Extension School, p. 12, http://nrs.harvard.edu/urn-3:HUL.InstRepos:42004235, accessed on November 18, 2020.
56 Atatürk, quoted in Rahman A. et al. (2015), "The Consequences of Ataturk's Secularization of Turkey," *Asian Social Science,* Vol. 11, No. 21, July 6, 2015, p. 351.
57 Atatürk, quoted in Armstrong (1961), pp. 199–120, quoted in ibid., p. 352.
58 Atatürk (1927), quoted in Akgül (2019), op. cit., p. 12.
59 Atatürk, quoted in Hayati (1994), "Mustafa Kemal Atatürk," http://www.columbia.edu/~sss31/Turkiye/ata/hayati.html, accessed on April 5, 2021.
60 Sansal, B. (2020), "Ataturk's Reforms: The Father of Turkey," *All About Turkey,* https://www.allaboutturkey.com/ataturk-reforms.html, accessed on November 22, 2020.
61 Halil (1997), op. cit., p. iii.
62 Eisenstadt, S. N. (1984), "The Kemalist Regime and Modernization: Some Comparative and Analytical Remarks," in Landau, J. M., ed. (1984), op cit., p. 9.
63 Ibid., p. 14.
64 Halil (1997), op. cit., p. 12.
65 Akural, S. M. (1984), "Continuity and Change in the Turkish Bureaucracy," in Landau, ed. (1984), op. cit., p. 147.
66 Hayati (1994), op. cit.
67 Ibid., p. 14.
68 Hayati (1994), op. cit.
69 Akural, S. M. (1984), "Continuity and Change in Turkish Bureaucracy," in Landau, ed. (1984), op. cit., p. 147.
70 Atatürk quoted in ibid.
71 Giritli, I. (1984), "Kemalism as an Ideology of Modernization," in Landau, ed. (1984), op. cit., p. 253.
72 Karabelias, G. (2009), "The Military Institution, Ataturk's Principles, and Turkey's Sisyphean Quest for Democracy," *Middle Eastern Studies,* Jan. 2009, Vol. 5, No. 1, (Jan 2009), p. 58.
73 Ibid., p. 58.

74 Ibid., pp. 58–59.

75 Akgül, (2019), op. cit., p. 57.

76 Sansal (2020), op. cit.

77 Ibid.

78 Akgül (2019), op. cit., p. 15.

79 Hayati (1994), op. cit.

80 Ibid.

81 Turkish Ministry of Press Broadcasting and Tourism (1961), *The Life of Ataturk* (Ankara: TMPBT), pp. 117–125, cited in Bay (2011), p. 162.

82 Mango, A. (1999), *Atatürk* (New York: Overlook), p. 40, cited in Akgül (2019), op. cit., p. 21.

83 Gröningen Growth and Development Center (2018), Maddison project database, p. 22, https://www.rug.nl/ggdc/historicaldevelopment/maddison/releases/maddison-project-database-2018, cited in Akgül (2019), op. cit., p. 21.

84 Ibid., p. 22.

85 Ibid.

86 Iyriboz, Y. quoted in Bay (2011), p. 167.

87 Ibid., p. 182.

88 Atatürk (1923), Bursa Speech, quoted in Akgül (2019), op. cit., p. 61.

89 Hayati (1994), op. cit.

90 Akgül (2019), op. cit., p. 12.

91 Unal, B. (2015), "Education Policies During Atatürk Period," *Procedia – Social and Behavioral Sciences* 174 (2015), pp. 1712–1722, https://cyberleninka.org/article/n/609501, accessed on November 16, 2020.

92 Özodaşık, M. (1999), *Cumhuriyet Dönemi Yen Bir Nesil Yetiştirme Çalışmaları (1923–1950)* (Konya: Çizgi Kitabevi), cited in ibid., p. 1718.

93 Atatürk, quoted in Koçer, H. A. (1981), *"Türk Eğitim Tarihimizde Atatürk'ün Yeri,"* Atatürk Devrimleri ve Eğitim Sempozyumu (9–10 Nisan), Ankara, cited in ibid., p. 1718.

94 Özodaşık (1999), op. cit., p. 1718.

95 Atatürk quoted in Akyüz, Y. (1995), *"Atatürk ve Eğitim,"* Ankara: Atatürk Araştırma Merkezi Yayınları. cited in ibid., p. 1718.

96 Atatürk quoted in Yağcı (2007), cited in ibid., p. 1718.

97 Atatürk quoted in Akkutay, U. (2006), *"Atatürk'ün Milli Devlet ve Milli Eğitim Görüşü,"* Atatürk Döneminden Günümüze Cumhuriyet'in Eğitim Felsefesi ve Uygulamaları Sempozyumu Bildirileri (16–17 Mart 2006) (Ankara: Gazi Üniversitesi Rektörlüğü), cited in ibid., p. 1718.

98 Akgül (2019), op. cit., p. 16.

99 Özodaşık (1999), op. cit., pp. 1718–1719.

100 Adem, M. (2006), "Cumhuriyet Dönemi Eğitim Politikaları (1923–2006)," Atatürk Döneminden Günümüze Cumhuriyet'in Eğitim Felsefesi ve Uygulamaları Sempozyumu Bildirileri (16–17 Mart 2006) (Ankara: Gazi Üniversitesi Rektörlüğü), cited in Özodaşık, M. (1999), op. cit., p. 1719.

101 Atatürk quoted in Par-Önen (1987), cited in ibid., p. 1719.

102 Atatürk quoted in ibid., p. 1719.

103 Ergun, M. (1997), *Atatürk Devri Türk Eğitimi* (Ankara: Ocak Yayınları), cited in ibid., p. 1719.

104 Yücel, H. A. (1994), *Türkiye'de Orta Öğretim* (İstanbul: Kültür ve Turizm Bakanlığı Yayınları), cited in ibid., p. 1719.

105 Karakütük, K. (2006), *"Cumhuriyet'in İlk Yıllarında Kırsal Türkiye'de Eğitimin Durumu ve Eğitim Seferberlikleri,"* Atatürk Döneminden Günümüze Cumhuriyet'in Eğitim Felsefesi ve Uygulamaları Sempozyumu Bildirileri 16–17 Mart 2006 (Ankara: Gazi Üniversitesi Rektörlüğü), cited in ibid., p. 1720.

106 Geray, C. (1978), *Halk Eğitimi*, Genişletilmiş 2. Baskı (Ankara: İmaj Yayıncılık), cited in ibid., p. 1720.

107 Ergun (1966), op. cit., cited in ibid., p. 1720.

108 Geray (1978), op. cit., cited in ibid., p. 1720.

109 Karagözoğlu, G. (1994), *"Atatürk'ün Eğitim Savaşı"* I. Uluslararası Atatürk Sempozyumu Açılış Konuşmaları Bildirileri 21–23 Eylül 1987 (Ankara: Atatürk Araştırma Merkezi), cited in ibid., p. 1720.

110 Karakütük (2006), op. cit., cited in ibid., p. 1720.

111 Karagözoğlu (1994), op. cit., cited in ibid., p. 1720.

112 Koçer, H. A. (1967), *Türkiye'de Öğretmen Yetiştirme Problemi* (Ankara: Milli Eğitim Bakanlığı Yayınları), cited in ibid., p. 1720.

113 Ergun (1966), op. cit., cited in ibid., pp. 1720–1721.

114 Winter, M. (1984), "The Modernization of Education in Kemalist Turkey," in Landau (1984), op. cit., p. 193.

115 Ataturk, quoted in Hayati (1994), op. cit.

116 Ibid.

117 Ibid.

118 Kinross, P. (1964), *Atatürk: The Rebirth of a Nation* (London: Weidenfeld and Nicholson), p. 390, cited in Bay (2011), p. 161.

119 Atatürk, quoted in Turkish Ministry of Press Broadcasting and Tourism (1961), op. cit., pp. 215–217, cited in Bay (2011), p. 161.

120 Akgül (2019), op. cit., p. 30.

121 Ibid., p. 17.

122 Armstrong, H. C. (1932), *Grey Wolf – Mustafa Kemal: An Intimate Study of a Dictator,* cited in Akgül, (2019), op. cit., p. 57.

123 Şengör, C. (2014). *Dahi diktatör*. Istanbul: Ka Kitap, cited in ibid., p. 57.

124 Erdoğan, M. (1998). Cumhuriyet ve demokrasi. In H. C. Güzel (Ed.), *Cumhuriyet II Siyasal Değerlendirme*. Ankara: Yeni Türkiye, cited in ibid., p. 57.

125 Mango, A. (1999), *Atatürk* (New York: Overlook), cited in ibid., p. 58.

126 İnalcık, H. (2007). *Atatürk ve Demokratik Türkiye* (İstanbul: Kırmızı Yayınları), cited in ibid., p. 58.

127 Hotham, D. (1972), *The Turks* (London: John Murray), cited in in ibid, p. 58.

128 Atatürk, quoted in ibid., p. 59.

129 Akgül (2019), op. cit., p. 59.

130 Volkan, V., and Itzkowitz, N. (1986). *The Immortal Atatürk: A Psychobiography* (London: University of Chicago Press), cited in ibid., p. 60.

131 Hotham (1972) op. cit., p. 23, cited in ibid, p. 60.

Chapter 5
Lessons Learned

Leadership Characteristics Reviewed

In their book *The Leadership Challenge*, Kouzes and Posner claimed to identify five "evergreen"[i] characteristics of admired leaders:[1] integrity, forward-looking, inspiring, competent, and intelligent. Tables 5.1 to 5.5 compare Elizabeth Tudor, Napoleon, and Atatürk against these characteristics.

We continue by assessing Elizabeth Tudor, Napoleon and Atatürk in terms of whether they demonstrated the traits of *ethical* and *unethical* leadership discussed in Chapter 1 in Tables 5.6 to 5.9.

We now assess whether Elizabeth, Napoleon, and Atatürk demonstrate the characteristics of *effective* and *ineffective* leadership discussed in Chapter 1 in Tables 5.10 to 5.12.

Lessons Learned

By comparing the careers of Elizabeth Tudor, Napoleon, and Atatürk, we draw important lessons regarding admired leadership: the need for integrity; being forward-looking; being flexible; having the intellectual curiosity needed to "connect the dots"; consistent image management; and, above all, having operational competence.

Need for Integrity

Kouzes and Posner consistently rank integrity as the attribute people put first in their requirements of admired leaders. But integrity can mean many different things. Kouzes and Posner define integrity as follows:

> To act with integrity, you must first know who you are. You must know what you stand for, what you believe in, and what you care about . . .[2]

They discuss leaders' values and personal credibility and how followers perceive the integrity of leaders, making the important point that values determine how people

---

[i] These top five characteristics remained unchanged from 1987 to 2007 across the countries surveyed: Australia, Canada, Denmark, Japan, Korea, Malaysia, Mexico, New Zealand, Singapore, Sweden, and the US.

https://doi.org/10.1515/9783110707878-006

behave. Dissonance between people's values and what they are asked to do damages perceptions of integrity:

> Values also motivate. They keep us focused on why we're doing what we're doing and on the ends towards which we are striving. Values are the banners that fly as we persist, as we struggle, as we toil . . .[3]

Leaders modeling espoused values signal to others what they can expect. It minimizes surprises that erode trust:

> You cannot lead through someone else's values, someone else's words. You cannot lead out of someone else's experience. You can only lead out of your own. Unless it's your style, your words, it's not you – it's just an act. People don't follow your position or your technique. They follow you. If you are not the genuine article, can you really expect others to want to follow you?[4]

Table 5.1: Integrity.

Elizabeth Tudor	Napoleon Bonaparte	Mustafa Kemal Atatürk
As a Renaissance, unmarried, female monarch, in weak and divided England, her survival depended on mastery of deception, dissimulation, prevarication and circumvention. She stuck to some guiding principles throughout her reign: 1. The good of her people: "Nothing, no worldy [sic] thing under the sun, is so dear to me as the love and goodwill of my subjects."[5] 2. Reconciling the interests of her Protestant and Catholic subjects so that religion should not be the cause of civil war. 3. Neutralizing the threats to English independence of Valois France and Hapsburg Spain and the Holy Roman Empire; playing them off against each other by remaining unmarried.	Before accepting Emperorship: 1. He lived by republican reforming principles. He explained what he had achieved in Italy: "Religion, the feudal system, and monarchy have in turn governed Europe for twenty centuries, *but from the peace you have just concluded dates the era of representative governments.*"[7] [Emphasis ours] 2. He promoted unity; creating a single Legion d'Honneur rewarding both military and civilian excellence equally, allowed 40,000 Royalists to return to France, agreed the Concordat with the Pope to avoid a religious civil war and to emancipate Protestants and Jews.[8]	Atatürk never asked subordinates to do things he himself had not done. In battle he led from the front. He had a clear purpose to overthrow the Sultan, abolish the caliphate, and destroy Ottoman institutions that prevented the modernization of Turkey: 1. He "had no respect for the leaders. He quarreled with them all . . . His brother officers disliked him as a self-opinionated, sneering fellow. His criticisms were always salty and bitter, with no humor to sweeten them."[10] 2. He opposed corruption, rent-seeking, and abuse of privilege. 3. He focused unremittingly on education and remained personally involved in teaching and promotion of the Latin alphabet.

Table 5.1 (continued)

Elizabeth Tudor	Napoleon Bonaparte	Mustafa Kemal Atatürk
4. Settling the succession without abrogating her freedom of action. 5. She believed that she would have to account for her actions at the Last Judgment, and this guided her behavior.[6]	By 1811 Napoleon was no different from other European monarchs and his family ruled the vassal states of the French Empire. He attempted to justify this by claiming that only his family could secure the gains of the revolution: "In establishing a hereditary nobility Napoleon had three aims: (1) to reconcile France with Europe, (2) to reconcile the old France with the new, (3) to wipe out in Europe the remnants of feudalism by associating the idea of nobility with that of public service and disassociating it from any feudal concept."[9]	4. He was authoritarian, but envisaged Turkey becoming a democracy and attempted to create democratic institutions. 5. He did not benefit personally from his position as President and worked for the benefit of the nation he wanted to create.

Table 5.2: Forward-Looking.

Elizabeth Tudor	Napoleon Bonaparte	Mustafa Kemal Atatürk
Elizabeth developed alternative scenarios and planned for varying outcomes as reported by the French ambassador: "It is not unusual to behold princes form great designs, *but to regulate the conduct of them, to foresee and guard against all obstacles in such a manner that, when they happen, nothing more will be necessary than to apply the remedies prepared long before – this is what few princes are capable of*". Duc de Sully[11] [Emphasis ours]	"Of all our institutions public education is the most important. *Everything depends on it, the present and the future. It is essential that the morals and political ideas of the generation which is now growing up should no longer be dependent upon the news of the day or the circumstances of the moment.* Above all we must secure unity: we must be able to cast a whole generation in the same mould".[12] [Emphasis ours]	Atatürk's objective was radical. His aim was to: 1. Break the hold of the Ottoman past on Turks. 2. Remove the dead hand of Islam (as he saw it) as far as modernization was concerned. 3. Create a new nation of Turks from the ruins of the Ottoman empire. 4. Create a fairer, meritocratic, and more egalitarian society. 5. Emancipate women.

Table 5.2 (continued)

Elizabeth Tudor	Napoleon Bonaparte	Mustafa Kemal Atatürk
1. She settled the succession by choosing Mary, Queen of Scots' son James, and at the same time neutralized the threat posed by his mother and keeping the Scots "onside". 2. She limited support of the Dutch rebels, using them as proxies in the struggle with Spain and avoiding open war, which was the likely result had she accepted the Dutch offer of becoming their Queen. 3. Her support of privateers helped bankrupt Spain, allowed her to pay off the national debt, financed the development of the English navy, and allowed her plausible deniability when challenged by Spain.	As a republican reformer, Napoleon was responsible for: 1. Code Napoleon; 2. Administrative restructuring of France to a centrally directed, but devolved departmental administration; 3. Unified education system; 4. Making peace with the Catholic church; 5. French central bank and stock exchange; 6. Paris fire brigade and paved roads; 7. Building three canals, upgrading three ports, upgrading roads across the Alps; 8. Creating the Legion d'Honneur as a unifying symbol of performance 9. Putting French finances on a sound footing through the creation of the central bank and reform of taxation.	6. Make education the primary driver of change; abandoning Arab script and adopting a newly created Latin one. 7. Establish political and economic institutions that would outlive him. By limiting his military ambition to creating a Turkish only state rather than regaining what the Ottoman empire had lost, he made peace with all of the Ottomans' enemies, kept defense spending low, and kept Turkey neutral.

Table 5.3: Inspiring.

Elizabeth Tudor	Napoleon Bonaparte	Mustafa Kemal Atatürk
"She certainly is a great queen and were she only a Catholic, she would be our dearly beloved daughter. Just look how well she governs! *She is only a woman, only mistress of half an island, and yet she makes herself feared by Spain, by France, by the Empire, by all!*" Pope Sixtus V[13] [Emphasis ours]	"I used to say of Napoleon that his presence on the field made the difference of forty thousand men." Duke of Wellington[15] "After the Italian campaign, Napoleon's name was on everybody's lips: From Graz to Bologna people are talking about	"Ataturk's feats as strategist and field commander in both the First World War and Turkey's War of Independence would have sufficed to ensure his place among major world leaders. However, he will probably be remembered even more as the builder and modernizer of the Republic, a

Table 5.3 (continued)

Elizabeth Tudor	Napoleon Bonaparte	Mustafa Kemal Atatürk
Elizabeth's speech to the soldiers at Tilbury in 1588 is one of the great speeches in English history: "Let tyrants fear. I have always so behaved myself that, under God, I have placed my chiefest strength safeguard in the loyal hearts and goodwill of my subjects; and therefore I am come amongst you as you see, at this time, not for my recreation and disport, being resolved, in the midst of heat and battle, to live or die amongst you all, and to lay for my God and for my kingdom and for my people, my honour and my blood, even in the dust. *I know I have the body of a weak and feeble woman, but I have the heart and stomach of a king, and of a king of England too,* and think foul scorn that Parma or Spain, or any prince of Europe should dare to invade the borders of my realm; to which rather than any dishonour shall grow by me, *I myself will take up arms, I myself will be your general, judge, and rewarder of every one of your virtues in the field. I know already for your forwardness you deserve rewards and crowns; and we do assure you, in the word of a prince, they shall be duly paid you*".[14] [Emphases ours]	only one person. Friends and enemies alike agree that Bonaparte is a great man, a friend of humanity, a protector of the poor and unfortunate. In all the stories the people tell he is a hero; *they forgive him everything except his sending to France Italian works of art*".[16]	role that demanded vision, determination and endless patience."[17] "Like George Washington, Atatürk has remained 'great in war, great in peace, great in the hearts of his fellow countrymen.'"[18]

Table 5.4: Competent.

Elizabeth Tudor	Napoleon Bonaparte	Mustafa Kemal Atatürk
Elizabeth Tudor successfully: 1. Avoided a religious civil war and delayed the rise of Puritanism 2. Settled the succession without marrying or having a child 3. Neutralized and eventually eliminated the threat of Mary, Queen of Scots 4. Neutralized the Spanish threat 5. Successfully managed the changing economic environment 6. Supremely mastered image management 7. Delayed Parliament's attempts to limit the powers of the Crown.[19] (For further details, see Table 5.10)	"I have no words to describe Buonaparte's merit: much technical skill, an equal degree of intelligence and too much gallantry, there you have a poor sketch of this rare officer . . ."[20] Napoleon's achievements included a modern civil code of law, the introduction of prefects in the administrative system, emancipation of the Jews and guaranteed property rights for the new owners of Church and émigré lands. But he was not a French George Washington. "To the role of legislator and founder of his country's liberty, he ultimately preferred that of conqueror."[21] (For further details, see Table 5.10)	"Probably no other twentieth-century leader did more for his country than Mustafa Kemal Atatürk. He brought Turkey independence, changed its alphabet and culture, and created a secular democracy. And probably no twentieth-century general had any better battlefield instincts, skill, or discipline, proving himself under fire at every level of command. And certainly, none so adroitly mixed revolutionary politics with military vision. Yet now, almost a century after his great achievements, he is nearly forgotten in the West, and even in Turkey his legacy is in dispute and his achievements threatened."[22] General Wesley Clark (For further details, see Table 5.10)

Table 5.5: Intelligent.

Elizabeth Tudor	Napoleon Bonaparte	Mustafa Kemal Atatürk

At age 10, Elizabeth gave her stepmother her translation of Queen Margaret of Navarre's *Le Miroir de l'Âme Pecheresse* into poetic English as a present.[23]
    At age 14, she was able to hold her own with her tutor, Roger Ascham, the leading scholar in England, who said:
    "I teach her words and she me things. I teach her the tongues to speak, and her
	"Seizing the essential point of subjects, stripping them down of useless accessories, developing his thought and never ceasing to elaborate it till he had made it perfectly clear and conclusive, always finding the fitting word for the thing, or inventing one where the image of language had not created it, Napoleon's conversation was ever full of interest . . .	Atatürk was brilliant at mathematics. At age 18, he graduated second in his class and entered Constantinople's War College, where one of the officers told him:
		    "You are not going to be an ordinary officer like the rest of us; you are going to change the country's destiny. Don't think I'm flattering you; *I see in you the signs of ability and*

Table 5.5 (continued)

Elizabeth Tudor	Napoleon Bonaparte	Mustafa Kemal Atatürk
modest and maidenly look teaches me works to do. For I think she is the best disposed of any in all Europe."[24] At 26, she was able to influence the Marian bishops and the Presbyterian divines in agreeing to the Thirty-Nine Articles, Act of Uniformity, and Act of Supremacy. Every day she allocated three hours for reading histories and philosophy in Latin and Greek. She gave impromptu speeches in Latin, French, and Italian that were better than those of the French and Italian ambassadors she received.	Yet he did not fail to listen to the remarks and objections which were addressed to him . . . and I have never felt the least difficulty in saying to him what I believed to be the truth, even when it was not likely to please him."[25] Prince von Metternich "From the fact that the First Consul always presided over the Council of State, certain people have inferred that it was servile and obeyed him in everything. On the contrary, *I can state that the most enlightened men of France . . . deliberated there in complete freedom and that nothing ever shackled their discussions. Bonaparte was much more concerned to profit from their wisdom than to scrutinize their political opinions.*"[26] [Emphasis ours]	*intelligence which great men who are born to rule show even in their youth.*"[27] [Emphasis ours]

Table 5.6: Ethical/Unethical Leadership: Benevolence and Callousness.

Elizabeth Tudor	Napoleon Bonaparte	Mustafa Kemal Atatürk
Benevolence[ii]		
When a deputation of judges came to pay their respects after her coronation, she commanded them to:	In his early years, Napoleon believed: "I have ensured the happiness of a hundred	Atatürk avoided vindictiveness and was magnanimous in making peace with the Russians, Armenians, and Greeks

ii *Benevolence:* This is the ultimate test set by Confucius and is interpreted as being magnanimous, having empathy, being able to connect to individuals and nature, and affirming the value of the universe and the ecology.

Table 5.6 (continued)

Elizabeth Tudor	Napoleon Bonaparte	Mustafa Kemal Atatürk
"Have a care over my people . . . They are my people. Every man oppresseth them and [de]spoileth them without mercy. They cannot revenge their quarrel nor help themselves. *See unto them, see unto them, for they are my charge."*[28] [Emphases ours]	families. What pleasure to die surrounded by one's children and able to say: 'I have had a hard life, but the state will benefit from it; through my worries my fellow citizens lie calmly, through my perplexities they are happy, through my sorrows they are gay.'"[31]	preventing grievances that could undermine the stability of the newly-created Turkish state.
Her "Golden Speech" in 1601 showed that what mattered to her throughout her reign was her love for her people and their love for her:	"In the retreat from Palestine, he was concerned about the wounded:	Atatürk emancipated women:
"I do assure you there is no prince that loves his subjects better, or whose love can countervail our love. *There is no jewel, be it of never so rich a price, which I set before this jewel: I mean your love. For I do esteem it more than any treasure in riches; for that we know how to prize, but love and thanks I count invaluable.* And though God hath raised me high, yet this I count the glory of my crown, that I have reigned with your loves."[29] [Emphasis ours]	All horses, mules and camels will be given to the wounded, the sick and plague-stricken who show any signs of life. Everyone not sick goes on foot, starting with me."[32]	"One of the necessities of today is to ensure the rise of women in every way. Therefore our women will be scholars and scientists and go through all the degrees the men do . . . If a social organization is content to meet contemporary requirements with only one of the two sexes, that social organization loses more than half its strength . . . Our women, like us, are intelligent and intellectual human beings . . . Let them show their faces to the world, and let their eyes look on the world carefully, there is nothing to be feared in this."[34]
	Napoleon was acutely conscious of the need to improve the living standards of the French people and did much to help in times of trouble. He understood the importance of economics for ordinary people:	
Elizabeth recognized the need to pass Poor Laws in 1563, 1572, 1576, 1597, and 1601 to help the poor who had been forced off the land by Enclosures. These acts represented a major change in that the State recognized its social obligation to look after the poor for the first time. The acts of 1597 and 1601 endured into the 19th century.[30]	"I fear insurrection caused by a shortage of bread – more than a battle against 200,000 men."[33]	He also gave the Turks a sense of their own identity and was able to give them back their self-respect, without which modern Turkey could not have been created.
	In the winter of 1806–7, when times were hard for the silk makers of Lyons, he spent money from his privy purse to keep them going; in 1811, he secretly advanced money to weavers of Amiens to help them pay their workers.	

Table 5.6 (continued)

Elizabeth Tudor	Napoleon Bonaparte	Mustafa Kemal Atatürk
Callousness[iii]		

Elizabeth was ruthless, but she was not callous. She did not like war, regarding it as an expensive waste.	Napoleon did not worry about the casualties his campaigns created.
	
	    In the words of General de Gaulle: "Napoleon left France crushed, invaded, drained of blood and courage, smaller than he had found it . . . Napoleon exhausted the French people's good will, abused their sacrifices, covered Europe with tombs, ashes and tears."[35]
		Atatürk famously commanded the 57th regiment to die at Gallipoli and they followed his orders to the last man.
		
		    However, he was always concerned that his men were properly equipped and provisioned before they went out to fight.

Table 5.7: Ethical/Unethical Leadership: Fairness and Corruption.

Elizabeth Tudor	Napoleon Bonaparte	Mustafa Kemal Atatürk
Fairness[iv]		

Elizabeth's guiding policy in domestic matters was to find a middle ground. She was more interested in compromise than in being ideologically correct.
 	
    She rewarded people for their performance, with the possible exception of Essex who, in her own words, had wasted the money she had provided him for the Irish war.
	Napoleon replaced a corrupt, rent-seeking Ancien Regime with a meritocratic system in the military, church, and civil service.
	
	    As he said:
	
	    "Every private in the French army carries a *field-marshal's baton* in his knapsack."[36]
	
	    His educational reforms were designed to achieve a level playing field for graduates from the "Grandes Écoles" and students who had passed the "baccalaureat" at the end of their studies in the lycée.
		Atatürk applied certain principles to the chain of command: Accurate information was essential; he did not allow his subordinates to tell him what they thought he wanted to hear; he imposed discipline and held individuals accountable.
		
		    "Wars are made by people. An army's value is determined by the value of its officers. The commander is a person who has creative powers."[37]
		
		    He did this across cultures without distinguishing between Turk, Arab, or Berber.

---

iii *Callousness:* A condition where the leader and some followers are unkind or uncaring, ignoring the needs and wants of most members of the group for which they are responsible.

iv *Fairness:* This is when decisions taken by the leader are seen to be just and fair because they do not favor cronies or friends at the expense of others who equally or more qualified.

Table 5.7 (continued)

Elizabeth Tudor	Napoleon Bonaparte	Mustafa Kemal Atatürk
Corruption[v]		

Elizabeth was not corrupt, though many of the people she granted licenses to were. The money she made from her investments in supporting privateering benefited the State directly:
 	
1. It helped build a superior naval capability to that of Spain without costing the Exchequer:
 	
  Alongside diplomacy, Elizabeth supported and licensed men who had previously been pirates in English waters, turning them into state-sponsored privateers practicing legal piracy against England's enemies. These men gained valuable experience on the seas and, when needed, used their military skills to strengthen the diminutive Royal Navy.[38]
2. The surplus went to pay off the national debt and allowed her to invest the rest in The Levant Company.
	Napoleon changed the rules and made himself Emperor, he did not profit *personally* from his exalted position, although his family did.
	
	By the end of his career he conflated personal glory with that of France, and put personal interest ahead of public interest.
	
	  "He was not a French George Washington. 'To the role of legislator and founder of his country's liberty, he ultimately preferred that of conqueror.'"[39]
		Atatürk allowed a certain amount of corruption among his followers, but he personally was incorruptible and did not profit from his position. From the start of his career, he turned down opportunities to benefit from his position:
		"After Ozdes admitted he had been offered plundered gold, Kemal snapped, 'Do you want to be today's man or tomorrow's?' 'Tomorrow's of course,' replied Ozdes. 'Then you can't take the gold,' said Kemal."[40]

---

v *Corruption:* This is when the leader and followers lie, cheat or steal; but above all put self-interest ahead of public interest and are prepared to cloak their action in self-serving hypocrisy.

Table 5.8: Ethical/Unethical Leadership: Open-Mindedness and Insularity.

Elizabeth Tudor	Napoleon Bonaparte	Mustafa Kemal Atatürk
Open-mindedness[vi]		
As far as religion (the single most important issue she had to deal with) was concerned, Elizabeth was unusually open-minded for her times. She said:	Napoleon's attitude to religion demonstrated open-mindedness and a willingness to adapt to the circumstances in which he found himself:	Atatürk was committed to dismantling the backward looking and insular approach of the Sultanate and Caliphate.
"There is only one Jesus Christ. The rest is a dispute over trifles;"[41] and in addition, she was not interested in creating "Windows into men's souls." As long as subjects were loyal and law-abiding, that was sufficient.[42]	"My policy is to govern men as the majority wish. That, I believe, is the way to recognize sovereignty of the people. It was . . . by turning Muslim that I gained a hold in Egypt, by turning ultramontane that I won over people in Italy. If I were governing the Jews, I should rebuild Solomon's temple."[43]	His exposure to Western ideas and the fact that he came from Macedonia, the part of the Ottoman empire in the greatest flux meant he understood the necessity for change. His exposure to the Arabs and their resentment of the Sultanate made him realize the difference between being Muslim and loyalty to the state.
Having inherited a bankrupt Treasury, Elizabeth needed to think "out of the box" to mend her finances. Parliament was increasingly unwilling to provide funds. Money was always a problem throughout her reign. By inventing an early form of public-private partnership through her investments in and endorsement of privateering, Elizabeth was able to pay off the national debt she inherited and finance the Dutch and Irish wars, though she was still out of pocket when she died.	"The people is sovereign; if it wants religion, respect its will."[44] "Seizing the essential point of subjects, stripping them down of useless accessories, developing his thought and never ceasing to elaborate it till he had made it perfectly clear and conclusive, always finding the fitting word for the thing, or inventing one where the image of language had not created it, Napoleon's conversation was ever full of interest . . . Yet he did not fail to listen to the remarks and objections which were addressed to him . . . and I have never felt the least difficulty in saying to him what I believed to be the truth, even when it was not likely to please him."[45] Prince von Metternich	His recognition of the importance of equality for women reflected his open-mindedness: "If henceforward the women do not share in the social life of the nation, we shall never attain our full development, incapable of treating on equal terms with the civilizations of the West."[46]

---

vi *Open-mindedness:* This occurs when the leader is willing to think "out of the box" to reflect changed contexts.

Table 5.8 (continued)

Elizabeth Tudor	Napoleon Bonaparte	Mustafa Kemal Atatürk

Insularity[vii]

Elizabeth Tudor	Napoleon Bonaparte	Mustafa Kemal Atatürk
At the beginning of her reign, Elizabeth emphasized that she was "mere English" in contrast to her half-sister Queen Mary (half Spanish) and her rival Mary, Queen of Scots (half Scots and French). This was to reinforce why her claim to the throne was unchallengeable. Her education and upbringing were as cosmopolitan as possible in terms of her exposure to other languages and philosophies of Europe. However, she never travelled outside England and did not understand Ireland and its needs with unfortunate results.	Napoleon did not understand that the war with England was a global struggle where control of the seas was as important as control of the continent, giving them a staying power only matched by the Russians. He failed to recognize the importance of naval supremacy and the strategic significance of the defeats in the Battles of the Nile, Copenhagen, and Trafalgar and their impact on his attempt to eliminate English ability to finance their allies. As a result, he concentrated on European land battles because he failed to understand why the English war party would never make peace with him, especially after the execution of the Duc d'Enghien outraged many in Europe and strengthened the alliance against him.	Atatürk's agenda was to modernize and create a new nation state where none had existed before with a secular sense of identity based on western values and the ideal of national self-determination, answering the question: "Who is a Turk?" He included the Kurds in his vision; however, from a Greek or Armenian perspective, he clearly was insular. The ruthless manner in which he delegitimized the role of Islam would alienate people in the Anatolian heartland, providing a fertile foundation for a revival of Islamic parties in the 21st century.

---

vii *Insularity:* The leader and some followers minimize or disregard the impact of actions of the health and welfare of the "other" – that is the people outside their organization but who are affected by its actions.

Table 5.9: Ethical/Unethical Leadership: Mercy and Ruthlessness.

Elizabeth Tudor	Napoleon Bonaparte	Mustafa Kemal Atatürk
Mercy[viii]		
Elizabeth forgave Mary, Queen of Scots many times over the years (1569, 1571, 1572, 1583), even though she persisted in plotting to overthrow Elizabeth. Despite the fact that Catholics were regarded as potential traitors after Pope Sixtus V excommunicated her and encouraged Elizabeth's assassination, there was no widespread persecution of Catholics, even though the Recusancy Act was passed in 1581. Only 250 Catholics were executed or died in prison in the 22 years that followed.[47]	On a few key occasions Napoleon showed leniency toward his enemies and pardoned two who had betrayed him, following in the footsteps of Augustus, whom he admired.	After the peace agreement with Greece, Atatürk's exchange of populations gave the Greeks of Ionia a second chance by allowing them to go to Greece rather than adopting genocidal policies. Nevertheless, it was ethnic cleansing at a time when such practices were acceptable.
Ruthlessness[ix]		
In 1570, Elizabeth instructed the Earl of Sussex to put down the Northern Rebellion and make an example of the rebels. Between 600 and 700 commoners were executed and 200 gentry forfeited their estates. The Duke Norfolk was demoted, The Earl of Northumberland was captured by the Scots, handed over to the English, and executed. A second revolt be Lord Dacre was ferociously put down.[48]	Napoleon expected single-minded focus on achieving a goal regardless of the personal cost: "Great extremities require extraordinary resolution. The more obstinate the resistance of an army, the greater the chances of assistance or of success . . . How many seeming impossibilities have been accomplished by men whose only resolve was death!"[49]	On the battlefield, Atatürk was prepared to sacrifice the 57th Regiment to prevent the ANZAC landing, establishing a bridgehead at Gallipoli. Turning towards his regiment, Kamal issued his most famous order: 'I do not expect you to attack, I order you to die! In the time which passes until we die, other troops and commanders can take our place!'[50]

---

viii *Mercy:* This is the situation where the leader shows compassion and forgiveness towards followers and enemies over whom he/she has the power to punish them for mistakes made; giving people a second chance.

ix *Ruthlessness:* This is the quality of not thinking or worrying about any pain caused to others when deciding what needs to be done; single-minded focus on achieving the objective regardless of the cost.

Table 5.9 (continued)

Elizabeth Tudor	Napoleon Bonaparte	Mustafa Kemal Atatürk
Mary, Queen of Scots was spared, against the advice of her Council, because Elizabeth did not want to execute a monarch. In 1572, after the failed Ridolfi plot, the Duke of Norfolk was executed. However, Mary, Queen of Scots was once again forgiven. Instead, Elizabeth tried to get the Scots to try Mary, Queen of Scots for the murder of Lord Darnley. The Scots would only agree if English soldiers were present at the scaffold, implicating Elizabeth. She abandoned the idea and Mary lived to plot another day. In 1585, after the failure of the Babington plot, Elizabeth initially agreed to Burghley's request that the conspirators should be disembowelled and then drawn and quartered while they were still alive. However, she relented and allowed the remaining seven conspirators to be drawn and quartered after they were dead.	However, his judicial murder of the Duc D'Enghien was both ruthless and misguided, uniting European states in resisting him. He showed no mercy to the King and Queen of Prussia after the Prussian defeats at Jena and Auerstädt in 1806 and executed Turkish officers in Palestine.	Atatürk was prepared at times to use judicial murder and execution to achieve his ends.

Table 5.10: Effective/Ineffective Leadership: Competence and Incompetence.

Elizabeth Tudor	Napoleon Bonaparte	Mustafa Kemal Atatürk
Competence[x]		
Working closely with Gresham (founder of the Royal Exchange), Elizabeth	In undertaking these projects, he involved leading experts, listened carefully to what they had to suggest, and	Atatürk had a remarkable grasp of the political big picture as well as of the intimate details of battlefield topography.

---

x *Competence:* Competent leaders and followers exercise an appropriate balance of skill/will to achieve desired outcomes.

Table 5.10 (continued)

Elizabeth Tudor	Napoleon Bonaparte	Mustafa Kemal Atatürk
successfully replaced the debased currency she inherited. Her fluency in Latin, Greek, Italian, and French combined with her mastery of detail, allowed her to dispense with secretaries and interpreters when dealing with or corresponding with ambassadors and foreign monarchs. Her deep knowledge of theology allowed her to hold her own in the discussions between the Marian bishops and Presbyterian divines culminating in the Thirty-Nine Articles, Act of Uniformity, and Act of Supremacy in 1559. She adopted a strategy of asymmetric warfare against Spain by supporting the Protestants in Holland and by encouraging and investing profitably in naval commercial ventures that weakened Spain's Transatlantic and Asian trade and built a strong English naval capability at little cost in time to defeat the Spanish Armada. She had a detailed knowledge of what was happening in mainland Europe and in England: "She was the wisest woman that ever was, for *she understood the interests and dispositions of all the princes in her time*, and was so perfect in	implemented them accordingly, based on fact-based analysis. "In thirteen months, Napoleon had scored a series of victories which outshone all the combined victories in Italy during the past 300 years. With an army of never more than 44,000 Napoleon had defeated forces totalling four times that number: he had won a dozen major battles, he had killed, wounded or taken prisoner 43,000 Austrians, he had captured 170 flags and 1,100 cannon."[52] Napoleon was extraordinarily competent and detail-oriented with a grasp of the big picture and an eye for detail both of the battlefield and for people, rejecting the use of executive summaries. He built administrative, legal, educational, economic, and scientific institutions that still define France today. Having established the need to rebuild France's finances, he established the French central bank, the Stock Exchange (Bourse), and instituted a new system of tax collection. In order to protect shipping from the English navy, he built three canals linking the north of France to the Mediterranean.	More important, he knew when to stop fighting and make peace with the Ottomans' hereditary enemies, allowing Turkey to focus on peaceful development. He defined and built a modern nation state out of the ruins of the Ottoman Empire and left it with functioning institutions that are only being challenged now by political Islam. His focus on educational reform and his personal involvement in the implementation of teaching the new Turkish script, ensured that the transition from Arabic script to the new script was achieved in record time. He personally spent time with linguists to establish the best way of matching the Turkish language with the new script, given the difficulties experienced with the Arabic script, to make it easier for people to read and write. He was an expert image manager.

Table 5.10 (continued)

Elizabeth Tudor	Napoleon Bonaparte	Mustafa Kemal Atatürk
her knowledge of her own realm that *no councillor she had could tell her anything she did not know before.*"[51] Lord Burghley [Emphasis ours] She was an expert image manager.	When the English blockaded France, cutting off sugar from the West Indies, he replaced sugar cane with sugar beet planted in the north of France.[53] He was an expert image manager.	

Incompetence[xi]

Elizabeth Tudor	Napoleon Bonaparte	Mustafa Kemal Atatürk
Although Elizabeth had excellent political advisers that she trusted (Burghley, Cecil, and Walsingham) in her Council, with whom she worked for most of her reign, she chose her military commanders (Leicester and Essex) based on her emotional relationships with them, rather than their skills as soldiers. The results were failure in Holland (Leicester) and costly defeat in Ireland (Essex).	Napoleon made four fundamental errors of strategy: 1. He failed to appreciate that England was a global strategic contest and not amenable to any negotiated settlement that he would be willing to propose. 2. He tried to fight a two-front war in Spain. 3. He invaded Russia without appreciating logistical implications. 4. He humiliated Austria and Prussia, ensuring that they would seek revenge when the opportunity arose. In addition, he violated his own *tactical* battlefield principles during the Battle of Waterloo, leading to defeat.	Atatürk was not incompetent militarily or politically. However, not being an economist, his economic policies left much to be desired, leading to excessive state involvement and too great an emphasis on import substitution – both fashionable solutions in the 1930s. He failed to institute an effective democratic system with a loyal opposition, despite trying to do so, and resorted to establishing a one-party state.

---

xi *Incompetence:* This is where leaders and followers lack the skill and/or will to sustain effective action.

Table 5.11: Effective/Ineffective Leadership: Flexibility and Rigidity.

Elizabeth Tudor	Napoleon Bonaparte	Mustafa Kemal Atatürk
Flexibility[xii]		
Flexibility lay at the heart of Elizabeth's approach to all major questions. She never adopted positions that backed her into a corner. Through skillful prevarication, obfuscation, and unexpected changing of her mind, she was able to keep her options open until the last minute, frustrating her advisers. "If men were prepared to believe that she was a 'mere woman' weaker and less intelligent than they, Elizabeth was willing to encourage this underestimation, which only made her stronger because her opponents were wholly unprepared for what her formidable intellect and will could throw at them."[54]	Napoleon innovated on the battlefield and in developing new administrative solutions; during his republican period he was willing to listen to all and surrounded himself with leading intellectuals. Most important of all, in negotiating the Concordat with the Pope, he demonstrated a willingness to compromise that saved France and Europe from another war of religion.	Militarily, Atatürk showed great ability to operate in different and demanding strategic and tactical situations. Diplomatically, he made peace with all of the Ottoman Empire's historic enemies on terms that meant Turkey could remain neutral when World War II was declared. He sought the advice of leading global experts, but once he had made up his mind, he did not welcome further discussion.
Rigidity[xiii]		
Elizabeth showed rigidity in that: 1. She would be Supreme head of the Anglican Church so that she could appoint bishops. She showed flexibility in the title by using the word "governor" to get around theological objections.	Napoleon's inability to understand that the other European powers would never accept the imposition by France of a universal political approach, whether it was republican (pre-1804), or imperial (post-1804) was a fatal intellectual flaw.	Atatürk tended to dominate discussions using the force of his intellect and personality to browbeat others into accepting his point of view. Throughout most of his career he was sure of his position, believing that he had the right answers whereas his adversaries were wrong. Events proved him right in most cases.

xii *Flexibility:* This is the ability to adapt to changing strategic contexts, tactical situations, and operational needs.
xiii *Rigidity:* Rigidity occurs when leaders and followers are stiff and unyielding. Although initially competent, they are unable or unwilling to adapt to new ideas and circumstances.

Table 5.11 (continued)

Elizabeth Tudor	Napoleon Bonaparte	Mustafa Kemal Atatürk
2. She insisted on keeping the episcopacy. 3. She insisted until the end on not executing Mary, Queen of Scots because she believed that monarchs could not be tried by their subjects. 4. Once she decided getting married would harm England, she successfully resisted all domestic and foreign political pressures as well as her own emotional inclinations and never married.	His inability to understand that England would never make peace with France as long as it was the dominant power in Europe was a fatal strategic error. His humiliation of Austria and Prussia was a serious tactical error.	His hostility toward Islam and everything the Ottoman state represented informed his insistence on a level of secularism, matched only by France's rigid approach to the subject.

Table 5.12: Effective/Ineffective Leadership: Self-control and Intemperance.

Elizabeth Tudor	Napoleon Bonaparte	Mustafa Kemal Atatürk
Self-control[xiv]		
From a very early age, Elizabeth realized that her life depended on being able to control her feelings and words: All her training and experience, her self-discipline and abnegation, her loneliness and sorrows endured had been for this 'crown imperial,' which was hers of right. She was determined never to give it up and for the rest of her life self-preservation became her first care.[55]	Napoleon does not appear to have normally lacked self-control; his apparent garrulousness was a carefully practiced art to put informants at ease. His thriftiness was extreme and he was regarded as personally incorruptible.	Atatürk exhibited great self-control and did not allow his exalted position as effective dictator to go to his head. He was personally incorruptible.

---

xiv *Self-control:* The ability to remain calm and make rational decisions under pressure. "I cannot trust a man to control others who cannot control himself." Robert. E. Lee.

Table 5.12 (continued)

Elizabeth Tudor	Napoleon Bonaparte	Mustafa Kemal Atatürk
Her self-control was sometimes affected by a need to reassure herself that she was the most beautiful woman in her court; and occasionally by her feelings toward Leicester and later Essex.		
Intemperance[xv] The levels to which Elizabeth showed her feelings for Leicester and later for Essex were perhaps unwise. When angered by them or other nobles, she could be terrifying, making it clear that she was her father's daughter. However, her anger did not last.	Twice Napoleon had very serious outbursts of fury with unfortunate results: 1. With the English ambassador during the Treaty of Amiens negotiations 2. With Talleyrand, turning him into a mortal enemy. He did not realize that although his anger did not last, the damage it did could be permanent.	Atatürk drank too much and eventually it killed him.

Many definitions of integrity focus on honesty, and, as in the latest Kouzes and Posner survey in the US in 2020, conflate "integrity" with "honesty." The definition of integrity we prefer is:

> The convictions of a person of integrity determine what they will say and do at any given time. They intentionally direct their conduct according to their understanding of what is right and wrong. **Authenticity** marks the heart of integrity. Their internal character remains consistent regardless of external conditions.

> Integrity includes the quality of being honest, but **honesty** does not always demonstrate integrity. The difference is the inner commitment to being trustworthy and communicating the truth without deception. An integrated person lives without duplicity and hypocrisy.[56]

---

xv *Intemperance:* This is when a leader lacks self-control and is abetted by followers who allow self-destructive behavior to continue.

Elizabeth Tudor and Atatürk demonstrated integrity as defined above;[xvi] Napoleon did not, as we hope becomes clear:

1. **Elizabeth Tudor** was Machiavellian and focused on the ends she desired and was flexible about the means she adopted. She learned from an early age that her survival depended on mastering deception, dissimulation, prevarication, and circumvention. In her diplomatic entanglements and potential marriage negotiations, it would have been incompetent to make honesty at all costs her priority; in her strategy of weakening Spain using privateers, plausible deniability was fundamental.

Her objectives reflected her most profound beliefs. Her guiding lights were to avoid religious civil war; defend the political interests of England; and settle the succession while maximizing her freedom to operate as long as she lived. Finally, her religious convictions led her to judge all her actions against what would happen to her at the Last Judgment.

Her subjects did not know exactly how she would behave on any given day or on any given issue, but they had a clear view of her priorities. They believed that she was a benevolent ruler by the standards of her time; did not seek a "window into men's souls"; and that she was an English nationalist of great personal physical courage and intelligence who only required loyalty and law-abiding behavior from her subjects. They were mesmerized by her mastery of rhetoric and her consistent and coherent image management which was authentic and consistent with her fundamental beliefs. She understood the importance of consistency and coherence to project integrity in her three interpersonal roles of figurehead, leader, and communicator, as defined by Henry Mintzberg.[57] She was recognized as personally incorruptible.

2. **Napoleon** needs to be assessed in two stages; when he was a servant of the French Republic before he became Emperor; and as a monarch after he became Emperor. The tragic lesson of the change in Napoleon's character is that he chose a different path from George Washington:

> He was not a French George Washington. "To the role of legislator and founder of his country's liberty, he ultimately preferred that of conqueror."[58]

When serving the Republic in his early career and as First Consul, he modeled integrity and was admired across Europe as a "great man." Particularly in Italy, where Italians were grateful for the creation of the Cisalpine and Ligurian republics. In this period, Napoleon lived by republican reforming principles and most of his reforms had the good of the French people in mind.

---

xvi Using this definition, Hitler had great integrity. As Churchill remarked correctly about Hitler, he told the world exactly what he intended to do in *Mein Kampf*. Having integrity per se does not necessarily lead to morally good outcomes.

Once he became Emperor, he changed from being a servant of the Republic to seeing himself as its master, and as the potential master of all Europe.

> He conceived of power and glory as the purpose of his being, and the pursuit of those qualities as overriding all considerations, political as well as moral.[59]

As he himself put it:

> Power is my mistress. I have worked too hard at her conquest to allow anyone to take her away from me.[60]

The unifying link between the two periods of his career was his belief that France should regain its position as the leading country in continental Europe. As long as Napoleon lived by his republican reforming principles, he was generally successful.

We believe the change in his goals was the result of his believing that as Emperor he was free to do as he chose; whereas as First Consul, he served the needs of the French Republic. The extra freedom and power went to his head and led him to stop listening to his advisers. He became arrogant and abusive, creating the coalition that destroyed him. He was unable to successfully navigate the risk that all COOs face when they become CEOs, and become *responsible for creating the strategic framework in which they operate*, as opposed to COOs who *deliver within the strategic framework set by others*. We are tempted to conclude that Napoleon was an extraordinary COO, but a fatally flawed CEO, proving Lord Acton's dictum that "absolute power tends to corrupt absolutely . . . "

3. **Atatürk,** unlike Elizabeth Tudor, did not have to resort to dissimulation, prevarication, and deception to achieve his ends. He made it clear that he believed Ottoman administration was corrupt and incompetent and that what the country needed was radical modernization, secularization, and westernization. Once he learned in Tripolitania, in his dealings with Arabs and Berbers, that being a loyal subject to the caliph as a Muslim was not the same as being loyal to the Turks, he compartmentalized the two concepts.

He overthrew the Ottoman dynasty and then ended the caliphate, focusing on creating and defending an ethno-nationalist, secular Turkish state, limited to the geographical area of what is now modern Turkey, and letting the rest of the Ottoman empire go – using the exchange of populations in the Treaty of Sèvres to render the Greek and Armenian Christian minorities politically insignificant.

To achieve his desired modernization, secularization, and westernization objectives, he promulgated the "six arrows" of Kemalism: Republicanism, Populism, Nationalism, Laicism (Secularism), Statism, and Reformism. His unified national secular education program, his replacement of the Arabic alphabet with the Latin, his emancipation of women, and his change in people's dress code supported the same objective – to abandon a backward-looking Ottoman, Muslim, and rent-seeking system of monarchical governance and adopt a forward-looking western-ized secular republican system in its place.

Like Elizabeth Tudor, Atatürk understood the importance of consistency and co-herence in his roles as figurehead, leader, and communicator; and was recognized as personally incorruptible.

Being Forward-Looking

A visionary leader, provides direction to make the world a better place for their fol-lowers by defining a sustainable mission and vision, and articulating what followers can expect. Leaders often attain power by focusing on the past, peddling a nostalgic interpretation of an imagined, as opposed to actual, past. The problem with back-ward-looking policies is that it is difficult to turn back the clock and recreate condi-tions that either never really existed, or that are no longer relevant. Although trying to recreate a past golden age is an effective platform for campaigning, it often proves to be a poor basis for governing.

1. **Elizabeth Tudor** was not a radical reformer like Atatürk or Napoleon. Her focus was on conserving and building the Tudor legacy. Her reign was one of incremental change rather than "great designs." Whenever radical change threatened to destabi-lize the state and her rule, she attempted to reconcile traditional thinking with the challenges posed by changing economic, political, or religious circumstances. This can be seen in her gradualist approach to religion; to the changing basis of political power in Parliament, which reflected the rise of the gentry and London's Protestant merchants; and the growth of Puritanism.

Elizabeth's strategic success was as an incrementalist who knew when to bend to pressures and when to stand firm. This was the result of her remarkable ability to imagine different scenarios and to ensure that she had appropriate resources in place to deal with problems as they arose. Her ambitions were realistic and limited to defending English interests. In the words of the French ambassador in 1601 at the end of her reign:

> To regulate the conduct of [great designs], to foresee and guard against all obstacles in such a manner that, when they happen, *nothing more will be necessary than to apply the remedies pre-pared long before – this is what few princes are capable of.*[61]   [Emphasis ours]

One area of policy that she did not deal with effectively was Ireland where she failed to resolve the long-standing problems that had been generated by Pope Adrian in 1155 from his Bull *Laudabiliter* granting English monarchs the right to annex Ireland – a problem that continues to bedevil Anglo-Irish relations.

She encouraged English commercial and naval expansion in the Americas and the East Indies, leading, for good and ill, to the creation of the largest empire in history and the growth of the most powerful company in the world in its heyday, the British East India Company.[62] Her patronage of the arts and, in particular, the theatre, contributed to the growth of English as a leading language in the world. It is unlikely that she realized how "great" these designs would become.

2. **Atatürk** was a revolutionary whose mission and vision was, by definition, radical. His ambition was to break the hold of the Ottoman past and Islam on the development of the Turkish nation he aimed to create. As a military commander, he energized the defeated remains of the Ottoman empire in Anatolia into an effective fighting force to defeat occupying armies and, thereby, create a new nation. An ethno-nationalist, he created a Turkish sense of identity based on secular independence from Islam, limited to Turkey only; was western-looking and based on a fairer, more meritocratic, and more egalitarian society where women were emancipated. His vision, like that of Napoleon, was to use a unified, modernized national education system as the primary driver of change, by abandoning the Arabic alphabet and replacing it with the Latin, making it easier for Turks to read and write.

He transformed Turkey from an Ottoman monarchical, multi-ethnic state, united by Islam and the caliphate, to a Turkish-Kurdish ethnic, secular proto-democracy.

By limiting his ambition to the territory that makes up modern Turkey rather than trying to regain the lands of the Ottoman empire, he was able to allocate the resources necessary for his grand design. He ended centuries of enmity with Turkey's neighbors, and invested in industrialization and modernization rather than the armed forces.

3. **Napoleon** in his period as a republican reformer sought to heal the divisions created by the Revolution between the adherents of the Ancien Regime and the beneficiaries of the Revolution. His vision was of a united/unified France that would regain its seat at the top tables of Europe. To do this, he believed that a whole generation needed to be recast in the same mode; and believed that a unified national educational curriculum was essential to its achievement. He saw it was necessary to make peace with the Catholic church and to rebuild France's finances.

He overhauled the French administrative system of government to give it a centrally directed but devolved prefectural system of local government; rationalized the tax system; established the central bank and stock exchange; and created the Code Napoleon – France's civil code that still applies today. He overhauled France's roads, built three canals and upgraded three ports, and built new roads across the Alps.

As Emperor, his failure to consider the consequences of his treatment of Talleyrand; his humiliation of Austria and Prussia that would turn them into revanchist regimes; his failure to appreciate the long-range strategic importance of naval warfare; his lack of understanding of the motives of England and Russia; and his disastrous invasion of Russia are evidence of his inability to look far enough forward to understand that his desire to impose a French Empire on Europe was bound to fail. This resulted from the conflation of his desire for personal military glory and power with the interests of France as a nation. A forward-thinker like Talleyrand could see clearly the two things were separate, whereas Napoleon either could not or would not.

Flexibility

"Flexibility" is ambiguous. It can mean the ability to bend without breaking, like the bamboo in a typhoon that uproots the stronger, more rigid trees. It can mean the willingness to "go with the flow" and become the hallmark of a person lacking integrity. In assessing Elizabeth Tudor, Napoleon, and Atatürk, we use the word to mean willingness to compromise and reconcile conflicting perspectives and strategic and operational imperatives:

> Strategy [flexibility] generally refers to an organization's ability to respond to changes in its environment both rapidly and at low cost. In the (limited) sense that strategy is an unchanging commitment to something, it is the antithesis of flexibility . . . *adaptability and alignment; flexibility and firmness. The words are different though the dilemma remains the same.*[63]
>
> [Emphasis ours]

From a business perspective we recognize the need to resolve such dilemmas:

> For a company to succeed over the long term it needs to master both adaptability[xvii] and alignment[xviii] – an attribute that is sometimes referred to as ambidexterity.[64]

Ambidexterity in our view is also the hallmark of successful generals – it differentiates those who are tactical geniuses who win battles but lose wars from those who know when to retreat or make peace in order to secure long-term gains.

1. **Elizabeth Tudor:** The essence of Elizabeth's philosophy was to avoid making commitments. She tried to keep her options open till the last moment, whether discussing marriage, negotiating with Parliament, or dealing with Mary, Queen of Scots.

Her approach to religion was to seek compromise on matters of theology, reconciling wherever possible the views of the Marian bishops, her Catholic subjects, and Protestant subjects and advisers. She neutralized the increasingly strident demands of the Presbyterians; however, on the issue of to whom did the Anglican church answer, she was firm that the power to appoint bishops was hers, while being flexible regarding her title.

Her naval strategy was based on outsourcing the supply of sailors and co-opting privateers and their ships, maximizing her access to fit-for-purpose ships, and fit and capable crews, while minimizing the fixed costs to her exchequer – a perfect

---

xvii Adaptability recognizes changing circumstances that demand changed responses.
xviii Alignment demands allocation of resources to achieve a fixed goal.

example of ambidexterity that had the additional advantage of allowing her plausible deniability while adhering to her objective of weakening Spain and building the best naval capability in Europe.

2. **Napoleon:** On the battlefield, Napoleon was a master of tactics; adapting to the conditions and circumstances facing him. As a result, until 1812, he was able to outthink, outmaneuver and outfight his enemies. However, from 1812 onward, he lost this skill, adopting an attempt to impose a French empire on all Europe. He refused to deviate from this dream, ignoring Talleyrand's admonition that it would fail.

As a reformer, he showed administrative imagination both in his dealings with the Italians after the Italian campaign in creating the Cisalpine and Ligurian Republics, demonstrating a spirit of compromise that allowed a role for the losing Italian aristocrats. He demonstrated the same willingness to compromise and recognize the validity of his opponents' positions in inviting the exiled Royalists back to France and in negotiating his Concordat with the Pope.

Upon becoming Emperor, his obsession with personal glory achieved through war limited his ability to compromise and be flexible, leading him to humiliate Austria and Prussia after their defeats, rather than offer generous terms, as he had in Italy.

3. **Atatürk:** Like Napoleon, Atatürk was a master of flexibility on the battlefield, evidenced by his willingness to retreat into the Anatolian heartland to draw in the Greek army; the antithesis of his approach at Gallipoli, where he ordered the 57th regiment to die rather than retreat. In diplomacy, his approach was accommodating and to make peace with Turkey's hereditary enemies.

As far as his political philosophy and platform of the six arrows of Kemalism was concerned, he sought the advice of globally recognized experts, but once he had made up his mind, he did not welcome further discussion. In his rejection of Islam in order to secularize Turkey, he was obdurate. There was no room or role for it. This obstinacy alienated the rural Anatolian heartland.

Intellectual Curiosity

Intellectual curiosity is the acquisition of general knowledge and wanting to understand the underlying mechanisms and structures of philosophical and operating systems, mathematical relationships, languages and cultures, and history. Intellectually curious people are better able to "connect the dots" because they are more aware of the existence of such dots.

1. **Elizabeth Tudor:** Being well-read is an essential ingredient in acquiring knowledge and understanding. At the age of thirteen, Elizabeth was already writing commentaries on Plato's *Republic*, Cicero's orations, Thomas More's *Utopia,* and the New

Testament in Greek. At fourteen, she was able to hold her own with her tutor, Roger Ascham, reputed to be the leading scholar in England:

> I teach her words and she me things. I teach her the tongues to speak, and her modest and maidenly look teaches me works to do. For I think she is the best disposed of any in all Europe.[65]

She was fluent in Italian and French and well-read in the works of both. She was musical, a good archer, and an excellent dancer. Throughout her reign, she devoted three hours every day to reading histories and the classics of her time. In June 1602, she translated the Latin poet Horace's "Art of Poetry," but was too old to complete her translation of Ovid's "Art of Love" from Latin.[66] When she was twenty-six years old, her grasp of theology was sufficient to allow her to hold her own against Anglican bishops and Presbyterian divines.

Her mastery of underlying principles, detail, and languages meant that she did not need secretaries or interpreters when dealing with ambassadors or her advisers in the Council. As Lord Burghley, the Chancellor with whom she worked for forty years, reckoned:

> "She was the wisest woman that ever was, for *she understood the interests and dispositions of all the princes in her time,* and was so perfect in her knowledge of her own realm that *no councillor she had could tell her anything she did not know before.*" Lord Burghley[67] [Emphasis ours]

2. **Napoleon:** Napoleon had good mathematical ability and a lawyer's attention to detail (inherited from his lawyer father). He was fascinated by how things worked and analyzed data to find the optimal deployment of battlefield resources. As an administrator he surrounded himself with leading experts in their respective fields and listened to what they had to say before implementing their suggestions.

> *Napoleon was probably the best-read emperor the world has ever seen.* As a young man he particularly enjoyed Plutarch's *Lives of the Noble Grecians and Romans*, and in exile on Saint Helena one of his favourites was *Paul et Virginie* by Jacques-Henri Bernardin de Saint-Pierre. *But he was also keen not to be separated from reading matter while on campaigns, so wisely commissioned various travel libraries which were put together by his personal librarian* Antoine-Alexandre Barbier.

> *These contained hundreds of volumes and covered military tactics, history, geography and religion as well as novels, poetry and plays.* In addition to these, he also ordered a smaller, more manageable travel library in a wooden box resembling a large book measuring around 15 by 10 inches, stocked with French classics in appropriately bespoke smaller format.[68]
>
> [Emphases ours]

His intellectual curiosity is illustrated by his leadership of the expedition he led to Egypt in 1798. He added improving science and anthropology to increase France's understanding of Egypt and its storied history as one of the expedition's objectives. Thus, the expedition was to be both a military conquest and a scientific discovery. To this end, Napoleon took with him scholars, scientists, and artists.[69] Napoleon's discovery program yielded new insights into ancient Egypt and Nubia and found the Rosetta stone that allowed historians to interpret Egypt's hieroglyphics for the first time.[70]

3. **Atatürk:** During his early years in Western Turkey, Atatürk was exposed to French political thought and read widely in Turkish, German, French and English. His reading covered the military, ethnographic, and diplomatic history of the Ottomans; histories of Austro-Hungary, the Balkans, and of French trade, British, and German involvement in the Near East, as well as books on Russia's objectives in its wars with Turkey. He read French and German books on anthropology, sociology; and biographies of important men, like Palmerston (who served twice as British Prime Minister in the 19th century), and their impact on the Turkish question; all correspondence on the Balkans, its wars, and correspondence relating to World War I, including Russian correspondence. He read German histories of the rise of the Turkish empire from its impact on Venice up to the Crimean War and to its decline as the "sick man of Europe." He read about the conquest of Constantinople by the Crusaders in 1204, and books on Christianity and Islam.[71]

During his Presidency, Atatürk invited leading experts in the fields of economics, anthropology, psychology, and linguistics to advise him on how best to modernize Turkey. He worked closely with them to learn what he needed to know to modernize the Turkish language, free it from its Arabic and Persian heritage, and develop an appropriate Latin script; and create a Turkish identity in which emancipated women could play their part.

Image Management

1. **Elizabeth Tudor** was expert in image management. She understood that from the moment she woke to the time she went to bed; she was on show.[72] Aware of the importance of appearances, she controlled her image throughout her reign; paying close attention to costume, hairstyles, and jewelry.[73] She encouraged public association of her with biblical heroes that had saved the Israelites from their enemies. Presenting herself as the Virgin Queen[74] allowed her to become a semi-divine object of veneration by her subjects who needed a replacement for Catholic worship of the Virgin Mary. Her image appeared in woodcuts, brooches, badges, medals, and coins. Miniatures were worn like icons by both sexes to demonstrate loyalty and deference to their Queen.[75] The ultimate tribute to her was Spenser's *The Faerie Queen.*

Elizabeth dominated her court with her collection of dresses and jewelry, her exuberant dancing, and her virtuosity in Latin; *more than any English sovereign, she showed herself to her subjects.*[76] She took care to appear before commoners as well as courtiers; touring the country twenty-five times a year, traveling in great style. Locals were treated to free displays of pageants and fireworks. She never missed an opportunity to make great speeches, emphasizing how special she was. At the same time, she maintained the common touch, silencing the crowd to listen to the words of welcome by a child whose task was to greet her in verse.[77]

The most important speech she gave to establish her special place in the hearts of her subjects was at the Tilbury military encampment during the naval battles with the Spanish Armada in 1588, where against the advice of her councilors given the real threat of assassination, she went wearing the armor of a cavalry officer, looking resplendent on her horse.

2. **Napoleon** realized that his ability to gain and stay in power depended on his popularity with the French people and, to keep that, it was not enough to win battles. He set out to control what the French saw and read about him. He began by issuing copper, silver, and gold medals celebrating his victories. Printmakers and engravers were instructed to create idealized images of him, his family, and his generals, as well as scenes of his victories, Egyptian treasures, and his coronation.

    He used his Bulletins of the Great Army to target French citizens, his soldiers, and his opponents with messages that presented him in the best light. His exaggerations led to the phrase "lie like a bulletin." Besides using the Bulletin to promote himself, he also used the press to his advantage, including in Egypt where he took printing presses with him to produce newspaper reports to impress people in France, but also to influence the locals and bring them to his side.

    > Finding treasures such as the Rosetta Stone, created a love for everything Egyptian and it did not take long for Egyptomania to be the rage throughout Europe, and particularly in France. In general, people were fascinated by everything Egyptian, and the scientific achievements in Egypt also resulted in an interest in craniology or phrenology, whereby the human skull was studied in the hope of determine a person's intelligence and characteristics . . .

    > *Finding the Rosetta Stone and other Egyptian treasures did not just enhance France's scientific reputation, it also enhanced Napoleon's. Every time someone thought of Egypt, it brought Napoleon to mind, particularly after he began promoting the use of Egyptian imagery in France after his return.* Two architects, Charles Percier and Pierre-François-Léonard Fontaine, were appointed to create this new style that thereafter was closely associated with the Napoleonic period.

    > What the architects developed employed war and militaristic elements. *It also embraced classical symbols from Roman emperors that included the eagle, palm leaves, and laurel wreaths. Also used in this new look were sphinxes, eagle heads, bees, the horn of plenty, and winged lions and, of course, the incorporation of Egyptian motifs. These symbols made a connection between Napoleon and the glory of earlier times.*[78]   [Emphases ours]

3. **Atatürk** developed and promulgated Kemalism with its six ideological arrows as the basis of the revolutionary changes he wanted to achieve. He used statues of

himself to dominate public spaces, a radical innovation given the Islamic prohibition of statues on the grounds they were idols:

> When we consider that every city and town in Turkey today has at least one monument of
> Atatürk located in one of its most important public spaces; that *all public and private pri-*
> *mary, middle and high schools possess a bust of him in front of which the student body ritually*
> *musters every Monday morning and Friday evening to chant the national anthem; that apart*
> *from statues and busts, his portraits or photos hang in every government office and state*
> *building, as well as in nearly all private offices, shops and workshops; and that his name has*
> *been bestowed upon boulevards, parks, stadiums, concert halls, bridges, forests, airports and*
> *educational institutions . . .* monumental statues of Atatürk constitute one of the most wide-
> spread instruments of the state elite-driven project of modernity in Turkey. By the time Ata-
> türk died in 1938, hundreds of busts, statues and monuments of him had been erected in
> the most important public spaces in Istanbul, Ankara and other major cities in Turkey.
>
> *They exemplify one of the most effective instruments of the elite-driven projects of modernity by*
> *revealing the ways in which Atatürk and his political elites attempted to establish a new official*
> *public culture and official history. They have been instrumental in the formation and reproduc-*
> *tion of Turkish nationalism since the beginning of the Turkish republic.*[79]   [Emphases ours]

He used every opportunity to appear in public classes as the teacher of peasants
and children, showing them how to read and write using the Latin alphabet
that replaced the traditional Arabic script. This reinforced the meaning of Atatürk as the "Father of the Turks," the surname he adopted when surnames became mandatory.

Operational Competence

Operational competence is a combination of effectiveness in delivering stated objectives and goals, and ethical behavior in achieving those goals:
1. **Effectiveness in delivery:** Table 5.4 summarized the competence of Elizabeth
   Tudor, Napoleon and Atatürk. This was broken down into its component parts
   in Tables 5.10–5.11:
   a. *Competence and incompetence:* Table 5.10 showed that Elizabeth, Napo-
      leon, and Atatürk were all competent across a wide range of subjects, but
      failed in some areas: Elizabeth in her choice of military commanders; Napo-
      leon in four strategic areas and during the battle of Waterloo; and Atatürk
      in his choice of economic policies.
   b. *Flexibility and rigidity:* Table 5.11 showed that Elizabeth was flexible as a matter
      of policy, delaying commitment to the last possible moment, seeking compro-
      mise on matters of religion, except for insisting on keeping bishops, appoint-
      ing, and controlling them. She remained unmarried regardless of the domestic
      and international pressures on her to marry and give birth to an heir, and re-
      sisted demands to execute Mary, Queen of Scots for as long as possible. Before

he became Emperor, Napoleon showed flexibility in battle, in negotiating the creation of the Cisalpine and Ligurian Republics in Italy, in Egypt regarding Islam, and in reaching the Concordat with the Pope. After he became Emperor, he stopped listening, refusing to accept that England would never make peace as long as France was the European hegemon, persisting in trying to impose a French empire on the rest of Europe. Atatürk was flexible militarily, diplomatically, and politically with the exception of his treatment of Islam.

   c. *Self-control and intemperance:* Elizabeth, Napoleon, and Atatürk were all capable of great self-control. Elizabeth's and Napoleon's outbursts of anger were sometimes exaggerated to make a point. Napoleon became less self-controlled after becoming Emperor. Atatürk's lack of self-control was that he drank too much, which eventually killed him.

2. **Ethical behavior:** Tables 5.6–5.9 compared Elizabeth Tudor's, Napoleon's and Atatürk's ethics in behavior:

   a. *Benevolence and callousness:* Table 5.6 showed that Elizabeth was benevolent and not callous; and that Napoleon and Atatürk were both benevolent and callous.

   b. *Fairness and corruption:* Table 5.7 showed that Elizabeth rewarded people for their performance, but allowed elites to continue rent-seeking through licensing, even though she herself was not corrupt. Napoleon and Atatürk replaced corrupt rent-seeking ancien regimes with meritocracies and were personally incorruptible.

   c. *Open-mindedness and insularity:* Table 5.8 showed that Elizabeth, Napoleon, and Atatürk were all open-minded. However, despite being cosmopolitan intellectually, Elizabeth and Atatürk were ethno-nationalists seeking insular solutions to their countries' problems. Napoleon's insularity manifested in his inability to understand that naval supremacy was critical if he was to defeat England – winning land battles in continental Europe could not.

   d. *Mercy and ruthlessness:* Table 5.9 showed that Elizabeth, Napoleon, and Atatürk could be merciful, but were ruthless at times. However, once he was Emperor, Napoleon was merciless in his dealings with Prussia and Austria, ensuring they would seek revenge.

Relevance in Current Conditions

We consider the relevance of lessons learned in today's business environment and how they are still relevant (perhaps with additions):

Integrity

Integrity is a more complicated subject than many realize. The election of Donald Trump in 2016 as President of the US and the rise of Boris Johnson to Prime Minister of the UK in 2019 following his successful Brexit campaign in 2016 based on half-truths, suggest that *integrity is not that important in winning elections or achieving power.*

Electorates in both countries knew the character of both men and still chose them to lead their countries, suggesting that consistency in appealing to a vocal minority of the electorate and feeding them what they wanted to hear, rather than facts was critical to their success. Perhaps this is because campaigning does not require integrity; but depends on mastery of rhetoric. As Mario Cuomo, the 52nd Governor of New York state, put it:

> You campaign in poetry. You govern in prose.[80]

Once in power, integrity assumes greater importance; it is the way in which followers and opponents evaluate the performance of leaders against what they said would deliver. *Repeated failure to adhere to declared values, a track record of U-turns and inconsistencies leads to a breakdown in the trust* of followers, as Mr Johnson's government discovered with his mishandling of the coronavirus pandemic in 2020:

> There's a palpable difference between being governed by people you don't agree with, and being governed by people who you wouldn't trust with even the most basic pragmatic decisions.

> There have been too many cock-ups, too much cronyism, too many U-turns, too much overpromising.[81]

Over time, integrity matters because a disconnect between the promised vision and the actual delivery fractures the bond between leaders and led. *Yet, Integrity without power is impotent and serves little purpose.*

Being Forward-Looking

Change is constant; it is crucial for business leaders to understand how likely changes would affect the viability of their organizations. This demands an awareness of megatrends in:
1. Demographics and economics – their impact on politics at global, national, regional and local levels.
2. Social changes and their likely impact on demand for an organizations' goods and services, and on the supply of suitably skilled labor.
3. Technological developments, their pace and likely impact on economies, industries, competitors, and organizational business models.

4. Legal and regulatory governance issues affecting organizations' freedom to operate with respect to the environment, health and safety, competition, and customer protection.

Responding effectively to megatrends requires imagining futures and development of appropriate plans, based on a realistic appreciation of what is possible, given the resources available and the ability of an organization to change.

Flexibility

Being forward-looking is only of value if an organization can adapt to deal with the identified changes in context created by awareness of such changes. Organizations can only change when leadership and top management:
1. Understand changing contexts, implications, and how they affect the ability of organizations to achieve their objectives.
2. Are willing and able to review their strategic goals, strategies, and tactics as a result.
3. Understand when to embrace or resist change, considering resources available to overcome obstacles, and likely objections by internal and external stakeholders.
4. Communicate the need for change fully and effectively to engage the whole organization in the effort.

Intellectual Curiosity

Intellectual curiosity is required to understand megatrends that determine organizational sustainability. It depends on being widely read and curious about what is happening outside the boundaries of the organization and professional disciplines. To be effective, "connecting the dots" requires certain skills:
1. **Analytical skills:** Being numerate, and understanding the limitations of qualitative and quantitative analysis.
2. **Systems thinking:** Having awareness of network and emergent properties of systems; including recognizing the interdependence of systems and, for example, the consequences of focus on efficiency at the expense of resilience (demonstrated by the impact of covid-19 on global supply chains).
3. **"Helicopter management":** Being capable of seeing the "big picture" while at the same time appreciating that the "devil is in the details."
4. **Integrative synthesis:** Being able to pull it all together, considering both the specialist and generalist points of view – the approach of successful polymaths like Elon Musk.[82]

Image Management

Personal image management is no different in principle from brand management. It depends on the same four pillars of branding:[83]

1. **Function:** Answers the question "What are the Mission, Vision and Values offered to followers?" so that they know what they are attempting achieve, by when and how and can assess over time whether they were achieved, and if not, was it because they were unrealistic fantasies or realistic objective that have been missed because of operational incompetence.
2. **Personality:** Answers the question "What is it like to do business with this person?" and includes the OCEAN personality traits, trustworthiness, reliability, as well as empathy and temper, but above all consistency of behavior and competence in delivery; and that there is no distinction between public and private behavior.
3. **Differentiation:** Answers the question "What makes the leader different, more effective than other people, in ways that are relevant to potential and existing followers."
4. **Source of authority:** Answers the question "Why should followers believe leaders?" by documenting their background, experience and track record, with track record of delivering what they have promised being the most important.

Operational Competence

Operational competence requires integrity, being forward-looking, flexibility, intellectual curiosity, and image management in leaders; it also includes a number of management skills that are contextually determined:

1. **Sector familiarity:** Understanding the economic dynamics of a sector and the strengths and weaknesses of the competition.
2. **Marketing and sales:** Having capability in developing products and services that suit sustainably profitable segments and achieving appropriate levels of coverage of buyers (directly or indirectly with convincingly suitable sales propositions).
3. **Research and development:** Ensuring existing product and services are kept up to date with latest technology and customer demands; and creating new products and services that are adopted by customers and non-customers.
4. **Supply chain:** Ensuring supply of raw materials of appropriate cost and quality; focusing on efficiency, reliability, and safety of inbound and outbound logistics and manufacturing, minimizing their environmental impacts.
5. **Finance:** Ensuring sustainable sources of funding, optimizing use of working capital and treasury, based on accurate and timely cost, management, and financial accounts.

6. **Risk:** Minimizing and mitigating systemic, reputation, environmental, business, and operation risks, including cybersecurity.
7. **Project management:** Negotiating and agreeing desired outcomes, allocating resources and responsibilities accordingly, with agreed individual accountabilities and due dates; followed up to ensure timely, "fit for purpose" delivery.
8. **Negotiation:** Ensuring "win-win" results if protagonists do business with each other on a regular basis so that there are no hard feelings despite the need to compromise; being willing to negotiate in "winner takes all" mode, if it is indeed a zero-sum game.
9. **HR:** Ensuring succession planning and talent management; objective performance appraisal, reward, and recognition systems that reflect agreed values; ensuring effective recruitment, retention, and dismissal programs that reflect current and future organizational design needs.
10. **IT:** Ensuring accurate, timely, and robust systems to support all processes and their information requirements in easily accessible and understandable, scalable form.

Summary

Although Elizabeth Tudor left an indelible image of the glory and success of her reign, from an institutional point of view, her only legacy was the Anglican church. Despite his tragic flaws and ultimate failure in his lifetime, Napoleon's operational competence in establishing institutions and building infrastructure for France has left a legacy that survives unchallenged up to the present day. Atatürk was operationally competent in all areas that he wished to change and died a success. However, his inflexibility with regard to the role of Islam in the new secular nation he created has led to his legacy being challenged in today's Turkey.

If the ultimate definition of effective and admired leaders is the enduring legacy they leave behind, then the most important contributor seems to be operational competence; incorporating, as it does, integrity to some extent; being forward-looking, flexible, and intellectually curious; supported by good image management and key managerial skills.

In Part 2 we explain that effective leadership is managerial and how leadership and management and strategies and tactics are, in reality, on a continuum and are not discrete activities; though they are often separated in the literature for convenient analysis.

This is why we discuss the morally neutral techniques of effective leadership in Part 3, but *focus in the last chapter on the role of ethics in achieving morally justifiable outcomes.*

References

1 Kouzes, J. M., and Posner, B. Z. (2007), *The Leadership Challenge, 4th Edition* (San Francisco: John Wiley & Sons), pp. 30, 31.

2 Ibid., pp. 50–51.

3 Ibid., p. 53.

4 Ibid., p. 58.

5 Elizabeth I (1559), quoted in Cartwright, M. (2020), "Elizabeth I and the Power of Image," *Ancient History Encyclopedia Foundation*, May 29, 2020, https://www.ancient.eu/article/1562/elizabeth-i–the-power-of-image/, accessed on October 26, 2020.

6 Weir, A. (1988), *Elizabeth the Queen* (London: Jonathan Cape), p. 55.

7 Napoleon quoted in Cronin, V. (1979), *Napoleon* (London: Collins), p. 143.

8 Talleyrand (1801), quoted Bernard, J. F. (1973), *Talleyrand: A Biography* (London: Collins), p. 236.

9 Napoleon's third person memorandum dictated in St. Helena after 1815.

10 Armstrong, H. C. (1933), *Gray Wolf: Mustafa Kemal, An Intimate Study of a Dictator* (New York: Minton Balch), p. 2, quoted in Bay, A. (2011), *Atatürk: Lessons in Leadership from the Greatest General of the Ottoman Empire* (New York: Palgrave Macmillan), p. 39.

11 Duc de Sully (1601), quoted in Weir (1988), op. cit., p. 471.

12 Napoleon quoted by Molé, Mathieu Louis, Count (1923), *The Life and Memoirs of Count Molé*, Edited by the Marquis de Noailles, 2v (London:), 61. Cited by http://www.napoleon-series.org/research/society/c_education.html#20, accessed on January 3, 2021.

13 Sixtus V (1588), quoted in Weir (1988), op. cit., p.399.

14 Weir (1998), op. cit., p393.

15 Knowles, E., ed. (1999), *The Oxford Dictionary of Quotations: Major New Edition* (Oxford, England: Oxford University Press), p. 809, #19.

16 Arndt, E., quoted in Cronin (1979), op. cit., p. 137.

17 Landau, J. M. (1984), "Introduction: Ataturk's Achievements: Some Considerations," in Landau, J.M., ed. (1984), *Atatürk and the Modernization of Turkey* (New York: Routledge), p. ix.

18 Landau (1984), op. cit., p. xii.

19 Weir (1988), op. cit., p. 487.

20 Jacques Coquille Dugommier's dispatch to the Minister of War, quoted in Cronin (1979), op. cit., p. 77.

21 Barber, T. (2020), "Napoleon & de Gaulle – a history of France's larger-than-life heroes," *The Financial Times*, July 15, 2020, https://www.ft.com/content/ffb576be-4363-4d1f-81d1-6e283f7f7381, accessed on April 5, 2021.

22 General Wesley Clark, quoted in ibid., p. xiv.

23 Williams, N. (1972), *Elizabeth I, Queen of England* (London: Sphere Books), p. 9.

24 Roger Ascham quoted in ibid., p. 16.

25 Prince von Metternich quoted by Markham, F. (1963), *Napoleon*, cited in Axelrod, A. (2011), *Napoleon: CEO: 6 Principles to Guide & Inspire Modern Leaders* (New York: Sterling), p. 200.

26 Comte de Plancy, quoted in Cronin (1979), op. cit., p. 193.

27 Atay, F. R. (1982), *The Atatürk I Knew* (Istanbul: Yapi ve Kredi), p. 27, cited in Bay (2011), op. cit., p. 27.

28 Elizabeth I (1558), quoted in Williams (1972), op. cit., p. 72.

29 Elizabeth I (1601), quoted in Axelrod, A. (2000), Elizabeth I CEO, (Paramus, New Jersey: Prentice Hall), p. 147.

30 Ibid.

31 Napoleon, quoted in Cronin (1979), op. cit., p. 53.

32 Napoleon, quoted in ibid., p. 163.

33 Quoted in Markham, F. (1963), *Napoleon,* cited in Axelrod (2011), op. cit., p. 40.

34 Turkish Ministry of Press Broadcasting and Tourism (1961), *The Life of Atatürk* (Ankara: TMPBT), pp. 215–217, cited in Bay (2011), op. cit., p. 161.

35 De Gaulle, C. (1938), in *France and Her Army* (London: Hutchinson, 1945 translation), quoted in Barber (2020), op. cit.

36 Napoleon, http://lifequoteslib.com/authors/napoleon_bonaparte.html, accessed on December 9, 2020.

37 Atatürk quoted in Ertuna, H. (1985), *1911–1912 Osmanli-Italyan Harbi ve Kolgasi Mustafa Kemal* [The Turco-Italian War of 1911–1912 and Major Mustafa Kemal] (Ankara: Kultur ve Turizm Bakanligi Yayinalri), 101, cited in Bay (2011), op. cit., p. 64.

38 Snyder, A. J. (2006), "The Politics of Piracy, Pirates, Privateers, and the Government of Elizabeth I," *Department of History, University of North Carolina, Wilmington,* p. 3, https://libres.uncg.edu/ir/uncw/f/snydera2006-1.pdf, accessed on October 19, 2020.

39 Barber (2020), op. cit., https://www.ft.com/content/ffb576be-4363-4d1f-81d1-6e283f7f7381, accessed on December 7, 2020.

40 Mango, A. (2002), *Atatürk: The Biography of the Founder of Modern Turkey* (New York: Overlook), 58, cited in Bay (2011), op. cit., p. 35.

41 Weir (1988), op. cit., p. 54.

42 Weir (1988), op. cit., p. 59.

43 From a speech by Napoleon to the Council of State, quoted in Cronin (1979), op. cit., p. 212.

44 "The people is sovereign; if it wants religion, respect its will." Address to an assembly of priests in Milan in 1800.

45 Prince von Metternich quoted by Markham (1963), cited in Axelrod (2011), op. cit., 200.

46 Kinross, P. (1992), *Atatürk: A Biography of Mustafa Kemal, Father of Modern Turkey* (New York: William Morrow/Quill), p. 14, cited in Bay (2011), op. cit., p. 161.

47 Ibid., p. 335.

48 Ibid., pp. 210–212.

49 *Military Maxim LXVII.*

50 Goncu, G., and Aldogan, S. (2006), *The Canakkale War: The Homeland is beyond the Trenches* (Istanbul: MB Publishing), pp. 41–42.

51 Burghley quoted in Weir (1988), op. cit. p. 487.

52 Ibid., pp. 126–127.

53 Nuwer, R. (2012), "Blame Napoleon for our Addiction to Sugar," *Smithsonian Magazine,* December 4, 2012, https://www.smithsonianmag.com/smart-news/blame-napoleon-for-our-addiction-to-sugar-152096743/, accessed on December 9, 2020.

54 Axelrod, A., (2000), op. cit., p.242

55 Weir (1988), op. cit., p. 49.

56 "What is the Meaning of Integrity?" *Accountable2You,* June 17, 2019, https://accountable2you.com/action/meaning-of-integrity, accessed on December 16, 2020.

57 Mintzberg, H. (1975), "The Manager's Job: Folklore and Fact," *Harvard Business Review,* 1975, pp. 49–61, cited in Pugh, D. S., and Hickson, D. J. (1996), *Writers on Organizations* (London: Penguin Books), p. 30.

58 Barber (2020), op. cit., https://www.ft.com/content/ffb576be-4363-4d1f-81d1-6e283f7f7381, accessed on December 7, 2020.

59 Bernard, op. cit., p. 196.

60 Napoleon, quoted in ibid., accessed on November 13, 2020.

61 Duc de Sully (1601), quoted in Weir (1988), op. cit., p. 471.

62 Blakemore, E. (2019), "How the East India Company became the world's most powerful business," *National Geographic,* September 6, 2019, https://www.nationalgeographic.com/culture/

topics/reference/british-east-india-trading-company-most-powerful-business/, accessed on December 20, 2020.

63 "Flexibility," *The Economist*, October 9, 2009, https://www.economist.com/news/2009/10/09/flexibility, accessed on December 20, 2020.

64 Birkinshaw, J. (2004), "Building Ambidexterity into an Organisation," *Sloan Management Review*, Summer 2004, quoted in ibid.

65 Roger Ascham quoted in ibid., p. 16.

66 Williams (1972), op. cit., p. 349.

67 Burghley quoted in Weir (1988), op. cit. p. 487.

68 Johnson, A. (2018), "What did Napoleon read? Inside the French Emperor's travelling campaign library," *The Independent*, June 25, 2018, https://www.independent.co.uk/arts-entertainment/books/features/napoleon-bonaparte-what-read-books-emperor-library-campaigns-a8415776.html, accessed on December 20, 2020.

69 Bernard (1973), op. cit., p. 203.

70 Ibid., p. 157.

71 "Books Atatürk Read," *Atatürk'le okumak,* https://ataturkleokumak.istanbul.edu.tr/, accessed on December 21, 2020.

72 Ibid., p. 61.

73 Cartwright, M. (2020), "Elizabeth I and the Power of Image," *Ancient History Encyclopedia Foundation,* May 29, 2020, https://www.ancient.eu/article/1562/elizabeth-i–the-power-of-image/, accessed on October 26, 2020.

74 Ibid.

75 Cartwright (2020), op. cit.

76 Axelrod (2000), op. cit., p. 52.

77 Ibid., p. 69.

78 Walton, G. (2019), "How Napoleon Controlled His Image," https://www.geriwalton.com/how-napoleon-controlled-his-image/, accessed on December 22, 2020.

79 Gur, Faik (2013), "Sculpting the nation in early republican Turkey," *Historical Research* 86 (232), May 2013, https://www.researchgate.net/publication/263347049_Sculpting_the_nation_in_early_republican_Turkey, accessed on December 22, 2020.

80 Cuomo, M. (1985), Interview *The New Republic,* April 4, 1985, https://en.wikiquote.org/wiki/Mario_Cuomo, accessed on December 25, 2020.

81 Williams, Z. (2020), "Panic, paucity and pessimism: life on Plague Island UK," *The Guardian,* December 23, 2020, https://www.theguardian.com/world/2020/dec/23/people-seem-more-afraid-life-on-plague-island-uk, accessed on December 24, 2020.

82 Simmons, M. (2018), "People With 'Too Many Interests' More Likely to Be Successful According to Research", *Observer,* May 3. 2018, https://observer.com/2018/05/people-with-too-many-interests-more-likely-successful-polymath-entrepreneurship-antifragile/, accessed on February 20, 2021

83 Based on Young & Rubicam's *Brand Asset Valuator.*

Part 2: **Leadership is Managerial**

In Part 1 we looked at the history of our ancestors regarding leadership and selected the careers of three of history's most admired political leaders to explore, England's Elizabeth Tudor, France's Napoleon Bonaparte, and Turkey's Mustaf Kemal Atatürk. In Chapter 5, we evaluated their leadership to see what lessons could be learned from their experiences. Using those lessons, we now show that leadership and management form a continuum and that strategy and tactics do the same.

https://doi.org/10.1515/9783110707878-007

Chapter 6
Managerial Leadership

Strategy, Tactics, and Polynesian "Wayfinding"

In Chapter 5, we concluded that the most important characteristic of effective leadership is operational competence. Elizabeth Tudor, Napoleon Bonaparte and Mustafa Kemal Atatürk were examples of leaders with extraordinarily high levels of operational competence because they understood that strategy cannot be separated from tactics and that, as Machiavelli argued, effective execution is what matters.

Strategy and tactics form part of a continuum, and the example of Polynesian "Wayfinding" supports this case.

Strategy

Setting strategy addresses five questions:[1]
1. *"What is our objective?"*
2. *"Why do we need to change what we are doing?"*
3. *"What do we need to change, in order to achieve our goal(s)?"*
4. *"Who needs to do what, in what sequence, and by when? How will we identify the need for correction and take action if it is needed?"*
5. *"How will we know when we have succeeded?"*

What is measured describes organizational priorities. As Peter Drucker said, *"People don't do what management expects, they do what management inspects!"*

Tactics

Tactics[2] deal with the intermediate steps required to meet agreed strategic goals. Tactics and strategy are not separated by a bright line and interact continuously. Their relationship is easier to understand by using sailing as a metaphor. Once a voyage begins, "tactical" considerations predominate, because conditions change constantly. A ship goes off course and must make corrections to arrive at its intended port of call. If the ship encounters headwinds, "tacking" is needed. Like tactics, tacking consists of short-term actions in response to changing external conditions to get back on course. Captains (at all organizational levels) must know their ultimate destination, how far they have been driven off course by changed conditions, and what to do to get back on course.

https://doi.org/10.1515/9783110707878-008

Polynesian "Wayfinding"

"Wayfinding"[3] illustrates this process, and explains how Polynesians sailed the Pacific in outrigger canoes to settle the islands in the South and Central Pacific. "Wayfinding"[i] has two elements that are tightly integrated: (1) setting strategy by designing a reference course; and (2) tactics to hold that course and find land:

1. **Strategy:** Before sailing, the "wayfinder" assesses available resources and designs a course to reach a destination, given the capabilities of the canoe, winds, currents, and weather conditions anticipated along the way. The reference course is the most feasible way of reaching the destination. The "wayfinder" chooses the best time to sail, taking account of the reference course.
2. **Tactics:** Holding a course and finding land:
   a. *Holding a course:* The "wayfinder" back-sights on land, lining up two landmarks until they disappear. Once on the open ocean, the movements of celestial bodies, the direction of the wind and clouds, the time of year, currents, and the movements of the ocean swell are observed to provide direction. Sun and moon rising and setting also provide clues to direction. At night, stars rise at points on the eastern horizon and set at points in the west. Using these clues, the "wayfinder" estimates the distance and direction traveled. The starting point, departure time, estimated speed of the craft, and approximate distance to destination are known. During the voyage, wind will likely drive the canoe off course – the wayfinder estimates how far, and makes appropriate corrections.
   b. *Finding land:* The "wayfinder" does not need pinpoint accuracy to find a destination because Pacific islands come in screens[ii] (groups). When the "wayfinder" reaches any island in the target screen, he can redirect the canoe to reach the desired island.

From the above, we can extrapolate the metaphor to successful leadership and managerial processes:

1. Defining, communicating, and engaging support for a mission
2. Ensuring organizational alignment to deliver the mission by evaluating the current state and resources of the organization, and its strategic, tactical, and operational context

---

i "Wayfinding" is non-instrument navigation and weather prediction using the sun, moon, and stars; sky and cloud patterns; ocean currents and swells; and maritime fauna as guides.
ii For example, the Tuamotu Archipelago stretches 550 miles north to south and 500 miles east to west; the Society Islands stretch 160 miles north to south and 310 miles east to west. Thus, while sailing to Tahiti from Hawai'i, the "wayfinder" can target a 400-mile-wide screen of islands between Manihi in the western Tuamotus, and Maupiti in the eastern Society Islands.

3. Determining milestones and measures, taking corrective action, or revising the mission depending on changes in context and conditions
4. Engaging stakeholders effectively

Looking at each of the above in turn:

Defining, Communicating, and Engaging Support for the Mission

A sustainable mission and vision have to be defined, protecting both the organization's financial viability and its long-term social license to operate. Four questions must be answered:
1. *What do the top team and owners (the governing coalition of the business) want to do?*
2. *What will society allow the organization to do?*
3. *Does it make economic sense?*
4. *Does the organization have the competencies required to succeed? Or can it realistically acquire them?*

Answering these questions combines commercial and ethical judgments. Henry Ford answered all four questions:

> I will build a motor car for the great multitude . . . it will be so low in price that no man making a good salary will be unable to own one – and enjoy with his family the blessing of hours of pleasure in God's great open spaces. When I'm through everybody will be able to afford one, and everyone will have one. The horse will have disappeared from our highways, the automobile will be taken for granted and we will give a large number of men employment at good wages.

Ford was explicit about mission and vision. He defined the beneficiaries: "the great multitude;" he defined the difference in their lives he would make: "enjoying God's great open spaces with their families;" he even defined his measures of success: everyone would own a car and the "horse will have disappeared from the highways," solving the horse manure crisis,[iii] and a "large number of men would be employed

---

[iii] "It might be difficult for people today to imagine, but in 1894 everything that took place on the streets was either horse-powered or human-powered. Vehicles and machines came much later. Horses performed the hardest duties, and both New York and London were home to approximately 200,000 horses. Today we might think that horses are cute, but in those times, the situation was much more complicated.

In a day, a horse could produce a bucketload of urine and several bucketloads of manure. In all major cities around the world, streets were – to a greater or lesser degree – covered with wet slush of horse excrement, the stench of which overwhelmed the city. The "cherry on top" was the fact that the life span of overworked horses was around three years, which meant that over 50,000 horses died annually. Since their bodies were massive and there was no machinery to remove them,

at good wages." He succeeded beyond his wildest dreams (and as a result, replacing one environmental problem with another). He invented a new way of assembling cars, answering the fourth question about necessary competencies – without which he would not have been able to mass produce the cars.

Effective "wayfinders" answer three questions: "Who does the organization serve?" "What products/services will it offer?" and "How will it provide these products/services?" A good mission statement:

1. *Has clear focus,* understood by all, so they know what markets the organization is in, and, just as important, the markets it is *not* in.
2. *Is differentiated and compelling.*
3. *Reflects a proper understanding of the competition for market margin.*
4. *Allows flexible responses to changing circumstances.*
5. *Protects the organization's long-term social license to operate.*

Ensuring Organizational Alignment

Effective "wayfinders" translate the mission into a vision that engages heads, hearts, and hands,[iv] communicating what success will look and feel like. The vision provides a clear "line of sight" to the mission so that all can understand their roles, responsibilities, and "what is in it for them," with milestones, targets, and due dates, with the consequences of failure clear.[4]

The difference between realizing the vision and having it remain an aspiration depends on ensuring five key elements are suitably aligned to achieve the mission and vision shown in Figure 6.1. They are: *"Purpose"* – what the organization exists for, *"Principles"* – the values it lives by, *"Power"* – the organizational design and power structure it adopts, *"People"* – who make things happen, and *"Processes"* – the systems and procedures that govern its operations, holding it together.

---

often the only available solution was to allow the corpses to rot until they could be removed in smaller pieces.

. . . In 50 years, every street in a city would be buried under three meters of manure, and the cities would be rendered uninhabitable. International conferences were held, and scientists were asked to tackle the problem, but to no avail – there was no reasonable solution.

Today we know that the solution was found quite soon after the problem had culminated. However, it did not come from scientist's; instead, the source of the solution was innovation, or rather from cars that were invented through innovation." Kracht. A. (2020), "The Great Horse Manure Crisis Reveals Something Unexpected", *Science and Philosophy*, October, 3, 2020, https://medium.com/science-and-philosophy/the-great-horse-manure-crisis-reveals-something-unexpected-90f80fa71e52, accessed on February 20, 2021."

iv The reason why it is important to engage all three is that the mission must be defensible rationally, but it must also excite and engage stakeholders and, in particular, employees; and it must be practical and implementable so employees know what they have to do.

Aligning the organization to achieve the mission and vision

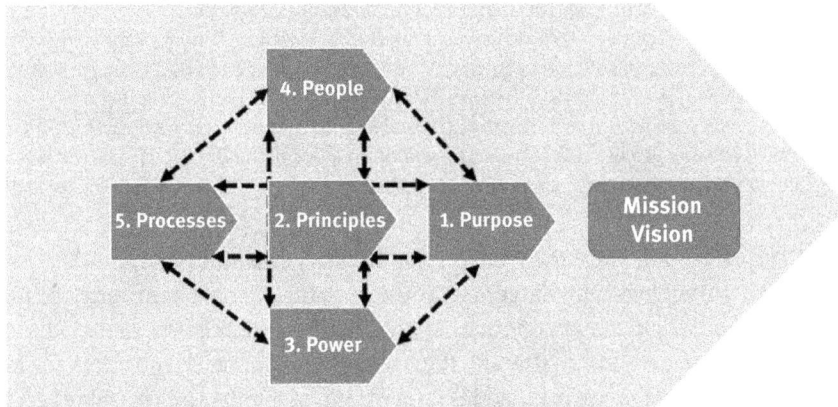

Source: Zinkin, J. (2014), *Corporate Directors Onboarding Program*, Kuala Lumpur, April 16, 2014

Figure 6.1: The "Five P" Framework.

Figure 6.1 shows mission and vision can only be achieved if the "Five Ps" are aligned. If any one of the "Five Ps" is misaligned, the mission and vision will not be achieved. The "Five Ps" interact with each other, either reinforcing or weakening the organization's ability to set priorities, and allocate resources appropriately. Working harmoniously together, they define and reinforce acceptable behavior and values. Working at cross purposes, they create conflict and undermine the values of the organization. The "Five Ps" cover:

1. **"Purpose":** The best way for "wayfinders" to ensure that the enterprise's "purpose" is aligned with their mission and vision is to answer six questions: 1) who are our intended beneficiaries, 2) what difference are trying to make in their lives, 3) what value will place on that difference, 4) how will we make that difference, 5) how will it cost, and 6) what return can we expect as a result?

2. **"Principles":** These are the *values* at the heart of the way the organization functions. They determine what kind of business it does and with whom it is done. The "principles" determine:
a. *What the company stands for and its culture:* Some companies have reputations for honest dealing, creating quality products, treating their employees well, and being good corporate citizens. Others do not. The difference comes from their "principles" – the values they profess and live by.

   Companies get what they expect: if they do not believe employees will work based on trust, collaboration, and values, but based only on greed and self-seeking, they will develop reward and recognition systems that reinforce such behavior. The reverse is also true:

How we do business – and what business does to us – has everything to do with how we think about business, talk about business, conceive of business, practice business. If we think, talk, conceive, and practice business as a ruthless, cutthroat, dog-eat-dog activity, then that, of course, is what it will become. And so, too, it is what we will become, no matter how often (in our off hours and personal lives) we insist otherwise. If, on the other hand, business is conceived – as it often has been conceived – as an enterprise based on trust and mutual benefits, an enterprise for civilized, virtuous people, then that in turn, will be equally self-fulfilling. It will also be much more amiable, secure, enjoyable, and last, but not least, profitable.[5]   [Emphases ours]

b. *The "tone at the top" and the "tone in the middle":* It is not enough to exhort employees to behave with integrity. The top management team must think carefully about the code of conduct, review it on a regular basis, and give the compliance function/internal audit the authority, resources, and tools to do their job properly, and always model the desired behaviors in themselves and others.

c. *Careers of employees and how they are treated:* Talent management must ensure the people who are recruited and promoted share the organization's values.

d. *Whether an organization is a "responsible citizen":* If a company is to maintain its social license to operate, the needs of the communities in which it operates and the impact the company has on the environment must be considered.

e. *Values that translate into measurable and observable behavior:* To mean anything, values must be translated into measurable behavior – discussed in employee appraisals and personal development plans. This requires values to be *translated from normally used abstract nouns into action statements,* describing desired behavior and performance expectations; and *embedded into the code of conduct* for all employees to internalize values.

3. **"Power":** This deals with organizational design, job descriptions, roles and responsibilities, and reporting relationships, as well as how people are treated.

The most appropriate organizational design will be determined by the business strategy agreed by the "wayfinders." "Wayfinders" must ensure that whatever organizational design they approve will be sufficiently flexible to avoid the problem of "stuckness" when conditions change.

Trompenaars and Hampden-Turner identified four organizational design archetypes, each with unique contextual cultural characteristics.[6] Their four organizational design archetypes are "Incubator," "Family Firm," "Guided Missile," and "Eiffel Tower." Figure 6.2 shows how the four archetypes relate to each other:

The horizontal axis represents a cultural continuum showing the difference in organizational focus on people versus tasks:

"INCUBATOR"	**Egalitarian** – Achieved Status	"GUIDED MISSILE"

| **People:**
– Particularist
– Relationships
– "Social" | *Fulfillment* oriented

Person oriented | *Project* oriented

Role oriented | **Task:**
– Universalist
– Rules
– "Instrumental" |

"FAMILY FIRM"	**Hierarchical:** – Ascribed Status	"EIFFEL TOWER"

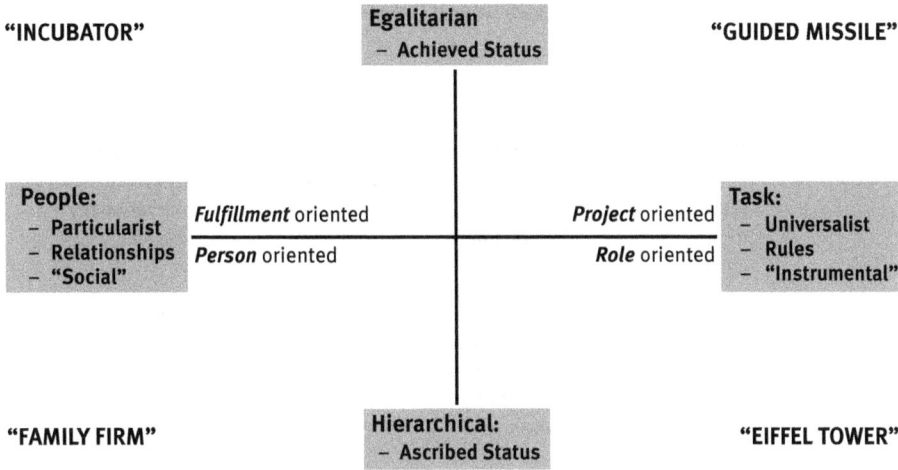

Figure 6.2: Four Organizational Archetypes.
Source: Based on Trompenaars, F., and Hampden-Turner, C. (2006), *Riding the Waves of Culture: Understanding Cultural Diversity in Business,* 2nd Edition (London: Nicholas Brealey Publishing), pp. 157–181.

a. *People:* On the left, the organization is people-oriented. Its employees believe that what matters are personal relationships and preserving relationships is more important than obeying rules or what is in a contract. They are "particularists" finding reasons why *"in these particular circumstances, the rules do not apply."* They feel being at work is a social activity as much as a process of completing tasks. Such organizations are most likely to be found in Southern and Eastern Europe, Asia, Africa, and Latin America.

b. *Task:* On the right, the organization is task-oriented. Its employees are "universalists" who believe that rules matter more than relationships and that they apply universally, regardless of relationships or seniority. The organization is "instrumental" because people and resources are allocated to fulfill tasks, once completed, the teams are disbanded and reallocated to the next task. Such organizations are most likely to be found in Northern Europe and the English-speaking world.

The vertical axis represents a cultural continuum showing the difference in organizational focus on equality versus hierarchy. It also shows how status is regarded. Egalitarian organizations tend to grant status based on people's latest actual achievements, whereas hierarchical organizations tend to ascribe status based on the performance history of individuals since they joined the organization.

The differences in organizational culture in the four archetypes affect employee relationships and attitudes. Failure to understand the differences can lead to misunderstanding, discord, poor performance, and waste. Table 6.1 compares the four different organizational cultures.

Table 6.1: Characteristics of the Four Organizational Cultures.

Behavioral Characteristics	Incubator	Family Firm	Guided Missile	Eiffel Tower
Employee relationships	*Diffuse,* spontaneous relations arising from shared creative processes	*Diffuse*, intuitive, holistic, lateral, and error correcting	*Specific,* problem-centered, professional, practical, cross-disciplinary	*Specific*, logical, analytical, vertical, and rationally efficient
Attitude to authority	Status *achieved* by individuals exemplifying creativity and growth	Status *ascribed* to parent figures who are close and powerful	Status *achieved* by project group members who contribute to targeted goal	Status *ascribed* to "superior" roles who are distant yet powerful
Ways of thinking and learning	*Diffuse,* process-oriented, creative, ad hoc, inspirational	*Diffuse*, intuitive, holistic, lateral, and error correcting	*Specific,* problem-centered, professional, practical, cross-disciplinary	*Specific*, logical, analytical, vertical, and rationally efficient
Attitudes to people	*Diffuse,* co-creators	*Diffuse,* family members	*Specific,* specialists and experts	*Specific*, human resources
Ways of changing	Improvize and attune	"Father" changes course	Shift aim as target moves	Change rules and procedures
Ways of motivating/ rewarding	*Management by enthusiasm* Participating in the process of creating new realities	*Management by subjectives* Intrinsic satisfaction in being loved and respected	*Management by objectives* Pay or credit for performance and problems solved	*Management by job description* Promotion to greater position, larger role
Criticism and conflict resolution	Must improve the idea, not negate it	Turn other cheek, save others' faces; do not lose power game	Constructive, task-related only, then admit error and correct fast	Criticism is accusation of irrationality, unless there are procedures to arbitrate conflicts

Source: Based on Trompenaars, F., and Hampden-Turner, C. (2006), *Riding the Waves of Culture: Understanding Cultural Diversity in Business,* 2nd Edition (London: Nicholas Brealey Publishing), p. 178.

Understanding the organizational cultural contexts that exist or are desired is critical. We have defined these four archetypes in their purest form to highlight the differences between them. In reality, organizations often are unique blend of these four archetypes, making it even more difficult for "wayfinders" to know where they stand and which behaviors and values they need to consider carefully. Understanding the context is therefore even more critical, if they are to be effective.

4. **"People":** There are three questions "wayfinders" must ask:
a. *Do we have the right number of people?* "Wayfinders" must consider the current business strategy and supporting socio-technological infrastructure and how they expect it to evolve over time. This will determine the number of jobs/roles needed to fulfill the agreed mission and vision.
b. *Do our people have the right skills and competencies to do the job properly?* "Wayfinders" must insist there is an up-to-date and forward-looking competency dictionary to assess the current skills base of their key employees. Despite the rapid pace of change that renders many competencies obsolete, and the fact that developing competency dictionaries is a backward-looking exercise and therefore not a very good guide to what competencies are likely to be needed in the future, there is an "evergreen" set of core competencies, in particular leadership competencies, that always apply.
c. *Do our people have the right character to work in line with our principles?* Organizations often hire and promote people based on their ability to meet targets they are set, their past track record, or their list of competencies, without considering whether they have the right character to fit with the principles espoused by the organization. Yet, what all "wayfinders" must emphasize is *how* results are achieved. This is as or more important than *what* results are achieved. Otherwise, they risk being guilty of "the folly of rewarding A while hoping for B."[7]
d. *Do we have the right kind of CEO for today's environment?* Based on a five-year INSEAD (Institut Européen d'Administration des Affaires) study of twenty CEOs,[8] it was concluded that:

> In management, as in other fields, collaboration has long since replaced individual genius as the principal source of creativity. Trying to apply the old model of determining strategy in the corner office and issuing orders is simply ineffective and inefficient today. From "Commander-in-Chief," the CEO has become "Chief Enabler of the Organization." His or her role is to *enable* other employees to perform."[9]

The surveyed CEOs believed "Enabling CEOs," whose style may be best suited to "business as usual" operating conditions, had to: reduce uncertainty, encourage collaboration, remove organizational barriers, create autonomy for employees,[v] support

---

v This advice may seem obvious to people who live in "low power distance" cultures; it goes against everything people who live in "high power distance" cultures believe about leadership.

but challenge employee thinking, educate employees, stay in touch with business and the outside world, and be role models: In short:

> The enabling CEO tries to keep things simple and fight organizational complexity in all its forms. He or she makes as few decisions as possible, doesn't meddle in office politics or power struggles and challenges staff by setting high standards and asking tough questions. Such leaders support their followers with resources, attention and mentoring – energising the whole organization."[10]   [Emphasis ours]

When it comes to a crisis, however, "Enabling CEOs" need to be able to change their style to that of "Crisis CEOs." Such CEOs must ensure solutions are found quickly.[11] The INSEAD study offered advice to potential "Crisis CEOs": accept crises happen and be prepared, mitigate risks, stay calm, act quickly, organize "teaming" collaboration by cutting across formal organizational boundaries, and pay attention to people and their emotions.

In a crisis, CEOs must become even more attentive to the ideas and feelings of their employees. They make themselves available to provide support and advice where needed, communicating with warmth and humor, exhibiting a confidence and optimism they may not feel:

> The CEOs we interviewed don't make a drama out of crisis. Being ready to move when it's least expected and adopting a different behaviour pattern at short notice stands them in good stead for the day when unforeseen circumstances arise.[12]

5. **"Processes":** These are the glue that binds the organization together: strategic planning, budgeting and financial reporting, approved policies and procedures – regularly inspected for lapses and loopholes and taking corrective action. Processes include all forms of internal formal and informal feedback mechanisms. Measurement and remuneration processes should align with the mission and vision. Three critical processes that present considerable difficulty are succession planning, talent management, and developing people.

a. *Planning succession:* Even very large organizations have difficulty implementing succession planning in practice. The suggested theoretical approaches are impossible to implement in most SMEs (small- and medium-sized enterprises) and family firms. Corporate governance codes urge listed companies to have board and key position succession plans:

Planning succession for boards:[13]
The duties of all directors (including but not limited to independent non-executive directors)[vi] are generally divided into "fiduciary" and "statutory." As "fiduciaries" they have to consider the interests of all members of the company (the shareholders) and

---

vi This brief summary of directors' responsibilities is correct for most jurisdictions but is inevitably a generalization. Legal advice should be taken about the requirements of particular jurisdictions.

act in good faith in their interests, be independent of conflicts of interest (or declare them). Statutory duties bind them to ensure compliance with reporting and regulatory requirements.

In addition to executing fiduciary and statutory duties it is considered desirable that they have relevant, diverse business and life experience, a wide circle of contacts, and strategic insight.[14]

Directors generally cannot be appointed by the Board or the CEO in most jurisdictions. Directors are appointed by the shareholders (to whom they owe their duties). The Board can suggest candidates – but the decision of who to appoint is not theirs.

Planning succession for the company:

Large companies generally have plans for CEO succession, and business critical positions:

i.   *CEO succession:*[15] This is the critical human resource responsibility of boards:

> CEO succession planning is a core responsibility of the board . . . the evidence suggests that boards are not uniformly effective in carrying out this function . . . the skill and care with which a board plans for a CEO departure and identifies a qualified successor can provide important insights into the general care with which they exercise their oversight responsibilities and the overall quality of governance at the firm.[16]

Planning CEO succession is difficult and often fails – consider HP with three failed CEOs in a row – Carly Fiorina,[17] Mark Hurd,[18] and Leo Apotheker.[19] Recruiting a CEO has to combine three elements: the rational, political, and emotional.[20]

> At the end of the day, courage, candor and common sense lie at the heart of effective CEO succession. Planning is critical, tools and methodologies are important, but in the final analysis, successful transitions rest upon the ability of proud and powerful business professionals to have these essential, hard conversations each step of the way.[21]

When considering who to choose as a CEO, it is important to remember there are four leadership roles: "captains," "navigators," "engineers," and "shipbuilders." Large organizations, unlike most smaller firms, can afford to fill the roles with specialists:[22]

The "captain" has to establish a code of conduct, and integrate crew activities by inspirationally articulating the mission, defining responsibilities, setting the timetable, and deciding when corrective action is required, as well as saving the crew and the ship in a crisis. The captain is not a superhero but the focus of energy around whom the crew rally.

> Part of our difficulty with appreciating the role that effective executive leadership can play in learning is that all of us are used to the "captain of the ship" image of traditional hierarchical leaders. However, when executives act as teachers, stewards, and designers, they fill roles that are much more subtle, contextual, and long term than the traditional model of the power-wielding hierarchical leader.[23]

The "navigator," in discussion with the captain, charts the route, accounting for wind, weather forecasts, tides, currents, and safe channels, reconciling the need for speed with economy and safety:

> To navigate is to chart a course for getting from where you are to where you want to go. Getting there is the process of planning, recording, and controlling the course and our progress to our destination . . .
>
>   . . . optimizing the response of your vessel and crew to the changing conditions of wind, water, tides and currents, and the needs of the crew and condition of the vessel itself.[24]

In business, "navigators" are likely found in staff functions, developing and stress-testing key assumptions of the plan, examining scenarios. They look at trends and their impact on the business, establish early warning signals, and advise the "captain" when conditions change.

The "engineer," called "line leaders" by Peter Senge, is relied on by "captains" and "navigators" to keep the ship moving:

> However, engaging local line leaders may be difficult. As pragmatists, they often find ideas like systems thinking, mental models, and dialogue intangible and 'hard to get their hands around' . . .
>
> . . .. Again, and again, we have found that healthy, open-minded skeptics can become the most effective leaders and, eventually, champions of this work. They keep the horse in front of the cart by focusing first and foremost on business results. *Such people invariably have more staying power than the "fans" who get excited about new ideas but whose excitement wanes once the newness wears off.*[25]   [Emphasis ours]

Senge's point about the temporary excitement of "fans" for new ideas are important caveats. Boards and top management teams, are persuaded by "big picture" ideas *before* they are applied. Line managers and "engineers," on the other hand, are more likely to be "detail oriented" pragmatists *interested in how the idea works in practice.* "Captains" and "navigators" need to remember this when communicating new ideas to "engineers" if they are to avoid the wary reaction of "yet another flavor of the month initiative" or the risk of misunderstanding legitimate "engine room" obstacles to adopting the latest, impractical management fad.

The "ship-builder" is the planner, enterprise risk manager, and auditor who ensure appropriate processes, and procedures, creating an appropriate organizational infrastructure. If a ship is not built appropriately, the mission and crew will be at risk, the *Titanic* was a flawed design.[26]

Having different people fill these four roles is expensive. Small organizations, like a Polynesian "wayfinding" crew, have "wayfinders" who undertake all of the four leadership roles. "Wayfinders" decide the destination and crew, they chart the course and make the necessary corrections, they do hard, manual work sailing the canoe, and they also design and build their canoes.

ii. *C-suite minus 2 and pivotal staff:* Succession planning for key employees in large organizations is best defined as:

A deliberate and systematic effort by an organisation to ensure leadership continuity in key positions, retain and develop intellectual and knowledge capital for the future, and encourage individual advancement.[27]

Typical ways of ensuring there is a qualified supply of candidates for these key positions is to engage in elaborate personal development planning, including training initiatives, coupled with leadership assessment exercises to decide what might be the best next moves over a one-, three-, and five-year timetable. These can be divided into "traditional" methods of moving existing employees within an organization to new positions as and when required, and "alternative" approaches such as job rotations (employees filling various positions for short periods to help them gain experience), talent pools (spreading the role by appointing many employees across more positions), and outsourcing.[28]

iii. *Planning Succession in SMEs and family firms* is challenging. There are family and organizational issues; legal, financial, and tax issues; and barriers to succession to consider in coming to practical solutions.[29] Resourcing issues make it impractical for SMEs and family firms to adopt the approach taken by large organizations. Succession planning in SMEs can best be described as:

The transfer of a business that results from the owner's wish to retire, or to leave the business for some other reason. The succession can involve a transfer to members of the owner's family, employees, or external buyers. Successful succession results in a continuation of the business, at least in the short term.[30]

There is, an old saying, "From rags to riches to rags in three generations." There is a great deal of truth in this.[31] By the third generation, family members may lack talent, or are no longer interested in going into the family business. There may be family feuds about inheritance and priorities. Family-controlled businesses that have hired professional managers to continue the vision can prosper for many generations.[32]

b. *Managing talent*: Talent management addresses all levels of the organization. The current view endorses the importance of the boards of large firms working with management, shown in Table 6.2.

Table 6.2: Four Steps in Talent Management.

Steps in the Process	Board's role	CEO's role	HR's role
Step1: Develop talent strategy and define who is "talent"	Ensure strategy satisfies *agreed* business strategy, vision, values and culture.	Agree board impact of business strategy on talent needs. Align strategy to satisfy business strategy, vision, values, and culture. Identify current and *future* needs.	Develop future-focused strategy with CEO. Agree *future* roles and responsibilities and their impact on talent with CEO.

Table 6.2 (continued)

Steps in the Process	Board's role	CEO's role	HR's role
Step 2: Identify pivotal positions and competencies	Approve pivotal positions identified by CEO. Ensure competency models deliver business strategy, vision, values, and culture.	Determine number of pivotal positions. Agree key current and future competencies to satisfy business strategy, values, and culture.	Identify future pivotal positions. Update competency models to reflect future business needs.
Step 3: Identify and develop talent pipeline	Get to know each high potential candidate. Assess external options for leadership.	Agree talent pipeline based on individual appraisals. Provide career enhancing opportunities for high potential candidates. Agree individual talent development plans. Provide performance feedback and progress reviews to identified talent.	Develop up-to-date training needs analysis. Reflect strategy in recruiting. Recruit and develop external talent. Agree replacement chart with CEO and top management.
Step 4: Monitor and evaluate	Ensure succession planning, talent management, and competency modeling[vii] are regular board items. Require high potential candidates to present to board meetings.	Evaluate effectiveness of talent management and leadership development activities. Report regularly to board on progress. Take part in evaluating individuals' progress.	Update talent management, leadership development, and succession planning progress annually. Review high potentials and their readiness to move to next role. Report on program status and individuals' progress.

Source: Zinkin, J. (2014), *Rebuilding Trust In Banks: The Role of Leadership and Governance* (Singapore: John Wiley & Sons), pp. 188–189.

---

vii In the rapidly changing contexts created by modern technology and global competition, some argue that trying to define required competencies is not helpful because they are the formalization of past success factors. However, we believe there are four "evergreen" leadership competencies every successful "wayfinder" must possess: the ability to manage change; the ability to adapt; the ability to be creative; and the ability to develop people.

Boards of large organizations should check whether their business strategy is vulnerable to failures in closing gaps between current and future organization design and current and future talent:

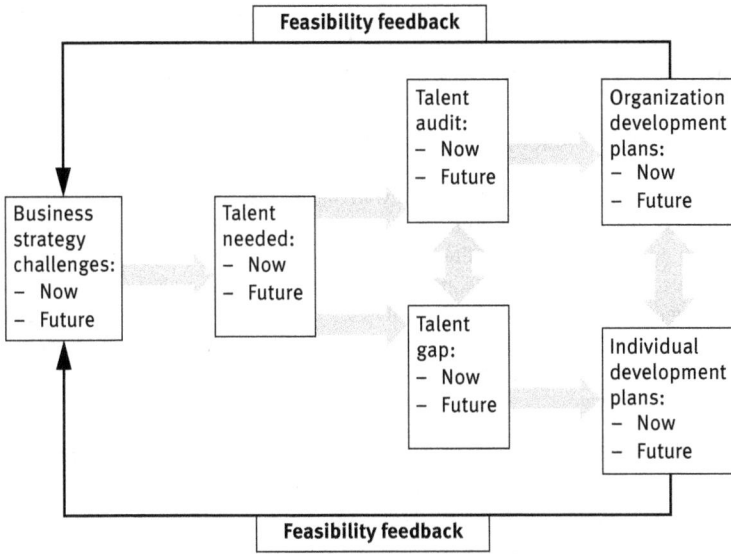

Figure 6.3: Feasibility Feedback for Business Strategy.
Source: Zinkin, J. (2014), *Rebuilding Trust in Banks: The Role of Leadership and Governance* (Singapore: John Wiley & Sons), p. 186.

To minimize the risk of strategic failure, *it is essential to undertake regular "feedback loop" reviews and environmental scans,* shown in Figure 6.3, and *change the business strategy if the gaps prove to be serious,* rather than sticking with it and hoping all will be well.

c. *Developing people:* The late Jack Welch said that effective leaders and managers, "wayfinders" as we prefer to call them, had to have the "Four Es": *energy,* the ability to *energize* others by articulating a vision and inspiring them, the ability to *execute,* and the *edge* to make difficult decisions.[33] It is evident that in Jack Welch's mind, leading was not separate from managing. We agree that effective "wayfinders" need these "Four Es" plus a fifth: "Empathy" – *the ability to engage with another person's point of view, even if not agreeing with it.* Being able to demonstrate these "Five Es" demands careful development of subordinates by their superiors.

"Wayfinders" must develop proper engagement skills in their subordinates to help them also become effective "wayfinders" with the "Five Es." The following are the most important engagement skills:[34] recognizing the importance of mental models, climbing the ladder of inference correctly, balancing quality advocacy with quality inquiry, mastering the "skill/will" model, stopping putting "square pegs into round holes," and navigating transitions:

i.   *Recognizing the importance of mental models:* This requires an appreciation that we all have our own mental models and boundaries of rationality determined by our experiences. Failure to recognize this leads to people talking past each other, digging themselves into ever deeper trenches of miscommunication.

Mental models are of fundamental importance:

> Any society, so long as it is, or feels itself to be, a working society, tends to invest in itself: a military society tends to become more military, a bureaucratic society more bureaucratic, a commercial society more commercial, as the status and profits of war or office or commerce are enhanced by success, and institutions are framed to forward it. Therefore, when such a society is hit by a general crisis, it finds itself paralysed by the structural weight of increased social investment. *The dominant military or official or commercial classes cannot easily change their orientation: and their social dominance, and the institutions through which it is exercised, prevent other classes from securing power or changing policy.*[35]   [Emphasis ours]

The "legacy effect" is similar. All organizations have founding principles that may become irrelevant to the current context as a natural result of the passage of time, the growth of the business, the rise of new competition, changes in society and regulation, and the points in the quote above. While "legacies" are crucial to success (they encapsulate founding beliefs and values, they articulate "who we are," "what we stand for," and "how we do business"), they can create boundaries to the rationality of those in the business and lock in groupthink when "out of the box thinking" is essential for change and survival. Past success reinforces the power of legacies to imprison creative, divergent thinking. This is a key contribution to the failure of leaders. Great initial success increases the danger of future failure, consider the disastrous final acts in the business careers of Stan O'Neal (Merrill Lynch), Jimmy Cayne (Bear Stearns), Dick Fuld (Lehman Brothers), and Fred Goodwin (Royal Bank of Scotland) in the Global Financial Crisis,[36] and the political catastrophe inflicted on Germany as result of Adolf Hitler's actions in World War II.[37]

The extent to which inappropriate mental models can pose problems in everyday operational situations is illustrated by the following examples:

–   *"Stonecutter" syndrome:* The parable of the consultant visiting a quarry to observe stonecutters working. One is disgruntled and working slowly. Asked what he is doing. He responds: "Can't you see, I am cutting stones!" The consultant sees another stonecutter who is cheerfully working more productively. Struck by the difference in the attitude and performance of the two men, he asks the second stonecutter what he is doing. This time the answer is, "I am doing something really important, I am helping build a cathedral!" Mental models determine attitudes.

- *"Hammer" syndrome:* Also known as the person being a "one trick pony." In these circumstances, superiors only know one way to do things (they only have a hammer to solve the problem), the problem must be a nail. "Wayfinders" who think like this will force-fit solutions, to the detriment of the organization.
- *"Oasis in the desert" syndrome:* Occurs when the organization identifies symptoms of a problem without understanding the interconnectedness of the root causes, and comes up with a partial solution that does not work, because it ignores the other systemic causes of the problem. The temptation to jump into action without fully understanding the implications of that action is always great. It should be avoided as long as "wayfinders" do not understand the root causes of the problem.

ii. *Climbing the ladder of inference correctly:* Using the proper process to avoid jumping to conclusions before the evidence warrants them. "Wayfinders" must avoid jumping to conclusions by first gathering relevant data; second, classifying, categorizing, and summarizing it to give it meaning; third, making assumptions; fourth, drawing conclusions based on either deductions or inferences; and fifth, based on evidence supporting their conclusions, adopting beliefs that allow them to take appropriate action. "Wayfinders" must continually scan the environment and be ready to revise views based on new information.

iii. *Balancing quality advocacy with quality inquiry:* Understand the difference between well and poorly balanced advocacy, and inquiry. Practice high quality advocacy and inquiry and avoid low quality advocacy and inquiry, as shown in Table 6.3.

Table 6.3: Balancing Quality Advocacy and Inquiry.

Advocacy: Making Statements	Inquiry: Asking Questions
High quality advocacy:	**High quality inquiry:**
1. Stating a point of view	1. Seeking to understand
2. Explaining the thinking	2. Stating current point of view
3. Providing examples	3. Genuinely probing reasoning
4. Encouraging challenge	4. Listening attentively
5. Listening attentively	
Low quality advocacy:	**Low quality inquiry:**
1. Forcing a point of view	1. Not seeking to understand
2. Failing to explain	2. Not stating current position
3. Failing to give examples	3. Sounding interrogative
4. Not asking for feedback	4. Listening poorly
5. Listening poorly	

Source: Zinkin, J. (2015), "Performance-Driven Leadership," *Star Newspaper Senior Management Program, Kuala Lumpur, Malaysia, September 1, 2015.*

vi. *Mastering the "Skill/Will" model:*[38] The "Skill/Will" model is a two-by-two matrix with "skill" ranging from low to high on one axis, and "will" ranging from low to high on the other. The model can be modified to analyze contextual performance drivers to help followers do better. In our modification, we see a richer set of inputs for "wayfinder" leaders, because there are now five scenarios instead of the four, shown in Table 6.4.

Table 6.4: Mastering the "Skill/Will" Model to Maximize Performance.

Skill	Will	Performance	Performance Drivers	"Wayfinder" Development Input
Low	Low	Low	Finds out job is harder than it seemed, will drops	**Direct:** Tell, show, do. Terminate?
Low	High	Low	New to the job, does not know how to perform, eager to learn and perform	**Direct:** Tell, show, do. Invest, follow up
Some	High	Moderate	As skill develops, will grows. Follower overestimates level of skill and wants to attempt higher levels of performance independently	**Coach:** Explain, discuss, plan next steps together, follow up
High	Low	Adequate, but could improve	1. Burnout may be the cause 2. Development required to meet raised expectations	**Support:** Probe, listen, encourage, follow up
High	High	High	Both skill and will are high and follower is an expert	**Delegate:** Agree on outcomes, empower, follow up, stretch

v. *Stopping putting square pegs in round holes:* This tendency manifests itself in two ways: (1) Believing the only way to progress in an organization is to become a manager of other people, and (2) force-fitting people into unsuitable roles, ignoring the impact of default personalities on productivity.

The number of people who really do not want to manage other people is surprisingly high.[39] There may be two factors to explain this. The first is the lack of training of managers in managing others:

A recent study by CareerBuilder.com shows that a whopping 58 percent of managers said they didn't receive any management training. Digest that for a second. *Most managers in the workforce were promoted because they were good at what they did, and not necessarily good at making the people around them better.* This statistic obviously unveils a harsh reality. We have a bunch of leaders who aren't trained on how to lead.[40]

The second is that many people actually do not like managing others because it takes them away from what they love, which is "doing" rather than getting others to do:

Why do we reward success on the job with a promotion *out* of the job and into management? . . . Companies continue to cling to the notion that one of the *only* mechanisms they have to acknowledge employees' talent is to make them managers and then to continue to promote them into ever-higher levels of management – reflecting the misguided assumption that being good at something also means being able to (and wanting to) manage others doing the same thing. Once in management, its trappings . . . don't really satisfy many of us who, like me, miss the *doing* . . .[41]

One of the most common mistakes of this type is to promote the best salesperson to become an indifferent sales manager, damaging performance twice over: once, by losing the results of the best salesperson, and twice, by putting them in a position where they can demotivate their subordinates. This is because of a failure to recognize that the skills, involvement, and aptitudes needed are quite different. However, it is sometimes important for the development of individuals to put them in a role that will give them new skills or broaden their horizons, but where they will feel uncomfortable because the new role does not fit their default personalities.

This will create added stress and, therefore, it is wise to recognize this, and to discuss it frankly with them during their personal development plan review. This helps them understand that they will find the new position more stressful, but that it will be time limited, and gives them the option to consider whether they really want the role as part of their career development.

One possible way to avoid making such a mistake is to invest in two career ladders: (1) the traditional managerial ladder which has an ever-increasing number of people to be managed as individuals climb the ladder, and (2) a parallel functional ladder where individuals grow and are promoted based on their technical expertise, allowing them to focus on what they do best and like doing.

vi. *Navigating transitions:* Organizations undergoing change must find ways of navigating the transition. No matter how beneficial the change is, it will be painful for some. A comment like, "Something must be wrong. Still after three months Jim is resisting changes in the system," shows the individual or organization is not navigating the transition well. It may be ignoring the effect of S.A.R.A.H (shock, anger, rejection, anxiety, and hope) on individuals, as they are forced to transition from their comfort zone, and where there is only the promise of an uncertain future. People need time to mourn endings, to move into neutral, and accept new beginnings gradually. Effective change can be understood by using the "Bridges" model, shown in Table 6.5.

Table 6.5: The "Bridges" Model for Navigating Change.

Focus	Endings	Neutral	New Beginning
Tasks Results and focus	**Storming** Making sense, understanding purpose, goals, roles, benefits	**Norming** Setting processes, "unwritten rules," short-term wins emphasized	**Performing** Creativity, openness, participation, effectiveness, and results
People Hearts and minds	**Emotional** Shock, confusion, fear, anger	**Ambivalent** Anger-rejection-acceptance, neither joy nor sadness	**Rational** Acceptance, help, productivity, positive, forward-looking
Engagement	**Communicate** Purpose and care	**Focus** Short-term and focus on positives	**Reinforce** New structure and heart

Source: Based on Bridges, W. (1991), *Managing Transitions*, cited in "Bridges' Transition Model: Guiding People Through Change," *MindTools*, Emerald Works, https://www.mindtools.com/pages/article/bridges-transition-model.htm, accessed on April 20, 2020.

Assessing the Environmental and Organizational Context

In assessing the contextual constraints on an organization, the environment is often divided into "external" and "internal" domains. Such division is potentially as problematic as the contrasts made between "leadership" and "management," or "strategy" and "tactics." However, with that caveat in mind, it is convenient to consider the techniques of assessment for "external" and "internal" environments separately.

1. **External Environmental Constraints** are best dealt with using PESTLE and "Five Forces" analysis:
a. *PESTLE analysis* is commonly used to understand the exposures of organizations. PESTLE[42] considerations are both fixed and variable, and interact continuously:
   i. *Political impacts:* Is a society democratic or authoritarian? Is "big" or "small" government preferred? Is laissez-faire economics or state control preferred? Government structure determines how business will be done. These constraints tend to be fixed or change only slowly. *Variable impacts require awareness of changing circumstances.* These issues are subject to frequent change. They manifest in legislation and regulations, and affect operational assumptions.
   ii. *Economic trends:* Global, national, and local events affect the economic perceptions of the organization's stakeholders, demand for products and services, and the social license to operate.

iii. *Social change:* Difficult to analyze, social change is gradual – until it is not! It is driven by changes in demographics, psychographics, education, income, life-stage, and life expectancy. All affect demand for products and services, the supply of suitably skilled employees, and the organizations' "social license" to operate, as societies and communities change their attitudes.

iv. *Technological change:*[43] Technological change can strengthen or weaken an organization's core competences. Disruptive technological change can render them obsolete. Disruptive technologies are game-changers[44] and an existential threat to organizations.

v. *Legal impacts:* Lack of clarity regarding legal obligations, or rights, or cross border operations leading to jurisdictional conflicts are problematic.

vi. *Environmental impacts:*[45] The challenges for organizations in these areas are consequential for stakeholders.

b. *"Five Forces"*: Porter's insight is that "wayfinders" have to worry about more sources of competition than just their head-to-head competitors. The amount of money a company makes from a given product market is determined by "Five Forces,"[viii,46] all competing for the market margin available in a given product market and whether it is a "blue" or "red" ocean:[47]

i. *Immediate head-to-head competitors:* Their strength and numbers determine the market share a company secures, and how much money it can make. It is affected by *supplier power* that determines how much margin they capture and *customer or buyer power* that determine pricing freedom and how much the loss of any single customer can hurt the bottom line.

ii. *The interaction between suppliers, a company, and its customers determines the attractiveness of any market.* Market attractiveness depends on new entrants and barriers to entry. The resulting increased competition reduces profitability. The ability of alternatives and substitutes to satisfy customers has the same effect. Both reduce profitability, or may render organizational competencies irrelevant.

2. **Internal Environmental Constraints** can be of two kinds: obstacles, and objections.

a. *Obstacles* are typically a lack of resources or bottlenecks. They are quantifiable and decisions can be made almost algorithmically.

---

viii The "Five Forces" are the profitability pressures created by 1) head-to-head competitors competing directly with the company's products or services, 2) suppliers of inputs to the company as it makes its products and services, 3) buyers of the outputs of the company, 4) new entrants who increase competitive capacity in the market, and 5) alternatives and substitutes that can replace the company's products and services.

b. *Objections* are concerns about a proposed course of action based on qualitative judgments. In business contexts, most objections are essentially qualitative in nature and can lead to intra-organizational conflict.

"Wayfinders" need to understand whether problems arise from obstacles, can be addressed by allocating resources, or are the result of objections that arise from differences of opinion. *Throwing more resources at barriers created by objections in the mistaken belief they are obstacles, will not solve the problem and wastes scarce resources.* Dealing with objections requires listening to what objectors say, to understand why they say it, to recognize that they have a different point of view, and to address their concerns articulately or change the planned course of action.

3. Impact of Business Life Cycle

Employment philosophies and conditions differ depending on whether the organization is an "Incubator," "Family Firm," "Guided Missile," or "Eiffel Tower." The four life-stages of organizations will also determine what kind of leaders/managers are likely to be most effective:

a. *Start-Ups* share many of the characteristics of an "Incubator." The mental models about the importance of vision, of testing new ideas, of "moving fast and breaking things;" and learning from the breakages, the type of relationships, and how to measure performance only apply to start-ups.

Relationships between people tend to be *diffuse*. It is too early in start-ups to talk of careers and, as a result, management style is "management by enthusiasm." Those accustomed to *specificity* in thought processes, measuring performance, in relationships and predictability will find it difficult to adjust to the context of a start-up. Those accustomed to *diffuseness* in thought processes, performance measurement, personal relationships, and unpredictable outcomes will flourish.

The challenge in a start-up is to turn ideas into practice.

b. *Growth stage* shares many features with the start-up. As time passes and predictability begins to matter, organizations (other than "Family Firms" and owner-managed businesses), will begin focusing on processes, procedures, and predictability of outcomes. Vision still matters, as does management by enthusiasm, but less than in start-ups.

In the case of "Family Firms," what will matter most is the temperamental and social fit with the founder and family. In "Family Firms," individuals need to be comfortable with a philosophy of "management by subjectives" where goals and objectives can change on a whim of the owner of the firm. Those uncomfortable with these contextual requirements will be forced out of the organization.

The primary focus in the growth stage is to create scalable value and start accumulating value for later extraction and distribution to shareholders.

c. *Maturity stage:* When organizations reach maturity, it hardly matters whether they started out as "Incubators" or "Family Firms," what matters is stability, order, and predictability. Most organizations choose between becoming a "Guided Missile" or an "Eiffel Tower." Instead of the *diffuse* approach to relationships, tasks, and performance measurement, those employed find themselves working in cultures where *specificity* replaces *diffuseness*. The key difference between the "Guided Missile" and the "Eiffel Tower" is the flexibility with which objectives and tasks change. "Guided Missiles" respond to changing contexts and situations more rapidly than "Eiffel Towers" because their environments are subject to greater competition, customer choice, and, in the case of multinationals, national cultural variations. A premium is placed on adaptability and "helicopter vision."[48]

The key challenges in mature, process-driven organizations remain the same: mastering the politics, how to "tell truth to power," and how to "think out of the box," lest they become trapped in an ossified culture because of the legacy effect.

The challenge in mature organizations is how to best reconcile the need to create value, extract value, and distribute it sustainably.

d. *Decline stage:* In the decline stage, effectiveness requires a short-term focus on optimizing the bottom-line, ruthlessly cutting costs and eliminating people who have done nothing wrong other than being in the wrong place at the wrong time. Most people are temperamentally ill-suited to doing this, letting the organization drift gradually downward, at first slowly, and then rapidly as it approaches bankruptcy.

The main business priority is extracting the maximum value in the shortest time, focusing on cash.

Effective Stakeholder Engagement

Ensuring effective stakeholder engagement with the vision and mission needs different approaches to "external" and "internal" stakeholders, another artificial dichotomy adopted for convenience (e.g., employees are also shareholders, voters, and may have relatives who work in suppliers or customers). Again, subject to the caveat, external stakeholders' livelihoods do not (usually) depend on accepting "wayfinder" proposals, whereas employees' livelihoods often depend on complying.

Key stakeholders in a business organization include creditors, customers, directors, employees, government (and its agencies), owners (shareholders), suppliers, unions, and the community from which the business draws its resources.[49]

Stakeholders can be divided into three groups:[50]

1. *Primary stakeholders have a direct impact on the fortunes of the company.* They include all members of the company value chain – customers (sources of revenue); members of the company supply chain (determinants of costs); shareholders; investors; and creditors (sources of funding); and past, current, and

prospective employees (past and future sources of labor). Regulators impose costs on doing business.

2. *Secondary stakeholders are involved with the activities or consequences of organizational activity.* Often service providers, auditors, lawyers, consultants, and advisers, they include three types of endorsers of the company's license to operate: *government* – enforcing regulation, *civil society* – community, NGOs, and advocacy groups, and *trade/industry associations* – lobbying for or against the company's actions. Secondary stakeholders provide early warning signals of change in the organization's strategic freedom.

3. *Tertiary stakeholders are the "commentariat"* who influence primary and secondary stakeholders by changing or reflecting the climate of opinion. They include analysts, rating agencies, academics, mainstream and social media, and, competitors.[ix]

Stakeholder engagement needs a comprehensive plan: identifying and assessing stakeholders, planning communications, and engagement. All stakeholders need to know "what is in it for them" – professionally, in terms of career, and personally, in terms of extra work and personal risk. Stakeholders wear different hats at different times, so, when engaging stakeholders, leaders must understand which hat their audience is wearing. Effective engagement seeks to build trust and confidence, solicit support and build alliances, and create goodwill.[51]

Summary

Setting strategy is about providing a mission, direction, and a plan to achieve it. Tactics are the short-term actions required on the organization's journey toward agreed goals, objectives, and destination to get back on course as a result of the impact of changing external and internal conditions.

Sailing is a powerful metaphor to understand the relationship between strategy, tactics, and operations. Sailors have to appreciate and respond to changing conditions to achieve goals, just as "wayfinders" must. *It is the context that determines the strategy, and the changing context determines the timing, and appropriateness of the tactics.* Polynesian "wayfinding" illustrates this in practice.

---

ix During Congressional investigations into the BP Deepwater Horizon disaster in the Gulf of Mexico, ExxonMobil and Chevron tried to argue they operated more safely than BP and that such a disaster could not have happened in their companies. In fact, their disaster response systems were equally likely to lead to the same results. The only claim they could perhaps make was they would have stopped operations quicker than BP. Goldenberg, S. (2010), "We could not have stopped Gulf oil gusher, ExxonMobil chief tells Congress," *The Guardian*, June 15, 2010, https://www.theguardian.com/environment/2010/jun/15/exxon-bp-oil-gusher-congress accessed on August 13, 2018.

Internal conditions matter. "Wayfinders" must distinguish between obstacles and objections. Obstacles are resource bottlenecks. Objections require changing people's minds.

"Wayfinders" are responsible for defining and agreeing on their organization's mission, establishing what top management want to do and society will allow, establishing whether the opportunity is worthwhile, and ensuring the organization has the required competencies and flexibility to avoid strategic "stuckness." When translating mission into vision, they provide a clear, differentiated, and emotionally compelling business focus, optimizing the organization's long-term license to operate.

They can do this by using the "Five P" framework to ensure organizational alignment of their "Purpose," "Principles," "Power," "People," and "Processes" with the mission and vision, recognizing there are four different organizational archetypes that will determine how best to achieve their goals. They are "Incubator," "Family Firm," "Guided Missile," and "Eiffel Tower."

We believe it is essential for "wayfinders" to appreciate the likely impact the different contexts will have on their ability to be effective whether it is for defining the mission and vision, ensuring appropriate organizational alignment or recognizing which of the four archetypal organizations they are working in.

"Wayfinders" make things happen through people. They need to recognize the four complementary types of leaders: "captains," "navigators," "engineers," and "shipbuilders." Large organizations employ specialists, allowing them to achieve mastery of their roles. In small organizations, an individual may have to execute all the roles.

Succession planning can only be applied imperfectly in even the largest organizations, and hardly ever in most SMEs. In publicly listed organizations, it divides into what is urged by codes of conduct and what is required for organizational success. It affects CEOs, their subordinates, and pivotal employees. CEO succession planning is a critical responsibility of boards.

Succession planning in SMEs and family firms is challenging, resource constraints often make it impossible. In family firms, the owner may want to transfer the organization to family members, potentially a risk to the organization. Some family firms have appointed professional managers and achieved multi-generational sustainability.

Managing talent is a four-step process which integrates people strategies into the business strategy. Effective "wayfinders" develop subordinates to have the "Five Es" of effectiveness: enthusiasm, the ability to energize others, the edge needed to make tough decisions, the ability to execute, and empathy. "Wayfinders" must recognize the importance of mental models and seek to challenge their own. "Wayfinders" can help employees navigate the transition from their comfort zones to the discomfort zone of uncertain promise and future potential using the "Bridges" model. Effective "wayfinders" need to remember the four life-stages of any organization (start-up, growth, maturity, and decline) require different types of skill and personality to achieve success.

Effective stakeholder engagement depends on accurate stakeholder identification, and assessment. Stakeholders may be advocates, supporters, spectators, saboteurs, or adversaries and need to be engaged accordingly. "Wayfinders" have the possibility of exercising more direct control over internal stakeholders. Engaging stakeholders effectively depends on planned and repeated effective communication. Supporters need to be mobilized, spectators energized, saboteurs neutralized, and adversaries opposed. Achieving these objectives requires appropriate, articulate advocacy.

References

1 Zinkin, J. (2019), *Better Governance Across the Board: Creating Value Through Reputation, People and Processes* (Boston/Berlin: Walter deGruyter Inc.), p. 141.

2 Smith, R. (2020), "Strategy vs. Tactics: The Main Difference & How To Track Progress of Both," *ClearPoint Strategy* https://www.clearpointstrategy.com/strategy-vs-tactics/, accessed on April 1, 2020.

3 "Polynesian Wayfinding," *Polynesian Wayfinding Society*, http://www.hokulea.com/education-at-sea/polynesian-navigation/polynesian-non-instrument-wayfinding/, accessed on March 18, 2020.

4 For a more detailed discussion, see Zinkin, J. (2014), *Rebuilding Trust in Banks: The Role of Leadership and Governance* (Singapore: John Wiley & Sons), pp. 136–140.

5 Solomon, R. C. (1999), *A Better Way to Think About Business: How Personal Integrity Leads to Corporate Success* (New York: Oxford University Press), p. xxii.

6 Trompenaars, F., and Hampden-Turner, C. (2006), *Riding the Waves of Culture: Understanding Cultural Diversity in Business,* 2nd Edition (London: Nicholas Brealey Publishing), pp. 157–181.

7 Kerr, S. (1995), "On the folly of rewarding A while hoping for B," *Academy of Management Executive,* February 1995, 9, p. 1.

8 Shekshnia, S., Kravchenko, K., and Williams, E. (2018), *CEO School: Insights from 20 Global Leaders,* quoted in *INSEAD Knowledge: Leadership and Organisations,* May 9, 2018 https://knowledge.insead.edu/sites/all/themes/knowledge2015/, accessed on July 31, 2018.

9 Ibid.

10 Ibid.

11 Ibid.

12 Ibid.

13 Zinkin. (2019), op. cit., pp. 220–221.

14 Pierce, C. (2016), "Trends in Corporate Governance," quoted in *The Handbook of Corporate Governance,* edited by Richard Leblanc (Hoboken, NJ: John Wiley and Sons), p. 41.

15 Zinkin. (2019), op. cit., pp. 225–228.

16 Larcker, D. P., and Tayan, B. (2016) "CEO Succession Planning," quoted in Leblanc (2016), op. cit., p. 155.

17 La Monica, P. (2005), "Fiorina Out, HP Stock Soars," *CNN Money,* February 10, 2005, https://money.cnn.com/2005/02/09/technology/hp_fiorina/, accessed on July 31, 2018.

18 Worthen, B., and Wing-Tan, P. (2010), "H-P Chief Quits in Scandal," *Wall Street Journal,* August 7, 2010, https://www.wsj.com/articles/SB10001424052748703309704575413663370670900, accessed on July 31, 2018.

19 Goldman, D. (2011), "HP CEO Apotheker Fired, Replaced by Meg Whitman," *CNN Money,* September 22, 2011, https://money.cnn.com/2011/09/22/technology/hp_ceo_fired/index.htm, accessed on July 31, 2018.

20 Nadler, M. (2016), "CEO Succession: An Owner's Guide for Directors," cited in Leblanc (2016), op. cit., p. 121.

21 Ibid, p. 140.

22 This section is based on Zinkin. (2019), op. cit., pp. 324–326.

23 Senge, P. (1995), "Rethinking Leadership In The Learning Organization," *The Systems Thinker,* https://thesystemsthinker.com/rethinking-leadership-in-the-learning-organization/, accessed on September 5, 2018.

24 Wohl, R. A., and Wohl, L. (2011), *Navigating Organizations Through the 21st Century: A Metaphor for Leadership* (Bloomington: Indiana: Xlibris), pp. 24–25.

25 Senge (1995).

26 Kelly, G. (2012), "Titanic Anniversary: The Myth of the Unsinkable Ship", *BBC Future,* April 2, 2012, https://www.bbc.com/future/article/20120402-the-myth-of-the-unsinkable-ship, accessed on March 17, 2021.

27 Rothwell, W. (2001), *Effective Succession Planning: Ensuring Leadership Continuity and Building Talent From Within,* 2nd edition (New York: AMACOM), 6, quoted in Ip, B., and Jacobs, G. (2006), "Business Succession Planning: A Review of the Evidence," *Journal of Small Business and Enterprise Development,* Vol. 13, No. 3, 2006, p. 327.

28 Ip and Jacobs (2006), op. cit., p. 339.

29 Ibid., p. 330.

30 Martin et al. (2002), *SME Ownership Succession – Business Support and Policy Implications* (London: Small Business Service), 6 quoted in ibid., pp. 326–327.

31 May, P. (2019), "Owner Strategy," *PWC.*

32 Zinkin, J. (2020), *The Challenge of Sustainability: Corporate Governance in a Complicated World* (Boston/Berlin: Walter de Gruyter Inc.), p. 46.

33 Krames, J, A., and Pratt, A. "Jack Welch and the 4 Es of Leadership," *What Makes A Good Leader,* http://www.whatmakesagoodleader.com/Jack-Welch.html, accessed on April 19, 2020.

34 Zinkin, J. (2015), "Performance-Driven Leadership," *Star* Newspaper Senior Management Program, Kuala Lumpur, Malaysia, September 1, 2015.

35 Trevor-Roper, H. (1965), *The Rise of Christian Europe* (London: Thames and Hudson), p. 184, quoted in Jay, A., (1994), *Management and Machiavelli: Discovering a New Science of Management in the Timeless Principles of Statecraft* (Amsterdam/Oxford/ Sydney/ Toronto: Pfeiffer & Company), p. 80.

36 Zinkin (2014), op . cit., pp. 25–46.

37 Fest J. C. (1973), *Hitler* (London: Weidenfeld & Nicholson).

38 Ibid.

39 Torres, N. (2014), "Most People Don't Want To Be Managers," *Harvard Business Review,* September 18, 2014, https://hbr.org/2014/09/most-people-dont-want-to-be-managers, accessed on September 10, 2019.

40 Sturt, D., and Nordstrom, T. (2018),"10 Shocking Workplace Stats You Need To Know," *Forbes,* March 8, 2018, https://www.forbes.com/sites/davidsturt/2018/03/08/10-shocking-workplace-stats-you-need-to-know/#67941965f3af, accessed on September 10, 2018.

41 Kreamer, A. (2012), "What If You Don't Want to Be a Manager?" *Harvard Business Review,* December 13, 2012, https://hbr.org/2012/12/what-if-you-dont-want-to-be-a, accessed on September 10, 2018.

42 For a more detailed discussion of PESTLE, see Zinkin (2019), op. cit., pp. 143–152.

43 For a detailed discussion of technological change, see Zinkin, (2020), op. cit., pp. 108–123.

44 Deloach, J. (2019), "Disruptive Innovation Tops List of Threats to Companies – Is Your Organization Thinking and Acting Digital?" *Corporate Compliance Insights,* March 29, 2019, https://www.corporatecomplianceinsights.com/disruptive-innovation-tops-list-of-threats-to-companies-is-your-organization-thinking-and-acting-digital/, accessed on April 1, 2020.

45 For a detailed discussion of environmental impacts, see, Zinkin (2020), op. cit., pp. 53–76.

46 Based on Zinkin (2019), op. cit., pp. 153–156.

47 Mauborgne, R., and Kim, W. C. (2004), *Blue Ocean Strategy* (Boston: Harvard Business Press).

48 Bridges, W. (1991), *Managing Transitions,* cited in "Bridges' Transition Model: Guiding People Through Change," *MindTools,* Emerald Works, https://www.mindtools.com/pages/article/bridges-transition-model.htm, accessed on April 20, 2020.

49 Business dictionary, http://www.businessdictionary.com/definition/stakeholder.html#ixz z25ahfNRnm, accessed on August 13, 2018.

50 For a detailed discussion on Stakeholder Engagement, see Zinkin (2019), op. cit., pp. 272–280.

51 Based on 2018 Edelman Trust Barometer: The State of Trust in Business, http://cms.edelman.com/sites/default/files/2018-02/2018_Edelman_Trust_Barometer_State_of_Business.pdf, accessed on August 13, 2018.

—

Part 3: **"Leadership Techniques"**

In Part 3, we discuss the techniques "wayfinders" can learn to be both effective and ethical. We begin by discussing Volatility, Uncertainty, Complexity, and Ambiguity (VUCA) and how to keep things simple, how best to use two leadership models to maximum effect, and how to communicate effectively. We conclude with a discussion on how "wayfinders" can reconcile duty-based and consequential ethics to make ethical and effective decisions.

https://doi.org/10.1515/9783110707878-009

Chapter 7
Dealing with Volatility, Uncertainty, Complexity, and Ambiguity

There are many issues where the multiplicity of interacting phenomena makes confident predictions of outcomes problematic. Important and interrelated questions are:

1. How will environmental change affect society?
2. Is the "neoliberal economy" with rising levels of income inequality, and brittle supply chains sustainable?
3. How will "Industry 4.0" (the impact of AI and robotization on employment and employability) manifest itself?
4. How will increasing polarization of society fueled by social media play out?
5. What long term impact will the covid-19 pandemic will have on society?

The ability of individuals to affect outcomes depends on their position in the leadership of organizations.[1] Whether they only manage themselves or manage others, they will be affected by the answers, but will be unable to do much to change them. If they manage other managers, their ability to influence outcomes will be greater, but still limited. As they move up the decision-making pyramid, challenges posed by VUCA have wider and more enduring organizational and societal impact.

VUCA and Decision-Making

VUCA has four components: volatility, uncertainty, complexity, and ambiguity. The concepts are interrelated. We need to be clear about what each of the terms in the VUCA acronym means:

Volatility is how fast changes occur, and the increase or decrease in the rate of change.

Uncertainty is "a situation in which something is not known, or something that is not known or certain."[2]

Complexity is "when the whole is made up of interrelated parts so that simple cause-and-effect chains are replaced by complicated, rapidly changing, interdependent forces and events."[3] Emergent properties (those which a complex system has, but which the individual members do not)[i] and network effects (increasing

---

i An example is that salt is composed of sodium and chlorine atoms – neither of which tastes "salty."

https://doi.org/10.1515/9783110707878-010

usage of a system leading to exponential growth of usage) are properties of complex systems.

Ambiguity is when "words or ideas are capable of being interpreted in more than one way."

Volatility

There are six different types of volatility that need to be managed in a business setting.

1. **Political Volatility:** The political environment is changing faster and the rate of change seems to be accelerating. Neoliberal economic assumptions about the benefits of globalization and free trade are increasingly challenged.[4] Changing political consensuses makes deciding on a business's best course of action challenging. In the UK, there is Brexit;[5] in France, the rise of the "gilets jaunes";[6] in Italy,[7] Germany,[8] and Spain[9] the traditional parties of left and right are losing the center ground to the Greens on the left, and to nativist, xenophobic parties on the right. The Middle East is destabilized by Sunni-Shia struggles for power between Iran supported by its proxies in Yemen, Syria, and Lebanon; and Saudi Arabia supported by the US, Egypt, and the Gulf States;[10] as well as by the Israeli-Palestinian conflict over land.[11] In Asia there are rising tensions between India and Pakistan over Kashmir,[12] North Korea and Japan over missile tests,[13] trade tensions between South Korea and Japan;[14] and the challenge posed by an assertive China to India in the Himalayas; as well as to Vietnam, the Philippines, Indonesia, and Malaysia over the South China Sea.[15] A revanchist Russia[16] seeks to destabilize Western democracies[17] and is pushing the boundaries of asymmetrical warfare in Eastern Europe in the Ukraine,[18] while testing NATO's commitment to defending the Baltic states.[19] The risk of war by mistake remains real in Eastern Europe, Northeast Asia, South Asia, and the Middle East. There is also the ever-present impact of migrants from North Africa and the Eastern Mediterranean destabilizing domestic politics in the EU;[20] and of refugees and migrants trying to enter the US from Central America.[21]

"Wayfinders" have to deal with ever faster political change as a result, and chart courses to deal with it.

2. **Economic Volatility:** Economic volatility usually manifests in currency volatility as a result of diverging growth rates, inflation, and interest rates – for example, the problems faced by Turkey[22] or Argentina.[23] It can also be the result of punitive sanctions, as with Iran.[24]

Every ten years or so, economic volatility results from a major financial crisis.[25] However, it is more likely to be the result of changing long-term growth assumptions globally, regionally, or nationally. Only rarely is it the result of a "black swan" event, like the covid-19 pandemic.

3. **Social Volatility:** Social volatility is a symptom and a cause of political and economic volatility. Increased social volatility in Europe has resulted from decisions about immigration, austerity after the Global Financial Crisis (GFC), and rising inequality and unemployment in the developed world caused by globalization. Social volatility is exaggerated by the rise of social media[26] providing an echo chamber for resentment and outrage.[27]

4. **Technological Volatility:** Schumpeter's "creative destruction"[28] is integral to capitalism. However, technological innovation usually causes less volatility than social innovation because it is adopted more slowly.

5. **Legal and Regulatory Volatility:** Legal and regulatory volatility are closely connected to political volatility – for example, nationalization or privatization of utilities[29] or the break-up of oligopolies like the tech giants,[30] and the impact of competition watchdogs on mergers and acquisitions.[31] Equally, changes proposed in the role of unions,[32] and health and safety legislation form part of the political cycle.

6. **Environmental Volatility:** Environmental issues have the longest time horizons, but they appear to be shortening and resulting in extreme weather events, disasters, and emergencies for which organizations are often not prepared.

Uncertainty

Uncertainty covers the same six political, economic, social, technological, legal, and environmental issues. The lack of predictability is what makes them so difficult for "wayfinders" to handle when making decisions that cannot be easily reversed.

1. **Political Uncertainty:** Currently, political uncertainty is high. The neoliberal consensus following the fall of the Berlin Wall in 1989 appears to be giving way to challenges to global institutions and norms with weakened governments having to deal with hung legislatures, and growing discontent with the economic and social status quo.

2. **Economic Uncertainty:** Decision-makers have always considered macroeconomic variables. The consequences of Covid-19 – with its impact on both demand and supply – and the viability of financial services are uncertain.

3. **Social Uncertainty:** Social uncertainty is displayed in changing values, changing demographics, and social media.
a. *Changing values:* How people behave toward each other, what they do with their education and disposable income, their attitudes to work and retirement are, in large part, determined by the values they adopt from role models and how they

modify these values – based on their life experiences and the economic opportunities they see before them.

After the GFC (Global Financial Crisis), electorates in the US and UK appeared to feel marginalized by elites who disregarded their sufferings arising from the GFC,[33] which destroyed trust in institutions (political, business, media, and experts in general).[34]

Demagogic, post-truth politics, and the dissemination of "fake news" has left electorates uncertain of "the truth," untrusting of authority, and preferring to believe social media echo chambers.[35]

b. *Changing demographics:* Demographics determine demand for products and services. "Wayfinders" should understand the threats and opportunities presented by any change in demographics: their share of the market, whether customers and prospects have more or less disposable income than previously, whether changes in education and lifestyle affect their demand for products and services and their willingness to work for the organization.

When organizations implement policies designed to eliminate discrimination, "wayfinders," tasked with implementation, have to recognize the feelings of those who believe, even if it is unjustifiable, that they are being disadvantaged. Failure to do so will only lead to further division and dissent within their organizations.

c. *Social media:* Social media is driven by algorithms designed to maximize the user's engagement and interest. As early as 2011, *The Atlantic* was concerned that the internet might be more suited for the propagation of lies than the truth.[36]

As long as social media is driven by a business model that seeks maximum engagement to satisfy advertisers' demands for attracting potential customers, it will continue to be source of social uncertainty and harm. It is notable that some advertisers are now seeking changed policies from social media companies because the market segments they seek to serve are alienated or angered by active social media influencers.

4. **Technological Uncertainty:** Technological uncertainty arises from disruptive innovations where decision-makers must consider whether what is being proposed has the capacity to render their business model obsolete. Disruptive technologies pose an existential threat.

Established companies have much to fear from upstart disrupters, who threaten their dominance by introducing new products based on a different business model. They should in theory be prepared to change their business models before the upstarts do it to them, as the late Jack Welch, one-time CEO of GE put it:

If the rate of change on the outside exceeds the rate of change on the inside, the end is near.[37]

Incumbents find it difficult to follow this advice. Effective evolution is often blocked by the "Innovator's Dilemma."[38] Vested interests will fight changes when it is not obvious that required change benefits them. And when it becomes obvious that change is required, it may be too late to do anything about it, as examples like Xerox's, Nokia's, or Sony's falls from grace make clear. There are, however, two conditions where delaying adopting disruptive technologies developed by competitors makes sense:

a. *When the technology is "bleeding edge,"* where unknown unknowns affect the safety of the offer. In these circumstances, it is often better to be second to market. The Comet was the first passenger jet. It set the technical standards for jet performance for sixty years, until the Boeing 787 Dreamliner's launch in 2009.[39] The Comet's test flight was in 1949, and its first commercial flight was on May 2, 1952. The Comet 1 flew until 1954. It was twice as fast as piston-engine rivals, loved by passengers and airlines. In 1954, however, two Comets crashed, the result of metal fatigue caused by how the hull skin was riveted on the roof of the plane under a painted-over plate. It was impossible to spot the crack's growth in time before it caused the hull to fail and the plane to break up on its 1,290th flight.

   Neither the designers of the Comet nor the industry knew enough about metal fatigue thresholds in an aluminum skin before the tests undertaken by the Royal Aircraft Establishment's safety experts. The plane was operating "beyond the limits of knowledge."

   As a result of the delays, the four lost years allowed Boeing to develop a bigger capacity jet and capture the market created by the Comet.[40]

b. *When rates of adoption are slow:* Advocates of generic disruptive technologies sometimes expect them to be implemented earlier than is practical. This may be the result of teething problems causing the new technology to underperform in its introductory phase, or of it being too expensive initially. It may be the result of path dependency where the initial technological, capital, or skills "infrastructure" is lacking. It may be the result of effective pushback by vested interests.

When faced with operational technological uncertainty, "wayfinders" need answers to decide: "Will what is being proposed work?" "How far have we pushed the technology envelope?" and "What is preventing us from doing it?"

a. *Pushing the technology envelope beyond its known limits:* The essential errors leading to the NASA space shuttle *Challenger* disaster were the focus on speed and cost, combined with the belief they were not pushing the envelope too far and too fast because each incremental step had worked, anesthetizing them to the fear of cumulatively small errors leading to catastrophic failure through a process called the "normalization of deviance."[41]

   Design failure crises occur in civil engineering, about every thirty years.[42] For example, when engineers develop new approaches to bridge-building, they push the frontiers of their understanding to create more aesthetically satisfying bridges, or bridges with longer spans to cross wider rivers. When the first such innovative bridge is built, the designers are careful to document all their assumptions about how the design is supposed to work, erring heavily on the side of caution. Once the new structural approach has proved successful, the next generation of designers push the envelope gradually, lengthening the spans or making new trade-offs to increase the beauty of the structure. However, at some point, they run the risk of taking their success in improving upon the original innovation one step too far – literally building a bridge too far – at which point the bridge collapses, sometimes with fatalities:

> The accidents happened not because the engineer neglected to provide sufficient strength as prescribed by the accepted design approach, but because of the unwitting introduction of a new type of behavior. *As time passed during the period of development, the bases of the design methods were forgotten and so were their limits of validity. Following a period of successful construction, a designer, perhaps a little complacent, simply extended the design method once too often."*[43]   [Emphasis ours]

Given this tendency to push the design envelope to the point of failure, justified by a track record of previous success,[44] decision-makers must be certain that past successes are not a recipe for future failure.

b. *Lacking internal processes to ensure success:* Once "wayfinders" are certain that the technology envelope is not going to be torn, they must ensure internal processes are not going to block progress toward desired outcomes. This requires ensuring that the right ideas are selected for further investment. Surprisingly, most organizations have too many creative ideas, rather than too few, when it comes to new products.[45]

Typically, organizations fail to select well – playing it safe to minimize uncertainty, they spread resources too thinly, instead of concentrating on projects with the likely best returns, or they fail to allocate/reallocate sufficient resources each year to long-term projects because of uncertainty, with resulting stagnation.

5. **Legal Uncertainty:** Legal certainty is a foundational rule of law.[46] To exist, five conditions must apply: 1) laws and decisions must be made public, 2) they must be unambiguous, 3) court decisions must be binding, 4) retroactivity of laws and decisions must be limited, 5) and legitimate interests and expectations must be protected.[47]

a. Decision-makers must consider carefully whether they should do business in jurisdictions where legal certainty does not exist. The short-term benefits of privileged access may be outweighed by long-term economic costs and reputational damage. Sanctions and trade wars cause legal and regulatory uncertainty.

b. Decision-makers need to remember the law reflects what society *was* thinking, legal change inevitably lags societal expectations.

6. **Environmental Uncertainty:** The scientific community is certain that global warming is taking place and is taking place faster than expected.[48]

Complexity

Few appreciate the impact of complexity on system behavior, or how it can manifest. Decision-makers need to practice systems thinking.

A simple example of how complexity can make guaranteeing a satisfactory result difficult is to analyze what it takes to enjoy a refreshing glass of milk. Failure at any stage to meet standards will lead to a bad experience:

Stage 1: Suppliers of feed and veterinarians must ensure that farmers' cows are in good health. *Failure to do so could lead to either the milk being of poor quality or carrying bovine tuberculosis.*

Stage 2: Farmers must ensure that cows are kept in good conditions, are properly fed and cared for according to the instructions of the feed suppliers and veterinarians. *Failure by any single farmer to do this could contaminate the entire supply chain.* Milk must be kept fresh, safe, and clean.

Stage 3: The milk haulers must test the milk to ensure it passes the required tests and must ensure that the trucks that will take the milk from the farms to the dairies are clean and can keep the milk chilled. *Failure here could lead to further contamination on its journey to the dairies.*

Stage 4: The dairies test milk on arrival, blending it from different suppliers, pasteurizing and then homogenizing it according to pre-set sanitary and performance standards that must be met at each stage in the process. The dairies use cartons supplied by packaging companies that must satisfy exacting performance standards; they pack the different milks (fresh, UHT (ultra-high temperature processed), whole, 2%, non-fat, etc.) according to grade, fat content, flavor, and pack size, labeling the resulting different milks with the appropriate branding and their sell-by dates. The milks are then ready to be delivered according to orders collated by retail chain and outlet. They are then stored in appropriate conditions, waiting to be collected at the designated time. *Failure to meet the required standards in any of these steps will lead to milks that are not fit for human consumption.*

Stage 5: The distributors who may belong to the dairies or to the retail chains collect the milks, check their condition, and deliver them to retail outlets according to orders placed, making sure the orders are handled correctly so there is minimum damage and that the milks are delivered within the agreed time, kept at the right temperatures throughout their journey (in the cold chain if the milks are fresh, as opposed to UHT which are put in sterilized, shelf-stable containers). *Failure to meet pre-set standards will lead to either damaged goods or spoiled product, unfit for human consumption.*

Stage 6: The retailers hold the milks in appropriate conditions, rotating them onto the shelves in line with their sell-by dates, removing those that have gone past their sell-by dates. *Failure to meet the pre-set standards will lead to product unfit for sale.*

Stage 7: The drinkers will take their cartons home and put them in their refrigerators if the milk is fresh, or in their pantries if UHT. Paying attention to the sell-by dates, they will open the cartons and enjoy a good glass of milk. They will then close the cartons, making sure they are properly sealed and put them back in the appropriate part of the refrigerator, away from fish and aromatic foods. *Failure to ensure that the cartons once opened are stored correctly in the refrigerator will likely lead to the milk being tainted by other food nearby, failure to keep it at the right temperature to drink before it has lost its freshness will spoil the taste. Even failure to make sure the glass has been properly washed and rinsed can spoil the experience.*

If such an apparently simple act as enjoying a glass of milk to its fullest is the result of this complex chain of events, where multiple actors must perform as expected and where their interactions affect the system to meet demanding standards, imagine, for example, how much more complex the chain of events and interactions required to achieve desired outcomes is for chemical plants, power grids, and finance (which are "tightly coupled" systems), and transport systems, whose effectiveness people often taken for granted. Two engineering examples make the case:

1. Piper Alpha Disaster, July 6, 1988: *Piper Alpha* was an oil production platform in the North Sea operated by Occidental Petroleum (Caledonia) Limited. It began production in 1976, but on July 6, 1988, it was the site of the world's most lethal offshore disaster – 167 oil rig workers died.

> *The defining characteristic of a tightly coupled process is that once it starts, it's difficult or impossible to stop*: a domino-toppling display is not especially complex, but it is tightly coupled. So is a loaf of bread rising in the oven . . .

> But what if a system is both complex and tightly coupled. *Complexity means there are many different ways for things to go wrong. Tight coupling means the unintended consequences proliferate so quickly that it is impossible to adapt to the failure or try something different.* On Piper Alpha, the initial explosion need not have destroyed the rig, but it took out the control room, making evacuation difficult, and also making it almost impossible to override the diver-safety catch that was preventing the seawater pumps from starting automatically. Although the rig's crew had, in principle, shut down the flow of oil and gas to the platform, so much pipework had been damaged that gas and oil continued to leak out and feed the inferno. Each interaction was unexpected. Many happened within minutes of the initial mistake. There was no time to react.[49] [Emphases ours]

2. US and Canada Blackout, August 14, 2003: The August 14, 2003, blackout in a large part of the US Midwest and Northeast and in Ontario, Canada, is an excellent example of a system that was "tightly coupled, as well as interactively complex,"[50] hence, the cascade of failures in eight US states and the province of Ontario. It affected an estimated 50 million people and 61,800 megawatts of electric load in Connecticut, Massachusetts, Michigan, New York, Ohio, Ontario, Pennsylvania, and Vermont. It took four days before power was restored in some parts of the US, and parts of Ontario suffered rolling blackouts for more than a week. Estimates of the costs in the US were US$4 billion to US$10 billion. Millions of office workers were stranded, Cleveland was left without water, twenty-two nuclear power plants were shut down, sixty-five fires were the result, and in New York City alone, first responders had to rescue people from eight hundred elevators:

> The details of the causes of the outage show the familiar string of interacting small errors. It was a hot summer day and demand was high, but that was not unusual. The device for determining the real-time state of the power system in the Midwest Independent Service Operator (MISO) had to be disabled because a mismatch occurred. The device . . . was corrected, but the engineer failed to re-engage it on going to lunch. Normally, this would not be a problem . . . but it just so happened . . . that forty-five minutes later . . . an alarm to indicate an untoward event at FirstEnergy began to malfunction . . . But the failure was of the sort that when the backup server came on, the program was in a restart mode, and under these conditions the software program failed. Moreover, it failed to indicate it had failed, so the operators were unaware that it was not functioning properly.
>
> Meanwhile in the MISO, the state estimator was restarted after lunch, but again indicated a mismatch . . . At this point there was no untoward event that the program would warn about . . . Independently, faulty tree-trimming practices and the hot weather caused one of the FirstEnergy's lines to go down . . . Finally the MISO noticed and took the tripped line out of service, but FirstEnergy's failed program did not allow FirstEnergy to know of either the trip or that the line was taken out of service. Three more lines shorted out on trees because of FirstEnergy's cutbacks in maintenance, but the utility's computers showed no problems. FirstEnergy only became aware when its own power went out . . . and had to switch to emergency power. By then in just seven minutes of cascading failures, eight states and parts of Canada blacked out."[51]

Clearly, being interconnected creates enormous additional levels of complexity in the grid. This is made even more complicated when grids begin to depend on renewable sources of electricity supply. They may be available in abundance when the sun is shining or when the wind is blowing or both. But what happens at night if the wind is not blowing? There is no supply, yet there is plenty of demand. In such circumstances, the grid must rely on power generated from fossil or nuclear fuels or from power that has been stored in batteries or in dams. Choosing the optimal configuration for present and future needs depends on relative prices of the different sources of supply in the spot and futures markets for power, affected in turn by the impact of future subsidies and taxation policies on the best estimates of projected future demand. This itself is a function of economic growth on the one hand, and improvements in energy efficiency on the other, and on the projected long-run return on investments in the different sources of supply, which are capital intensive with long-term payoffs subject to assumptions of the likely cost of capital.

The complexity is even greater when we remember that all these different supply chains need to operate as an integrated system and they will have to serve 10 billion people by the middle of the century.[52]

To understand how complex systems work, their interdependencies, and the consequences of failure in their interconnected elements requires considerable technical expertise and time. The impact of Covid-19 is an example of unpredictable and far-ranging consequences when complex and tightly coupled systems break down, with nobody knowing where or how the dominoes are going to fall. Only experts appreciate complex systems. There is a risk that pressures on decision-makers lead them to excessive reliance on oversimplified analyses. Reports are prefaced with executive summaries that may deny busy decision-makers the opportunity to discuss and debate the details, leading to decisions taken without due attention being paid to the need to avoid the threats to good decisions, discussed in more detail in Chapter 8.

Ambiguity

An example of ambiguity in action was UN Resolution 242, adopted unanimously by the UN Security Council on November 22, 1967, which ended the Six Day War between Israel and Egypt, Jordan, and Syria. The ambiguity was in the difference in the English and French versions of the resolution, which allowed both the Israelis and the Arabs to agree to a ceasefire based on their different interpretations about territorial withdrawal by the Israeli army. Based on the English version, the Israelis understood it to mean "from not all" the occupied territories, whereas the Arabs using the French version understood it to mean withdrawal "from all" occupied territories. This ambiguity allowed the parties to stop fighting, but did nothing to resolve the conflicting objectives of the Israelis and Palestinians.

"Wayfinders" may be presented with ambiguity of corporate purpose, ambiguity over values and codes of conduct, ambiguity over different stakeholder priorities, ambiguity over forecasts and interpretations of facts, and ambiguity of communicating to different audiences.

1. *Ambiguity of Corporate Purpose*: For many years, the ambiguity of corporate purpose could be summed up in the contrasting philosophies of Peter Drucker and Milton Friedman. Drucker argued that the purpose of business was "to create and maintain satisfied customers," whereas Friedman argued that it was "to maximize shareholder value." This disagreement was complicated by arguments over time horizons. Was the purpose of business to achieve either or both of these apparently irreconcilable objectives in the short or long term? The view of investors

crystallized around the need to focus on short-term profits, regardless of unintended consequences.[53]

The present consensus has shifted back toward Drucker's view that maximizing profit is not the main purpose of business with the US Business Roundtable's Declaration on August 19, 2019, that the purpose of the corporation is to promote an economy that serves all Americans. Whether this change of heart is real or PR whitewash, only time will tell.

2. *Ambiguity of values and codes of conduct*: Often companies that have mission, vision and values statements use single words to describe the desired values – for example, "Integrity", "Teamwork" and so on, without describing the expected behavior associated with each value and the circumstances in which certain behavior is permissible or forbidden, leaving to the employees to guess exactly what they are allowed or not allowed to do. More seriously, often little thought is given to whether the five or six designated values may contradict each other. For example, "We expect our employees to learn from their mistakes" and "Get it right the first time" – the former encouraging them to experiment, while the latter's focus on TQM (total quality management) appears to contradict it. To make matters more complicated, it is also often not clear which value has priority.

3. *Ambiguity between Stakeholder Priorities*: The parallels between the 2019 Business Roundtable Declaration and Johnson & Johnson's 1943 *Credo* in Table 7.1 are striking.

Unlike the US Business Roundtable's declaration, the *Credo* avoids ambiguities of priority between stakeholders. In the *Credo*, customers come first, then employees, then communities, and finally shareholders. It also makes it clear that shareholders are only entitled to a fair return and not the maximum return.

4. *Ambiguity of Facts*: It is difficult for generalists to know what to make of disagreements between specialists about how to interpret the facts. Bona fide experts disagree about epidemiology, the economy, the stock market, the impact of AI on employment, about nutrition, wellness, and health. In part, this is because as new facts emerge, different conclusions are the result, and in part this is because it is not clear whether what has been observed is correlation rather than causation.[54] It also arises partly from a lack of systems thinking – understanding how emergent and network properties appear – in essence, the problem of siloed thinking.

5. *Ambiguity of communicating to different audiences*: Companies have many different audiences and their interests can differ markedly. Effective communication needs to recognize these differences, while at the same time remembering that regardless of the audience, there is a common core of messaging that must reflect the company's purpose and values and its brand promise. This requires an integrated communication architecture to reconcile these differences and ambiguities to create a credible and coherent set of communications, appropriate to each audience. (This is discussed in detail in Chapter 10.)

Table 7.1: J&J's *Credo* and Business Roundtable Declaration Compared.

Johnson & Johnson *Credo* (1943)	Roundtable Declaration (2019)
We believe our first responsibility is to the patients, doctors and nurses, to mothers and fathers and all others who use our products and services. In meeting their needs everything we do must be of high quality. We must constantly strive to provide value, reduce our costs and maintain reasonable prices. Customers' orders must be serviced promptly and accurately. Our business partners must have an opportunity to make a fair profit.	Businesses play a vital role in the economy by creating jobs, fostering innovation and providing essential goods and services. Businesses make and sell consumer products, manufacture equipment and vehicles, support the national defense, grow and produce food, provide health care, generate and deliver energy, and offer financial, communications and other services that underpin economic growth.
We are responsible to our employees who work with us throughout the world. We must provide an inclusive work environment where each person must be considered as an individual. *We must respect their diversity and dignity and recognize their merit.* They must have a sense of security, fulfillment and purpose in their jobs. Compensation must be fair and adequate and working conditions clean, orderly and safe. We must support the health and well-being of our employees and help them fulfill their family and other personal responsibilities. Employees must feel free to make suggestions and complaints. There must be equal opportunity for employment, development and advancement for those qualified. We must provide highly capable leaders and their actions must be just and ethical.	While each of our individual companies serves its own corporate purpose, we share a fundamental commitment to all of our stakeholders. We commit to: – *Delivering value to our customers.* We will further the tradition of American companies leading the way in meeting or exceeding customer expectations. – *Investing in our employees.* This starts with compensating them fairly and providing important benefits. It also includes supporting them through training and education that help develop new skills for a rapidly changing world. *We foster diversity and inclusion, dignity and respect.* – *Dealing fairly and ethically with our suppliers.* We are dedicated to serving as good partners to the other companies, large and small, that help us meet our missions.
We are responsible to the communities in which we live and work and to the world community as well. We must help people be healthier by supporting better access and care in more places around the world. We must be good citizens – support good works and charities, better health and education, and bear our fair share of taxes. We must maintain in good order the property we are privileged to use, protecting the environment and natural resources.	– *Supporting the communities in which we work.* We respect the people in our communities and protect the environment by embracing sustainable practices across our businesses. – *Generating long-term value for shareholders,* who provide the capital that allows companies to invest, grow and innovate. We are committed to transparency and effective engagement with shareholders.

Table 7.1 (continued)

Johnson & Johnson *Credo* (1943)	Roundtable Declaration (2019)
Our final responsibility is to our stockholders. Business must make a sound profit. We must experiment with new ideas. Research must be carried on, innovative programs developed, investments made for the future and mistakes paid for. New equipment must be purchased, new facilities provided and new products launched. Reserves must be created to provide for adverse times. *When we operate according to these principles, the stockholders should realize a fair return.* [Emphases mine]	Each of our stakeholders is essential. We commit to deliver value to all of them, for the future success of our companies, our communities and our country. [Emphases mine]

Source: Johnson, R.W. (1943), "Our Credo," *Johnson & Johnson website,* https://www.jnj.com/credo/, accessed on December 8, 2019,
Business Roundtable (2019), "Business Roundtable Redefines the Purpose of a Corporation to Promote 'An Economy That Serves All Americans'," *Business Roundtable,* August 19, 2019, https://www.businessroundtable.org/business-roundtable-redefines-the-purpose-of-a-corporation-to-promote-an-economy-that-serves-all-americans, accessed on December 16, 2019.

Moving from VUCA 1.0 to VUCA 2.0

Past approaches to VUCA, were reactive – Bill George, former CEO of Medtronic, called these VUCA 1.0.[55] For the future, he recommended a two-pronged approach – one that still deals with VUCA *reactively* to limit the impact of VUCA-based risk (VUCA 1.0), plus *proactively* building on VUCA 1.0 strategies to create a sustainable future – an approach he called VUCA 2.0. Stage 1 for each of the elements is reactive, designed to limit the impact of VUCA-based risk, while stage 2 is proactive, designed to create a sustainable future, despite the greater difficulties posed by VUCA now.

Volatility + Vision + Values

Stage 1 seeks to minimize the risk posed by volatility to "business as usual" models by building slack and redundancy into processes and systems, stockpiling inventory and talent on a "just in case" basis (which needs to be reconciled with "just in time" and "lean management" thinking). The desirable level of investment is determined by the level of risk.[56]

While *volatility* is a reality of business, it's far more predictable than most leaders believe. The causes of seasonal fluctuations, supply chain disruptions, natural disasters or shifts in demand are often out of your control and can lead to major month-to-month revenue or cost disruptions. But it's possible to see and heed early warning signs. *Leaders who seek clarity about internal and external conditions and track those with high potential to create disruption are better able to recognize volatile conditions and respond accordingly.*[57]   [Emphasis ours]

Stage 2 is a proactive approach to volatility, focusing on developing an "evergreen" vision that is sufficiently well crafted that it can withstand the vagaries of volatility, minimized but not eliminated by an effectively implemented stage 1:

Today's business leaders need the ability to see through the chaos to have a clear vision for their organizations. They must define the True North of their organization: its mission, values, and strategy. *They should create clarity around this True North and refuse to let external events pull them off course or cause them to neglect or abandon their mission, which must be their guiding light.*[58]   [Emphasis mine]

If the organization is to develop an "evergreen" vision and set of values which are the basis of its code of conduct it must define its mission (discussed in detail in Chapter 6). The organizational design, the number of people and their associated skills, and the processes adopted may have to change to meet new conditions, but the mission, vision, and values should not.

Uncertainty + Understanding

The traditional approach to uncertainty in VUCA 1.0 is to invest in information, to collect, interpret, and share it, supported by a knowledge management infrastructure in more sophisticated organizations. Such structural changes reduce the levels of uncertainty.[59]

Dealing with uncertainty proactively requires decision-makers to use contrarian thinking regarding business model assumptions – to listen to customers and non-customers, to engage with employees and suppliers and academics and innovation centers:

Listening only to information sources and opinions that reinforce their own views carries great risk of missing alternate points of view. Instead, leaders need to tap into myriad sources covering the full spectrum of viewpoints by engaging directly with their customers and employees to ensure they are attuned to changes in their markets. *Spending time in the marketplace, retail stores, factories, innovation centers, and research labs, or just wandering around offices talking to people is essential.*[60]   [Emphases ours]

While it makes sense for decision-makers at the top of the leadership pipeline to be involved in these processes, there are real difficulties for them in acquiring up-to-date and accurate information. "Wayfinders" build upon the reactive approach of

VUCA 1.0 to achieve the proactive approach of VUCA 2.0 by testing contrarian hypotheses in meetings and by being better at interpreting probabilities:

1. **Testing contrarian hypotheses:** The best ways to deal with uncertainty are to test contrarian hypotheses, as well as developing a range of plans or scenarios combined with appropriate pre-mortems and suitable contingency plans as a result. There are three process ways of getting around this problem to generate constructive contrarian challenge:

a. *The "Alfred Sloan Solution":* Alfred Sloan, the founder of General Motors, understood the importance of robust, constructive challenge in improving the quality of decisions. His solution to the problem, which he introduced after his first board meeting where all the directors had agreed with what was being proposed, was to ask them to return with "reasons why not" at the next board meeting:

> If we are all in agreement on the decision – then I propose we postpone further discussion of this matter until our next meeting *to give us time to develop disagreement and perhaps gain some understanding of what the decision is all about.*[61]   [Emphasis ours]

Not all committee Chairs have the self-confidence or ability to synthesize complex arguments as quickly as Alfred Sloan, and so there are very few committees that operate in this way. However, there is a process solution to this problem.

b. *Rotating "Devil's Advocacy":* The purpose of this approach is to achieve the same result as Alfred Sloan's approach:

> The advantage of such a process is clear: the ensuing discussion *focuses on all the reasons why the decision might be undesirable, highlighting what could go wrong; and as a result, forcing the board to improve the proposal to overcome identified defects, develop contingency plans in case those defects cannot be eliminated and materialize later, or to reconsider adopting the idea.*

> The benefit of making it an ad hoc rotating process, is no single [committee member] gets tarred with the negative halo of always being the naysayer 'Devil's Advocate.' Making who will be called upon to argue the case against the proposal ad hoc ensures all [committee members] are well-prepared for the discussion. *However, to be able to do their "due diligence" on proposals put before them, they will need to understand the real costs of doing business; the financial assumptions of the budget and how the objectives, KPIs and resulting targets and outcomes have been derived.*[62]   [Emphases ours]

If directors have to rely on management, the problem of information asymmetry arises, if they have to depend on external experts, there is a question of costs and they are still not off the hook, as is clear from the following words of Lord Goldsmith, the UK Attorney General, during the debate on the 2006 Companies Act:

> As with all advice, slavish reliance is not acceptable, and obtaining of outside advice does not absolve directors from exercising their judgment on the basis of such advice.[63]

In this case, there is a structural solution to the problem.

c. *Board "Cabinet Secretariat":* Fifty years ago, Unilever's Chief Executive Office (the "Special Committee") had the so-called Special Committee Secretariat to serve it. The secretariat answered to the Special Committee only. It was led by a director-level ex-line manager who understood line management issues, but who had been a senior civil servant in the Indian Civil Service before India's independence. He understood the importance of being seen to be neutral in any argument between executive directors over strategic direction and allocation of resources. His role was to create informed discussion by providing well-researched facts neutrally rather than to exercise power.[64] This structural solution provided board members with all the arguments and facts, based on a *detailed understanding of the workings of the businesses and the board dynamics they needed to challenge management* (unlike external consultants). It also allowed management to discuss their draft proposals with the secretariat that could point out where their cases were weak, sending them back to management for improvement before being finally presented to the board. It achieved the same purpose as Alfred Sloan's method, without having to wait until the next board meeting.

2. **Interpreting probabilities better:** There is plenty of evidence to suggest that human beings are bad at understanding probabilities,[65] (this is discussed in detail in Chapter 8). Given that so few people are comfortable with probabilities and that dynamic probabilistic decision trees are often used in determining which of a number of scenarios is likely to yield the best risk-adjusted expected values of the courses of action under consideration, it may be necessary for the "board cabinet secretariat" to work with management in interpreting them to directors. Then the directors may feel sufficiently confident to challenge probabilistic assumptions robustly.

Complexity + Courage + Commitment

The traditional reactive approach to dealing with complexity in VUCA 1.0 is to invest in specialists and resources to try to understand its causes and consequences better, to simplify[ii] the business by eliminating sources of complexity, and to build in redundancy so that if things go wrong there is backup to keep things going.

When things go wrong and lessons are learned, the other solution is to add in safety measures to make sure that the same mistakes cannot happen again. The problem with this approach is that the operation of the whole system is ignored:

---

ii The "elevator pitch" and instructions to have PowerPoints with only three bullets per slide that are only a dozen slides long are examples of oversimplification that ignore the "devil is in the details" which may lead to difficulties later on.

Galileo described an early example of this principle in 1638. Masons at that time would store stone columns horizontally, raised above the soil by two piles of stone. The columns often cracked in the middle under their own weight. The 'solution' was to reinforce the support with a third pile of stone in the centre. But that didn't help. The two end supports would often settle a little, and the column, balanced like a see-saw on the central pile, would then snap as the ends sagged.[66]

"Tightly coupled complex systems" create what engineers call a new "failure mode." Dealing effectively with complexity needs more than the reactive simplification of VUCA 1.0. Bill George makes the point that courage is also needed to challenge received wisdom:

Now more than ever, leaders need the courage to step up to these challenges and make audacious decisions that embody risks and often go against the grain. They cannot afford to keep their heads down, using traditional management techniques while avoiding criticism and risk-taking. In fact, their greatest risk lies in not having the courage to make bold moves. This era belongs to the bold, not the meek and timid.[67]

While it may be true that leaders need to show courage and challenge conventional wisdom, such advice should not be translated into a justification for foolhardiness.

Ambiguity + Adaptability

Ambiguity will always exist and it makes for inefficiency:

The costs of operating with ambiguity are enormous. Ambiguity in the form of a vague job posting leads to an underperforming hire. Ambiguity about the purpose of a project results in wasted time and money. Ambiguity about a customer "requirement" leads to unnecessary features that bring no benefit because the so-called "requirement" wasn't one.

And unlike volatility, uncertainty, and complexity – all genuine realities that are mainly outside of your control – ambiguity is man-made. *People create ambiguity.*
          Fortunately, they can also abolish it with clarity.[68]   [Emphases ours]

The task for "wayfinders" is to minimize the impact of ambiguity and to determine where ambiguity is permissible and where it is not. This is where clarity of "purpose" is essential, so that everybody in the organization knows what business the organization is in, and, just as important, what business it is not in. Everybody knows who the organization wishes to do business with and how, what it stands for, and how it treats its beneficiaries and employees – in other words, its "principles" or values.

Whatever is "evergreen" must be unambiguous. Consequently, the organization's "purpose" must be unambiguous and so must its "principles." Otherwise its code of conduct will be meaningless.

That does not mean, however, that there can be no adaptation to meet changing circumstances. So, in moving from VUCA 1.0 to VUCA 2.0, "wayfinders" must find a judicious blend of that which is "evergreen," clear, and unambiguous: its "purpose" and "principles"; and those factors that can be adapted to suit new conditions: its organization design, the number of employees and their desired competencies, and policies, procedures, and processes.

The need to adapt is the result of unforeseen combinations of volatility, uncertainty, and complexity. The best way to create adaptive capacity is to develop multiple business plans with strong balance sheets that do not "bet the business," where failure is survivable rather than an experience that bankrupts the business, allowing organizations to learn from trial and error.[69]

> If ever there were a need for leaders to be flexible in adapting to this rapidly changing environment, this is it. Long-range plans are often obsolete by the time they are approved. Instead, *flexible tactics are required for rapid adaptation to changing external circumstances, without altering strategic course. This is not a time for continuing the financial engineering so prevalent in the past decade. Rather, leaders need multiple contingency plans while preserving strong balance sheets to cope with unforeseen events.*[70]   [Emphasis ours]

Summary

Decision making is more complicated than ever because we do not know what the impact of the Covid-19 pandemic will be, how climate change will affect us, whether the neoliberal economy is sustainable in its current form, whether employment is sustainable, given the impact of "Industry 4.0," and how these issues will affect the political and social fabric of society. They have made dealing with VUCA and its four components of volatility, uncertainty, complexity, and ambiguity more complicated.

Volatility undermines the "business as usual" assumptions as a result of its appearance in politics, where there are more potential problems than before, in economics and social conditions, where governments have to deal with the results of Covid-19 to help economies recover from their deep downturns and revive employment. Its immediate impact is less critical in creating technological, legal, or environmental volatility.

Uncertainty leads to unpredictability which makes it essential that decision-makers avoid making irreversible decisions – an approach to decision-making that Elizabeth Tudor mastered to great effect throughout her reign. There is great political and economic uncertainty currently, but the more important long-term considerations are the effect of changes in social values, changes in demographics and the effect of social media on political discourse. Technological uncertainty, however, impacts across sectors – and in organization-specific ways. Decision-makers must decide whether potential improvement in their offers has pushed them beyond known technological limits, as a result of the "normalization of deviance" effect, without realizing it. And that instead of "pushing the envelope," they are "tearing it." Legal uncertainty only matters in a limited number of circumstances and decision-makers need to recognize that the long-term risks may outweigh the short-term rewards of doing business in conditions where legal uncertainty prevails. As far as environmental uncertainty is concerned, the long-term risks may be existential, and the short-term ones raise the cost of insurance and funding.

Complexity presents the greatest difficulty in VUCA, particularly if a system is complex and "tightly coupled." In such circumstances, decision-makers only realize what can go wrong when the system fails. Many of the systems we take for granted are not as resilient as we think. Perhaps one benefit of Covid-19 is that it is teaching decision-makers to treat complexity with the respect it deserves.

Ambiguity is a source of inefficiency. Unfortunately, decision-makers are faced with ambiguity of corporate purpose, ambiguity between stakeholder priorities, ambiguity in facts, and ambiguity in roles.

In the future, decision-makers will need to move from VUCA 1.0 to VUCA 2.0.

As far as volatility is concerned, they must reconcile being flexible when faced by volatility. They can no longer assume business as usual in changing contexts even if they remain dedicated to their mission, vision, and values.

To deal with uncertainty, decision-makers need to deploy resources to get as much information and analysis as possible, and they will have to increase their level of understanding by adopting contrarian thinking processes (the "Alfred Sloan solution," "rotating devil's advocacy," or the "board cabinet secretariat") to test their understanding of what could happen, based on a number of different scenarios, supported by strong balance sheets. They will also need to learn to interpret probabilities better (covered in Chapter 8).

As far as complexity is concerned, there are no easy answers, only hard work. *Decision-makers must master the details and this means taking the time needed to achieve a granular level of understanding instead of relying only on the executive summary.* Commitment to the business at hand is essential, as is the courage to ask the difficult questions and engage in constructive challenge so that dominant or charismatic CEOs do not get away with taking reckless risks that could destroy the business.

In dealing with ambiguity, decision-makers should use the "Five P" framework (discussed in Chapter 6) to establish where it is permissible and where it is not. At all levels of decision-making, "wayfinders" should insist on maximizing clarity: clarity of purpose, clarity of how success is defined, clarity of timelines and of accountability. They should also insist that whatever is "evergreen" – the mission, vision, and values (the organization "purpose" and "principles") – cannot be ambiguous. Everything else (organization design, staffing, and processes) is adaptable to reflect changes in context.

References

1 Charan, R., Drotter, S. and Noel, J. (2011), *The Leadership Pipeline: How to Build the Leadership Powered Company* (San Francisco, California: Jossey Bass), pp. 15–29.

2 Cambridge Dictionary, https://dictionary.cambridge.org/dictionary/english/uncertainty, accessed on November 26, 2019.

3 Zinkin, J. (2019), "Emerging Risk and Future Board: Boardroom Governance in a VUCA world," *SIDC, presentation* to B.A.T. Malaysia Berhad Board, November 27, 2019.

4 Roubini, N. (2019), "The Global Consequences of a Sino-American Cold War," *Project Syndicate,* May 20, 2019, https://www.project-syndicate.org/commentary/united-states-china-cold-war-deglob alization-by-nouriel-roubini-2019-05?barrier=accesspaylog, accessed on November 25, 2019.

5 Inman, P. (2019), "U.K. companies hit by sharpest activity drop since Brexit vote," *Guardian,* November 22, 2019, https://www.theguardian.com/business/2019/nov/22/uk-service-sector-suffers-sharpest-drop-since-brexit-vote?utm_term=RWRpdG9yaWFsX0J1c2luZXNz, accessed on November 26, 2019.

6 Caldwell, C. (2019), "The People's Emergency," *The New Republic,* April 22, 2019, https://newre public.com/article/153507/france-yellow-vests-uprising-emmanuel-macron-technocratic-insiders, accessed on November 26, 2019.

7 Horowitz, J. (2019), "Italy's Government Collapses, Turning Chaos Into Crisis," *New York Times,* August 20, 2019, https://www.nytimes.com/2019/08/20/world/europe/italy-pm-giuseppe-conte-re sign.html, accessed on November 26, 2019.

8 Karnitschnig, M. (2019), "5 Takeaways from Germany's regional elections," *Politico,* September 3, 2019, https://www.politico.eu/article/5-takeaways-regional-elections-brandenburg-saxony/, accessed on November 26, 2019.

9 "Spanish election results: Socialists win most seats, PP and Vox make huge gains, C's collapse," *The Local,* November 10, 2019, https://www.thelocal.es/20191110/spanish-election-results-exit-poll-shows-socialist-lose-seats-pp-and-vox-make-huge-gains, accessed on November 26, 2019.

10 Rashad, M., and Kalin, S. (2019), "Trump, Saudi Arabia Warn Iran Against Middle East Conflict," *Reuters,* May 19, 2019, https://www.reuters.com/article/us-saudi-oil-emirates-tanker/trump-saudi-ara bia-warn-iraq-against-middle-east-conflict-idUSKCN1SP01C, accessed on November 26, 2019.

11 Mladenov, N. (2019), "'Multi-generational tragedy' in Israel and Palestine demands political will for two-state solution," *United Nations,* October 28, 2019, https://news.un.org/en/story/2019/10/1050091, accessed on November 26, 2019.

12 "Kashmir unrest could lead Pakistan, India to 'accidental war'," *Al Jazeera,* September 10, 2019, https://www.aljazeera.com/news/2019/09/kashmir-unrest-lead-pakistan-india-accidental-war-190910140000666.html, accessed on November 26, 2019.

13 "North Korea launches two possible 'ballistic' missiles into sea, Japan says," *Reuters,* October 31, 2019, https://www.cnbc.com/2019/10/31/north-korea-launches-two-projectiles-japan-and-south-korea-say.html, accessed on November 26, 2019.

14 "Japan and South Korea promise to work on bilateral ties amid escalating trade tensions," *Reuters,* October 24, 2019, https://www.cnbc.com/2019/10/24/japan-and-korea-promise-to-work-on-bi lateral-ties-trade-tensions.html, accessed on November 26, 2019.

15 Heydarian, R. (2019), "Unopposed no more: Beijing's ambitions in the South China Sea increasingly draw U.S. attention," *South China Morning Post,* https://www.scmp.com/news/china/diplomacy/arti cle/3037095/unopposed-no-more-beijings-ambitions-south-china-sea, accessed on November 26, 2019.

16 Plokhy, S., and Sarotte, M, E. (2019), "The Shoals of Ukraine: Where American Illusions and Great Power Politics Collide," *Foreign Affairs,* November 22, 2019, https://www.foreignaffairs.com/articles/united-states/2019-11-22/shoals-ukraine, accessed on November 26, 2019.

17 Taylor, M.L. (2019), "Combating disinformation and foreign interference in democracies: Lessons from Europe," *Brookings,* July 31, 2019, https://www.brookings.edu/blog/techtank/2019/07/31/combating-disinformation-and-foreign-interference-in-democracies-lessons-from-europe/, accessed on November 26, 2019.

18 "The U.S. and Russia: A Lesson in Asymmetry," *Stratfor Worldview,* July 28, 2017, https://worldview.stratfor.com/article/us-and-russia-lesson-asymmetry, accessed on November 26, 2019.

19 Judson, J. (2019), "Do the Baltics need more U.S. military support to deter Russia?" *Defense News,* July 16, 2019, https://www.defensenews.com/land/2019/07/15/do-the-baltics-need-more-us-military-support-to-deter-russia/, accessed on November 26, 2019.

20 Smale, A. et al. (2015), "Migrants Cross Austria Border from Hungary," *New York Times,* September 4, 2015, https://www.nytimes.com/2015/09/05/world/europe/migrant-crisis-hungary.html?hp&action=click&pgtype=Homepage&module=first-column-region&reg, accessed on November 26, 2019.

21 Doctors Without Borders (2019), "The facts about the humanitarian crisis in Mexico and Central America," February 5, 2019, https://www.doctorswithoutborders.org/what-we-do/news-stories/news/facts-about-humanitarian-crisis-mexico-and-central-america, accessed on November 2019.

22 Goodman, P.S. (2019), "Turkey's Long, Painful Economic Crisis Grinds On," *New York Times,* July 8, 2019, https://www.nytimes.com/2019/07/08/business/turkey-economy-crisis.html, accessed on November 26, 2019.

23 Perez, S., and Dube, R. (2019), "Why Argentina Faces an Economic Crisis. Again." *Wall Street Journal,* September 25, 2019, https://www.wsj.com/articles/why-argentina-faces-an-economic-crisis-again-11569422388, accessed on November 26, 2019.

24 "Six charts that show how hard U.S. sanctions have hit Iran," *BBC News,* May 2, 2019, https://www.bbc.com/news/world-middle-east-48119109, accessed on November 26, 2019.

25 "Financial crises occur about once every decade," *The Financial Times,* March 23, 2015, https://www.ft.com/content/5148cd1e-cf01-11e4-893d-00144feab7de, accessed on November 26, 2019.

26 Nye, J.S. (2018), "Is Fake News Here to Stay?" *Project Syndicate,* December 5, 2018, https://www.project-syndicate.org/commentary/fake-news-part-of-the-background-by-joseph-s–nye-2018-12, accessed on December 2, 2019.

27 Rueb, E. S., and Taylor, D. B. (2019), "Obama on Call-Out Culture: 'That's Not Activism,'" *The New York Times,* October 30, 2019, https://www.nytimes.com/2019/10/31/us/politics/obama-woke-cancel-culture.html, accessed on April 5, 2021.

28 Schumpeter, J.A. (1950), *Capitalism, Socialism and Democracy, Third Edition* (New York: HarperCollins).

29 Labour Party (2019), "It's Time for Real Change," https://labour.org.uk/manifesto/, accessed on November 26, 2019.

30 Copeland, R. (2019), "Breakup of Tech Giants 'On the Table,' U.S. Antitrust Chief Says," *The Wall Street Journal,* October 22, 2019, https://www.wsj.com/articles/breakup-of-tech-giants-on-the-table-u-s-antitrustchief-says-11571765689, accessed on November 26, 2019.

31 Meredith, S., and Browne, R. (2018), "All you need to know about Fox, Comcast and Disney's battle to own Sky," *CNBC,* September 20, 2018, https://www.cnbc.com/2018/07/18/disney-comcast-and-fox-all-you-need-to-know-about-one-of-the-biggest.html, accessed on November 26, 2019.

32 Rainey, R. (2019), "How Elizabeth Warren would boost labor rights," *Politico,* October 3, 2019, https://www.politico.com/news/2019/10/03/how-elizabeth-warren-would-boost-labor-rights-024199, accessed on November 26, 2019; Labour Party (2019), op. cit.

33 Stiglitz, J.E. (2010), "U.S. Does Not Have Capitalism Now: Stiglitz," *CNBC,* January 19, 2010, https://www.cnbc.com/id/34921639, accessed on December 2, 2019.

34 Edelman (2018), "2018 Trust Barometer: The State of Trust in Business," p. 5.

35 Jackson H., and Ormerod, P. (2017), "Was Michael Gove right? Have we had enough of experts?" *Prospect,* July 14, 2017, https://www.prospectmagazine.co.uk/magazine/michael-gove-right-about-experts-not-trust-them-academics-peer-review, accessed on December 2, 2019.

36 Rosen, R, J. (2011), "Truth, lies and the Internet," *The Atlantic,* December 29, 2011, https://www.theatlantic.com/technology/archive/2011/12/truth-lies-and-the-internet/250569/, accessed on December 3, 2019.

37 Welch, J. https://www.goodreads.com/quotes/185636-if-the-rate-of-change-on-the-outside-exceeds-the, accessed on September 27, 2018.

38 Christensen, C. (1997), *The Innovator's Dilemma* (Boston, MA: Harvard Business Review Press).

39 Paur, J. (2009), "Boeing's 787 Is as Innovative Inside as Outside," *Wired,* December 24, 2009, https://www.wired.com/2009/12/boeing-787-dreamliner-interior/, accessed on March 12, 2020.

40 Withey, P. (2019), "The deHavilland Comet Disaster," *Aerospace Engineering,* July 1, 2019, https://aerospaceengineeringblog.com/dehavilland-comet-disaster/, accessed on December 5, 2019.

41 Meigs, J. B. (2016), "Blame BP for Deepwater Horizon. But Direct Your Outrage to the Actual Mistake," *Slate,* September 30, 2016, http://www.slate.com/articles/health_and_science/science/2016/09/bp_is_to_blame_for_deepwater_horizon_but_its_mistake_was_actually_years.html, accessed on July 26, 2018.

42 Petroski, H. (2012), *To Forgive Design: Understanding Failure* (Cambridge, Mass: Belknap Press).

43 Sibly, P.G., and Walker, A.C. (1977), "Structural Accidents and Their Causes," *Proceedings of the Institution of Civil Engineers,* 62, Part 1: pp. 191–208, quoted in Petroski (2012), op. cit., p. 339.

44 Ibid.

45 Ibid.

46 Fenwick, M., and Wrbka, S. (2016), "The Shifting Meaning of Legal Certainty," Fenwick, M., Wrbka, S. (eds.), *Legal Certainty in a Contemporary Context* (Singapore: Springer), https://link.springer.com/chapter/10.1007/978-981-10-0114-7_1, accessed on December 6, 2019.

47 Maxeiner, J.R. (2008) "Some Realism About Legal Certainty in Globalization of the Rule of Law," *Houston Journal of International Law,* Vol. 31, No. 1 (2008), pp. 27–46.

48 Lombrana, L. M. (2019), "Global Warming Prediction Sounds Alarm for Climate Fight," *Bloomberg Climate Changed,* December 3, 2019, https://www.bloomberg.com/news/articles/2019-12-03/global-temperature-headed-toward-5-degree-increase-wmo-says?utm_medium=email&utm_source=newsletter&utm_term=191205&utm_campaign=climatechanged, accessed on December 6, 2019.

49 Harford, T. (2011), *Adapt: Why Success Always Starts With Failure* (London: Little Brown), pp. 185–186.

50 Perrow, C. (2007), *The Next Catastrophe* (Princeton: Princeton University Press), p. 213.

51 Ibid., p. 212.

52 Dirks, G. (2020), in an email to the author on January 20, 2020.

53 Perrow, C. (2011), *The Next Catastrophe: Reducing Our Vulnerabilities to Natural, Industrial and Terrorist Disasters* (Princeton: Princeton University Press), p. 144.

54 Dirks, G. (2020), in an email reply to the author on January 21, 2020.

55 George, B. (2017), "VUCA 2.0: A Strategy for Steady Leadership In An Unsteady World," *Forbes,* February 17, 2017, https://www.forbes.com/sites/hbsworkingknowledge/2017/02/17/vuca-2-0-a-strategy-for-steady-leadership-in-an-unsteady-world/#85e137713d84, accessed on December 16, 2019.

56 Bennett, N., and Lemoine, G.J. (2014), "What VUCA Really Means For You," *HBR,* January-February 2014 Issue, https://hbr.org/resources/images/article_assets/hbr/1401/F1401C_A_LG.gif, accessed on December 18, 2019.

57 Martin, K. (2019), "Managing VUCA IS Easier Than You Think," *Forbes,* April 25, 2019, https://www.forbes.com/sites/karenmartin/2019/04/25/managing-vuca-is-easier-than-you-think/?sh=1d905a3757ea, accessed on April 5, 2021.

58 George, B. (2017), "VUCA 2.0: A Strategy For Steady Leadership In An Unsteady World," *HBS Working Knowledge,* featured in *Forbes*, February 17, 2017, https://www.forbes.com/sites/hbswor kingknowledge/2017/02/17/vuca-2-0-a-strategy-for-steady-leadership-in-an-unsteady-world/ #7d64970d13d8, accessed on December 19, 2019.

59 Bennett and Lemoine (2014), op. cit.

60 George (2017), op. cit.

61 Sloan, A., quoted in Zinkin (2019), op. cit., p. 341.

62 Zinkin (2019), op. cit., p. 341.

63 Lord Goldsmith, U.K. Attorney General quoted in Zinkin (2019), op. cit., p. 58.

64 Based on conversations between the author's late father, who headed up the Special Committee Secretariat, and the author.

65 Sorrel, C. (2016), "People Are Really Bad at Probability, And This Study Shows How Easy it to Trick Us," *Fast Company,* June 27, 2016, https://www.fastcompany.com/3061263/people-are-really-bad-at-probability-and-this-study-shows-how-easy-it-is-to-trick-us, accessed on December 22, 2019.

66 Harford (2011), op. cit., p. 187.

67 George (2017), op. cit.

68 Ibid.

69 Harford (2011), op. cit., pp. 18–20.

70 George (2017), op. cit.

Chapter 8
Reconciling VUCA with the Need for Simplicity

In Chapter 7, we showed how VUCA poses difficulties for "wayfinders" and suggested ways of improving decision-making by moving from a reactive VUCA 1.0 to a proactive VUCA 2.0. Why is dealing with VUCA so difficult? The answer lies in our evolution as a social species which affects our ability to embrace change, the ways we process information, make decisions, and in how, in seeking to avoid complexity and ambiguity in communications, we can over-simplify.

Humans as a Social Species

Even in cultures that claim to value individualism above community (discussed in Chapter 9), people have always been members of collectives. As anthropologists and marketeers know, individuals are members of many collectives simultaneously, defined by: humanity as a whole; by nation, ethnic group, tribe, family, religion, language and gender within and across nations; by wealth, class, education, and disposable income; within the workplace by occupation, roles and responsibilities; by communities, voluntary associations, hobbies and interests; by self-proclaimed identity and chosen ideology; and also by lifestyle, lifestage, etc. Collectives manifest as interest groups that may, or may not, cooperate to achieve common goals, or fight to defend their interests.

Just as physical evolution is the result of the exploitation of new niches arising from continual environmental change, social entities, including human collectives, display *competition*, *cooperation*, and *altruism* in acquiring resources needed to thrive in changing conditions.[1] Success is ultimately measured in terms of a collective's long-term survival, and share of the niche occupied.

Competition

Competition is the first pillar of collective success at the cellular, genetic, collective, and species level.[2] It is popular to assume all that matters for collectives to flourish is that they win in a "social Darwinian"[i] "survival of the fittest," and that consequently

---

i Social Darwinian thinking is not Charles Darwin's, but Herbert Spencer's idea. It was popular in the US in the late 19th century as justifying the rampant inequality of the "Gilded Age":

> In 1889, seven-tenths of the national wealth belonged to one three-hundredths of the people. After acquiring the means of obtaining such riches, it was only natural that this faction of Americans strove to keep their new lives. In order to do so, they had to look for a justification to explain the problems that were peaking [sic] through the gilded cover of success.

https://doi.org/10.1515/9783110707878-011

the selfish, self-centered behavior of narcissistic leadership and followership is the ideal. Such a superficial analysis ignores the role of cooperation, altruism, and adaptability in the success of the collective.

Cooperation

Cooperation is the second pillar of success and comes in two forms: (1) collaboration, and (2) alliances.

1. **Collaboration** is not quite the same as cooperation (though most people and dictionaries regard them as synonymous). The difference is shown in Table 8.1.

Table 8.1: Cooperation and Collaboration Defined.

Cooperation is defined as: British English (Collins English Dictionary)	Collaboration is defined as: British English (Collins English Dictionary)
1. "Joint operation or action"	1. "The act of working together to produce a piece of work, especially a book or some research"
2. "Assistance or willingness to assist"	2. "A piece of work that has been produced as the result of people or groups working together"
3. "The combination of consumers, workers, farmers, etc., in activities usually embracing production, distribution, or trade"	3. "The act of helping an enemy who is occupying your country during a war"[4]
4. "Beneficial but inessential interaction between two species in a community"	
American English: (Collins English Dictionary)	**American English** (Merriam Webster Thesaurus)
1. "The act of cooperating, joint effort or operation"	1. "The state of having shared interests or efforts (as in social or business matters)"
2. "The association of a number of people in an enterprise for mutual benefits or profits"	2. "The work and activity of a number of persons who individually contribute toward the efficiency of the whole"[5]
3. "An interaction between organisms that is largely beneficial to all those participating"[3]	

Many of the elite faction of America found this justification in social Darwinism and used the social theory to excuse the exploitation of workers, the poor living conditions, the corruption, racism, imperialism, and the general use of other's failures to promote progress. [Emphases ours]

Vales, S. (2004), ""Everybody Drinks Water": Mark Twain's Critique of Social Darwinism," *Honors Projects* Paper 2, https://digitalcommons.iwu.edu/history_honproj/2/, accessed on September 3, 2020.

From a work perspective, the difference between cooperation and collaboration is that collaboration requires that all parties involved understand how the different roles and responsibilities fit together in delivering a project with agreed milestones, accountabilities, and outcomes:

> To start truly *collaborating*, here are two steps that you should take:
>
> First, consider the goal you're trying to achieve. Map out the end-to-end work that you think will be needed to get the outcome you want. What will your team be responsible for? What will you need from other teams in the organization? As you create this map, *sketch out the possible sequencing of activities and timing that might be required. You want to create an explicit framework that will serve as a collaboration contract. When people know what's needed, in what form, and by when, they can then tell you whether it's possible or not, and then you can have a real dialogue about what can be done.*
>
> Second, convene a working session with all of the required collaborators from different areas of the company to review, revise, and make commitments to this collaboration contract . . . *get all of the needed collaborators in the room together as early as possible to work through the plans, make adjustments, and find ways to share resources and align incentives.*[6]   [Emphases ours]

To overcome the potential internal barriers created by departmentalization, departments must collaborate so that participants in a joint project understand what all are required to do and by when; the resource implications and bottlenecks that have to be overcome to complete their agreed joint projects to specification, on time, and on budget; and have an agreed upon project plan timeline with its critical path and agreed accountabilities. Cooperation alone allows things to go wrong at the handover interfaces.

2. **Alliances** are where there is

> . . . an arrangement between two or more people, groups, or countries by which they agree to work together to achieve something.[7]

Altruism

Altruism is "disinterested and selfless concern for the well-being of others" when dealing with people, and as "behavior of an animal that benefits another at its own expense."[8] It is sometimes suggested that altruism only occurs in humans,[9] but altruism is observed among animals and insects and in the plant and fungal kingdoms.[10]

Such behavior is of no benefit to the individual animal or insect, but does benefit the collective through the survival of genes, and/or memes. Similar behavior exists at the cellular level.[11] Altruism, like competition, and cooperation creates an evolutionary advantage for genes or memes ensuring their long-term survival.

How Humans Adapt to Change

Adaptability is a biological and cultural feature ensuring long-term survival. When examining human collectives and their ability to adapt, we need to consider the barriers to, and enablers of, change.

1. **Barriers to Change:** The most important barriers are previous success, and the resulting ideology, cultural features, vested interests, inertia, and ignorance:

a. *Ideology can be either a barrier or an enabler.* It is a barrier to change when it is used to promote or defend existing vested interests. It is an enabler when it forms the basis of reform or revolution. "Ideology" involves the adoption of "superordinate goals," which are appeals to altruism encouraging individuals to consider the interests of the collective.

   Perhaps the earliest recorded example of ideology as both a barrier to, and enabler of, change was Socrates' "Noble Lie" in Plato's *Republic,* where he proposed a foundational myth to justify a ruling hierarchy,[12] similar to a caste system.[13]

b. *Cultural differences:* Every societal organization has its own foundation myth:

   > All human groups operate around shared narratives, which create identity, meaning, and core values and shape the epistemology through which they interact with the broader environment. All these are deeply anchored in the minds of its members, and frame their outlook, their opinions and their decisions, consciously or unconsciously.[14]

These shared narratives (memes) shape behavior, even to the point of followers/members of the collective being willing to lose their lives for apparently little in return. The foundation myth for any culture is likely to be a major barrier to change, best expressed as the legacy effect where people's reaction to any suggestion of change is "That is not who we are!" or "That is not how we do things!" or "That would be a violation of our values!" Cultural differences can create serious impediments to change through misunderstandings arising from five differences in belief systems, and behavioral axioms (discussed in Chapter 9).

c. *Vested interests:* Machiavelli was quite clear about the importance of vested interests as a barrier to change proposed by challengers to the status quo:

   > The innovator makes enemies of all those who prospered under the old order, and only lukewarm support is forthcoming from those who would prosper under the new. Their support is lukewarm partly from fear of their adversaries, who have existing laws on their side, and partly because men are generally incredulous, never really trusting new things unless they have tested them by experience. In consequence, whenever those who oppose changes can do so, they attack vigorously, and the defence made by the others is only lukewarm . . .[15]   [Emphasis ours]

   In meetings, people in authority can hinder change by using eleven techniques to watch out for depending on their positions and the context[16] shown in Table 8.2.

Table 8.2: Eleven Techniques to Hinder Change.

---

1. Using meetings to slow things down
2. Insisting on "my way or the highway" in discussions
3. Putting on Edward De Bono's "black hat"[17] to criticize things before they happen and shut ideas down
4. Misleading people by being too nice to them so they do not realize they must change
5. Thinking that participants have agreed to what is being proposed when they have not
6. Emphasizing the past and heritage at the expense of thinking positively about the future
7. Valuing contributions to the discussion based on seniority/rank of the speaker (especially in "high power distance"[18] cultures)
8. Defending their silos (their micro-collective) to the detriment of the organization (the macro-collective)
9. Adopting a top-down style of management that demotivates/alienates the people who have to make the policies work
10. Attacking speakers personally rather than discussing how to build on their ideas
11. Sowing dissension between participants

---

d. *Inertia and ignorance* are powerful forces to prevent change, particularly when reinforced by fear of the unknown and of failure.[19] Ignorance prevents change as a result of lack of understanding that there are other ways of being, and doing. Inertia results from individuals' unawareness of their heuristics, which prevent them from thinking differently. "There are three levels of an organization's ability to change:

> i. The slowest to change is the collective knowledge that is shared between the members of the community involved . . . The main barrier to such change is that *the perspective of the community is limited by the things it has never thought about and which it therefore has no way to describe, analyze or conceptualize.* Breaking through that barrier is itself a major invention/innovation. But there can also be conscious barriers, for example through the protection of intellectual property rights.
>
> ii. At the level of the individual one has to take tacit knowledge ("know-how") into account, which has either been subsumed under more conscious conceptual knowledge and customs or resides in the physical, neuro-muscular behavior of the human body. *It is difficult to change as it is not embedded in our conscious memory but is exercised as routine, without conscious thought.*
>
> iii. But the individual also has conscious knowledge ('know that'), which is subject to conscious learning and is therefore the easiest and quickest to change. It actively involves the conscious mind, planning and changing behavior. *Yet one must remember that such conscious knowledge is also limited by its boundary with the unknown–those processes, questions, and challenges that one has never thought about. It is in this domain that changes are made most easily.*[20] [Emphases ours]

VUCA only makes matters worse, as will become clear, when we discuss the impact of neuroscience on how people make decisions.

2. **Enablers of Change:** The three most important enablers of change are megatrends, "ideas whose time has come," "way-finders" capable of overcoming the barriers to change, and effective implementation (discussed in detail in Chapter 9).

a. *Megatrends:* These are long-term changes that affect the relevance and sustainability of the organization or collective. Sustainability presents four challenges that require organizations to consider changing what they do. They are: 1) climate change; 2) the possibility that globalization is in reverse as a result of the pandemic on the one hand, and the protectionist approaches to trade on the other; 3) the challenge to employment and employability, accelerated by the pandemic and the advent of "Industry 4.0"[ii] and 4) the viability of the "social contract"[iii] everywhere, highlighted by the rise in inequality, and the selective way climate change and the Covid-19 pandemic affect the poorest and most disadvantaged in society.

Whether organizations realize it or not, the pressures for change arising from megatrends, coupled with changes in demographics are irresistible. Organizations will change or fail.

---

ii "Industry 4.0" refers to the impending fourth industrial revolution created by the adoption of automation and artificial intelligence.

iii **Social contract**, in political philosophy, *an actual or hypothetical compact, or agreement, between the ruled and their rulers, defining the rights and duties of each.* In primeval times, according to the theory, individuals were born into an anarchic state of nature, which was happy or unhappy according to the particular version. They then, by exercising natural reason, formed a society (and a government) by means of a contract among themselves.

> . . . Social-contract theories had their greatest currency in the 17th and 18th centuries and are associated with such philosophers as the Englishmen Thomas Hobbes and John Locke and the Frenchman Jean-Jacques Rousseau. What distinguished these theories of political obligation from other doctrines of the period was their attempt to justify and delimit political authority on the grounds of individual self-interest and rational consent. *By comparing the advantages of organized government with the disadvantages of the state of nature, they showed why and under what conditions government is useful and ought therefore to be accepted by all reasonable people as a voluntary obligation.* These conclusions were then reduced to the form of a social contract, from which it was supposed that all the essential rights and duties of citizens could be logically deduced.   [Emphasis ours]

Editors of Encyclopaedia Britannica (2019), "Social Contract," *Encyclopaedia Britannica, Inc.,* August 5, 2019, https://www.britannica.com/topic/social-contract, accessed on September 3, 2020.

A gradual change in economic orthodoxy that may take decades to manifest also constitutes a "megatrend," like a glacier, it creates ineluctable pressure to reinterpret ideas in response:

> Politicians, administrators, citizens, business leaders, political activists, and the media may not make intellectual consistency their primary concern, but they do understand and frame their arguments and plans in light of broad understandings about how the world works and should work. Opinions and beliefs may be guided by material needs or desires, but material needs and desires are likewise influenced by intellectual understandings. *Ideas play a critical role by putting a thumb on the scale in favor of some arguments and against others, they reshape the world, if not perfectly in their own image, then still in ways that are powerfully different from how the world would look without them.*[21] [Emphasis ours]

Megatrends affect politics and the economy as societies struggle to adapt to changes. There will be new ideas on how best to respond changing the role of government, emphasizing the importance of public health, and redefining which roles and jobs in society are truly essential.

b. *Ideas whose time has come:* Pressures created by megatrends force the re-examination of assumptions and finding solutions to new problems, breaking the mental prison created by the "basin of attraction,"[22] reflecting myth and legacy. As a result, the "new normal" will encourage the adoption of ideas whose time has come, a phenomenon best expressed by Victor Hugo when he wrote:

> There is one thing stronger than all the armies in the world, and that is an Idea whose time has come[23]

There is, however, an important caveat regarding the likelihood of new ideas becoming paradigm shifts that change the way people think about the world:

> The political world of make-believe mingles with the real world in strange ways, for the make-believe world may often mold the real one. In order to be viable, *in order to serve its purpose, [however,] a fiction must bear some resemblance to fact. If it strays too far from fact, the willing suspension of disbelief collapses.* And conversely it may collapse if facts stray too far from the fiction.[24] [Emphasis ours]

For example, independence from colonial powers after 1945 was "an idea whose time had come" as result of three factors:

i. The US actively undermining the former colonial powers' attempts to reassert their dominion.[25]

ii. The realization that white men were not superior after all – the result of the Japanese defeating the Russians in 1905[26] and the Americans, Dutch, French, and British and their dramatic capture of their East and Southeast Asian colonies in 1941.[27]

iii. The exhaustion of the European colonial powers after World War II.[28]

The unifying idea of the leaders of independence movements across Asia and Africa was freedom from occupying colonial powers and rejection of their cultural manifestations (language, monuments, and history) in the hope that what would replace them would be a clear unified new national identity. In almost every case, the dreams of the leaders and supporters of independence movements were not achieved because their struggles were more *coalitions against* an outdated idea rather than *coalitions for implementing* a new vision:

> Considering all that independence seemed to promise – popular rule, rapid economic growth, social equality, cultural regeneration, national greatness and, above all, an end to the ascendancy of the West – *it is not surprising that its actual advent has been anticlimactic. It is not that nothing happened, that a new era has not been entered. Rather, that era having been entered, it is necessary now to live in it rather than merely imagine it, and that is inevitably a deflating experience.*
>
> The signs of this darkened mood are everywhere: in nostalgia for the emphatic personalities and well-made dramas of the revolutionary struggle, in disenchantment with party politics, parliamentarism, bureaucracy, and new class of soldiers, clerks, and local powers, in uncertainty of direction, ideological weariness . . . *a dawning realization that things are more complicated than they look, that social, economic, and political problems, once thought to be mere reflexes of colonial rule, to disappear when it disappeared, have less superficial roots.*[29]
>
> [Emphases ours]

This insight is about the structural, and contextual impediments to achieving the vision of charismatic "great men," who might have been great visionaries, but were poor implementers because *the reality is that governing is not the same as rebelling, campaigning, or philosophizing.*[iv,30]

Ideas may lie dormant for decades, even centuries, as the Renaissance proved, only to spring into life where the economic and cultural conditions are favorable, starting slowly but growing to become an irresistible force.

The video in 2011 of a young Tunisian setting himself on fire, desperate as a result of long-term economic problems, was the meme that triggered the failed Arab Spring in Egypt and Syria. The video of the last nine minutes of George Floyd's life was the meme that revitalized "Black Lives Matter," crystallizing systemic racial injustice.

Just as super-spreader incidents turned a local Covid-19 epidemic in Wuhan into a global pandemic, so the video memes in Tunis and Minneapolis were spread by social media to "infect" the minds of millions elsewhere. Such memes reflect ideology as a response to stress, similar to the causes of the French Revolution:

> In one sense. . .ideology is a response to strain. But now we are including *cultural* as well as social and psychological strain. *It is a loss of orientation that most directly gives rise to ideological activity, an inability . . . to comprehend the universe of civic rights and responsibilities in which one finds oneself located . . .* The reason why the French Revolution was, at least up to its time, the greatest incubator of extremist ideologies, "progressive" and "reactionary," in

---

iv Plato's "Letter VII" provides an insight into the power struggle in contemporary Sicilian Syracuse and his own failure to put into practice his theory of philosopher-king when he was adviser to the tyrant Dionysius. Plato, *Phaedrus and Letters VII And VIII* (London: Penguin Books, 1973), pp. 115–150.

human history was not that either personal insecurity or social disequilibrium were deeper or more persuasive than at many early periods – though they were deep and pervasive enough – but because the central organizing principle of political life, the divine right of kings, was destroyed. *It is a confluence of sociopsychological strain and an absence of cultural resources by means of which to make sense of the strain, each exacerbating the other, that sets the stage for the rise of systematic (political, moral, or economic) ideologies.*[31]   [Emphases ours]

The Arab Spring and Black Lives Matter have in common that they have no central administrative/managerial driving force. This is their strength in protest (nothing to decapitate), but, in the case of the Arab Spring, their fatal flaw in government. For memes to do more than infect millions of human minds to the detriment of their hosts, they need channels of effective communication (transmission), provided by social media. To move from being an emotional driving force to effective government, they need the organizing principle of effective leadership.

c. *Effective leaders*: Effective leaders understand the importance of responding to ever-changing context (discussed in Chapter 7) by reconciling two types of leadership with deploying managerial skills (discussed in Chapter 9). They appreciate there is more to being effective than relying on charisma:

> *The enormous concentration of social energies that charismatic leadership can, whatever its other defects, clearly accomplish, dissolves when such leadership disappears.* The passing of the generation of prophet-liberators in the last decade has been nearly as momentous, if not quite as dramatic, an event in the history of the new states as was their appearance in the thirties, forties, and fifties.[32]   [Emphasis ours]

There are structural and contextual impediments to achieving the goals of "great men" who might have been great visionaries, but poor implementers. To be effective in governing, "great men" have to be good organizers as well as charismatic visionaries, delegating tasks to competent followers who make the difference between fantasy and reality. As a result, few historians now endorse the "Great Man" theory as a complete explanation of history.

> Most historians grafting away in the archives will end up taking a position of pragmatic compromise, which acknowledges the power of individuals but makes sense of it through contextualisation . . .[33]

This raises the question: "Why are the ideas of charismatic and populist leaders so powerful?"

Epidemiology provides part of the answer by explaining how ideas are transmitted. Great prestige leaders are "super-spreaders of ideas" or of memes that colonize the minds of others, as "ideological-cultural viruses," that propagate and spread independently of their originators.[34] For example, Plato's transformation of Socrates' life and teachings; St. Paul's and St. Peter's transformation of Christianity after the death of Jesus;[35] the transformation of Buddha's agnostic ethical teachings into religion by his disciples; the different adaptations by Lenin, Mao,

Castro, and Ho Chi Minh of Marx's ideas; Gandhi's ideas put into practice by Nehru; or Martin Luther King's ideas transformed into Black Lives Matter fifty years after his death.

How Humans Make Decisions

Neuroscience helps explain how and why followers adopt ideas of leaders. The human brain has evolved over millennia to minimize the effort of processing information – to reduce cognitive load:

> Cognitive load that learners experience can be intrinsic, extraneous or germane . . . The level of intrinsic load for a particular task is assumed to be determined by the inherent difficulty of a certain topic and the level of element interactivity of the learning material in relation to a student's prior knowledge. *The more elements that interact, the more intrinsic processing is required for coordinating and integrating the material and the higher the working memory load* . . . Working memory load is not only imposed by the intrinsic complexity of the material that needs to be learned, it can also be imposed by the instructional design. For instance, unclear instructional procedures can impose extraneous load. Extraneous processing means that the learner engages in cognitive processing that does not support the learning objective.[36]   [Emphasis ours]

While this quote refers specifically to students and their ability to learn, the principles seem to apply to people in general when they are required to process information. The brain has to work harder,

> the more elements that interact, the more intrinsic processing is required for coordinating and integrating the material and the higher the working memory load.

It also has to work harder in order to make sense of the environment if instructions or messaging are unclear or confused, and it can be distracted by outside influences that have little to do with the task at hand. This has led it to split its work into two "systems" and in turn to the use of heuristics and biased decision-making.

System 1 and System 2

We like to believe we make decisions rationally, choosing between different points of view based on facts and logic. This postulated approach is largely illusory because of heuristics (mental shortcuts), biases (prejudices based on experiences), and the salience (relevance) of particular stimuli in particular situations.

Taking the time needed to evaluate the threat and decide whether to "fight or flee," could, and usually did, make the difference between life and death. As a result, the human brain developed unconscious, instinctive processes (System 1) to respond immediately to a situation that might be threatening. These subconscious processes are automatic and consume very little energy:

To survive physically or psychologically, we sometimes need to react automatically to a speeding taxi as we step off the curb or to the subtle facial cues of an angry boss. That automatic mode of thinking, not under voluntary control, contrasts with the need to slow down and deliberately fiddle with pencil and paper when working through an algebra problem.[37]

The unconscious mind works independently of the conscious mind (System 2) and is in "always on" mode, whereas the conscious mind only operates when it is asked to:

Systems 1 and 2 are both active whenever we are awake. System 1 runs automatically and System 2 is normally in a comfortable low-effort mode, in which only a fraction of its capacity is engaged. System 1 continuously generates suggestions for System 2: impressions, intuitions, intentions, and feelings. *If endorsed by System 2, impressions and intuitions turn into beliefs, and impulses turn into voluntary actions. When all goes smoothly, which is most of the time, System 2 adopts the suggestions of System 1 with little or no modification.*[38,v]   [Emphasis ours]

System 2's processing of facts, using logic and making connections between different data points is hard work,[39] creating a heavier cognitive effort and, as a result, requires more oxygen and glucose for the brain, which is why System 2 normally operates in low-effort mode, endorsing whatever System 1 comes up with. This division of labor between System 1 and System 2 is efficient and works well most of the time. System 1 works well *most of the time* but not all the time, because although its models of familiar situations are accurate, as are its short-term predictions, and its responses to challenges and threats are quick and appropriate, there are times when the existence of biases creates errors in specific conditions that System 2 needs to correct. One of the most important roles of System 2 is to stop people from acting on impulse and regain self-control.

When System 1 gets into difficulty and cannot provide satisfactory answers because its assumptions are violated, System 2 switches into high-energy mode. This happens when a problem requires working out to get to an answer, as in algebra or geometry or when an event is detected that does not fit with the unconscious expectations of System 1 – for example, Bugs Bunny cannot be seen in Disneyland and gorillas do not cross basketball courts in the middle of a game.

Yet when test subjects were shown mocked-up images of Bugs Bunny shaking hands with tourists in Disneyland, *some 40 percent subsequently recalled a personal experience of meeting Bugs Bunny in Disneyland.*[40]   [Emphases ours]

Researchers asked subjects to count the number of times ball players with white shirts pitched a ball back and forth in a video. *Most subjects were so thoroughly engaged in watching white shirts that they failed to notice a black gorilla that wandered across the scene and paused in the middle to beat his chest.* They had their noses so buried in their work that they didn't even see the gorilla.[41]   [Emphasis ours]

---

v The latest developments of Kahneman's theory are more complicated, but we think that the simplified presentation here provides useful insights to practitioners.

The gorilla experiment demonstrates that some attention is needed for the surprising stimulus to be detected. Surprise then activates and orients your attention: you will stare, and you will search your memory for a story that makes sense of the surprising event. System 2 is also credited with the continuous monitoring of your own behavior – the control that keeps you polite when you are angry, and alert when you are driving at night.[42]

Conflict between Systems 1 and 2 creates problems. It is logically impossible for the test subjects to have shaken hands with Bugs Bunny in Disneyland and yet they could remember meeting him there personally, somehow rationalizing to themselves after the event how that could be the case. Equally, in the case of the gorilla, the focus of System 2 was on the complicated task of counting the number of times the ball was being pitched, leaving no "space" for watching out for the gorilla. The mental effort of focusing created the equivalent of tunnel vision, blocking out the gorilla. It may help to compare and contrast the types of activity that are typical for each system shown in Table 8.3.

Table 8.3: System 1 and 2 Activities Compared.

System 1 (on "Autopilot")	System 2 (Requiring Effort and Concentration)
1. Detect that one object is more distant than another	1. Brace for the starter gun in a race
2. Orient to the source of a sudden sound	2. Focus on the gorilla in the baseball game
3. Complete the phrase "bread and . . ."	3. Focus on the voice of a particular person in a crowded and noisy room
4. Make a "disgusted face" when shown a horrible picture	4. Search memory to identify a surprising sound
5. Detect hostility in a voice	5. Maintain a faster walking speed than is natural for you
6. Answer 2 + 2 = ?	6. Monitor the appropriateness of your behavior in a social situation
7. Read words on large billboards	7. Count the occurrences of the letter "a" in a page of text
8. Drive a car on an empty road	8. Compare two washing machines for overall value
9. Find a strong move in chess (if you are a chess master)	9. Fill out a tax form

Table 8.3 (continued)

System 1 (on "Autopilot")	System 2 (Requiring Effort and Concentration)
10. Understand simple sentences	10. Check the validity of a complex logical argument
11. Recognize that a "meek and tidy soul with a passion for detail" resembles an occupational stereotype	

Source: Based on Kahneman, D. (2012), "Of 2 Minds: How Fast and Slow Thinking Shape Perception and Choice [Excerpt]," *Scientific American,* June 15, 2012, https://www.scientificamerican.com/arti cle/kahneman-excerpt-thinking-fast-and-slow/, accessed on August 31, 2020.

Heuristics and Sources of Inappropriate Decision-Making

The need to optimize the amount of energy and work done by the human brain means that we rely mainly on System 1 (the unconscious mind) rather than System 2 (the conscious mind). This manifests in two ways: operating on autopilot, for example when driving on a route we know by heart and, more important, by adopting useful sets of heuristics that normally allow us to deal with situations without applying the amount of work needed for cognitive processing demanded by System 2.

Most of the time, this works well, but sometimes the heuristics (shortcuts or rules of thumb) we use mislead us so that we end up making wrong decisions and being unwilling to recognize our mistakes. The causes of error are (1) the "rush to solve," (2) the cognitive biases that System 1 employs as rules of thumb, (3) rhetoric and logical fallacies, and (4) cognitive dissonance.

1. **"Rush to Solve":** This is the tendency to want to find an immediate solution to an apparent problem without:
   a. *Spending enough time on defining the problem properly,* identifying and agreeing objectives needed as a result of the problem. As a result, decision-makers may opt to solve the wrong problem or deal with symptoms as opposed to causes.
   b. *Considering possible alternatives* of interpretation of the facts and of possible courses of action to resolve the problem. As a result, decision-makers may fail to choose the best course of action, opting for a second-best solution, or worse still, the wrong solution.
   c. *Investing enough time and effort in gathering relevant data* as a result of either time or budgetary pressures, whose relevance can only be determined properly by doing steps (a) and (b) correctly. Many disastrous decisions have been taken on the basis of statements like "in the time available . . ." or "with the information we had available . . ." Perhaps the best-known example of this was the US invasion of Iraq to clear it of weapons of mass destruction it did not possess.

d. *Recognizing the impact of mental models.* These describe the brain processes people use to make sense of their world:

> Confronting the incredible complexity of the brain, a range of neuroscience theories have emerged to explain what is going on inside our heads. In business and other organizations, these interactions become even more complex, as individuals with their own mental models interact through group decision making or negotiation, and they are susceptible to biases . . .[43]

The mental models we have reflect our cultures, histories, family backgrounds, religious beliefs, education, personal experiences, and everyday routines and habits.[44] These frame how we approach other people and how well we listen to their points of view and are able to accept their arguments without climbing the "ladder of inference" inappropriately by jumping to conclusions, stereotyping, and indulging in the "stonecutter," "hammer," or "oasis in the desert" syndromes (discussed in Chapter 6).

e. *Reaching an appropriate conclusion.* This depends on taking the time to understand the facts and assumptions in a VUCA environment. There is the possibility of "analysis paralysis," and of reacting over-hastily as a result. In the face of volatility, where uncertainty will always exist, where there may be great complexity leading to unanticipated results, and reasonable disagreements may arise because of differing perspectives of the same issues, reaching an appropriate decision requires a "reframing" or restatement of the problem and what the protagonists are trying to achieve. Here are two examples of reframing:

> The first is about Tom Watson, the founder of IBM. One of his employees made a very costly error that cost the firm ten million dollars. The employee had to meet with Watson in his office. As the employee entered the office he said, "I suppose you want my resignation." Watson looked at him and said in disbelief, "Are you kidding? We just spent ten million dollars on your education."
>
> From this point forward, you can bet that Watson had both the attention and cooperation of the employee. This is reframing. *The mistake had already occurred and the money was lost, Watson chose to see this mistake as an opportunity to salvage some value from this employee . . .*
>
> The second example of reframing is about the psychoanalyst, Milton Erickson. Erickson was a master at helping his clients to solve their problems with reframing. In this example, a father brought his strong-willed daughter to see Erickson, so Erickson could "fix her." As the father explained, their daughter always had her own opinion to express rather than just listen to him or his wife and accept what they had to tell her. The father explained that he and his wife did not know what else to do with her . . .
>
> What did Erickson say? Erickson replied to the father, "Now isn't it good that she will be able to stand on her own two feet when she is ready to leave home?" This silenced the father as he understood the impact of Erickson's reframe. He now understood that his daughter's independence was not a problem to be eliminated. Rather, *his daughter's independence was an opportunity that he and his wife needed to channel appropriately so she would not accept poor treatment when she became an adult.*[45]   [Emphases ours]

f. *Articulating and documenting the rationale.* The final step in decision-making is to take the trouble to explain how the conclusion was reached: the assumptions used, the facts and how they were evaluated, so that if the results are not what was predicted, people can establish why the deviations occurred and take appropriate corrective action as a result.

2. **Cognitive Biases:** These are systematic patterns of deviation in decision-making, arising from the way the cognitive system works. They cause us to be irrational in the way we search for, evaluate, interpret, judge, use, and remember information, as well as in the way we make decisions. Biases can be "hot," i.e., based on emotion, or "cold," based on logic and facts. There are many cognitive biases and heuristics that we use to decipher what to do in an uncertain, complex, and ambiguous environment. Some of the most common ones are as follows (in alphabetical order).

a. *Availability:* The availability bias limits the alternatives considered or information gathered to the alternatives or information that come readily to mind. It is also known as "What you see is all there is" (WYSIATI).[46] WYSIATI makes it easier to create coherence and for us to accept a statement as true. It allows us to decide on partial information in a fast-moving world and avoid analysis paralysis. Much of the time it is a good enough heuristic to support reasonable actions, but it also makes us jump to conclusions too quickly.

b. *Anchoring:* This tendency is to anchor on an initial value and stay too close to it when attempting to adjust away from it while making final assessments. The most obvious example of anchoring occurs when "wayfinders" do their annual budgets based on the numbers of the previous year, instead of adopting "zero-based budgeting."

c. *Attribution:* Underestimating the impact of independent environmental or situational conditions on how people behave and to overestimate the impact of personality. For example, when a stranger is having a "bad hair day" and looks unhappy or angry as a result, the temptation is to believe that he is an angry or unhappy person, when the observed emotions are the result of a transient and temporary condition, caused by something that has just happened, such as hearing bad news on his mobile phone.

d. *Cognitive dissonance:* Cognitive dissonance occurs when people hold two or more contradictory beliefs simultaneously. This can occur when behavior does not reflect beliefs – we believe one thing, but do the opposite. This mental conflict and the resulting discomfort force us to pick between beliefs by justifying and rationalizing one while rejecting or reducing the importance of the others by rejecting, debunking, or avoiding new information:

> We tend to pick the belief or idea that is most familiar and ingrained in us. Changing our beliefs isn't easy, nor is changing the attitudes and behaviour associated with them. As a result, *we usually stick with the beliefs we already hold, as opposed to adopting new ones*

that are presented to us. In fact, many of us go further by avoiding situations or information that might clash with our existing beliefs to create dissonance.[47]

Cognitive dissonance has impact at the personal and systemic levels:

i. *Personal level:* At the personal level, the existence of cognitive dissonance can lead to decisions that are personally harmful:

> Rejecting, rationalizing, or avoiding information that conflicts with our beliefs can lead us to make poor decisions. *This is because the information is not rejected because it is false but because it makes us uncomfortable.* Information that is both true and useful can often have this effect. Decisions made in the absence of true and useful information can have harmful consequences. Smoking, for example, has been shown to cause cancer and contribute to various other chronic health conditions. Smokers often rationalize their detrimental decision to continue smoking by either denying evidence that supports its health risks or by considering themselves to be the lucky exception.[48]

ii. *Systemic level:* At the systemic level, cognitive dissonance can lead to social harm or political conflict. Climate change deniers exhibit one form of cognitive dissonance – the economic costs of accepting that it is real are too high for them. Cognitive dissonance in politics reflects people's inability to admit that their choices were wrong because of the impact such an admission would have on their values and belief systems:

> When we believe strongly in a political leader or ideology, we are more likely to dismiss information that does not support their message. *In other words, we often ignore or distort evidence that challenges our political beliefs.* This is part of the reason why it is so difficult to change someone's mind on political issues. *Voters are likely to remain loyal to their chosen candidates and party even when evidence that should challenge those loyalties is presented.*[49]   [Emphases ours]

The reason why people remain loyal to their political beliefs, parties and candidates even after discovering that promises made were empty or misleading is the pain of embarrassment when recognizing they got it wrong, so they find new reasons why they were right:

> *If people go through a great deal of pain, discomfort, effort, or embarrassment to get something, they will be happier with that "something" than if it came to them easily . . .* Why would people like anything associated with pain? . . . the answer was obvious: self-justification. The cognition that I am a sensible, competent person is dissonant with the cognition that I went through a painful procedure to achieve something – say, joining a group that turned out to be boring and worthless. Therefore, *I would distort my perceptions of the group in a positive direction, trying to find good things about them and ignoring the downside.*[50]   [Emphases ours]

One way by which people can cope with unresolved cognitive dissonance is to compartmentalize their lives:

> Psychologists define compartmentalization as *a defense mechanism that we use to avoid the anxiety that arises from the clash of contradictory values or emotions.* For example, a manager

can think of himself as nurturing and sensitive at home, but a hard-nosed tough guy at work. These two self-images can coincide because the manager compartmentalizes his life, creating what I call a "mental bureaucracy."

> . . . it's often easier to mentally file information as "work," "home," or "family," rather than try to see how it might apply to more than one of those categories. Similarly, *we compartmentalize our behavior and unconsciously act in certain ways when we're in different settings. This thought pattern also allows us focus on getting a task done at work even when we're worried about something in our personal lives.*[51]   [Emphases ours]

e. *Confirmation:* Human beings seek and give excessive credence to confirming information in the information gathering and evaluation steps and to then favor conclusions that are consistent with initial prejudices:

> Contrary to the rules of philosophers of science, who advise testing hypotheses by trying to refute them, people (and scientists quite often) seek data that are likely to be compatible with the beliefs they currently hold. *The confirmatory bias of [the unconscious mind] favors uncritical acceptance of suggestions and exaggerates the likelihood of extreme and improbable events.*[52]   [Emphasis ours]

Confirmation bias ignores evidence that does not support pre-existing beliefs or cherry picks items that support existing beliefs and expectations and ignores others. One of the unintended consequences of the planning process is that events that are sufficiently close to what has been expected are interpreted as confirming the assumptions of the planners, when in fact they are early warning signals of failure:

> *Most of your expectations are reasonably accurate and tend to be confirmed, partly because they are based on your experience and partly because you correct faulty assumptions whenever they have negative consequences.* The tricky part is that all of us tend to be awfully generous in what we treat as evidence that our expectations are confirmed. Furthermore, we actively seek out evidence that confirms our expectations and avoid evidence that disconfirms them . . . *You're less likely to do a more balanced search where you weigh all the evidence and look just as closely for disconfirming evidence in the form of tentative, modest behavior.* This lopsided search sets at least two problems in motion. First, you overlook accumulating evidence that events are not developing as you thought they would. And second, you tend to overestimate the validity of those expectations you now hold . . . *As pressure increases people are more likely to search for confirming information and to ignore information that is inconsistent with their expectations* . . . The tendency to seek confirmation and shun disconfirmation is a well-honed, well-practiced human tendency . . . All of us face an ongoing struggle for alertness because we face an ongoing preference for information that confirms.[53]   [Emphases ours]

f. *Gambler's fallacy:* This occurs when there is a "run of luck" that gamblers believe will continue, when the probabilities are that events will return to a norm defined by probabilities.

g. *Horns and halo:* These cause impressions of people in one area to influence how we see them in other unrelated areas. The halo effect means that people who are physically attractive tend to be regarded as being more knowledgeable and having better characters than people who are unattractive where the reverse (the horns effect) happens.

h. *Initial tendency:* This occurs when we rely on the initial assessment using our unconscious minds (System 1) to find an answer to a problem that requires calculation (System 2), and we jumped to the wrong initial conclusion. For example:

> Students at Princeton University were asked a simple brain teaser:
>
> "A bat and a ball cost $1.10 in total. The bat costs $1 more than the ball. How much does the ball cost?"
>
> Almost anyone who hears this question feels an initial tendency to answer "10 cents," because the total sum of $1.10 separates naturally into $1 and 10 cents, so that the answer "10 cents" sounds about right. The problem is that over half the people in the experiment ended up sticking with this initial estimate, leading them to answer this question incorrectly, since the right answer is that the bat costs $1.05, while the ball costs $0.05.[54]

i. *Ostrich effect:* This is related to confirmation bias and occurs when people avoid information they do not want to face. This might manifest physically, e.g., avoiding looking at or listening to news they do not like, through inattention, reinterpreting the information with "alternative facts" to forget the unpleasant implications, or forgetting on purpose.

> The main reason why people avoid information is to avoid the unpleasant emotional impact that they expect it to lead to, at least in the short term, even if this avoidance will lead to a greater emotional cost later on.[55]

j. *Overconfidence:* Overconfidence leads to suboptimal behavior in every step of the judgment process:

> Overconfidence: As the WYSIATI rule implies, neither the quantity nor the quality of the evidence counts for much in subjective confidence. *The confidence that individuals have in their beliefs depends mostly on the quality of the story they can tell about what they see, even if they see little.* We often fail to allow for the possibility that evidence that should be critical to our judgment is missing – what we see is all there is. Furthermore, *our associative system tends to settle on a coherent pattern of activation and suppresses doubt and ambiguity.*[56]
>
> [Emphases ours]

k. *Rhyme and reason:* This bias makes it easier for people to remember and repeat and therefore believe a statement that has a rhyme in it than an equivalent statement that does not. For example, the saying "woes unite foes" is treated as being more accurate because it is easier to remember than its equivalents: "misfortunes unite foes," "woes unite enemies" or "misfortunes unite enemies," even though they all mean the same thing.

l. *Self-serving:* This occurs when people claim credit for success even when they are helped by extraneous factors and blame others and the self-same external factors when things go wrong. A related problem arises when they are riding a wave of success, as illustrated by the January 28, 1986, *Challenger* disaster:

> Success breeds confidence and fantasy. When an organization succeeds, its managers usually attribute success to themselves or at least to their organization, rather than to luck. The organization's members grow more confident of their own abilities, of their manager's skills, and of their organization's existing programs and procedures. They trust the procedures to keep them appraised of developing problems, in the belief that these procedures focus on the most important events and ignore the least significant ones.[57]

This can lead to serious mistakes when it is combined with confirmation bias and the gambler's fallacy, as it did in the case of the *Challenger* and *Deepwater Horizon* disasters, discussed in Chapter 7.

m. *Stereotyping:* Stereotypes arise from the need to simplify complex information that is passed on from one person to another, typically about culture, gender, ethnicity, and profession, which become foci of bias:

> As it passes down a chain of individuals, social information that is initially random, complex and very difficult to remember becomes a simple system of category stereotypes that can be learned easily.

> According to Martin and colleagues, stereotypes may have negative consequences when they contribute to prejudice, but they can also help us make sense of the world around us, helping us in "the way we organize, store, and use information about other people."

> "For example, if we meet a stranger, stereotypes provide us with a foundation on which we can begin to build an impression of this person and therefore guide our behaviour towards them," says Martin.[58]

3. **Rhetoric and Logical Fallacies:** The ancient Greeks developed rhetoric as a technique to persuade people of a given point of view. It is not concerned with the truth of an argument but with the ability to change people's minds. It is a powerful, and morally neutral tool that has been used throughout the ages.

> *Where there are political parties there must be propaganda, and rhetoric and oratory become essential to the citizen of a democracy who wanted to compete for social or economic or political success.* Where rhetoric is supreme, the decision of the law-courts will be swayed by brilliant argument and appeals to the emotions, and so, in the law-courts it was persuasion, not truth, which prevailed. *A policy, a point of view, a moral principle or a religion came to be valued not for its truth, but for its popular appeal,* just as the goodness of an article in modern life is sometimes assessed by its sales. In the end the substitution of reason for tradition as the supreme criterion produced not freedom for the

individual, as had been hoped, but power for the few individuals who were skilled in the arts of salesmanship . . .

> . . . *For rhetoric – like propaganda and advertising – was the art of making others agree to a point of view whether that point was right or wrong. Indeed, the falser it was the greater the rhetorical success in persuading someone else to accept it: and conversely, the sounder a doctrine or a legal case or a political judgement, the more skill required to make it look ridiculous. Rhetoric, in fact, was the technique of making the worse appear the better and the better the worse cause . . . and it rapidly became the most highly developed science in all Greece.*[59] [Emphases ours]

Rhetoric uses words to convey meaning, deceive, persuade, or evoke emotions. Its effectiveness is determined by its relevance to situations or to individuals and their circumstances and emotional state. Protagonists (speakers, advertisers, and teachers) employ three basic approaches, appealing to:

a. *Ethos:* Here speakers seek to persuade the audience via their personal authority or credibility, or through the endorsement of their point of view by popular celebrities.
b. *Pathos:* This approach seeks to generate emotional responses (positive or negative) in the audience, using passionate pleas or convincing stories which may or may not be true, as long as they excite the relevant emotions in the listener or reader.
c. *Logos:* This approach uses logic to persuade by using facts and figures to make the case.

Effective persuaders use the three approaches differently depending on the topic, context, and audience, and often combine more than one approach. However, they often rely on three rhetorical steps. They develop and refine the arguments, make relevant connections between their arguments and the audience, and structure their arguments using "Pyramid Principle" or "message house" techniques.

Introductions are important because they let the audience know what the purpose of the discussion is. They should make the audience receptive, usually via anecdotes to engage the participants and explain why the topic is of interest, relevance, and importance to them, by showing that it has been neglected, ignored, or its effect on the audience is not properly understood.

Persuaders will not merely seek to make the best case they can for their own point of view, they will also seek to discredit opposing arguments by appealing to ethics, emotions, and logic using both legitimate and illegitimate techniques shown in Table 8.4.

Some leaders are expert in using illegitimate techniques and this needs to be recognized when dealing with their promises and arguments. They are especially

Table 8.4: Legitimate and Illegitimate Techniques of Persuaders.

Legitimate Techniques	Illegitimate Techniques
Alliteration: use of recurring initial consonant sounds, as in "ping pong"	*Ad hominem:* attacking the other person on personal grounds to discredit her or him rather than disproving the point being made as in "the Honorable Member is never lucky in the coincidence of his facts with the truth"
Allusion: referring to an event, place, or person to make a point, but without elaborating (similar to name-dropping)	*Alternative facts:* deliberately creating confusion by reinterpreting facts as representing something else or doctoring evidence for social media purposes
Amplification: repeating a word for additional emphasis, often using added adjectives, as in "love, real love takes time"	*Ambiguity:* using ambiguous language to give the appearance of being logical
Analogy: explaining one thing in terms of another	*Appeal to ignorance:* suggesting that a proposition is true because it has not yet been proved totally false as in "climate change is a hoax"
Anaphora: Repeating a word or phrase to create parallelism and rhythm, usually in music or poetry as in "water, water everywhere, nor yet a drop to drink"	*Appeal to pity:* as in one should feel sorry for others justifying what they do
Antanagoge: placing a compliment and criticism side by side, as in "damning with faint praise"	*Bandwagon fallacy:* "Everyone is doing it, so it must be OK," similar to groupthink where collective discussion stifles outlier views
Antimetabole: repeating words or phrases in reverse order, as in "ask not what your country can do for you – ask what you can do for your country"	*Causal fallacy:* failing to recognize that correlation is not causality
Antiphrasis: using words with opposite meanings for ironic or sarcastic effect as in "this essay is 100 pages short!"	*Circular argument:* making the conclusion the same as the assumption as in "If 'A' is true, then 'B' is true, then 'A' is true" – the same as a tautology
Antithesis: making a connection between two things as in "that's one small step for man, one giant leap for mankind"	*False dilemma:* positing a false "either or" situation when it is in fact a case of "both and"
Appositive: placing a noun or phrase next to another noun for descriptive purposes as in "Mary, Queen of Scots was executed" where "Queen of Scots" is the appositive noun	*Hasty generalization:* generalizing from the particular, as in using anecdotes and individual experience which are not statistically significant to try to prove a point
Enumeration: making a point with a list of details	*Red herring* introducing an irrelevant argument to confuse the issue
Epanalepsis: repeating something from the start of a clause or sentence at the end as in "always low price, always"	*Slippery slope:* drawing false long-term consequences from an initial condition as in "if we agree to this minor concession, we set a dangerous precedent and who knows where it could all end"
Epithet: an adjective describing a quality of the person as in "Richard the Lionheart"	
Epizeuxis: repeating one word for emphasis as in King Lear's "never, never, never, never, never"	*Straw man:* presenting an alternative approach that is an extreme case and therefore already rejected by it its proponents
Hyperbole: exaggeration	
Litotes: using a negative to emphasize a positive, usually a double negative for effect as in "she is not a bad cook"	

Table 8.4 (continued)

Legitimate Techniques	Illegitimate Techniques
Metanoia: correcting or qualifying a statement as in "you are the most beautiful woman in this town, nay the entire world"	*Sunk cost fallacy:* continuing with a failing course of action because of the previous investment in it, based on appeals to authority,
Metaphor: implied comparison by stating one is the other as in "the eyes are windows of the soul"	when at war where the dead are used as justification for continuing fighting as in "otherwise their sacrifice is pointless"
Metonymy: type of metaphor where what is being compared is referred to by something associated with it as in "the milk of human kindness"	*Tu Quoque:* as in "You too have made mistakes," justifying the speaker's mistakes, also known as "what aboutery" where false equivalence between two courses of action is drawn
Onomatopoeia: words that sound like what they are describing as in "popping of corks"	*Zero-sum fallacy:* when people are acculturated to believe in "win-lose" rather than "win-win"
Oxymoron: a two-word paradox as in "near miss" or "business ethics"	outcomes when negotiating, cooperating, or collaborating, reflecting a low level of trust
Parallelism: using words or phrases with a similar structure as in "like father, like son"	
Simile: comparing one object to another as in "float like butterfly, sting like a bee"	
Understatement: downplaying the importance of an idea	

adept at using the so-called "Noble Lie." The "Noble Lie" is both a legitimate technique ("noble") and potentially an illegitimate one ("lie"). Which it is, depends on how it is used.

"Noble lies" are particularly useful in creating foundation myths to bring separate collectives together for a supposed higher superordinate goal as in the case of:

a. 19th century Pan-Slavism in the Austro-Hungarian empire, leading to the creation of Yugoslavia and Czechoslovakia after World War I.[60]
b. Pan-Arab nationalism after end of World War II.[61]
c. The creation of a Muslim Pakistan unifying East Pakistan with West Pakistan, separated by a thousand miles of India in between, based on their shared Muslim religion.[62]

The objectives were noble, but the underlying reality that the different "nations" that were joined together shared sufficiently unifying long-term views of their identities and objectives proved to be false, and so the dreams failed. Yugoslavia broke up into its constituent states after the death of Tito and saw the worst genocide in Europe after World War II.[63] Even the calmer Czechs and Slovaks chose a friendly divorce.[64] Egypt and Syria are not just two separate states, but are enemies. East Pakistan broke away from West Pakistan after a bitter civil war to become Bangladesh.[65] Spain with its separatists in Catalonia, the United Kingdom with Scots seeking independence, the

Canadians with Quebec are the result of earlier unifying nationalist "noble lies" under stress.

Perhaps the noblest of "noble lies" is to be found in the American Declaration of Independence:

> We hold these truths to be self-evident, that all men are created equal, that they are endowed by their Creator with certain unalienable Rights, that among these are Life, Liberty and the pursuit of Happiness.[66]

It is ironic that at the time of the Declaration, women did not have the same rights as men, African Americans were slaves, and the indigenous people were being systematically killed or driven from their lands in violation of their "unalienable rights to Life, Liberty, and the pursuit of Happiness." The nobility of the vision is what makes America exceptional and a country that people wish to emigrate to, the reality of the injustices and inequality persisting in the US is what makes for its current divisions. Nevertheless, the undoubted power of the "Noble Lie" is demonstrated in the greater effectiveness of soldiers who believe their particular sacralized version of the truth:

> A fighter's identity must have fully "fused" with those of his brothers in arms. *The top priority of such fighters must . . . have shifted from family to another cause, a transcendental ideal that has become so "sacralised" that it would not be traded away for anything.* Artis's researchers identified fighters who had mentally downgraded their families to second or third place. *Some were Peshmerga, who most valued "Kurdeity" – a love for the homeland steeled with commitment to fellow Kurds and Kurdish culture. Many IS captives, for their part, had shunted their families into third place behind the caliphate and sharia. Units girded with those beliefs had fought on effectively even after seven-tenths of their comrades had fallen.*

> . . . Fanaticism has long been recognised as a plus in a soldier, be it the Zealots of ancient Israel, the Roman Catholic conquistadors of the Americas, or the Nazis' 12th SS "Hitler Youth" Panzer Division.[67]

Such is the power of the "Noble Lie" and therein lies its danger.

The Problem of Simplification

Chapter 7 makes it clear that "wayfinders" have to deal with VUCA, which makes effective decision-making itself complicated. It requires consideration of the interests of overlapping collectives with changing membership. These are all arguments against seeing the world in simple terms. Yet neuroscience demonstrates the human brain's propensity to default to rules of thumb that reflect our biases, and to succumb to rhetoric and its use of techniques of influence in order to win arguments (regardless of truth or falsehood). This means we have to find ways of keeping things simple, if facts are to be absorbed and accepted.

It is perhaps the most remarkable of the many achievements of Elizabeth Tudor, Napoleon, and Atatürk that they handled great uncertainty and complexity and the corresponding mastery of detail so well, while keeping things simple and understanding the importance of consistent image management.

People cannot handle more than five priorities, and most presentations by consultants[68] and "message houses"[69] used to develop advertising claims are premised on the idea of a single "governing thought/idea" supported by three lines of reasoning/ message to show why it is correct. Busy people expect to be told why they should pay attention and what is in it for them in the so-called "elevator pitch." Yet effective simplification requires careful thought and is time-consuming. Winston Churchill and many other famous people are supposed to have apologized for writing a long letter to a friend because they did not have sufficient time to write a short one. The first to do so was Blaise Pascal.[vi] Churchill did, however, say:

> Out of intense complexities intense simplicities emerge.[70]

Perhaps what Churchill meant was that no matter how uncertain, complex, and ambiguous the circumstances "wayfinders" face (i.e., VUCA), they must articulate and communicate clearly superordinate goals around which their followers can coalesce. In such circumstances, it is essential to have simplicity of message, supported by the most compelling arguments, properly structured to combine all the elements of rhetoric, appealing to both logic and emotions. However, *to be effective*, that is not enough. "Wayfinders" must not forget that the course of action needed to meet the agreed superordinate goals must reflect the complex realities of context. The devil is *always* in the details, something populist leaders tend to forget, which makes them ultimately ineffective.

Populist leaders harness the power of the "Noble Lie" to upend the political establishment and expert insiders in government. For example, in the UK, the appeal of taking back control in the name of recovering its sovereignty led to the Brexit referendum where many illegitimate tools of rhetoric were used to great effect to promote the "Noble Lie." The result:

> Populist revolutions are always in danger of falling into a familiar trap. Their leaders mobilise outsiders against insiders and neophytes against old hands. But *those who win find themselves*

---

vi The first person of many to use such an excuse was the French mathematician, Blaise Pascal who wrote in 1657: "Je n'ai fait celle-ci plus longue que parce que je n'ai pas eu le loisir de la faire plus courte." Which translates as: "I have made this longer because I have not had time to make it shorter." https://quoteinvestigator.com/2012/04/28/shorter-letter/, accessed on September 8, 2020.

running the country, which requires the services of clever, competent types. Recruiting and retaining such people does not come naturally to populists . . .[71]   [Emphasis ours]

Summary

Dealing with VUCA effectively is difficult because humanity has evolved as a social species. Collectives have been a feature of the human condition from empire to nation, ethnic group, tribe, family, religion, language, and gender, as well as by psychographics, lifestyle, and occupation. People can belong to different collectives simultaneously, each with different objectives and values, creating added uncertainty, complexity, and ambiguity.

The success of collectives is measured in terms of their longevity and share of the niches they occupy. Success depends not only on competition to determine the "survival of the fittest," but also on collaboration, altruism, and adaptability. The ability to adapt depends on how well collectives deal with barriers to and enablers of change.

The most important barriers to change are ideology, cultural differences, and the foundation myths upon which those differences are built; vested interests, inertia, and ignorance; and the difficulties for decision-making posed by VUCA.

There are three enablers of change: megatrends, "ideas whose time has come," and effective "wayfinders" capable of overcoming barriers to change. The megatrends that will determine the sustainability of collectives are climate change, the problems faced by globalization as a result of the pandemic and the growth of protectionism, the threat posed to employment by "Industry 4.0," and the threat to political systems posed by inequality, made worse by the unequal impacts of climate change and Covid-19.

"Ideas whose time has come" take time as the swings in economic thinking demonstrate. Such ideas, however, depend on effective implementation for their success. The experience of countries that threw off the colonial yoke shows that *being against something is not enough, people must have a clear idea of what it is they are for,* and that however powerful such ideas are as memes that are spread across the world via social media, they will only materialize if they are implemented by effective "wayfinders" who understand that *governing is not the same as rebelling, campaigning, or philosophizing.*

Populist leaders and their followers tend to believe in the "great man" theory of history. Such leaders are effective at mobilizing the masses based on appeals to emotion, but often prove to be less capable of delivering on their promise because the "devil is in the details." Such leaders appeal to the human desire for simple answers to complex questions, using heuristics and the evolutionary imperative to minimize cognitive load when acquiring and processing information for decision-making.

System 1 of the brain uses heuristics and biases – subconscious processes – that consume very little energy, whereas System 2 of the brain processes facts, using logic and making connections between different data points, consuming a great deal of energy as a result. One of the most important roles of System 2 is to stop people from acting on impulse alone and to regain self-control. System 1 applies when we operate on autopilot and System 2 complements it when we need to make an intellectual effort or concentrate.

The heuristics we use in System 1 work well *most of the time*. But they do lead us to make mistakes through the "rush to solve," cognitive biases, rhetoric and its associated illegitimate techniques, and the existence of cognitive dissonance.

"Rush to solve" errors are caused by not spending enough on defining the problem properly, failing to consider all possible alternatives, not getting enough relevant data, failing to appreciate the significance of our own and other people's mental models, and reaching wrong conclusions because of inappropriate framing of the issues.

Cognitive biases play an important role because they cause us to be irrational in the way we search for, evaluate, interpret, judge, use, and remember information.

Rhetoric can make matters worse because it is not concerned with the truth of an argument but with the ability to change people's minds by playing on emotions and manipulating biases. It is a powerful, morally neutral tool that can and has been misused throughout the ages. It uses words to convey meaning, deceive, persuade, or evoke emotions and its effectiveness is determined solely by whether the argument was won or lost. *There are legitimate and illegitimate techniques for winning arguments, and it is essential that effective "wayfinders" understand which techniques to use and to know when inappropriate techniques are being used against them.*

Populist leaders are experts in the use of illegitimate techniques (e.g., "alternative facts" and "Stop the Steal") and in particular the "Noble Lie" – a technique that is both legitimate ("noble") and illegitimate ("lie"). How it is used determines which it is. "Noble lies" are particularly effective in creating foundation myths to bring different collectives together to satisfy a higher superordinate goal. They work well as long as the underlying reality reflects the dream or vision. Perhaps the best example is the American Declaration of Independence's "we hold these truths to be self-evident . . ." Armies have always known the power of the "Noble Lie" and its ability to increase the fighting capacity of soldiers who believe their particular sacralized version of the truth. This is its power and its danger.

Effective "wayfinders" must deal with VUCA and they also have to deal with the different interests of overlapping collectives with changing membership. These are arguments against seeing the world in simple terms. Yet human evolution and neuroscience demand we find ways of keeping things simple if facts are to be absorbed and accepted. This requires structured communication with a single "governing thought" supported by three lines of reasoning and the ability to distill the argument down to the so-called "elevator pitch." It is therefore essential to have simplicity of message using the legitimate tools of rhetoric and the "Noble Lie" when creating superordinate goals around which people can coalesce. However, the simplicity of the message must not ignore the reality of the facts on the ground and that the "devil is in the details" that a VUCA-based approach will highlight.

Effective "wayfinders" must realize that reconciling VUCA with the need for simplicity can only be achieved by ensuring that simplicity of message does not mean over-simplification of understanding and paucity of planned actions to achieve the desired goals. *If the planned actions fail to deal with the VUCA realities on the ground, the "Noble lie" will be a lie, revealing incompetence.*

References

1 *Economist* (2020), "The viral universe: Viruses have big impacts on ecology and evolution as well as human health," *The Economist,* August 20, 2020, https://www.economist.com/essay/2020/08/20/viruses-have-big-impacts-on-ecology-and-evolution-as-well-as-human-health, accessed on August 20, 2020.

2 Ardrey, R. (1966), *The Territorial Imperative: A Personal Inquiry into the Animal Origins of Property and Nations* (New York: Atheneum).

3 Collins English Dictionary, https://www.collinsdictionary.com/dictionary/english/cooperation, accessed on August 27, 2020.

4 Ibid.

5 Merriam-Webster Thesaurus, https://www.merriam-webster.com/thesaurus/collaboration, accessed on August 27, 2020.

6 Ashkenas, R. (2015), "There's a Difference Between Cooperation and Collaboration," *HBR,* April 20, 2015, https://hbr.org/2015/04/theres-a-difference-between-cooperation-and-collaboration, accessed on August 27, 2020.

7 Macmillan Dictionary, https://www.macmillandictionary.com/dictionary/british/alliance, accessed on January 1, 2021.

8 Oxford English Dictionary, https://www.lexico.com/definition/altruism, accessed on August 27, 2020.

9 Dawkins, R. (1976), *The Selfish Gene* (Oxford: Oxford University Press).

10 Okasha, S. (2020), "Biological Altruism," *Stanford Encyclopedia of Philosophy* (Summer 2020 Edition), https://plato.stanford.edu/entries/altruism-biological/, accessed on August 27, 2020.

11 *Economist* (2020), op. cit.

12 Plato, *The Republic, Part IV, Book III,* Lee, H. D. P. translated (London: Penguin Classics, 1987), pp. 116–117.

13 Zinkin, T. (1963), *Caste Today* (Institute of Race Relations: Oxford University Press).

14 Van Der Leeuw, S., and Folke, C. (2020), "The Social Dynamics of Basins of Attraction," unpublished paper, p. 11.

15 Machiavelli, N. (1513), *The Prince* (Harmondsworth: Penguin Books, 1999), Chapter VI, 19.

16 Ulrich, D., Smallwood, N., Sweetman, K. (2008), *The Leadership Code: Five Rules to Lead By* (Boston: Harvard Business Review Press), p. 63.

17 De Bono, E. (1985), *Six Thinking Hats* (New York: Little, Brown and Company).

18 Hofstede, G. "The 6D model of national culture," https://geerthofstede.com/culture-geert-hofstede-gert-jan-hofstede/6d-model-of-national-culture/, accessed on August 29, 2020.

19 Van der Leeuw and Folke (2020), op. cit., p. 12.

20 Ibid., p. 9.

21 Kramer, L. (2018), "Beyond Liberalism: Rethinking Political Economy," *Hewlett Foundation Board Paper*, p. 5.

22 Van der Leeuw and Folke (2020), op. cit.

23 Hugo, V., Thoughts on the Business of Life, *Forbes Quotes*, https://www.forbes.com/quotes/9443/, accessed on July 15, 2020.

24 Morgan, E. (1988), *Inventing the People* (New York: W. W. Norton), pp. 13–14, quoted in Kramer (2018), op. cit., p. 7.

25 Beloff, M. (1957), "Anti-Colonialism in American Foreign Policy: Realpolitik and Illusion," *Commentary*, September 1957, https://www.commentarymagazine.com/articles/max-beloff/anti-colonialism-in-american-foreign-policyrealpolitik-and-illusion/, accessed on August 29, 2020.

26 History.com Editors (2018), "Russo-Japanese War," *History*, August 21, 2018, https://www.history.com/topics/korea/russo-japanese-war, accessed on August 29, 2020.

27 Royde-Smith, J. G., and Hughes, T. A. (2020), "World War II – Japanese Policy 1939–1941," *Encyclopaedia Britannica Inc*, August 27, 2020, https://www.britannica.com/event/World-War-II/Japanese-policy-1939-41, accessed on August 29, 2020, Royde-Smith, J. G and Hughes, T. A. (2020) "World War II – Pearl Harbor and the Japanese Expansion to July 1942," *Encyclopaedia Britannica Inc*, August 27, 2020, https://www.britannica.com/event/World-War-II/Pearl-Harbor-and-the-Japanese-expansion-to-July-1942, accessed on August 29, 2020.

28 CIA (1948), "The Break-Up Of The Colonial Empires And Its Implications For US Security," *CIA Historical Review Program*, September 3, 1948, https://www.cia.gov/library/readingroom/docs/DOC_0000258342.pdf, accessed on August 29, 2020.

29 Geertz, C. (2000), *The Interpretation of Cultures* (New York: Basic Books), pp. 234–235.

30 Reich, R. (2020), "Voters can replace a party that knows how to fight with one that knows how to govern," *The Guardian*, August 16, 2020, https://www.theguardian.com/commentisfree/2020/aug/16/us-election-democrats-republicans-trump, accessed on August 16, 2020.

31 Geertz (2000), op.cit., pp. 219–220.

32 Ibid., p. 235.

33 Miller, L. (2019), "Is There Still Value in 'Great Man' History," *History Today*, Volume 69, Issue 9, September 2019, https://www.historytoday.com/archive/head-head/there-still-value-%E2%80%98great-man%E2%80%99-history, accessed on August 18, 2020.

34 Dennett, D. (2002), "Dangerous Memes," *TED Talk*, https://www.ted.com/talks/dan_dennett_dangerous_memes?utm_source=tedcomshare&utm_medium=email&utm_campaign=tedspread#t-911385, accessed on July 15, 2020.

35 Loisy, A. (1948), *The Birth of The Christian Religion* (London: George Allen & Unwin)

36 Larmuseau, C. et al. (2019), "Combining physiological data and subjective measurements to investigate cognitive load during complex learning," *Frontline Learning Research*, Vol. 7, No. 2, p. 59, https://journals.sfu.ca/flr/index.php/journal/article/view/403, accessed on September 1, 2020.

37 Kahneman, D. (2012), "Of 2 Minds: How Fast and Slow Thinking Shape Perception and Choice [Excerpt]," *Scientific American*, June 15, 2012, https://www.scientificamerican.com/article/kahneman-excerpt-thinking-fast-and-slow/, accessed on August 31, 2020.

38 Ibid.

39 Sweller, J. (2010), "Element Interactivity and Intrinsic, Extraneous and Germane Cognitive Load," *Educational Psychology Review*, 22, April 23, 2010, pp. 123–138.

40 Edelman, G. (2000), *Universe of Consciousness: How Matter Becomes Imagination* (New York: Basic Books), cited in Wind, Y., Crook, C., and Gunther, R. (2005), *The Power of Impossible Thinking:*

Transform the Business of Your Life and the Life of Your Business (Upper Saddle River, NJ: Wharton School Publishing), p. ix.

41 Ibid., p. xiii.

42 Kahneman (2012), op. cit.

43 Wind, Crook, and Gunther (2005), op. cit., p. xlviii.

44 Ibid., pp. 209–233.

45 Tanner, R. (2020) "Reframing for Innovative and Creative Problem-Solving," *Management is a Journey*, March 16, 2020, https://managementisajourney.com/reframing-for-innovative-and-creative-problem-solving/, accessed on September 5, 2020.

46 Kahneman, D. (2011), *Thinking, Fast and Slow* (London: Allen Lane), p. 87.

47 "Why do we look for consistency in our beliefs?" *The Decision Lab*, https://thedecisionlab.com/biases/cognitive-dissonance/, accessed on September 8, 2020.

48 Ibid.

49 Ibid.

50 Aronson, E. (2007), "Why It's Hard to Admit to Being Wrong," *NPR*, July 20, 2007, https://www.npr.org/templates/story/story.php?storyId=12125926, accessed on September 8, 2020.

51 Askhenas, R. (2012), "Break Through Your Mental Bureaucracy," *Harvard Business Review*, February 28, 2012, https://hbr.org/2012/02/break-though-your-mental-burea.html, accessed on September 10, 2020.

52 Kahneman (2011), op. cit., p. 81.

53 Weick, K. E., and Sutcliffe, K. M. (2001) *Managing the Unexpected: Assuring High Performance in an Age of Complexity* (San Francisco: Jossey-Bass), pp. 34–35.

54 "Cognitive Biases: What They Are and How They Affect You," *Effectiviology*, https://effectiviology.com/cognitive-biases/, accessed on August 28, 2020.

55 "Cognitive Biases: What They Are and How They Affect You," *Effectiviology* https://effectiviology.com/ostrich-effect/, accessed on September 6, 2020.

56 Kahneman (2011), op. cit., pp. 87–88.

57 Weick and Sutcliffe (2001), op. cit., p. 55.

58 Hutchison, J. et al. (2014), "Cultural Stereotypes May Evolve From Sharing Social Information," *Association for Psychological Science*, July 24, 2014, https://www.psychologicalscience.org/news/releases/cultural-stereotypes-may-evolve-from-sharing-social-information.html, accessed on September 7, 2020.

59 Crossman, R. H. S. (1963), *Plato Today, 2nd edition* (London: Unwin Books), pp. 38–39.

60 Editors of Encyclopaedia Britannica (2013), "Pan-Slavism," *Encyclopaedia Britannica, Inc.*, October 15, 2013, https://www.britannica.com/event/Pan-Slavism, accessed on September 11, 2020.

61 Editors of Encyclopaedia Britannica (2020), "United Arab Republic," *Encyclopaedia Britannica, Inc.*, March 5 2020, https://www.britannica.com/place/United-Arab-Republic, accessed on September 11, 2020.

62 Sarkar, M. (2018), "Faith, fury and fear: The story behind one of history's greatest migrations," *CNN*, August 15, 2018, https://edition.cnn.com/2017/08/08/asia/india-pakistan-independence-timeline/index.html, accessed on September 11, 2020.

63 "The Break up of Yugoslavia: 1990–1992," *Office of the Historian*, https://history.state.gov/milestones/1989-1992/breakup-yugoslavia, accessed on September 11, 2020.

64 Engelberg, S. (1993),"Czechoslovakia Breaks in Two: To Wide Regret," *The New York Times*, January 1, 1993, https://www.nytimes.com/1993/01/01/world/czechoslovakia-breaks-in-two-to-wide-regret.html, accessed on September 11, 2020.

65 "Bangladesh War of Independence," *New World Encyclopedia*, https://www.newworldencyclopedia.org/entry/Bangladesh_War_of_Independence, accessed on September 11, 2020.

66 American Declaration of Independence, 1776.

67 "Predicting pugnacity: How to forecast armies' will to fight," *The Economist, Science & Technology,* September 5, 2020 edition, https://www.economist.com/science-and-technology/2020/09/05/how-to-forecast-armies-will-to-fight?utm_campaign=the-economist-today&utm_medium=newsletter&utm_source=salesforce-marketing-cloud&utm_term=2020-09-04&utm_content=article-link-1&etear=nl_today_1, accessed on September 5, 2020.

68 Minto, B. (1995), *The Pyramid Principle: Logical Writing, Thinking and Problem Solving* (London: Prentice Hall).

69 "Narrative Development," *Message House,* https://message-house.co.uk/narrative-development, accessed on September 8, 2020.

70 Churchill, W. (1997), *The Sayings of Winston Churchill* (London: Duckworth), p. 59.

71 Bagehot (2020), "The talent dearth in Britain's government," *The Economist,* July 18, 2020, https://www.economist.com/britain/2020/07/18/the-talent-dearth-in-britains-government, accessed on September 10, 2020.

Chapter 9
Combining two Leadership Models with Managerial Skills

Ask the participants at the start of any leadership program what they expect of leaders and the usual answers are: vision, empathy, charisma, decisiveness, and clarity of purpose. Rarely do they mention the ability to follow up, and almost never do they mention the so-called managerial skills and operational competence required to deliver the imagined future. This is an unfortunate consequence of the widely propagated belief that "leadership" and "management" are separate activities; and relates to the rise of populist, charismatic leaders (in both business and politics) who achieve power through slogans and bluster, but do not have the necessary experience, managerial skills, and understanding of how volatility, uncertainty, complexity, and ambiguity affect the implementation of their visions (discussed in Chapter 7). As a result, they fail to deliver the vision they promise.

The need to combine vision with tasks designed to achieve that vision (i.e., management) was recognized in 1730 and we would do well to remember the following when considering effective leadership:

> A Vision without a task is but a dream, a task without a Vision is drudgery,
> A Vision and a task is the hope of the world[1]

In other words, vision matters, but without the skills of execution, without operational competence, it will remain a dream. Equally, a task without a sense of direction will merely be pointless work for work's sake. Consequently, skills in both "leadership" and "management" define effective "wayfinders."

Leaders who only have vision but lack managerial skills to execute are at best philosophers like Marx, super-spreaders of ideas or memes that "infect" the minds of their followers – like Lenin, who then implement them – or they are merely dreamers and fantasists like Baron Munchausen. As we concluded in Chapter 5, the most important lesson learned from the careers of Elizabeth Tudor, Napoleon and Atatürk is that their operational effectiveness and attention to detail was the key to their greatness. It is the combination of both with vision that defines the effectiveness of "leaders" and the duration of their legacies.

Two Leadership Models

Effective leadership benefits both leaders and followers. Primitive leaders gained preferential access to scarce resources (land, livestock, and women), while their followers benefitted from the vision, direction, and dispute resolution they provided.

https://doi.org/10.1515/9783110707878-012

Success was measured in terms of territorial and reproductive gains and the ability to defend them.[2] Success led to imitation of leadership behaviors, and their perpetuation in the form of cultural memes, allowing the transmission of key success factors by non-genetic means through myth-making, ideological, and religious ideas. While memes generally benefit both leaders and led, *it is notable that it is the memes that persist.* There have been many examples where the demands of memes damage the individual interests of leaders and/or followers – for example, the Zealots at Masada,[3] Japanese kamikaze pilots in World War II,[4] the suicide bombers of Tamil Eelam,[5] and, recently, of followers of Al-Qaeda and Daesh.[6] This may also explain how investors and employees fall for scams.

Two Styles of Leadership

There appear to be two overarching models of leadership, which reflect two leadership styles – dominant and prestige[7] – each with "contrasting expressions, functions, histories, and neural and developmental pathways."[8] The two styles are defined by the way they use five different foundations of power and are constrained by a third element – collective disciplining.

1. **Dominant Leadership** evolved in primitive primates and hominids to resolve conflict and establish group hierarchy. Such leaders were alpha males, aggressive defenders of territory and social ranking, whom Hegel classified as "aristocrats," prepared to die in mimetic (dyadic) battles for territorial supremacy and mating rights – *to gain privileged access to limited resources for personal gain.* Philosophical and cultural support for the existence of this style of leadership comes from Muhammad Ibn Zafar,[9] Machiavelli,[10] and Hegel.[11]

Dominant leadership is authoritarian, top-down, coercive, and infinitely scalable because it depends on positional authority. Dominant leaders appoint others to implement their ideas from the positions to which they are assigned. Positional authority allows coercion of followers by use of threats and punishment. Thus, it is relatively straightforward for large collectives to adopt and develop dominant leadership.

Dominant leadership is built on three foundations:

a. *Legitimate power:* Legitimate (positional) power is formal *authoritarian* power based on the duties and position of an individual within an organization, delegated to the holder, accompanied by status symbols – i.e., a uniform, title, or imposing office.[12]

b. *Coercive power:* Coercive power is based on the ability to punish others by demoting them or withholding rewards. It is based on fear. It is the most obvious but least effective long-term form of *authoritarian* power as it creates resistance and resentment within those who experience it. Extensive use of coercive power is a sign of toxic leadership.[13]

c. *Reward power:* Reward power depends on the ability to confer rewards, typically benefits in kind, time-off, increases in pay or responsibility, and promotion. Reward power has two weaknesses. The first is whether rewarders have full control over the process or have to depend on others to confer the rewards in full. The need to negotiate with others undermines their authority and therefore their ability to project their power. The second is that rewards lose their ability to motivate as they hit diminishing returns over time. People become satiated quite quickly if rewards are repetitive.[14]

2. **Prestige Leadership** evolved in primitive hunter-gatherer societies to suit those leading foraging packs. Such leaders did not rely on long-term positional authority, their authority was task based so they could be at any level in the pecking order. In modern organizations they might be advisers outside the internal hierarchy. Their authority is personal. The primary objective for the hunter-gatherer group (according to Van Vught and Smith) is *to maximize successful foraging for the benefit of all in the group.* Philosophical support for existence of this type of leadership comes from Confucian, Taoist, and Buddhist ethical traditions, and from the Abrahamic religious heritage.

Such leadership is authoritative, bottom-up, empathetic, and difficult to scale. It depends on others' interpretations to scale up because the authority of prestige leaders is unique and impossible to replicate. Such leaders are often considered to be "humble, generous, competent, and inspiring."[15] Prestige leaders recruit followers through an emotional or intellectual bond created between them and others based on their ideas, wisdom, vision, and generosity.[16] *Although their behavior may be difficult to scale, their ideas and vision are infinitely scalable* (though they may be modified by dominant leaders who come after them).

Great prestige leaders are "super-spreaders of ideas" or of memes that colonize the minds of others as ideological-cultural viruses, to propagate their existence and spread independently of their originators.[17]

Prestige leadership is built on two foundations:
a. *Referent power:* Referent power is *authoritative* expertise or the ability to attract others and build a loyal cadre as a result of the charisma and interpersonal skills of the individual. It may be the result of a specific trait that is admired, creating opportunities for interpersonal influence because the follower would like to be associated with the leader's particular personal qualities and gains status from being associated with the individual. It is unstable on its own, but can be very effective when combined with coercive and reward power – hence the strength of the hold of cult leaders over their followers.[18]

b. ***Expert power:*** Expert power is *authoritative* and based on the particular and specialist skills and expertise of an individual and the organizations' need for them. The relevance of skills and expertise are determined by context and situation and is usually highly specific, limited to a particular area of expertise. Expert power is more valuable if it is difficult to transfer or replicate. It allows the expert to demonstrate superior understanding of the situation, suggest better solutions and outperform others. Expert power, like competencies, may have a limited shelf-life as organizational circumstances change.[19]

3. **Collective disciplining** constrained over-dominant leaders whose behavior threatened the viability of the primitive collective. Such leaders were either disciplined by the "village," expelled from the group, or, in extreme cases, killed.[20]

In modern organizations, the constraints placed on dangerous dominant leaders is achieved by the regulatory framework that determines what behavior is socially acceptable and internal processes decided by the board or its equivalent regarding agreed upon values, accepted behaviors, and codes of conduct to enforce them.

From Prestige to Dominant Leadership

There seem to be two imperatives that convert prestige leadership into dominant leadership: the impact of scale, and the need for continuity of either bloodline or "meme line."

1. **Impact of scale:** Given the unique characteristics of prestige leaders cannot be replicated, once their ideas or vision have created organizations with hierarchies, the need to allocate responsibilities, arbitrate between competing interests, and allocate resources to support those responsibilities forces organizations to turn to dominant leadership models to fulfill these roles. For example, when "Incubators" become successful "Guided Missiles" or "Eiffel Towers," the need for efficiency leads to standardization of processes, resulting in a move from "management by enthusiasm and co-creation" (ideally suited for prestige leadership) to "management by objective" or "management by job description" (more suited to dominant leadership). In the case of "Family Firms," as long as the founder is still running the business, the leadership role is a blend of both prestige (reflecting the founder's vision) and dominance (reflecting the need for fast decisions). Once the "Family Firm" is being run by the second or third generation, the balance between prestige and dominant leadership styles likely shifts toward dominance.

2. **Need for continuity:** Continuity comes in two forms: dynastic a (biological) need to keep hold of the organization, territory, or principality for the founding family; and the need to ensure ideological orthodoxy as the next generation adopts the ideas of the original "super-spreader of the memetic virus":

a. **Dynastic continuity:** The founders of the Chinese Han and Ming dynasties began their rise to power as prestige leaders, as did Napoleon. Yet, by the end of their careers they had become dominant leaders, validating Lord Acton's dictum that:

> Power tends to corrupt, absolute power corrupts absolutely. Great men are almost always bad men, even when they exercise influence and not authority, still more when you superadd the tendency or the certainty of corruption by authority.

Chinese explanations for the change in the dynastic founders of the Han and Ming dynasties from empathetic, collaborative prestige leaders who worked closely with their comrades in arms, only to end up as paranoid murderers of their key supporters, suggest that the reason for killing their close collaborators was the need to ensure that the empire passed to their children – hence the need to eliminate potential rivals. In these cases, we can suppose *the motive was to maintain privileged access to resources.*

b. **Ideological orthodoxy:** If the founders of ideologies and religions have in the main been prestige leaders, why do their ideas get adopted but are administered or implemented by increasingly authoritarian, intolerant, and dominant leader followers? The Albigensian Crusade, Spanish Inquisition, and the European wars of religion between Protestants and Catholics appear to be ruthless, intolerant perversions of Christ's teaching. The vicious infighting in both the early Soviet Union and in China, between the Chinese and Soviets or the Chinese and the Vietnamese are all battles for dominant control of followers of Marx's ideas that Marx did not foresee. Islam with its emphasis on brotherhood and the prohibition of war between Muslims, experienced the Sunni-Shia and Sunni-Ahmadiyya splits, the 10th century "closing of the gates of Ijtihad" led to an increasingly top-down, intolerant Sunni version of the Prophet's teachings, culminating in the ruthless Islamic State (Daesh) of the 21st century (justified as the true version of the Prophet's teachings, validating the previously prohibited murder of thousands of co-religionists).

Using Two Styles of Leadership

The effectiveness of leaders depends on adopting the style most appropriate to contextual factors and their ability to deploy dominant and prestige styles of leadership accordingly. This is influenced by individual personality traits, charisma, and contexts (cultural, organizational, and personal). With the passage of time, there is a tendency for individuals and organizations that begin with a prestige style of leadership to move to a dominant style as a result of the difficulties of scaling up prestige leadership as organizations grow, and as followers impose orthodoxy/orthopraxy on their prestige leader-founders' original ideas.

There are two ways to reconcile dominant and prestige styles of leadership: recognizing that both are more effective when they reflect the context and situation in which leaders find themselves, and in providing a structural resolution to the dilemma.

1. **Contextual and Situational Awareness:** Effective "wayfinders" realize that contextual and situational awareness determines which leadership style suits the conditions in which they find themselves. For example, "wayfinders" low down in an organization do not have the positional authority to practice dominant leadership based on coercion or reward power. They may have some limited legitimacy power offered by the position/role they fulfill. However, they have the opportunity to achieve prestige leadership through referent or expert power. This explains why there are leaders at all levels in organizations. From an initial opportunity to achieve prestige leadership, effective "wayfinders" are able to move up the leadership ladder, leveraging their prestige into positions that yield greater legitimacy power and may offer limited coercion and reward power. As they gain authority in the organization, their ability to wield coercion and reward power rises correspondingly.

Effective "wayfinders" recognize that different circumstances and contexts demand different styles of leadership and consequently they appreciate that they do not have to choose between the two styles but can reconcile them instead, based on where they are in terms of seniority, job function, and urgency of decision-making, illustrated in Figure 9.1.

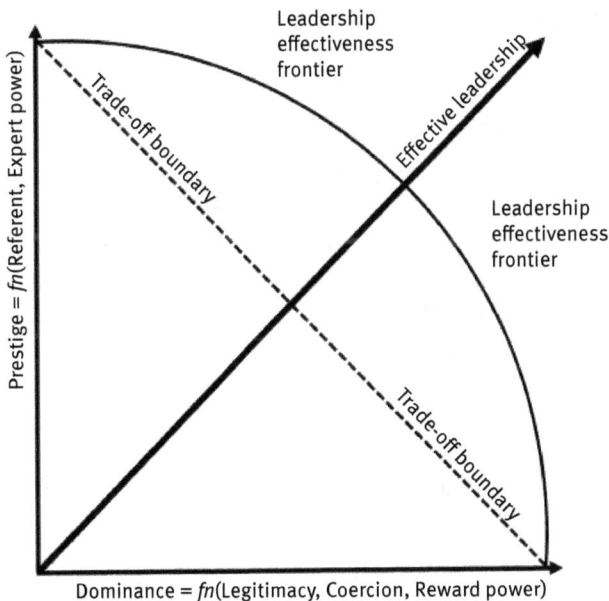

Figure 9.1: Effective Leadership Reconciles Two Styles of Leadership.

In Figure 9.1, the vertical vector shows how prestige leadership is a function of referent and expert power and how it tends to build over time, with referent power nearest to the origin and expert power building upon it. The further from the origin, the greater the power.

The horizontal vector shows how, over time, the effectiveness of dominant leadership increases with greater legitimacy, coercion, and reward power. Legitimacy (positional power) comes first, allowing individuals to use coercive power to achieve their goals, and finally using reward power once their goals have been achieved. The further from the origin, the greater the dominance leadership. The dotted line is the "trade-off boundary" that comes from regarding prestige and dominant leadership as being an "either-or" choice, whereas the "effective leadership" vector reflects the idea that it is a "both-and" activity. Effective leaders use both styles depending on their situations, circumstances, and contexts. This reconciliation allows them to achieve superior outcomes beyond the "trade-off boundary" up to the "leadership effectiveness frontier" to greater benefit for both leaders and led.

2. **Structural Resolution:** Some professional service firms have found a way of combining dominant and prestige leadership styles to great effect by creating three career ladders for their partners: rainmaking client leadership (dominant style), practice leadership expertise (prestige style), and administration (a combination of both styles, but predominantly dominant).

Cognitive Abilities and Innate Traits

The effectiveness of leaders depends on their cognitive abilities, which can be reinforced or weakened by their innate traits.[21]

1. **Cognitive skills:** Intellectual horsepower is built upon three foundations:
   a. *Thinking skills* which can be divided into skills of critical reasoning (numerical, verbal, spatial, emotional) and can be skills of analysis or synthesis. The experience of many leaders suggest that it is not essential for leaders to personally possess all of these skills provided that they surround themselves with people who possess such skills, and are willing to listen to their advisers.[22]
   b. *Ability to absorb new information* and to integrate it into new thinking and a coherent framework for its appropriate application.[23]
   c. *Avoiding the rush to judgment* in conditions of stress by using appropriate heuristics, recognizing the sources of bias,[24] and the difficulty of overcoming cognitive dissonance,[25] as a critical part of effective problem-solving (discussed in Chapter 8).

2. **Innate traits:** The five personality traits are captured in the OCEAN acronym:[26]

a. **Openness to experience** captures appreciation of art, emotions, adventure, heterodox ideas, curiosity, and variety in experiences. It reflects a person's level of intellectual curiosity, creativity, liking of novelty and variety, levels of imagination, independence, and dislike of routine. Table 9.1 compares high- and low-level openness traits.

Table 9.1: Levels of Openness Compared.

Person with High Level of Openness	Person with Low Level of Openness
Perceived as unpredictable or lacking focus. Individuals with high levels of openness are said to pursue self-actualization by seeking adrenaline highs and adventurous experiences (skydiving, gambling, living abroad).	Seeks fulfilment through perseverance, often characterized as being pragmatic, data-driven, and sometimes perceived as being dogmatic and closed-minded.

b. **Conscientiousness** captures the levels of efficiency and organization compared with being easy-going and carefree. It reflects an individual's tendency to be organized and dependable, show self-discipline, act dutifully, be achievement oriented, and to prefer planning to spontaneous behavior. Table 9.2 compares high- and low-level conscientiousness.

Table 9.2: Levels of Conscientiousness Compared.

Person with High Level of Conscientiousness	Person with Low Level of Conscientiousness
Often perceived as stubborn and obsessive.	Associated with flexibility and spontaneity, but also can appear sloppy and unreliable.

c. **Extraversion** measures individuals' preference to be outgoing and energetic compared with their preference for solitude and reservation. This appears in their levels of energy, positive emotions, assertiveness, sociability, need for stimulation in the company of others, talkativeness, and surgency (emotional reactivity in which extraverted individuals tend towards high levels of positive affect). Table 9.3 compares people with high- and low-levels of extraversion.

Table 9.3: Levels of Extraversion Compared.

Person with High Level of Extraversion	Person with Low Level of Extraversion
Often perceived as attention-seeking, domineering, and bordering narcissistic.	Has a reserved, reflective personality, often perceived as being aloof or self-absorbed.

d. *Agreeableness* describes the tendency of individuals to be empathetic, compassionate, and cooperative rather than suspicious and antagonistic toward others. It measures the level to which individuals are trusting and helpful toward others and whether they are good-tempered or not. Table 9.4 shows a comparison of agreeableness.

Table 9.4: Level of Agreeableness Compared.

Person with High Level of Agreeableness	Person with Low Level of Agreeableness
Often perceived as naïve or submissive.	Is often competitive and challenging and perceived as argumentative and untrustworthy.

e. *Neuroticism* describes the tendency of individuals to experience negative emotions easily such as anger, anxiety, vulnerability, and depression. It also refers to an individuals' degree of emotional stability and impulse control, sometimes referred as "emotional stability." Table 9.5 compares individuals with high- and low-levels of emotional stability.

Table 9.5: Levels of Emotional Stability Compared.

Person with High Level of Emotional Stability	Person with Low Level of Emotional Stability
Often perceived as having a stable and calm personality, but can appear uninspiring and unconcerned.	Often perceived as very dynamic, but with an excitable and reactive personality, leading them to be regarded as unstable or insecure.

3. **Charisma:** General charisma reflects a natural personal predisposition, based on observable expressive behavior, of affability and influence which is how most people think of it in everyday life.[27] General charisma is an important component of referent power and explains why some people (those with charisma) at all levels in organizations have the ability to influence others.

Surprisingly, charisma can be enhanced through learning[28] to increase the leadership effectiveness of individuals. There are twelve techniques that "wayfinders" can learn to enhance their charisma shown in Table 9.6.

Table 9.6: Twelve Techniques to Enhance Charisma.

Aristotle's Nine Verbal Techniques	*Connect, Compare, and Contrast* 1. *Use metaphors that people can relate to*: For example, Martin Luther King Jr.'s "I Have a Dream" speech where he compared the US Constitution to receiving an unreliable promissory note guaranteeing rights of liberty, life, and happiness, except for African-Americans who had been given a "bad check," marked with "insufficient funds."[29] 2. *Use stories and anecdotes:* Jesus used parables to great effect to get his teachings understood by his audiences. 3. *Use contrasts to reinforce the point*: For example, President Kennedy's "Ask not what your country can do for you – ask what you can do for your country."
	Engage and Distil 1. *Use rhetorical questions:* For example, Anita Roddick asked three questions when she founded The Body Shop: "How do you make business kinder? How do you embed it in the community? How do you make community a social purpose for business?"[30] 2. *Use three-part lists:* This is because "most people can remember three things, three is sufficient to provide proof of a pattern, and three gives an impression of completeness. Three-part lists can be announced – as in 'There are three things we need to do to get our bottom line back into the black' – or they can be under the radar, as in the sentence before this one."[31] Julius Caesar's "Veni, Vidi, Vici" ("I came, I saw, I conquered")[32] is perhaps the most famous example. The UK government used this approach to deal with the Covid-19 pandemic with their slogan "Stay at home, save lives, protect the NHS."
	Show Integrity, Authority and Passion 1. *Express moral conviction*: This gets the audience to align itself with the speaker's purpose and objectives, for example, Martin Luther King Jr., Nelson Mandela, and Mahatma Gandhi 2. *Channel the emotions of the group*: This is morally neutral since it depends on what the emotions of the group are; for example, many charismatic leaders have used hatred, mistrust, resentment, and fear of others to mobilize their supporters.
	Convey Confidence Goals Are Achievable 1. *Provide compelling statement of goals to be achieved* Logos (logic), Eros (material benefit), and Thymos (emotional arguments) to justify them 2. *Provide reassurance based on personal track record using Ethos* (speaker's credibility). (This is discussed further in Chapter 10.)

Table 9.6 (continued)

Three Non-Verbal Techniques[33]		
	1.	*Animated voice:* People who are passionate vary the volume with which they speak – whispering at appropriate points or rising to a crescendo to hammer home a point. Emotion – sadness, happiness, excitement, surprise – must come through in the voice. Pauses are also important because they convey control.
	2.	*Facial expressions* help reinforce your message. Listeners need to see as well as hear your passion – especially when you're telling a story or reflecting their sentiments. So be sure to make eye contact (one of the givens of charisma), and get comfortable smiling, frowning, and laughing at work.
	3.	*Gestures* are signals for your listeners. A fist can reinforce confidence, power, and certitude. Waving a hand, pointing, or pounding a desk can help draw attention.

Leadership charisma differs from general charisma:

> Charisma is rooted in values and feelings. It [is] influence born of the alchemy that Aristotle called the logos, the ethos, and the pathos, that is, to persuade others, you must use powerful and reasoned rhetoric, establish personal and moral credibility, and then rouse followers' emotions and passions. *If a leader can do those three things well, he or she can then tap into the hopes and ideals of followers, give them a sense of purpose, and inspire them to achieve great things.*[34]
>
> [Emphasis ours]

In a leadership context where the emphasis is on getting followers to act, it is important to remember charisma is morally neutral. Political leaders with great charisma can use it to inspire people to do good (for example, Mahatma Gandhi, Martin Luther King Jr., Nelson Mandela, and Mother Teresa) or harm (for example, Alexander the Great, Hitler, Mao, and Stalin). Sometimes the same charismatic leaders will deploy charisma in "good" or "evil" endeavors.

In a business context, the same dilemma appears with leaders who were originally great for their companies but became disasters as they were corrupted by power and previous success. Table 9.7 lists some examples of charismatic leaders who were good for their companies and those who were bad for their companies.

In short, charismatic leadership is neutral. Like many other skills, it can be used for good or evil and/or create or destroy value. It weakens judgment because it is based on charm and fear, it is addictive because leaders and followers seek the emotional gratification it provides at the expense of critical reasoning, and it can lead to intolerance, division, and tribalization.[39]

Table 9.7: Charismatic Leaders Who Had Different Types of Impact.

Positive Examples for Their Companies	Negative Examples for Their Companies
1. **Founders** – Branson, Richard (Virgin) – Jobs, Steve (Apple) – Ma, Jack (Alibaba, Ant Financial) – Musk, Elon (SpaceX, Tesla) – Schultz, Howard (Starbucks)	1. **Destroyed value** – Dunlap, Al (Scott Paper) – Fiorina, Carly (HP) – Levin, Gerald (AOL) – Mayer, Marissa (Yahoo) – Nardelli, Bob (Home Depot) – Sculley, John (Apple) – Smith, Roger (GM)
2. **Took value to the next level** – Browne, John (Amoco, Arco, BP) – Dimon, Jamie (JP Morgan Chase) – Iger, Bob (Disney)	2. **Disasters** – Cayne, Jimmy (Bear Stearns)[35] – Ebbers, Bernie (WorldCom) – Fuld, Dick (Lehman Brothers)[36] – Goodwin, Fred (Royal Bank of Scotland)[37] – Lay, Ken (Enron) – Mozilo, Angelo (Countrywide Financial) – O'Neal, Stan (Merrill Lynch)[38] – Skilling, Geoffrey (Enron)
3. **Turnaround successes** – Bethune, Gordon (Continental Airlines) – Gerstner, Lou (IBM) – Ghosn, Carlos (Nissan, Renault) – Iacocca, Lee (Chrysler) – Jobs, Steve (Apple) – Marchione, Sergio (Chrysler, Fiat) – Mullaly, Alan (Ford)	

Source: Based on Parker, G. (2016), "The 20 Greatest Business Comeback Stories of All Time," *Money Inc.*, https://moneyinc.com/greatest-business-comebacks/, accessed on July 27, 2020, Toscano, P. (2009), "Portfolio's Worst American CEOs of All Time," *CNBC*, April 30, 2009, https://www.cnbc.com/2009/04/30/Portfolios-Worst-American-CEOs-of-All-Time.html, accessed on July 27, 2020.

Required Managerial Skills of Leaders

To answer the question, "What managerial skills must effective "wayfinders" possess in a business environment?" we need to revisit the "Five P" framework (discussed in Chapter 6).

To use the metaphor of the human body, "purpose" represents the conscious mind at work defining what needs to be done, "principles" are the unconscious mind and its heuristics that define beliefs and values, "power" represents the skeleton and muscles that make things happen, "people" represent the blood that carries essential nutrients and oxygen to the different parts of the body so that the joints and muscles (departments) can fulfill the conscious and unconscious commands of the brain (head office), "processes" represent the central nervous system that translates the commands into messages of action throughout the body, providing essential feedback when things go wrong.

Failure by leaders to have clarity of purpose leads to directionless activity, failure to articulate principles leads to inappropriate heuristics (discussed in Chapter 8) and poor decisions, failure to design power properly leads to an inability to execute because of missing limbs or muscle weakness (institutions needed to execute), failure to appoint the right people is like suffering from pernicious anemia or viruses in the blood, and failure to integrate the whole with processes is like having motor neuron disease where the entire body is gradually paralyzed as the nervous system shuts down.

The answers to the question "what managerial skills must leaders have?" depend on departmental function and tasks, and where people sit in the leadership pipeline.

1. **"Purpose":** Effective "wayfinders" must have the skills and operational competence needed to answer five questions about their organization's purpose:
a. *Who are the beneficiaries of the organization and are their interests being satisfied?* The focus and detailed understanding will vary depending on the stakeholders concerned and level of seniority of "wayfinders":
   i. The top of the leadership pipeline will have to consider the interests of all stakeholders (customers, employees, suppliers, communities, regulators, and shareholders),
   ii. Sales and marketing will have to focus on customers,
   iii. HR and line management focus on employees to maximize engagement, productivity, and the appropriate level of skills,
   iv. Production and logistics focus on suppliers and regulators regarding occupational health and logistics, and environmental concerns,
   v. Finance considers profitability to satisfy shareholders and regulators through proper budgeting, cost accounting, and financial reporting,
   vi. Risk management ensures the risk appetite of the organization matches that of its shareholders,
   vii. R&D focuses on the relevance of the products and services offered and their relative value for money for existing customers.
b. *What is the organization trying to achieve and is it still relevant?* To do this, "wayfinders" must understand all customers *and non-customers*, megatrends that affect the organization and its industry, competition for market margin (head-to-head competitors, suppliers, buyers, alternatives, and substitutes), the impact of technology on the business model, and the ability to innovate to remain relevant. These are questions for the most senior "wayfinders" (department heads, unit heads, and enterprise leaders). They require a granular understanding of the organization's business model, where it creates and destroys value, and what can be done to change these relationships. This in turn demands an understanding of

opportunity costs, resourcing needs and likely availability, and their impact on future organizational design, employment, and competencies. For "wayfinders" to do this effectively, they need to have the relevant domain experience, technical competence and financial literacy – all managerial skills, as opposed to so-called leadership skills.

c. *What do customers and non-customers value and why does the organization fail to attract non-customers?* Senior "wayfinders" in marketing, sales, and R&D need the relevant domain experience and technical skills to be able answer these questions, as well as leadership skills if they are to ask appropriate questions and appreciate what the answers imply. Failure to have such experience can lead to being misled by misunderstanding the findings or by vested interests in the organization that are either resisting change or covering up past errors in basic assumptions about customer and non-customer dynamics. Perhaps the most important skills in answering these questions are:

   i. *The ability to imagine a different future* requires answering the questions "Why?" "Why not?" "What could we do differently?" recognizing that, "This is how we have always done things," or "We tried that and it did not work," are not satisfactory answers; and using Ishikawa's fishbone and the "Five Whys" analysis to get to the root causes.[i]

   ii. *The ability to connect dots* that are apparently unrelated, to create a new combination of ideas, existing processes or services to launch a disruptive game-changing offer[ii] that satisfies both existing customers and attracts non-customers.

---

i Ishikawa "fishbone" analysis, also known as cause-and-effect diagram is a diagram-based technique that combines mind-mapping with brainstorming to consider all possible causes of a problem. The diagram looks like a fish skeleton, hence the name. For details of how to use the technique, see "Cause and Effect Analysis", *MindTools*, https://www.mindtools.com/pages/article/newTMC_03.htm, accessed on March 17, 2021. The "Five Whys" analysis method was developed by Toyota: when a problem occurs, drill down to its root cause by asking "Why?" five times. Then, when a counter-measure becomes apparent, follow it through to prevent the issue from recurring.

ii For example, Admiral Hyman Rickover the "father of the nuclear navy," created an entirely new strategic weapon system by combining three tried and tested independent products in an unexpected way. Nuclear reactors and ICBMs had been successfully installed on land and submarines had been in use since the late 19th century. Rickover's genius was to combine the three into a totally new weapons system. The nuclear reactors gave the submarines unlimited reach on undersea patrols, allowing them to loiter undetected in strategically important places, the submarines provided an invisible launching platform for the ICBMs to take out key Soviet targets that the USSR could not track. As a result, the Soviets could not be sure that they would not suffer from a devastating retaliatory attack even if they destroyed all the land-based missiles and bombers the US had deployed. The net result: "Mutually Assured Destruction" that kept the peace, preventing the Cold War becoming a hot war. McLemore, C. and Jimenez, E. (2018), "Who is the Admiral Rickover of Naval Artificial Intelligence?" *War on the Rocks,* September 18, 2018, https://warontherocks.com/2018/09/who-is-the-admiral-rickover-of-naval-artificial-intelligence/, accessed on August 6, 2020.

d. *How will we know if we have succeeded in achieving our purpose?* This requires "wayfinders" at every level to understand the KPIs (key performance indicators) and how they fit together to achieve the agreed upon purpose in a timely fashion, distinguishing between input KPIs that are essential for successful project management, output KPIs to measure performance in meeting milestones, and outcome KPIs to measure impact effectiveness. Getting these KPIs right, and ensuring that they deliver the optimum critical path requires detailed systems thinking, domain understanding, and experience of the nature of the business, the interactions between its component parts, and what could go wrong in a tightly coupled complex system – all managerial skills reflecting operational competence.

e. *What is the plan and the assumptions on which it is based?* The plan provides a common "language" based in numbers that allows all the different "wayfinders" to appreciate what they are supposed to do, by when, and where they fit into the big picture. Effective planning requires regular review of assumptions, variances and progress, and follow on corrective actions. Without these being done correctly, systematically, with effective contingency plans to get back on track, "wayfinders" at all levels run the risk of failing to execute agreed upon objectives, demonstrating operational incompetence.

Answering these five questions requires "wayfinders" to have analytical, problem-solving, measurement, and financial skills that are fundamental to effective execution of the organizational purpose. In addition, every "wayfinder" needs to have decision-making skills capable of dealing with volatility, uncertainty, complexity, and ambiguity, requiring systemic thinking skills as well (discussed in Chapter 7), and be able to communicate resulting decisions effectively: what needs to be done, by whom, and by when (discussed in Chapter 10).

2. **"Principles":** As discussed in Chapter 6, "principles" refers to the organization's *"evergreen" values* that determine 1) what type of business the organization is willing to undertake, 2) the types of customers it is willing to serve, 3) the products and services it offers and how they are made, 4) how customers (internal and external) are treated, 5) what types of behavior and processes are expected, and what types are unacceptable (captured in the code of conduct). In other words, "principles" answer the questions: "Who are we?", "What do we believe in?", "What do we stand for?", "How should we do business?", "How should we behave?", "How should we treat people?", and "How should we measure performance to ensure ethical behavior?".

3. **"Power":** As discussed in Chapter 6, "power" refers to the organization's structure, roles, and responsibilities and how these could change over time as the strategic context changes. As a result, effective "wayfinders" need to be comfortable with organizational design, job evaluation, and the continuous review of managerial and functional core competencies, which may change over time, unlike leadership competencies

which are "evergreen." The leadership "evergreen" competencies are managing change, developing people, and being creative/imaginative.

Managing change depends on "wayfinders" imagining different futures at global, national, organizational, departmental, or even personal levels, or as Marshall Goldsmith put it, "bringing the future to the present."[40] However, this can only be achieved through defining value chain *desired* states across the organization's business model and comparing them with the value chain's *actual* state. This then provides "wayfinders" with gap analyses by element in the value chain to design project management programs to close the gap. The process is shown in Figure 9.2.

VALUE CHAIN *DESIRED* STATE:

GAP ANALYSES

VALUE CHAIN *ACTUAL* STATE:

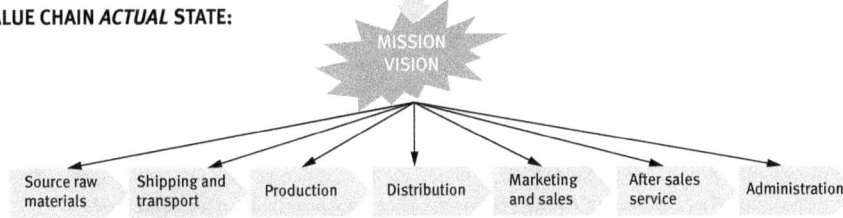

Figure 9.2: Managing Change – Bringing the Future to the Present.

Figure 9.2 illustrates the value chain desired state derived from the imagined future and compares it with the value chain actual state. The comparison provides the basis of the gap analyses for the differences in the new mission and vision and the existing ones and the corresponding shortfalls in each element of the value chain. Based on these gap analyses, "wayfinders" can then engage the people most familiar with current conditions at each stage in the value chain to determine what must be done to close the gaps, by when, and by whom, using stakeholder engagement skills (discussed in Chapter 6), standard project management, and critical path techniques to ensure that the imagined future becomes a current reality.

In so doing, it is essential "wayfinders" remember that managing transitions is always difficult. They should recognize the emotional pain such change may create and mitigate it by using S.A.R.A.H for empathy and the "Bridges model" to help people navigate the transition (discussed in Chapter 6).

4. **"People"**: Talented people are the lifeblood of organizations – without people, there is no organization. We recognize the aptness of the comparison with blood when we say, "We need new blood to encourage fresh thinking," as a justification for recruiting talent from outside, just as people need transfusions to prevent them from bleeding out or dying from blood disorders. However, that does not mean any blood will do. First, the blood type must match, second it must be free of disease that can be transferred from one person to another. It is the same when bringing new people into an organization. The equivalent check to matching blood type is that the new recruits must possess the experience and competencies needed to do the job for which they are being hired. The equivalent check to ensuring that no new virus is being introduced into the patient's system is to check that the values, belief systems, and (business) cultural backgrounds fit with the values and beliefs of the organization they are joining. There are five possible cultural mismatches that can have a material impact on "wayfinder" effectiveness, created by differences in belief systems:

a.   *Rules versus Relationships:*Universalists and Particularists have different underlying belief systems that lead to divergences in behavior, shown in Table 9.8.

Table 9.8: Differences between Universalists and Particularists.

Universalist Approach	Particularist Approach
Underlying beliefs:	Underlying beliefs:
1. What is good and right can be defined and always applies regardless of circumstances	1. Obligations are to relationships, considering special circumstances come first
2. No exceptions to applying rules, relationships do not matter	2. Waivers are necessary because special circumstances always exist
3. Level playing field is the basis of competition	3. Handicaps are the basis of competition
4. Only one reality – that which has been agreed in a legally binding document	4. Several realities exist based on changing circumstances and relationships
5. Legal contracts are easily drawn up	5. Legal contracts are easily modified
6. Trustworthy person honors their word or contract	6. Trustworthy person honors changing mutual ties
7. Particularists cannot be trusted to adhere to codes of conduct because they will always help their friends out when there is a problem	7. Universalists cannot be trusted because they put the code of conduct first and won't help their friends out when there is a problem

Table 9.8 (continued)

Universalist Approach	Particularist Approach
Resulting behavior:	**Resulting behavior:**
1. Focusing on rules rather than relationships – a deal is a deal	1. Focusing on relationships – relationships evolve and so the deal must evolve

2. Using legal proceedings to ensure promises are kept:
  a. Contract records agreement in principle and codifies *specific performance*
  b. Implies consent and provides recourse
  c. Introducing lawyers into the process signals failure to perform, is not acceptable, and expensive to remedy
  d. Contract takes the place of the relationship
	2. Keeping promises based on personal relationships:
	  a. Recognizing good relationships require *keeping the contract as diffuse as possible*
	  b. Relationships are more lasting
	  c. Seeking process of mutual accommodation, litigation should be avoided
	  d. Relationship takes the place of the contract

3. Striving for consistency and uniform procedures	3. Taking offense at detailed penalties and requirements in the contract for specific performance
4. Instituting formal ways of changing the way business is done	4. Building informal networks and creating private understandings
5. Changing the system so the system will change you	5. Modifying relations with individuals so that they modify the system
6. Signaling changes publicly	6. Pulling levers privately
7. Seeking fairness by treating all like cases in the same way	7. Seeking fairness by treating all cases on their special merits

Source: Based on Zinkin, J. (2020), *The Challenge of Sustainability: Corporate Governance in a Complicated World* (Boston: Walter de Gruyter), pp. 149–150.

b. *Managing and Measuring Performance:* The most important causes of disagreement between organizational cultures on managing performance come from differences in peoples' beliefs regarding time and how to measure performance. "Wayfinders" need to examine their own assumptions and beliefs regarding the right way to manage performance and recognize the people they supervise may have different beliefs and assumptions if they are to avoid unfortunate misunderstandings and unintentional conflict.

People spend time sequentially or synchronously. Which they choose depends on their assumptions and beliefs about the nature of time. Table 9.9 shows the differences in assumptions between sequential and synchronous approaches to time.

Table 9.9: Differences in Approaches to Time.

Sequential Approach	Synchronous Approach
Underlying beliefs:	**Underlying beliefs:**
1. Time is a scarce resource – "time is money"	1. Time is "space for relating with others"
2. Time is measurable and tangible	2. Time is like a "wide ribbon, intangible
3. Time is linear	3. Time is circular
Resulting behavior:	**Resulting behavior:**
1. Corporate ideal is the straight line and most rapid efficient route to achieving objectives	1. Corporate ideal is the interacting circle in which past experience, present opportunities, and future possibilities cross-fertilize
2. Focusing on the quickest way from A to B, efficiency is the driver	2. Focusing on developing long-term relationships: "What's the hurry?"
3. Leaving the past behind in the attempt to capture the immediate gains in the near future	3. Refusing to admit the need for change unless it can carry part of the heritage forward
4. Focusing on the agenda and each step one at a time	4. Pursuing multiple and often apparently distracting agendas
5. Seeing product or service as separate from the relationship	5. Seeing a product or service as part of an ongoing relationship
6. Insisting each step has its own sequence and its own 'due by' date, project management essential	6. Seeing separate steps as parallel parts of the whole rather than on their own
Performance Appraisal:	**Performance Appraisal:**
1. Employees feel rewarded by achieving planned future goals (MBO)	1. Employees feel rewarded by achieving improved relationships with supervisors/customers
2. Employees' most recent performance is the major issue, along with whether their commitments for the future can be trusted	2. Employees' entire histories with the firm and future potential are the contexts framing the review of current performance
3. Plan the career of employees jointly with them, stressing landmarks to be reached by certain times, and corrective actions if not achieved	3. Discuss with employees their final aspirations in the context of the company, in what ways can they be realized?

Source: Based on Zinkin, J. (2020), *The Challenge of Sustainability: Corporate Governance in a Complicated World* (Boston: Walter de Gruyter), pp. 150–151.

The second difference in approach to measuring performance can be a serious source of misunderstanding when appraising people. Some cultures are specific, breaking performance down into its constituent parts, whereas others are more diffuse when defining performance. Table 9.10 compares the two approaches.

Table 9.10: Specific and Diffuse Approaches to Performance.

Specific Approach	Diffuse Approach
Underlying beliefs:	**Underlying beliefs:**
1. Principles and consistent moral stands, independent of the person being addressed	1. Highly situational morality depending on the person and context
2. Private and business agendas are kept separate	2. Private and business issues are not kept separate
3. The language of performance contracts at work is specific	3. The behavior of the whole person in a relationship, including outside work, is diffuse
4. *"The Report leads to the Rapport"* a. Measurement of KPIs b. Facts/performance create trust	4. *"The Rapport leads to the Report"* a. Trust creates performance b. Trust provides access to the facts
5. Company is an "Instrumental" system designed to perform functions and tasks in an efficient way. People are paid for the tasks they perform.	5. Company is a "social" group of people working together. They have social relations with other people and with the organization
Resulting behavior:	**Resulting behavior:**
1. Operates on feedback and fact-based analysis	1. Reconciles contradictions in a complex world of networks
2. Seeks truth through analysis: deductive, inductive logic	2. Understands the need for balance, yin and yang coexist
3. Believes in individual responsibility/ accountability	3. Believes in group or team responsibility/ accountability
4. Works with business plans and budgets	4. Works with scenarios
5. Deals in *explicit* knowledge: a. Manuals b. Software c. Libraries d. Records e. SLAs and SOPs	5. Deals in *tacit* knowledge: a. Relationships b. Culture c. Understandings d. Who knows what e. Institutional memory
6. Communication: a. Direct, to the point, purposeful in relating b. Precise, blunt, definitive, and transparent	6. Communication: a. Indirect, circuitous, seeming "aimless" forms of relating b. Evasive, tactful, ambiguous, even opaque

Table 9.10 (continued)

Specific Approach	Diffuse Approach
Performance Appraisal:	Performance Appraisal:
1. Only as good as the last performance appraisal 2. Clear, precise, and detailed instructions assure better compliance, allowing employees to disagree in clear terms	1. Past contributions of employees taken into account 2. Ambiguous and vague instructions allow subtle, responsive interpretations through which employees can exercise personal judgment

Source: Based on Zinkin, J. (2020), *The Challenge of Sustainability: Corporate Governance in a Complicated World* (Boston: Walter de Gruyter), pp. 151–152.

c. *Determining Status:* There are two ways of looking at status. At one end of the spectrum are those who believe that status, like respect, must be earned. At the other end of the spectrum are people who believe that some people are entitled to status and respect regardless of what they do. Sociologists say people's status is either *achieved* or it is *ascribed.* Table 9.11 shows the two approaches to status.

Table 9.11: Achieved or Ascribed Status.

Status Is Achieved	Status Is Ascribed
Underlying beliefs:	Underlying beliefs:

1. Status through *Achievement* means you are judged on
  a. Measurement of performance: contracts and KPIs matter
  b. Track record
  c. Recent performance ("only as good as your last . . .") – technical know-how: *"What did you study?" "What do you know?"*
	1. Status through *Ascription* means you are judged on
	  a. What is attributed to you (birth, kinship, gender, age)
	  b. Educational record
	  c. Connections – technical know-who: *"Where did you study?" "Who do you know?"*

2. Individuals can be easily compared based on their ability to "Achieve more" in specific performance terms	2. Individuals are unique and cannot be easily compared with others in specific performance terms as there are other factors to be considered

3. "I am my functional role"
  a. Hierarchical relationships are functionally specific and *apply only at work*
  b. Success is universally defined according to performance benchmarks
  c. Relationships with others are instrumental – lasting as long as necessary to complete the task
	3. "I personify the organization, wielding its power"
	  a. Status is independent of task or function and hierarchical relationships *still apply outside work*
	  b. Role justified through "power to get things done"
	  c. Relationships are social – based on loyalty and affection

Table 9.11 (continued)

Status Is Achieved	Status Is Ascribed
4. Subordinates' status is independent of superior's status, rewards may be higher	4. Subordinates' status depends on superior's status, rewards must be less
5. Superiors know what questions to ask, but not the answers	5. Superiors are expected to know the answers and tell their subordinates
6. Universalist: the rules apply to everybody regardless of relationships	6. Particularist: waivers to the rules may be applied to preserve relationships
Career development philosophy:	**Career development philosophy:**
1. *High fliers* promoted on "Up or Out" basis	1. *Crown Princes* identified based on potential
2. "Only as good as last performance review" – latest performance best predictor of future performance	2. Exposed to different roles and responsibilities to elicit potential, mistakes tolerated
3. Measured on achievement of latest KPIs, earlier contributions discounted	3. Measured on earlier contributions as well as present performance
Resulting behavior:	**Resulting behavior:**
1. Individualistic, independent, and accountable	1. Communitarian, dependent, and waiting for instruction
2. Most senior managers are of varying age and have proved themselves in specific jobs	2. Most senior managers are qualified by their social background rather than past performance
3. Respect for superiors is based on how effectively their jobs are done and how adequate their knowledge	3. Respect for superiors is seen as a measure of commitment to the organization and its mission
4. Use of titles only when relevant to the competence you bring to the task	4. Extensive use of titles, especially to clarify status in the organization
5. Decisions are challenged on technical and functional grounds	5. Decisions only challenged by people with higher authority
6. MBO (management by objectives) and pay-for-performance are effective tools	6. 'Rice bowl'@[iii] and social rewards from superiors more effective than MBO

Source: Based on Zinkin, J. (2020), *The Challenge of Sustainability: Corporate Governance in a Complicated World* (Boston: Walter de Gruyter), pp. 154–155.

d. *Individualism versus Community:* The difference in the importance placed on individual or collective behavior matters. It affects attitudes toward individual accountability, competition versus collaboration, and the role of the individual in the community. Table 9.12 shows the two approaches.

---

iii "Rice bowl" is a Chinese term for livelihood.

Table 9.12: Individual Versus Community.

Individual	Community
Underlying beliefs:	**Underlying beliefs:**
1. *Person seeking fulfillment is solely responsible for choices made and convictions formed* in the creative, feeling, inquiry, and discovery processes	1. *Society nurtures, educates, and takes responsibility for the spirit engendered among its members* in the social discourse of living
2. Individual is self-made and inner-directed, based on 　a. Self-reliance 　b. Self-interest 　c. Achieving personal growth	2. The social system creates personal outer-directed success, based on 　a. Social concern 　b. Altruism 　c. National service and societal legacy
3. Competing is the basis of success	3. Cooperating is the basis of success
4. Shareholder value and profitability come first	4. Stakeholder value and market share come first
5. Government acts as referee	5. Government acts as coach
Resulting behavior:	**Resulting behavior:**
1. Competing all out as rivals	1. Collaborating as mentor-mentee
2. Achieving alone and assuming personal responsibility	2. Achieving in groups and assuming joint responsibility
3. Making decisions on the spot, as representatives of the organization	3. Referring decisions back to the organization, acting as delegates
4. Making decisions based on voting	4. Making decisions by consensus
5. Focusing on completing tasks	5. Focusing on building relationships
6. Talking about "I"	6. Talking about "We"
Managing people:	**Managing people:**
1. Giving people freedom to take personal initiatives	1. Holding up superordinate goals for all to meet
2. Trying to adjust individual needs to organizational needs	2. Seeking to integrate personality with authority within the group
3. Introducing individual incentives (MBO, pay for performance, etc.)	3. Paying attention to esprit de corps, morale, and cohesiveness
4. Expecting high job turnover and mobility	4. Having low job turnover and mobility
5. Seeking out high performers and champions for role models	5. Praising the whole group and avoiding showing favoritism

Source: Based on Zinkin, J. (2020), *The Challenge of Sustainability: Corporate Governance in a Complicated World* (Boston: Walter de Gruyter), p. 156.

e. *Levels of Trust:* History and culture determine the levels of trust between govern-ments, intermediate actors, businesses, and how businesses are established, run, and handed on to the next generation of "wayfinders."[41] Cultures can be classified as "high" or "low" trust, although how they arrived there may differ considerably.[42] Francis Fu-kuyama classified cultures according to trust as a reflection of their social capital (the ability to work together for a common purpose):

> The ability to associate depends, in turn, on the degree to which communities share norms and values and are able to subordinate individual interests to those of larger groups. Out of such shared values comes trust . . .[43]

The resulting difference in behaviors is shown in Table 9.13.

Table 9.13: Behavioral Differences According to Trust Levels.

High	Low
1. *No separation between ideation/conception and execution*[44]	1. *Separation between ideation/conception and execution*
2. Tripartite socio-political structures comprising State, civil society, and family[45]	2. Dual socio-political structures with strong State and strong family focus, but weak civil society focus[50]
3. Community/collective defined by shared ethical habits and reciprocal moral obligations, "win-win" outcomes	3. Community/collective defined by explicit rules and regulations and "win-lose" mentality
4. Reliance on community/collective to create social capital	4. Reliance on the State to create social capital
5. Solidarity within the economic community/group	5. Focus on individual self-interest at the expense of the community/group
6. Large scale, multinational "Guided Missile" firms not based on kinship or State support, managed by professional non-family members (Germany, Holland, Japan, Sweden, Switzerland, UK, and US),[46] in Germany and Japan supported by "family" firms in their supply chains	6. "Family" firms predominate (China, France, Hong Kong, Italy, South Korea, and Taiwan) and experience difficulty in creating large organizations that go beyond the family, State firms promote durable, globally competitive "Eiffel Tower" firms (China, France, and Italy),[51,iv]

---

iv In South Korea, the *chaebols* are large globally successful family-controlled firms managed by pro-fessional managers, sponsored originally by the State through the favorable allocation of credit to enter government targeted pillar industries. The State does not own them, unlike in China, France, or Italy. In Italy, in addition to the State owned "Eiffel Towers" designed to harness economies of scale, there are three cultures: In Lombardy, there is a high level of trust and there are large private enterprises operat-ing as "Guided Missiles." In the South, there is a low level of trust and family firms are small and weak. In Emilia-Romagna, there is a third group with similar characteristics to Germany's Mittelstand – glob-ally competitive family firms operating in specialist value adding niches.

Table 9.13 (continued)

High	Low
7. Reliance on business networks with shared assumptions about codes of practice and professional behavior: "These communities do not require extensive contract and legal regulation of their relations because prior moral consensus gives members of the group a basis for mutual trust."[47]	7. Low spontaneous sociability resulting in cooperation "only under a system of formal rules and regulations, which have to be negotiated, agreed to, litigated, and enforced,[v] sometimes by coercive means . . . Widespread distrust . . . imposes a kind of tax on all forms of economic activity . . . that high-trust societies do not have to pay."[52]
8. Workers organized on a more flexible and group-oriented basis with responsibility delegated to lower levels[48]	8. Workers fenced in by a series of bureaucratic rules minimizing individual responsibility, emphasizing hierarchy[53]
9. Within moral "insider" groups there is a high level of spontaneous trust, respect and equality not extended to outsiders (e.g., Germany,[vi] and in particular Japan)[49]	9. In countries dedicated to the belief "all men are created equal, groups comprise people with different backgrounds, beliefs, and moral standards. Instead of a trust-based moral community, there is law, formal equality and due process (e.g., US, France)"[54]

5. **"Processes":** This is where vision meets reality or as Americans would say, "Where the rubber meets the road." Effective "wayfinders" appreciate that their ability to deliver their vision depends on their understanding of how organizational policies need procedures, processes, contracts, and service level agreements to ensure that purchases of raw materials, intermediate finished goods, and final products satisfy performance specifications and are delivered to the right place at the right time. The same applies to services.

Effective "wayfinders" have a proper appreciation of the managerial skills needed to set priorities between conflicting needs to handle the processes to optimize sourcing raw materials, maximize productivity in production, maximize cost effectiveness and

---

v "French workers on the shop floor are reluctant to form teams spontaneously, their preference is to cooperate on the basis of formal rules established centrally by management or by centralized bargaining between management and labor. Labor relations . . . tend to suffer from the formalism, labor unions tend not to settle disputes with management locally but refer problems up the ladder of authority – ultimately to the government in Paris." Fukuyama, F. (1995), op. cit., p. 119.

vi "German superiors assume the opposite [from their French counterparts], namely that their subordinates want and are able to acquire the kind of knowledge about their jobs that allows them to work autonomously. The task of the German supervisor is thus not to tell those charged with execution how to do their work, but rather to indicate to them what needs to be done. Conversely, in return for not being hedged in by a thicket of rules, German subordinates must count on their supervisors not to make abusive use of their discretionary powers. *German society is 'High trust' because it discourages the separation of conception and execution.*" [Emphasis ours] Fukuyama, F. (1995), op. cit., p. 242.

customer satisfaction in logistics and distribution, maximize cost effectiveness of marketing, sales, and after sales service, and ensure that finance and administration maximize the long-term financial viability of the organization and minimize its risks.

Crises and disasters always reveal whether the leadership of an organization understands the importance of processes and whether they are masters of the necessary skills. The Covid-19 personal protective equipment shambles in the US[55] and the UK[56] illustrate what happens when leaders do not have an appreciation of the importance of connected processes between different government departments at the national, regional, and local levels. Just declaring that all public health frontline workers would get the equipment they needed when they needed it (the vision) did not translate into reality because the leadership, in both countries, did not deploy the required managerial skills, or have the operational competence to execute effectively.

At national levels, political leaders must appreciate that governing is not the same as campaigning, being on reality TV, or writing opinion pieces where stirring promises, entertainment, or amusing aphorisms matter more than the facts. Governing effectively is about dealing with facts and making difficult choices in complex changing conditions. This demands an appreciation of the constitutional, legal, financial, and procedural limits on executive action.

The same is true when leading any organization. If "wayfinders" are to execute effectively, they cannot escape the constraints created by the facts on the ground and the policies, procedures, and processes designed to allocate resources to achieve optimum, predictable outcomes in each element of the value chain, while at the same time ensuring that conflicting priorities between the different elements of the value chain do not undermine the organization's purpose.

Summary

The popular view that leadership and management are two separate activities has led to the rise of populist, charismatic leaders who rely on rhetoric to achieve power without having the necessary managerial skills to execute. Leaders who have vision but lack managerial skills are, at best, super-spreaders of memes who depend on others to implement their ideas which may be severely distorted as a result.

Effective leadership benefits leaders and the led. It depends on leaders utilizing both dominant and prestige leadership styles as context demands.

Dominant leadership offers leaders privileged access to limited resources for personal gain. It is authoritarian, top-down, positional, coercive, and infinitely scalable, reflected in the preponderance of dominant leaders in large organizations. It is founded on legitimacy, coercive, and reward power.

Prestige leadership evolved to maximize resources for the benefit of all members of the group. It is authoritative, bottom up, personal and collaborative, founded on referent and expert power. It is difficult to replicate because it depends on the unique characteristics, experience, and knowledge of individuals. Although the behavior of prestige leaders is difficult to scale, their ideas and vision are infinitely scalable because they are spread through memes that "infect" the minds of others.

There seem to be two imperatives that tend over time to convert prestige leadership into dominant leadership: the impact of scale and the need for continuity as organizations grow. This need for continuity comes in two forms – the dynastic (genetic and biological continuity) need to keep control for the founding family (be it for a principality or an enterprise), and the desire to preserve orthodoxy (beliefs, the ideological and meme continuity), and orthopraxy (behavioral continuity).

There are two ways to reconcile dominant and prestige styles of leadership to increase "wayfinder" effectiveness. The first is for the "wayfinder" to have a high level of contextual and situational awareness and to recognize when it is appropriate to employ each style. This demands an understanding of how referent and expert power build over time as individuals rise up the leadership pipeline to develop prestige power. It also requires an understanding of how the dominant style of leadership depends on increasing individual seniority (as result of rising prestige power) beginning with power of positional legitimacy, moving on to power of coercion that positional authority grants, culminating in reward power. "Wayfinders" who practice both styles depending on the context and situation are able to maximize their leadership effectiveness frontier.

The ability to practice both styles appropriately is determined by the cognitive abilities and innate traits of individuals, modified by their life experiences.

Cognitive skills that matter are the family of thinking skills (analytical, systemic, and problem-solving), the ability to absorb, analyze, and synthesize new information, and avoiding the rush to judgment under stress (discussed in Chapter 8). Five innate personality traits and their levels affect how people behave: openness to experience, conscientiousness, extraversion, agreeableness, and neuroticism.

Charisma is important and although it has been regarded as an innate talent, its effect can be enhanced by applying Aristotle's rhetorical techniques. Charisma's impact can be further heightened through three learnable non-verbal techniques: using an animated voice, facial expressions, and gestures. Charismatic leadership is morally neutral and can be used for evil (Hitler) or good (Nelson Mandela).

The managerial skills leaders must have if they are to be effective "wayfinders" can be determined by answering five questions about their organizational purpose: "Who are the beneficiaries of the organization?" "What is the organization trying to achieve and is it still relevant?" "What do customers and non-customers value and why does the organization fail to attract non-customers?" "How will we know if we have succeeded in achieving our purpose?" and "What is the plan, and its assumptions?"

As part of answering questions about organizational "purpose," effective "wayfinders" need to ensure they have an appropriate "power" structure to deliver the "purpose." This requires understanding organizational design, and competency audits to ensure that it is durable. This in turn requires change management skills to "bring the future to the present."

Once the "power" issues have been resolved, the organization must be populated with suitable "people." Finding such people does not only require determining their availability, career development, and affordability, it also requires appreciating the behavioral impact on organizational effectiveness of five important differences in belief systems regarding: rules versus relationships, managing and measuring performance, determining status, individualism versus community, and cultures with different levels of trust.

Finally, effective "wayfinders" must have a sound understanding of "processes" in order to set priorities between the conflicting needs of different elements of the organizational value chain if it is to support the overall mission, vision, and values. Inability to appreciate the importance of joined up processes, network effects, and emergent properties of systems will lead to failure to achieve the desired goals, and to the vision being at best an unachievable dream, at worst a nightmare.

References

1 From a Sussex church, 1730.
2 Ardrey, R. (1966), *The Territorial Imperative: A Personal Inquiry into the Animal Origins of Property and Nations* (New York: Atheneum).
3 Yadin, Y., and Brown, K. S. (1996), "Herod's Fortress and the Zealots Last Stand: A BYU Forum Address," *Brigham Young University Studies*, Vol. 36, No. 3, Masada and the World of the New Testament (1996–7), pp. 15–32.
4 "Kamikaze: Military Tactic," *Encyclopedia Britannica*, https://www.britannica.com/topic/kamikaze accessed on July 27, 2020
5 Kuruppu, K., and Overton, I. (2018), "Suicide terrorism in the Sri Lankan Civil War (1983–2009)," *Action on Armed Violence*, October 15, 2018, https://aoav.org.uk/2018/suicide-terrorism-in-the-sri-lankan-civil-war-1983-2009/, accessed on July 27, 2020.
6 Harmon, V. et al. (2018), "Causes and Explanations of Suicide Terrorism: A Systematic Review," *Homeland Security Affairs* 14, Article 9 (December 2018), https://www.hsaj.org/articles/14749, accessed on July 27, 2020.
7 Vugt, M., Hogan, R., and Kaiser, R. (2008). "Leadership, Followership, and Evolution: Some Lessons From the Past," *The American Psychologist*, 63, 182–96. 10.1037/0003-066X.63.3.182.
8 Van Vugt, M. and Smith, J. E. (2019), "A Dual Model of Leadership and Hierarchy: A Synthesis," *Trends in Cognitive Science*, Cell Press Reviews, November 23, 2020, p. 952, https://pubmed.ncbi.nlm.nih.gov/31629633/, accessed on July 11, 2020.
9 Ibn Zafar al Siqilli, M. (d.1190), *Sulwan Al-Muta' Fi 'Udwan Al-Atba* (Consolation for the Ruler During the Hostility of Subjects), in Kechichian, J. A., and Dekmejian, R. H. (2003), *The Just Prince: A Manual of Leadership* (Singapore/Kuala Lumpur: Horizon Books).
10 Machiavelli, N. (1513), *The Prince* (London: Penguin Classics, 1999).
11 Hegel, G.W.F. (1807), *The Phenomenology of Mind*, cited in Fukuyama, F. (1992), *The End of History and the Last Man* (London: Penguin Books), p. 192.
12 French, J. R. P., and Raven, B. H. (1959). "The bases of social power," In D. Cartwright (ed.), *Studies in Social Power* (Ann Arbor, MI: Institute for Social Research), pp. 150–167.

13 Ibid.

14 Ibid.

15 Van Vugt and Smith (2019), op. cit., p. 953.

16 Ibid., p. 956.

17 Dennett, D. (2002), "Dangerous Memes," *TED Talk*, https://www.ted.com/talks/dan_dennett_dangerous_memes?utm_source=tedcomshare&utm_medium=email&utm_campaign=tedspread#t-911385, accessed on July 15, 2020.

18 French and Raven (1959), op. cit.

19 Ibid.

20 Van Vugt and Smith (2019), op. cit., p. 962.

21 Loehlin, J. C., McCrae, R. R., Costa, P. T., and John, O. P. (1998)."Heritabilities of Common and Measure-Specific Components of the Big Five Personality Factors," *Journal of Research in Personality*, Vol. 32, No. 4, pp. 431–453, https://doi.org/10.1006/jrpe.1998.2225.

22 French and Raven (1959).

23 Ibid.

24 Kahneman, D. (2011), *Thinking Fast and Slow* (London: Allen Lane), pp. 71–88.

25 Aronson, E., and Tavris, C. (2020), "The Role of Cognitive Dissonance in the Pandemic," *The Atlantic*, July 12, 2020, https://www.theatlantic.com/ideas/archive/2020/07/role-cognitive-dissonance-pandemic/614074/?utm_source=newsletter&utm_medium=email&utm_campaign=atlantic-daily-newsletter&utm_content=20200715&silverid-ref=MzQxNTM3NDUyNjQzSO, accessed on July 16, 2020.

26 Ackerman, C. (2017), *Big Five Personality Traits: The OCEAN Model Explained*, *Positive Psychology*, June 23, 2017, PositivePsychology.com. https://positivepsychology.com/big-five-personality-theory.

27 Tshkay, O. et al. (2018), Charisma in Everyday Life: Conceptualization and Validation of the General Charisma Inventory," *Journal of Personality and Social Psychology*, 2018, Vol. 114, No. 1, p. 147.

28 Antonakis, J., Fenley, M., and Liechti, S. (2012), "Learning Charisma," *Harvard Business Review*, June 2012, https://hbr.org/2012/06/learning-charisma-2, accessed on July 27, 2020.

29 Ibid.

30 Ibid.

31 Ibid.

32 Caesar, J. (BCE47), in a letter to the Roman Senate after his victory at the Battle of Zela.

33 Antonakis Fenley and Liechti (2012), op. cit.

34 Ibid.

35 Zinkin, J. (2014), *Rebuilding Trust in Banks: The Role of Leadership and Governance* (Singapore: John Wiley & Sons), pp. 30–33.

36 Ibid., pp. 33–37.

37 Ibid., pp. 37–42.

38 Ibid., pp. 28–30.

39 Chamorro-Premuzic, T. (2012), "The Dark Side of Charisma," *Harvard Business Review*, November 16, 2012, https://hbr.org/2012/11/the-dark-side-of-charisma, accessed on July 27, 2020,

40 Goldsmith, M. (2008), *What Got You Here Won't Get You There* (London: Profile Books).

41 Fukuyama, F. (1995), *Trust: The Social Virtues and the Creation of Prosperity* (New York: Free Press Paperbacks).

42 Ibid.

43 Ibid., p. 10.

44 Ibid., p. 242.

45 Ibid., p. 55.

46 Ibid., p. 29.

47 Ibid., p. 26.
48 Ibid., p. 31.
49 Ibid., 252.
50 Ibid., p. 55.
55 Yong, E. (2020), "How the Pandemic Defeated America," *The Atlantic*, September 2020 Issue, https://www.theatlantic.com/magazine/archive/2020/09/coronavirus-american-failure/614191/?utm_source=newsletter&utm_medium=email&utm_campaign=atlantic-daily-newsletter&utm_content=20200803&silverid-ref=MzQxNTM3NDUyNjQzS0, accessed on August 12, 2020.
56 McTague, T. (2020), "How the Pandemic Revealed Britain's National Illness," https://www.theatlantic.com/international/archive/2020/08/why-britain-failed-coronavirus-pandemic/615166/#main-content, accessed on August 12, 2020.

Chapter 10
Communicating Effectively

Prakash Tandon[i] used to say:

> The surface area of our ears is four times that of our mouth. That is because listening is more important than talking.

Effective "wayfinders" understand that communication involves listening as well as talking. Listening is hard to do well:

> *Concentration while listening is a greater problem than concentration during any other form of personal communication. Actually, listening concentration is more difficult . . .*

> *Basically, the problem is caused by the fact that we think much faster than we talk.* The average rate of speech for most Americans is around 125 words per minute. This rate is slow going for the human brain . . . words play a large part in our thinking processes, and the words race through our brains at speeds much higher than 125 words per minute . . .

> It might seem logical to slow down our thinking when we listen so as to coincide with the 125-word-per-minute speech rate, but slowing down thought processes seems to be a very difficult thing to do. When we listen, therefore, we continue thinking at high speed while the spoken words arrive at low speed . . . To phrase it another way, we can listen and still have some spare time for thinking.

> The use, or misuse, of this spare thinking time holds the answer to how well a person can concentrate on the spoken word.[1]   [Emphasis ours]

What does this mean in practice? Imagine a conversation between superior A and subordinate B. A begins to explain something to B. B pays attention, listening to each word. But the words from A are reaching B's brain slowly, B begins to insert thoughts of his own into the narrative. Without realizing, B is side-tracked by thoughts "inserted" into A's stream of words. Usually, B does not lose the thread of A's argument. However, at some point, B will spend so much time on the side-track that, when he returns to what A is saying, A will have moved on. Now B finds it hard to understand A's point because steps in the argument have been missed. Consequently, B spends more time on the side-tracks, missing more of A's argument. B ends up having understood little of what was said.

---

i First Indian Chairman of Hindustan Lever.

https://doi.org/10.1515/9783110707878-013

Three techniques facilitate better listening:[2]
1. *Listen without judging while the argument is made.*
2. *Review, ask questions to clarify, and summarize periodically* to understand the meaning behind the words using "active listening" to look for meaning that has not been put into words – including non-verbal signals.
3. *Weigh the evidence when the argument is complete.*

Good listening requires practice.

Try to *understand the speaker's ideas rather than memorizing facts.* It is easier to remember facts by absorbing the ideas supported by them.

Confirmation bias causes individuals to only "hear" that part of the argument that confirms their existing beliefs:

"Three As"

Communications should reflect the:
1. Nature of the *audience*
2. *Attitude* of the communicator and of the audience
3. *Angle* advocated

Communication that focuses only on *angle* (content) is ineffective because the audience's willingness to accept the argument is affected by their perception of its relevance and appropriateness. The emotional context can block the message being heard, the *attitude* that the communicator wishes to project must take into account the attitudes of the audience.

Audience

The willingness of audiences to receive messages depends on their size and membership, levels of seniority and sophistication, and interests:

1. *Size and membership:* It is more difficult to communicate effectively with large, diverse audiences because they are less homogeneous with more conflicting interactions between subgroups. Effective "wayfinders" know the composition of audiences in advance and choose whenever possible to maximize homogeneity of seniority, capability, and experience.

2. *Seniority and sophistication:* Audiences can have members from different strata of seniority, sophistication, and experience. It is difficult to engage effectively with heterogeneous groups:

a. *Impact of different levels of seniority:* Elliot Jacques[3] claimed there are six real hierarchical boundaries set by time spans of three months, one year, two years, five years, ten years, and twenty years. The different time spans reflect different types of decision and levels of accountability. *Communication to each layer needs to reflect differences in role, responsibility, and time horizon.*

The six levels of the "leadership pipeline"[4] similarly reflect the different roles and responsibilities of individuals moving from managing themselves, to managing others, to managing managers, to becoming a functional manager, a business manager, group manager, and finally an enterprise manager. Communication should tailor the messaging for each hierarchical level.

b. *Impact of different levels of sophistication: People at the top of the "leadership pipeline" deal with multiple issues simultaneously, and need to make trade-offs. Often they choose between "least-bad" alternatives.* They are more open to conceptual presentations. They are more likely to accept arguments based on plausibility and, because they deal in longer time horizons, they are less concerned with the immediate need to answer the question, "What do I do differently on Monday?" Their cognitive process when deciding on an action is "Believe, Understand, Do." They are impressed by executive summaries and often move to action without considering the detail. When they communicate what they want to happen, they use a "Believe, Understand, Do" structure.

"Big picture" exhortation in top-down communication only works if implementers understand the answer to their question "What will I be doing differently on Monday?" Implementers' concerns relate to their responsibilities and their interests, in terms of reporting relationships or in terms of reward and recognition. Implementers are wary of initiatives from the head office. They operate with a mental model of "Do, Understand, Believe" not "Believe, Understand, Do."

Communication style and structure must reflect the nature of the audience.

3. *Interests:* Even in apparently homogeneous groups, all audience members do not have the same life, values, and purposes:

> The human tendency to absorb the values of one's immediate environment and project those values onto the entire world may work well enough for life in small, relatively isolated hunter-gatherer bands, but *it's absolutely disastrous for billions of people raised in a variety of different cultures and subcultures who must share a world in spite of their incompatible worldviews. Human moral psychology doesn't scale well.*[5]   [Emphasis ours]

Navigating uncertainty and ambiguity when audiences are looking for clarity and certainty that cannot exist is problematic. Recognizing this requires empathy and open-mindedness. "Wayfinders" need to show a compelling "line of sight" between their superordinate goals and the people upon whom they depend to make things happen in the way they want.

Attitude

Mismatching message and audience is a frequent source of communication failures. For example, lawyers intervening to protect an organization from litigation, when what is needed is a clear demonstration of contrition if there was wrongdoing or of humanity and control if the problem is an accidental tragedy. Michael Bishop, CEO of British Midland in 1989 after the crash on take-off of a Boeing 737–400 near Keg-worth, just off the M1 Motorway in England, killing 47 people, did it well:

> *Within five minutes of hearing the news, he had decided to be very publicly available to press and broadcast crews, giving the information as fast as he received it.* He distinguished himself by showing both humanity and control.
>
> *The first interviews were given on the phone in his car on the way to the scene.* He knew almost nothing about what had happened but he said as much as he could. *He spoke with compassion, saying he understood how the relatives of passengers must be feeling because he personally knew every member of the crew and the pilot was an old friend.*
>
> When he arrived, his priorities were to get the relatives of 74 injured passengers and crew to the hospitals concerned, and to provide immediate support to the bereaved. *Every family was allocated a carer who would organise somewhere for them to stay and look after their personal needs.*
>
> . . . *At 4am Bishop gave a press conference. He cut a highly sympathetic figure with his simple account of the action he'd taken in response to a 'profoundly distressing' accident.*[6]
>
> [Emphases ours]

There was no doubt about Bishop's attitude and priorities. He made himself available, on site as fast as he could, answered questions, controlled the narrative as a result, giving a press conference at 4:00 a.m. the following morning. *One year later, more people were flying on British Midland than before the crash.*

Attitude makes a difference:

> If I want things to be one way and you want things to be some other way, we might be able to reach some sort of compromise. But if I want things to be one way, and I believe that the way I want things is not *merely* the way I want things but also the way things *ought to be,* and if I believe further that it's *just plain to see* that my is *the way things ought to be* and that anyone who says otherwise must be *outright lying* or *wilfully refusing to see the truth,* and if you want things to be some other way and you're just as convinced of the *rightness* of your position as I am of mine, then what chance do we have of reaching a reasonable compromise?[7]

Effective "wayfinders" recognize the power of attitude and reduce the potential for attitudinal conflict through validation,[8] acknowledging that the "wayfinder" has heard and appreciated another person's contribution/participation in the discussion, even if he or she does not agree with it. Validation affirms the other person's value. It requires listening actively, deciding the best form of validation, and formulating a non-judgmental response. "Wayfinders" must focus on what is being said, control their biases, separate facts from emotions, and pick up cue words to act as leads into validation.[ii] Validating is not the same as agreeing:

> Agreeing means you think it's the right idea. Validating is showing respect for someone's having an idea and spending time thinking about it.[9]

Angle

When planning to communicate, the objectives, the audience and their interests, and the style of communication need to be considered. A useful structure is to ask the following questions:

1. What am I trying to achieve and why *now*?
2. Who do I need to get to agree with what I am proposing?
3. What are their issues and interests and how will what I am proposing affect them?
4. How good is my case, factually, and emotionally? Have I left anything out, are there any flaws in my argument?
5. Will I face obstacles (resource constraints) or objections (negative mindsets) and what plans do I have to deal with them? In the case of objections, who is on my side and why, and who is against my ideas and why?
6. How would I feel hearing what I am going to say if I were in their shoes?

It helps if the speaker's thinking style or tendency matches that of the audience.

When communicating with people who are being asked/instructed to do something, it helps to place them on the motivation matrix[10] shown in Table 10.1. People are motivated *by* mythos[iii] (beliefs or memes), ethos (credibility), pathos (emotion),

---

ii Common forms of validation: use of stock phrases like "good job," "active listening" paraphrasing to ensure common understanding, asking a meaningful question, recounting the person's success, using body language and physical presence in a non-threatening way, listening and avoiding the use of "but . . .," " using "and" instead.

iii "All human groups operate around shared narratives, which create identity, meaning, and core values and shape the epistemology through which they interact with the broader environment. All these are deeply anchored in the minds of its members, and frame their outlook, their opinions and their decisions, consciously or unconsciously." Van der Leeuw, S., and Folke, C. (2020), "The Social Dynamics of Basins of Attraction", unpublished paper, p. 11.

"Myth can be defined as what anchors a culture": "an incredibly complex dynamic between a society's cognitive and perceptual dynamics, its network structures and its environmental context, all interacting within the path-dependent trajectory that shaped its dynamics. As a function of these, a society defines its identity, shapes the epistemology through which it interacts with its environment, establishes its fundamental values and much more. All these are deeply anchored in the minds of its members, and determine their outlook, their opinions, and their decisions. This anchor is so complex that we cannot hope to unravel it, map it, understand it, or modify it." Ibid., pp. 6–7.

and logos (logic), and are motivated *for* achievement, recognition, power, or self-actualization. Understanding where they are will affect the *angle* of the communication.

Table 10.1: The Motivation Matrix.

	Motivated for:			
Motivated by:	**Achievement**	**Recognition/ Affection**	**Power**	**Self-Actualization**
Mythos Beliefs/ Memes	We have a high-performance culture, we thrive on challenge and meeting impossible targets	When we complete the project, we will join the teams in the company hall of fame	We are a high-performance organization where only high-performers get to the top	You only want to work for a leading organization where you are challenged to be your best
Ethos Credibility	The CEO expects your team to do this in two weeks	If we meet the deadline for creating a new program, the CEO will highlight our performance at the company's annual dinner	Having a track record of delivering difficult projects on time increases the chance of leading other teams	It is great to work for the best organization in the industry and to be recognized as such by my peers
Pathos Emotion	The CEO believes you can get this done on time and I know you are just the person for the job	If you meet the deadline for creating a new program, the CEO will present you with a special award to thank you at the company's annual dinner	You will be promoted and lead other teams if you get this done on time	Working for this organization, you will feel you can really make a difference and make the world a better place
Logos Logic/ Reason	The CEO gave us a tighter deadline which requires you to work harder When we meet it, you will get extra time off in compensation	If you meet the new deadline, the CEO will give you a pay increase at the annual performance review	High-performance teams have the best career prospects, meeting the deadline will help your career	There is more to work than just getting paid well, your work has a social purpose as well

Effective "wayfinders" use context to determine where people fit in the matrix and listen to how they talk about the future to understand their motivations and what *drives* them:[11]

1. *Ethos:* If they talk about execution or competitors and the biggest projects, ethos drives them.
2. *Emotion:* Enthusiasm is a positive sign, worry or being troubled is a negative sign that emotion drives them.
3. *Logic:* If they talk about process and resourcing required, logic drives them.

Context will determine what *pulls* them:[12]
1. *Achievement:* If comments are task oriented, they are attracted by achievement.
2. *Recognition:* If they talk about being the best or relative performance, they seek recognition.
3. *Power:* If they talk about dominating the competition, wanting to run the show or doing it in a particular way, they seek power.

Not everyone is motivated by money all the time[13] and not everyone is competitive in all situations. The best motivators will depend on the context and the activity.

The effectiveness of communicators depends in large part on their *ethos*:

> The Greek term *ethos* translates loosely into English as *ethics.* However, in communication at work, it is the idea that *credibility* of who you are persuades people. Master communicators know their ethos and use it to strengthen the influence of what they say."[14]

Ethos depends on background and culture; how the person thinks, and the communicator's ability to match thinking style to that of listeners; how the person listens and speaks; the organization the person represents, title, and experience; relationships and connections; appearance; and track record and performance.[15]

"Three Rs"

Review

Performance reviews are valuable two-way channels of communication: allowing a "line of sight" for each employee to the mission, vision, and values of their organization. They also allow "wayfinders" to get a feel for how their subordinates identify with the purpose and values of the organization. For performance reviews to be of value in developing subordinates, certain conditions must prevail.
1. *Principles must be translated into observable, measurable behaviors:* It is essential that principles (values) are translated from abstract nouns into action statements describing desired performance and behavior and the timelines involved. Personal development plans should communicate how the individual has performed, what improvements are necessary, and the timeline, as well as the training and resources that will be made available to help the individual achieve targets on the way

to meeting the organization's standards of performance in terms of objectively measurable KPIs.

2. *Performance reviews must reflect the organization's KPIs and timelines:* The organization's mission and vision determine its business strategy and KPIs with their associated project milestones, due dates, and timelines, broken down into standards and targets by division, department, and individuals.

3. *Feedback must be given appropriately:* Providing feedback at annual appraisals is not enough. Responsibility for success or failure should be attributed promptly, while the behavior being discussed is still fresh. This might be as simple as commenting informally on what was good or could be done better immediately after a meeting. If the issue is more serious, then a short meeting on the subject as soon as possible after the incident is leading practice. Discussion of performance issues should take place immediately in order to (1) nip a bad practice in the bud, and (2) enable the individual to get back on track.

Effective feedback will cover the following[16] by:

a. Reviewing what the agreed objectives were and the actual results,

b. Discussing what the individual/group has done well, focusing on the positives,

c. Identifying where there has been a problem, focusing on the implications/consequences of the behavior for other people, and identifying what could have been done better,

d. Agreeing on what has been learned from the experience,

e. Agreeing on the need for a change in behavior by identifying what the individual/group should continue doing, as well as what they should do differently/better,

f. Getting "buy-in" from the individual/group that they will change their behavior now that they understand the implications of the behavioral performance shortfall,

g. Agreeing on a timeline for improvement and follow up,

h. *Never making the behavior the basis of a personal attack.*

Recognition

Effective "wayfinders" remember that two of the most powerful words in the English language as morale boosters are "thank you." They do not make the mistake of failing to thank people for "just doing the job they are paid to do," as some superiors do. Even if they are doing their jobs, when they are doing them well, they should be thanked, as it provides important emotional feedback that what they do is noticed and appreciated.

Reward

How people are rewarded and what they are rewarded for are crucial communication signals in organizations. Effective "wayfinders" use rewards and punishment to control behavior. Rewards and punishment sit upon a motivation continuum stretching from demotivation to extrinsic and intrinsic motivation.

Much of the literature suggests that extrinsic and intrinsic motivators are antagonistic.[17] This is somewhat misleading for two reasons. First, intrinsic and extrinsic motivators overlap in their effect on behavior.[18] Second, the motivation continuum reflects Maslow's hierarchy of needs with the extrinsic motivators operating at the survival and safety levels of Maslow's hierarchy and they overlap with the intrinsic motivators at the belonging level; while the autonomy, mastery, and "making a difference" intrinsic motivators are examples of Maslow's esteem and self-actualization.[19] However, there are important limitations in relying on extrinsic motivators:

1. *Extrinsic and intrinsic motivators overlap*: Extrinsic motivation was initially defined as behavior performed in the absence of self-determination (i.e., that an external party was making someone do something that they otherwise would not have done). Intrinsically motivated behavior was held to be self-determined and autonomous, undermined by the application of extrinsic motivators. However, once we recognize that they both fit along a continuum and overlap, we realize that there are four type of motivation: external, introjected, identified, and intrinsic:

    a. *External reason* "means doing the target activities to comply with authorities."[20] As such, it reflects the need to comply. However, as armies know, the consistent application of external reasons when recruiting civilians can change their behavior to the extent that recruits internalize how they should behave so that it becomes "second nature" (System 1 consciousness) or in other words an instinctive Pavlovian conditioned reflex that does not require the use of the slow and effortful workings of the conscious mind (System 2 consciousness). In this sense the behavior has become intrinsic, because it is subconscious.

    b. *Introjected reason* "is framed in terms of internal, esteem-based pressures to act, such as avoidance of guilt and shame or concerns about approval from self or others. Individuals subsequently begin to internalize their reasons for the action."[21]

    c. *Identified reason* "occurs when a behavior is valued by the individual and is perceived as being chosen by oneself. It typically takes the form 'I want.'"[22] However, some argue that it is an extrinsic motivation because the activity it creates is a "means to an end" rather than the end itself. As such, it would include the two types of activity usually defined as intrinsic, namely "autonomy" and "mastery."

d. *Intrinsic reason* "involves doing an activity for fun or for inherent enjoyment in a self-determined way. It can be classified wholly into intrinsic motivation" – in other words, it only includes the concept of self-actualization.

The effectiveness of these four types of motivation is shown in Figure 10.1.

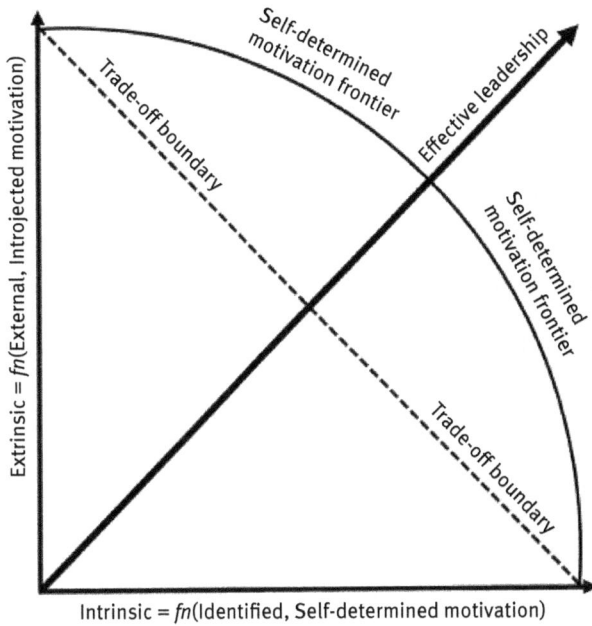

Figure 10.1: Reconciling Extrinsic and Intrinsic Motivation.

The vertical vector shows how extrinsic motivation becomes more powerful the further it is from the origin, beginning with external motivation and building introjected motivation upon it. The horizontal vector shows how intrinsic motivation becomes more effective the further it is from the origin, beginning with identified motivation and working up to self-determined or self-actualized motivation. Reconciling both approaches by recognizing how they overlap allows effective leadership to achieve more than if the traditional approach based on antagonism between the two types of motivation is used, shown as the trade-off boundary. Effective "wayfinders" recognize that is not a case of "either-or," but one of "both-and," depending on the context.

2. *Motivation continuum reflects Maslow's hierarchy of needs*: The external motivator's conditioned reflexes operate at the survival and safety levels of Maslow's hierarchy. Introjected motivators operate at the esteem level, identified motivators

operate at the respect level, while intrinsic motivators form the basis of self-actualization.

3. *Limitations on using extrinsic motivators*: Extrinsic motivators such as piecework pay for performance in factory conditions, for example, is highly effective when the work is repetitive and routine in nature. Even in these predictable conditions, extrinsic motivators can hit diminishing returns caused by people's natural tendency to materialistic satiety.[iv] However, that appears not to be the case for work that requires creativity, exercise of judgment, and dealing with unpredictable conditions. In such conditions, research done by Daniel Pink suggests that intrinsic motivators are much more powerful than extrinsic ones, such as bonus,[23] and that rewarding people by granting them autonomy (working out for themselves how best to get their job done), allowing them to achieve mastery (becoming expert in their role) by investing in their development, and giving them the freedom to make a difference is much more effective than relying on extrinsic motivators.

As an example of how reconciling both approaches can add value, consider invoicing. It is tedious, routine, and predictable, requiring both attention to detail and timely execution. In an example company, the invoicing function was split into four teams, competing with each other every month for which team could complete the *most invoicing* that was *both accurate and timely*. How they did the work was left up to them. The winning team's reward was an excellent lunch in a good restaurant with the finance director, and invoicing was made exciting by the competition and the daily published progress reports of each team. Such recognition is more effective if it is public, so that their colleagues can see them as role models in the particular circumstances for which they are being recognized, and appreciate better what is expected of them and what happens when they meet expectations.

"Four Cs"

Effective communication is built on clarity, consistency, consonance, and codes of conduct.

Clarity

To achieve effective implementation, clarity of purpose, of expectations, and of measurement are needed. Ambiguity of purpose leads to confusion and extra cost as people hedge their bets and make recommendations that waste time, effort, and

---

iv Satiety is defined as "the state of being completely satisfied, especially with food or pleasure, so that you could not have any more," Cambridge English Dictionary, https://dictionary.cambridge.org/dictionary/english/satiety, accessed on August 2, 2020.

money. Without clarity of expectations, people cannot know if they are on track, or what corrective actions are needed. Without clarity, people will not know "what's in it for them."

The problems the UK government faced in its handling of the Covid-19 pandemic (2020–2021) are an object lesson in the critical importance of clarity of purpose and of avoiding confused messaging, and of avoiding a series of U-turns in objectives and measurements. Initially, while there was still time to adopt a strict lockdown based on containment of the disease by testing, tracking, and tracing those who had been in contact with infected people, and by closing borders to entry of people from coronavirus hotspots, the British government chose to do none of them.[24] They were of two minds about the use of masks,[25] and whether their strategy was to allow the spread of the disease to achieve "herd immunity."[26] Their primary, limited objective was to ensure that the NHS (National Health Service) would not be swamped when the virus peaked, as had happened in Lombardy.

They did meet this objective by building five temporary hospitals designed to handle virus patients only,[27] and transferred hundreds of elderly patients already in the hospital back into nursing homes without checking whether they were likely to spread the disease there when they returned.[28] As a result, there was confusion,[29] delay, and unnecessary death – leading to the highest death rate in Europe.[30] Even when the government finally adopted its call to "Stay at Home, Save Lives, and Protect the NHS," the special adviser to the Prime Minister, who had set the rules, broke them and was defended by the Prime Minister and senior Cabinet ministers.[31]

As far as measurement expectations for the "test, track, and trace" strategy were concerned, the targets set by the government kept changing, their due dates kept being delayed and still they were not met.[32] Not surprisingly, public trust in the British government's handling of the virus collapsed.[33] It was a catalog of blunder after blunder.[34] What the pandemic debacle shows is that clarity of slogans is not enough once in government, where operational competence in delivery of outcomes is what matters. The success of the British government in vaccinating people was an example of operational competence that has helped restore the Prime Minister's and the government's credibility.[35] This is not surprising, given the conclusion in Chapter 5 that the most important characteristic of effective leaders is operational competence, based on the careers of Elizabeth Tudor, Napoleon and Atatürk.

"Wayfinders" need to communicate clearly what needs to be done, by whom, by when, what the expected performance standards and targets are, and stick to them, and engage implementers by making clear the consequences of success or failure.

Consistency

Consistency is:

> The quality of always behaving or performing in a similar way, or of always happening in a similar way.[36]

From a "wayfinder" perspective, there are three ways that "being the same" matters:

1. *Behaving in the same way over time.* If "wayfinders" behave in the same way over time, regardless of changes in their contexts and circumstances, that is a sign of the rigidity and inflexibility that warrants such comments as:

> A foolish consistency is the hobgoblin of little minds, adored by little statesmen and philosophers and divines . . .[37]

2. *Behaving predictably in the way decisions are made as an individual:* People do not like dealing with people who are unpredictable. What they look for is predictability, not necessarily of outcome, but in the way the person behaves, treats others, and processes information before making a promise. In these circumstances, consistency is a virtue:

> When you look at people who are successful, you will find that they aren't the people who are motivated, but have consistency in their motivation.[38]

3. *Communicating the same essential ideas across different divisions of the organization, adjusted for each audience:* Great brands are built and maintained through consistent communication with customers and prospects at every available touch point – internally and externally. Effective "wayfinders" understand this. They appreciate that they are responsible for ensuring behavior in line with organizational mission and values, making sure that every communication that internal and external customers receive, is consistent. This can only be achieved if the organization has built an integrated communication architecture, shown in Figure 10.2.

Figure 10.2 shows the linkage between the organizational mission vision and values and its promise which are the responsibility of the board and CEO. This provides the overarching roof, connected to the product and service brands – the foundation of the business operations – via the eight pillars, each with its respective audiences and different parts of the organization responsible for communicating with them. The key to successful integration is that "wayfinders" in each pillar and at each level of seniority must tell a clear and consistent set of stories internally and externally that flow directly from the organizational mission, vision, and values while reinforcing them at the same time.

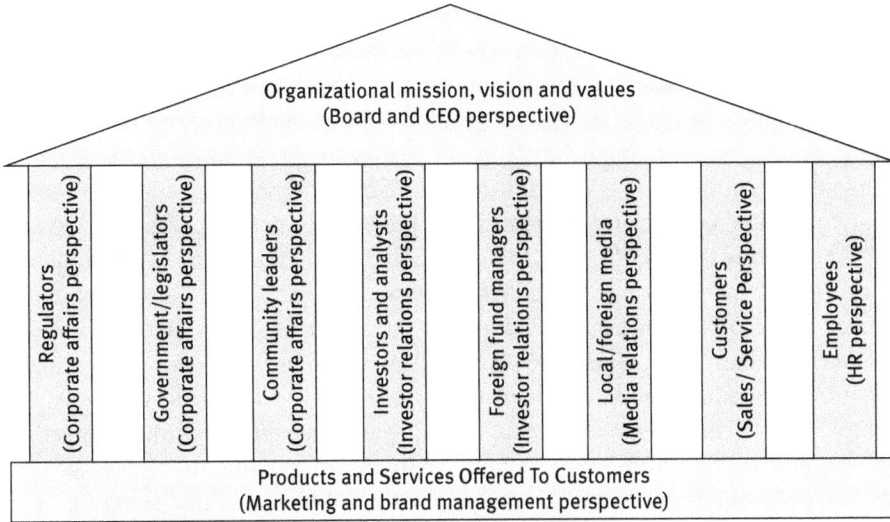

Figure 10.2: Integrated Communication Architecture.

Coherence

Coherence is important for three reasons:

1. *Organizational alignment to achieve the agreed on mission, vision, and values is essential* and can only be achieved if there is consonance between the "Five Ps" and the agreed on mission, vision, and values (discussed in Chapter 6).
2. *"Wayfinders" who do not follow the principles and the agreed processes,* undermine their own credibility and authenticity.
3. *Integrated communication requires coherence.* It is not possible to create and maintain an integrated communication architecture if there is dissonance between the different parts of the organization.

Codes of Conduct

Codes of conduct must reflect the "Principles" (desired organizational behaviors and values), "wayfinders" must act as role models to their subordinates or they will undermine them.

Summary

Effective communication is a two-way interaction, depending on the ability of "way-finders" to listen actively without judging, reviewing, clarifying, and summarizing to understand the meaning behind the words, and weighing the evidence when the argument is complete. It is difficult to do well because people speak more slowly than they think and because of their natural predisposition to confirmation bias.

Considering techniques, "wayfinders" should reflect the nature of the audience, the attitudes and prejudices of both speakers and listeners and their impact on the receptiveness of audiences, affected greatly by the angle or message involved and its contextual appropriateness. "Wayfinders" may find using the motivation matrix useful. It shows how people are *motivated by* mythos, ethos, pathos, and logos. The matrix shows people are *motivated for* attaining achievement, recognition/affection, power, and self-actualization. Effective communicators tailor their messages depending on which of 16 combinations of "motivated by" and "motivated for" best represents their intended audiences.

Effective communicators review performance to create a "line of sight" to the organization's mission, vision, and values ("principles"), provided the adopted principles are translated into observable, measurable behaviors, reflecting the core values of the enterprise, its KPIs and timelines, forming timely, constructive, and effective feedback for consistent improvement, recognizing each individual's performance objectively.

Effective communicators understand the importance of using appropriate rewards and that extrinsic and intrinsic motivators are part of a continuum and may overlap. Effective "wayfinders" realize they should use a combination of both, depending on context.

Considering content, effective communicators appreciate the importance of clarity of purpose and expected performance, and consistency of message across the organization and its various audiences, achieved by adjusting the same essential ideas to suit particular circumstances within the framework of an integrated communication architecture. Coherence of organizational alignment depends on consistency of messaging across divisions, as do personal credibility and authenticity of "wayfinders." Failure creates dissonance. Codes of conduct are an essential mechanism to minimize unpredictable behavior that could otherwise muddy the message.

References

1 Nichols, R. G., and Stevens, L. A. (1957), "Listening to People," *Harvard Business Review,* September 1957 Issue, https://hbr.org/1957/09/listening-to-people, accessed on June 9, 2020.
2 Ibid.
3 Jacques, E. (1990), "In Praise of Hierarchy," *Harvard Business Review,* January-February 1990, https://hbr.org/1990/01/in-praise-of-hierarchy, accessed on June 12, 2020.

4 Charan, R., Drotter, S. and Noel, J. (2011), *The Leadership Pipeline: How to Build the Leadership Powered Company* (San Francisco, CA: Jossey-Bass), pp. 16–26.

5 Greene, J. D. (2002), "The Terrible, Horrible, No Good, Very Bad-Truth about Morality and What to Do About it," Doctoral Dissertation, *Princeton Department of Philosophy*, June 2002, https://emil kirkegaard.dk/en/wp-content/uploads/Joshua-D.-Greene-The-Terrible-Horrible-No-Good-Very-Bad-Truth-about-Morality-and.pdf, accessed on April 5, 2021.

6 MediaFirst (2014), "Kegworth Plane Crash 25 Years On: A Media First Analysis," https://www.me diafirst.co.uk/blog/kegworth-plane-crash-25-years-on-a-media-first-analysis/, accessed on June 13, 2020.

7 Greene (2002), op. cit., pp. 233–234.

8 Becker, E. F., and Wortmann, J. (2009), *Mastering Communication at Work: How to Lead, Manage, and Influence* (New York: McGraw Hill Education), pp. 79–86.

9 Ibid., p. 90.

10 Based on ibid., p. 41.

11 Ibid., p. 45.

12 Ibid., pp. 45–46.

13 Pink, D. (2010), "Drive: The surprising truth about what motivates us," *RSA ANIMATE*, April 1, 2010, https://www.youtube.com/watch?v=u6XAPnuFjJc, accessed on June 13, 2020.

14 Becker and Wortmann (2009), op. cit., p. 19.

15 Ibid., pp. 23–25.

16 Ulrich, D., Smallwood, N., Sweetman, K. (2008), *The Leadership Code: Five Rules to Lead By* (Boston: Harvard Business Review Press), p. 75.

17 Hayamizu, T. (1997), "Between intrinsic and extrinsic motivation: Examination of reasons for academic study based on the theory of internalization," *Japanese Psychological Research* 1997, Vol. 39, No 2, pp. 98–108.

18 Ibid., p. 99.

19 Maslow, A. (1943), "A Theory of Human Motivation," *Psychological Review*, Vol. 50, No. 4, pp. 370–396.

20 Hayamizu (1997), op. cit., p. 99.

21 Ibid.

22 Ibid.

23 Pink, D. H. (2009), *Drive: The Surprising Truth About What Motivates Us* (New York: Riverhead Books).

24 Morales A. et al. (2020), "How the Alarm Went Off Too Late in Britain's Response Virus Response," *Bloomberg Businessweek*, April 24, 2020, https://www.bloomberg.com/news/features/2020-04-24/coro navirus-uk-how-boris-johnson-s-government-let-virus-get-away, accessed on June 16, 2020.

25 Bosely, S. (2020), "UK under pressure to rethink face masks in wake of WHO advice," *The Guardian*, June 5, 2020, https://www.theguardian.com/world/2020/jun/05/uk-under-pressure-to-rethink-face-masks-in-wake-of-who-advice, accessed on June 16, 2020.

26 O'Grady, C. (2020), "The UK backed off on herd immunity. To beat COVID-19, we'll ultimately need it.," *National Geographic*, March 20, 2020, https://www.nationalgeographic.com/science/2020/03/uk-backed-off-on-herd-immunity-to-beat-coronavirus-we-need-it/, accessed on June 16, 2020.

27 Day, M. (2020), "Covid-19: Nightingale hospitals set to shut down after seeing few patients," *British Medical Journal*, May 7, 2020, https://www.bmj.com/content/369/bmj.m1860, accessed on June 16, 2020.

28 Grey, S., and MacAskill, A. (2020), "Special Report: in shielding its hospitals form COVID-19, Britain left many more of the weakest exposed," *Reuters*, May, 2020, https://www.reuters.com/arti cle/us-health-coronavirus-britain-elderly-sp/special-report-in-shielding-its-hospitals-from-covid-19-britain-left-many-of-the-weakest-exposed-idUSKBN22H2CR, accessed on June 16, 2020.

29 Cushion, S. et al. (2020) "Coronavirus: public confused and suspicious over government's death toll information," *The Conversation*, May 19, 2020, https://theconversation.com/coronavirus-public-confused-and-suspicious-over-governments-death-toll-information-138966, accessed on June 16, 2020.

30 Euronews, "Coronavirus: Why is the UK's COVID-19 death toll higher than other EU countries?" *Euronews*, June 5, 2020, https://www.euronews.com/2020/05/06/coronavirus-why-is-the-uk-s-covid-19-death-toll-higher-than-other-eu-countries, accessed on June16, 2020.

31 "The damage Dominic Cummings has done to Boris Johnson," *The Economist*, May 28, 2020, https://www.economist.com/britain/2020/05/28/the-damage-dominic-cummings-has-done-to-boris-johnson, accessed on June 16, 2020.

32 Wright, M. (2020), "Test and trace will be in place 'by June', insists Michael Gove, as he reveals 17,000 contact tracers recruited," *The Telegraph*, May 17, 2020, https://www.telegraph.co.uk/news/2020/05/17/test-trace-will-place-june-says-michael-gove-reveals-17000-contact/, accessed on June 16, 2020.

33 Reuters (2020), "UK leads fall in global trust in government COVID responses: poll," *Reuters*, June 3, 2020, https://www.reuters.com/article/us-health-coronavirus-poll/uk-leads-fall-in-global-trust-in-government-covid-responses-poll-idUSKBN23B0H4, accessed on June 16, 2020.

34 Guardian Editorial (2020), "The guardian view of Boris Johnson's crisis: blunder after blunder," *The Guardian*, June 15, 2020, https://www.theguardian.com/commentisfree/2020/jun/15/the-guardian-view-of-boris-johnsons-crisis-blunder-after-blunder, accessed on June 16, 2020.

35 McClean, S., and Davey-Attlee, F. (2021), "Vaccine rollout is a much-needed win for UK after bungling its response", *CNN*, February 17, 2021, https://edition.cnn.com/2021/02/15/europe/uk-vaccine-rollout-target-gbr-intl/index.html, accessed on February 21, 2020.

36 Cambridge Dictionary (2020), "Meaning of consistency *noun* (being the same)," https://dictionary.cambridge.org/dictionary/english/consistency, accessed on June 16, 2020.

37 Emerson, R. W. (1841), *Essay on Self-Reliance*, https://www.goodreads.com/quotes/tag/consistency, accessed on June 16, 2020.

38 https://www.brainyquote.com/quotes/arsene_wenger_598799.

Chapter 11
Ethical and Effective Decision-Making

Readers will have realized by now that the discussions in the preceding chapters do not address the ethics of decision-making, they are focused on the techniques of effective leadership and management. Our premise is that those activities are morally neutral, and can be used for good or ill.[1]

We now consider some approaches to ethics from history and culture. We suggest how "wayfinders" can develop a six-step process to ensure that they have thoroughly considered whether their decisions are ethical as well as effective. This does matter because the *long-term* survival of organizations depends on decisions being effective *and* ethical.

Discussing ethics is difficult because different people define the term in different ways. Below, we very briefly review the development of ethical theory from its Aristotelian origin to the present day:

> Ethics, as the thought of Man about his action, is as ancient as Man itself . . .
>
> ethical systems changed through time, gaining more and new concepts to think about new human realities in the world and to communicate them. An example would be the constellation of four concepts needed in ancient Greek philosophy to explain moral life – good, end, happiness, and virtue – to which medievalism added the concept of God, modernity the concept of liberty, and contemporaneity the concept of responsibility . . . Ethics originally heteronomous, being given to Man (from a higher entity: Nature or God), becomes autonomous, being made by Man to Man. Finally, ethics turned out to be applied to many different concrete fields of human activity – engineering, media, economics, politics, etc. – but none more developed than in the biomedical (and environment) field through bioethics.
>
> . . . ethics has always been and still is a rationalization of human action (the logic underneath human actions) concerning the principles it is grounded on, the ends it aims toward, and the processes it entails.[2]

We also consider applied ethics:

> Applied ethics is a branch of ethics specific to a concrete social domain of activity, grounded on common morality and addressed to all people possibly involved in that activity.
>
> All applied ethics are of a theoretical-practical nature, having a double requirement: on the one hand, a sound theory to guarantee the objectivity of its justifications and the coherence of its orientations and, on the other hand, efficient and efficacious interventions in concrete situations to assure the real and satisfactory resolution of problems.[3]

https://doi.org/10.1515/9783110707878-014

Duty-Based and Consequential Ethics

Approaches to ethics can be considered under two broad headings, duty-based ethics where the ethics of an action are considered (focus on the means) and consequential ethics where the result of the action are evaluated (focus on the ends).

In Table 11.1, we compare and contrast the advantages and drawbacks of duty-based (deontological)[i] and consequential ethics. Both approaches have advantages and problems in application.

Table 11.1: Duty-Based and Consequential Ethics Compared.

Duty-Based Ethics	Consequential Ethics
Doing the "Right thing" has priority over achieving a desirable outcome: 1. Do the right thing because it is the right thing to do 2. If an act is wrong, it must not be undertaken, regardless of the good it could do	*Whether an act is right or wrong depends only on the outcome:* 1. The more an act produces good consequences, the better or more right it is 2. People should choose actions that maximize good consequences
Advantages 1. One set of rules regarding behavior for everyone regardless of the circumstances 2. Clarity and simplicity, individuals know what they are expected do and not to do 3. Easy to apply codes of conduct, rewarding or punishing behavior based only on what happened, without allowing for intent, purpose, and outcome 4. Predictable outcomes and speedy decisions	*Advantages* 1. Each decision considers current circumstances and its likely consequences 2. Actions are justified by the overall good they achieve 3. Behavior can be flexible provided it results in a good outcome; intent, purpose, and outcome are considered 4. Allows for particular circumstances to be considered

---

i "Deontology falls within the domain of moral theories that guide and assess our choices of what we ought to do. Within the domain of moral theories that assess our choices, deontologists – those who subscribe to deontological theories of morality – stand in opposition to *consequentialists*." "Deontological Ethics," *Stanford Encyclopedia of Philosophy*, October 17, 2016, https://plato.stanford.edu/entries/ethics-deontological/, accessed on May 23, 2020.

Table 11.1 (continued)

Duty-Based Ethics	Consequential Ethics
Drawbacks	*Drawbacks*
1. May fail to recognize differences between cultures and value systems, creating unnecessary misunderstanding between groups	1. In a complex, interconnected world with tightly coupled systems, it is often extremely difficult to establish what the consequences are going to be
2. May cause problems in cultures where relationships matter more than rules	2. Can create uncertainty and lack of predictability
3. Addresses form rather than substance in ambiguous situations	3. Often difficult to decide on suitable time horizons and appropriate cut-off points after which the consequences are no longer relevant to the decision
4. Rigidity and rash decisions based on simple assumptions unsuited to the complexity of prevailing circumstances	4. Takes time, undesirable analysis paralysis can result, when quick decisions are needed, based on incomplete or conflicting data
5. Can lead to ethical paralysis in situations where "ethical" actions will lead to "unethical" outcomes	

Six Ethical Approaches

We believe decision-makers should consider six approaches if they are to make ethical *and* effective decisions. They are virtue, effectiveness, mutuality, predictability, utility, and self-image ethics.

Virtue

Virtue-based ethics are the earliest form of ethics, associated with Aristotle and Plato in the West, and Confucius and Mencius in the East:

> Virtue ethics is currently one of three major approaches in normative ethics. It may, initially, be identified as the one that emphasizes the virtues, or moral character, in contrast to the approach that emphasizes duties or rules (deontology) or that emphasizes the consequences of actions (consequentialism).[4]

Three concepts define a virtuous person according to Aristotle: *arête* (excellence or virtue), *phronesis* (practical or moral wisdom), and *eudaimonia* (happiness or flourishing):

1. ***Excellence or virtue (arête)*** is a trait of character that defines how people behave. A virtuous person is one who acts and feels as he or she should:

> An honest person cannot be identified simply as one who, for example, practices honest dealing and does not cheat. *If such actions are done merely because the agent thinks that honesty is the best policy, or because they fear being caught out, rather than through recognising 'To do otherwise would be dishonest'... they are not the actions of an honest person...*[5]   [Emphasis ours]

2. ***Practical or moral wisdom (phronesis)*** is the caveat that people who only behave with *arête* could be virtuous to a fault – for example, being too generous or too honest:

> . . . someone's compassion might lead them to act wrongly, to tell a lie they should not have told, for example, in their desire to prevent someone else's hurt feelings. It is also said that courage, in a desperado, enables him to do far more wicked things than he would have been able to do if he were timid. *So it would appear that generosity, honesty, compassion and courage despite being virtues, are sometimes faults.*[6]   [Emphasis ours]

Practical or moral wisdom considers context. It appreciates that "the right thing to do" in one set of circumstances may not be in another. It reconciles practicing virtuous excellence with the need to foresee consequences. It addresses the overlap of virtue ethics and consequential ethics, recognizing the difficulty of adopting virtue ethics without considering potentially adverse consequences of an intended virtuous action.

3. ***Happiness or flourishing (eudaimonia)*** actions are defined by their contribution to the individual's happiness or flourishing/wellbeing. Plato and the Stoics believed that virtuous behavior on its own was sufficient to yield happiness, but Aristotle argued that luck and the possession of material things also mattered:

> According to eudaimonist virtue ethics, the good life is the *eudaimon* life, and the virtues are what enable a human being to be *eudaimon* because the virtues just are those character traits that benefit their possessor in that way, barring bad luck.[7]

Different cultural backgrounds may cause different behaviors in similar circumstances, e.g., Confucius and Mencius prioritize relationships above rules. They recommend morality based on the five cardinal virtues of benevolence, filial piety, trustworthiness, loyalty, and righteousness, with hierarchical interactions:[ii]

> *Morality among Chinese people is traditionally defined by relationally determined norms grounded in Confucian precepts that are shared by persons bound by particularistic ties rather than by reference to some abstract standards applying to autonomous individuals.* For instance, in seeking to be the ideal moral character, a junzi or cultivated gentleman in Confucian terms, a person must demonstrate a considerable number of desirable qualities, plus the five cardinal virtues of benevolence (ren), filial conduct (xiao), trustworthiness (xin), loyalty (zhong), and righteousness (yi), *in interactions with particular others in a highly defined hierarchical social order.*[8]   [Emphases ours]

1. ***Benevolence (ren)*** requires rulers to care for others and the examples used in Confucius' *Analects* are of treating people in the street as if they were guests, common people as if they were important attendants at sacrifices, being reticent and not dominating conversations, being respectful where the person lived,

---

ii The five cardinal Confucian relationships are ruler to subject, father to son, husband to wife, elder brother to younger brother, and friend to friend.

revering fellow workers, and being loyal in dealings with others.[9] In summary, having empathy and humility, being unselfish out of consideration of the needs of others. This is in contrast to Aristotle's definition of a "magnanimous man" who looked down on his social inferiors, spoke his mind regardless of the pain he caused, and was not humble,[10] but self-centred.

2. **Filial piety (xiao)** entails loyalty and deference to one's parents, ancestors, and by extension, to one's country and its leaders:

> In general, filial piety requires children to offer love, respect, support, and deference to their parents and other elders in the family, such as grandparents or older siblings. Acts of filial piety include obeying one's parent's wishes, taking care of them when they are old, and working hard to provide them with material comforts, such as food, money, or pampering.

> . . . parents give life to their children, and support them throughout their developing years, providing food, education, and material needs. After receiving all these benefits, children are thus forever in debt to their parents. In order to acknowledge this eternal debt, children must respect and serve their parents all their lives . . .

> . . . The tenet of filial piety also applies to all elders – teachers, professional superiors, or anyone who is older in age – and even the state. The family is the building block of society, and as such the hierarchical system of respect also applies to one's rulers and one's country. *Xìao means that the same devotion and selflessness in serving one's family should also be used when serving one's country.*[11]   [Emphasis ours]

3. **Trustworthiness (xin)** Confucius taught that it was the most valuable quality when advising a ruler. It qualified a gentleman to give advice to a ruler and a ruler or official to rule over others. Trustworthiness was more important than weapons or food for a ruler and more effective than strength or the ability to flatter in an individual. If the ruler could not be trusted, the state would fall:

> If the people do not find the ruler trustworthy, the state will not stand.[12]

> If your words are sincere and trustworthy and your actions are honorable and respectful, you will get on in the world even among the barbarian tribes. If your words are insincere and untrustworthy, if you act without honor and respect, how can you possibly get on in the world even in your own village? When you stand, you should always have this principle in front of you. When you drive you should have it carved upon the yoke of your carriage, only then will you truly be able to move ahead.[13]

4. **Loyalty (zhong)** Confucius regarded loyalty as a mutual obligation that required subordinates to speak up:

> Ji Kangzi asked: "What should I do to make the people respectful, loyal, and eager to follow me?" Confucius said: "Treat them with dignity, and they will be respectful. Show you are a good son and a loving father, and they will be loyal. Promote the good and teach those who lack ability, and they will be eager to follow you."[14]

> Confucius said: "Can you truly love someone if you are not strict with them? How can you be truly loyal to someone if you refrain from admonishing them?"[15]

5. ***Righteousness (yi)*** is related to public responsibility of officials as stewards who were not corrupt, emphasizing fairness and integrity in dealings. Confucius was clear corruption was not to be tolerated, insisting it was better to eat coarse rice, drink water, and sleep without a pillow than to achieve wealth and power corruptly.[16] However, Confucius saw righteousness as contextually determined:

> In regulating one's household, kindness overrules righteousness. Outside of one's house, righteousness cuts off kindness. What one undertakes in serving one's father, one also does in serving one's lord, because one's reverence for both is the same. Treating nobility in a noble way, and the honorable in an honorable way, is the height of righteousness.[17]

The common threads in the Aristotelian and Confucian approaches to virtue ethics are apparent. Differences in resulting behavior may result because the Aristotelian approach is essentially individualistic whereas the Confucian is communitarian. The Aristotelian "magnanimous man" comes across as more arrogant, more entitled, more insensitive to the feelings of others and more disdainful of ordinary people than the Confucian "benevolent man."[18]

Effectiveness

Although not the first,[iii] the most famous proponent of ethics focusing on effectiveness of rulers is Machiavelli, who developed a framework for analyzing what made rulers effective. It is intentionally amoral (as discussed in Chapter 1), concerned with what works in different contexts and given different objectives.

The Prince makes it clear that the ruler's goals and objectives are determined by historical antecedents and current political contexts. Constraints to action should be recognized and the "art of the possible" practiced.

A ruler establishing his rule, will have to behave differently from one who is secure and legitimate. Difficulties prospective rulers face when taking over a state depend on whether it was a well-established republic where its people value their freedom, or a principality where people are used to being ruled by a monarch. In either case, Machiavelli made it clear that *what matters first is to get and hold on to the levers of power by whatever means* determined by the historical/political contexts and to exercise that power by using situational management skills. Amoral behavior could be justified for "reasons of state."

> Fourteenth century Italy may well have required a harsh prince but, remarkably Machiavelli became more popular in the time since. Cromwell, Frederick the Great, Louis XIV, Napoleon, Bismarck, Clemenceau, Wilson, Stalin, Hitler, Roosevelt, De Gaulle, Churchill, Truman and a

---

iii The *Sulwan Al-Muta' Fi 'Udwan Al-Atba* (Consolation for the Ruler During the Hostility of Subjects) by the Sicilian Arab, Muhammad ibn Zafar al-Siqilli, focuses on the need to be effective and was written in the 12th century.

score of modern rulers referred to the Florentine's book as a source of practical guidance. Dictators and statesmen alike sought to implement his recommendations . . .

> . . . *Because Machiavelli's prince lacked justice, he could not rule with legitimacy. Yet, almost 350 years before the Florentine wrote his famous guidebook, a fellow Italian – but of Arab origin – underscored why a ruler could not govern without justice.*[19] [Emphasis ours]

Perhaps this need for justice[iv] to provide legitimacy was the reason why Machiavelli preferred republican government to princely government, a preference that is abundantly clear in the *Discourses*. In the *Discourses*, Machiavelli argued that challenge is important in helping the ruler make good decisions and that managed conflict of the type in the Roman Republic led to better decisions than monarchy.

It is useful to compare key elements of Machiavelli's approach to effectiveness with that of Ibn Zafar Al-Siqilli's, written some 350 years earlier, shown in Table 11.2.

Table 11.2: Machiavelli and Ibn Zafar Compared.

Machiavelli	Ibn Zafar
Political context	**Political context**
A corrupt Papacy was losing its moral authority and was too weak to unify Italy, yet retained just enough power to prevent either France or Spain from doing so. The result was continuous warfare between Italy's five principalities[v] amid rampant cruelty and debauchery.	Infighting in the 12th century between Sunni and Shia, Arabs and Persians brought about by the declining authority of the Caliphate created a power vacuum leading to Turkish, Norman, and Mongol conquests.
View of Human Nature	**View of Human Nature**
"Machiavelli's judgment is more categorical, he views human nature as selfish, aggressive and acquisitive, which places men in a condition of constant conflict and competition that would result in anarchy unless restrained by laws backed by a powerful ruler."[20]	"To Ibn Zafar, evil is generally inherent in human beings, which cannot be changed . . . [However], as a Muslim, he is inclined to acknowledge the possibility of moderating human passions through education and religious belief."[21]
Role of Religion	**Role of Religion**
Religion is an instrument of the state to promote obedience.[vi]	The role of the state is to promote religion.

---

iv The 1968 race riots in the US and the 2020 "I can't breathe" and "Black Lives Matter" demonstrations following the brutal homicide of George Floyd at the hands of the police, support the argument that, without justice, the legitimacy of regimes is built on weak foundations. Borger, J. (2020), "James Mattis condemns Trump's handling of George Floyd protests," *The Guardian*, June 4, 2020, https://www.theguardian.com/us-news/2020/jun/03/james-mattis-comdemns-trump-george-floyd-protests, accessed on June 5, 2020.

v Florence, Milan, Naples, Papal States, and Venice.

vi Machiavelli's view predates Marx's description that religion is "the opiate of the people."

Table 11.2 (continued)

Machiavelli	Ibn Zafar
Qualities of the Ruler	**Qualities of the Ruler**
"For Machiavelli, the virtuous prince is one who has the will as well as the ability to achieve power and establish a stable political order . . . Consequently, power becomes the supreme virtue, as 'Machiavellian' has come to mean."[22] As far as Machiavelli was concerned, the ruler did not need to have all the qualities Ibn Zafar sought, but instead it was enough that the ruler was *perceived* to have them. More important he must be prepared to go against these qualities if needed to hold on to power by becoming cruel, inhuman, and irreligious.	"Ibn Zafar could not have accepted Machiavelli's advocacy of power as the ultimate virtue . . . Accordingly he lists a long chain of moral and instrumental qualities ranging from trust in God, fortitude, patience, contentment, and self-denial to paternal affection, vigilance, courage, sagacity, foresight, generosity, firmness, impartiality, and righteousness."[23] Despite this list of virtues, Ibn Zafar recommended using artifice (*hila*), ruse (*makida*), and falsehood (*kazb*), but rejected the idea that appearance was enough. Most important was the creation of a just society.[24]
Choosing Advisers	**Choosing Advisers**
Machiavelli regarded choosing advisers to be "*of foremost importance.*"[25] "Rulers get the advisers they deserve for good rulers choose good ones, bad rulers bad ones. The easiest way of assessing a ruler's ability is to look at those who are members of his inner circle"[26] "When you see your advisor give more thought to his own interests than yours . . . then you can be sure such a person will never be a good advisor. You will never be able to trust him, for he who runs a government should never suggest anything that is not in the ruler's interests."[27] "The ruler, in order to get the best out of his advisor, should consider his advisor's interests, heaping honours on him, enriching him, placing him in his debt, ensuring he receives public recognition, so that he sees he cannot do better without him, that he has so many honours he desires no more, so much wealth he desires no more, so much status he fears the consequences of political upheaval."[28]	Ibn Zafar states a king's first duty is to choose "a faithful counsellor, from whose advice he may seek assistance in good as well as in adverse fortune" and that choice reflects the ruler's wisdom: "Counsel is the mirror of the intellect, if therefore you would like to know the capacity of anyone, ask for advice."[29] "If you would like to know whether good or bad prevails in the mind of a man, ask for his counsel." "Amongst faithful and far-sighted counsellors, he is most deserving of attention whose prosperity depends on your own, and whose safety is tied to yours. He who stands in such a position, exerting himself for your interests, will likewise serve and defend himself while fighting for you."[30] Ibn Zafar describes the *wazir* to the king of Persia as " . . . a man of mature years, astute, firm, clear-sighted, experienced in business, a theologian, and well-versed in languages, literature, science and the stratagems of war."[31] Good advisers must have the courage to speak truth to power, traitors are flatterers.[32]

Source: Based on Kechichian, J. A., and Dekmejian, R. H. (2003), *The Just Prince: A Manual of Leadership* (Singapore/Kuala Lumpur: Horizon Books), pp. 102–114.

When it comes to practical governance, both Machiavelli and Ibn Zafar agree on the following principles:

1. Refrain from oppressing the people,
2. Avoid being hated or despised as a result of behaving rapaciously,
3. Ensure the subjects have an interest in keeping their ruler in power,
4. Avoid excessive leniency,
5. Be vigilant and prepared for all possibilities, with adequate resources, reserves, funds, troops, and fortifications,
6. Learn from history and the actions of great men,
7. Always be ready to take advantage of opportunities in both war and peace,
8. Display strength of character, courage and nobility.[33]

The difference between Machiavelli and Ibn Zafar is summed up in Table 11.3.

Table 11.3: Machiavelli and Ibn Zafar's Summaries on Being a Prince.

Machiavelli: Ruler to be Feared	Ibn Zafar: Ruler as a Servant
" . . . One ought to be both loved and feared, but since it is difficult to accomplish both at the same time, I maintain it is much safer to be feared than loved, if you have to do without one of the two. Still a ruler should make himself feared in such a way that if he does not inspire love, at least he does not provoke hatred."[34]	"The most enslaved is the king, because he is bound to serve his subjects with body and mind. This is because the ruler must govern them, instruct them, defend them, provide for their prosperity, restrain the disobedient, assist the oppressed, ensure free movement, strengthen frontiers, devise and apply laws, collect excessive wealth and expend it for the public good, prevent revolution, eliminate civil discord and sedition. Besides all of this, the king stands in need of his subjects, endures various difficulties, must protect himself, carry on the duties of the state, seek out those who are able to give him good and honest counsel, and be prepared to repulse enemies."[35]

Mutuality

The concept of mutuality is to be found in all major ethical systems as the "Golden Rule":

> "Do unto others as you would have them do unto you" is the idea (also called the *law of reciprocity*) that may be the most universally applauded moral principle on Earth – the Golden Rule. Something like it appears in every major religion and ethical philosophy. The wording above is from the King James *Bible*, Matthew 7:12, however Hindu, Jewish, Buddhist, Confucian, and Zoroastrian versions of it appeared 3,000–500 years earlier . . .

. . . Similarly, around 500 BCE, Confucius wrote "What you do not want done to yourself, do not do to others." In contrast to the statement in Leviticus, which is found in the middle of a long list of rules, the Confucian rule has always been emphasized as a foundation of Confucian society.[36]

As far as ethics for decision-making is concerned, we are interested in the social contract ethics expressed in the "Golden Rule," which Rousseau re-interpreted[vii] as:

The essential point remains the same: that only where all are equally affected by the policy adopted can an equitable solution be expected:

'*The undertakings which bind us to the social body are obligatory only because they are mutual, and their nature is such that in fulfilling them we cannot work for others without working for ourselves . . . this admirable agreement between interest and justice gives to the common deliberations an equitable character which at once vanishes when any particular question is discussed, in the absence of a common interest to unite and identify the ruling of the judge with that of the party.*'

Provided this condition is met, nobody will deliberately vote for a burdensome law because it will be burdensome to him too: this is why no specific limitations on the 'general will' are needed . . . Among the various policies which would affect everyone in the same way, each person has to decide which would benefit himself the most – and, since everyone else is similarly circumstanced, he is automatically deciding at the same time which would benefit everyone else the most.[37]   [Emphases ours]

The concept of mutuality makes it possible to foresee whether there will be resistance to the imposition of rules on members of a community or employees of an organization. People are more likely to agree to decisions that limit their freedoms if they are perceived to be equal in application and beneficial to the group as a whole. This became apparent in the UK in 2020 during the Covid-19 pandemic where rules strictly applied to the public were waived for ministers and their advisers, causing resentment and a breakdown of trust.[38]

Predictability

Decision-makers should provide clarity and predictability for those affected by their decisions if there is to be order and consistency in the way people implement decisions. People need a mix of laws, regulations, rules, and operating procedures to let them know what they can and cannot do, how they are expected to act, the penalties they face for breaking those laws and rules, and guidance on the best ways to do what is asked of them.

---

vii Rousseau, Jean-Jacques (1712–1778), published in 1762, *Of the Social Contract, Principles of Political Right.*

The German philosopher, Immanuel Kant, provided a comprehensive framework[viii] for setting rules, recognizing the need for predictability that satisfied the demands of fairness. He divided rules into two types: *maxims* and *imperatives*. He argued that since humans are rational, actions always aim at some sort of end or goal, captured by a *maxim* – a subjective rule or policy of action explaining what a person is doing and why.[39] Even when doing something as apparently simple as having a coffee, the process or "script" may differ. For example, ordering a cup of coffee in Starbucks is quite different from ordering one in a restaurant. To avoid making a process mistake in enjoying a coffee, the customer must know the appropriate procedure to achieve a predictable experience and outcome. *Maxims* describe such procedural steps. Kant's *hypothetical imperatives* describe how people *ought* to behave and are the basis of standard operating procedures, which are generally applicable, for example, to anyone wishing to get a coffee, but would not be appropriate for people who do not want a coffee, nor can they be identical in every environment where coffee is served. *They are customized to suit the context* and circumstances of each outlet.

Kant also provided a predictable set of rules called *categorical imperatives*. These are formal rules describing how people *should behave without making any reference to their actions*. Categorical imperatives are those that all should adopt, regardless of the circumstances involved.[ix]

Categorical imperatives apply to people no matter what their goals and desires may be, unlike hypothetical imperatives that apply to people only if they have desires that they want to satisfy, defining how to satisfy those specific desires. *The categorical imperative to help others in need does not apply to people only if they desire to help others in need, and the duty not to steal is not suspended if they have some desire that they could satisfy by stealing.*

Utility

Utilitarianism focuses actual, direct, and indirect consequences of decisions by attempting to measure the pleasure and pain created. It views the most important goal for humanity as maximizing pleasure and minimizing pain.[x] However, that does not

---

viii Kant, Immanuel (1724–1804), wrote in 1781/1787 *Critique of Pure Reason*.
ix The need for this universalist approach in certain circumstances is demonstrated by the anger and outrage felt by the British public in May 2020 when they discovered that Dominic Cummings, an unelected special adviser to Boris Johnson, the British Prime Minister, broke the pandemic lockdown rules, rules which he had put in place, because he felt they did not apply to him, a position defended by the Prime Minister. Bagehot (2020), "Dominic Cummings and Boris Johnson: united by a shared contempt for rules," *The Economist*, May 28, 2020, https://www.economist.com/britain/2020/05/28/dominic-cummings-and-boris-johnson-united-by-a-shared-contempt-for-rules, accessed on June 5, 2020.
x Utilitarianism reflects the thinking of Jeremy Bentham (1746–1832) and John Stuart Mill (1806–1873).

mean it is enough for a majority to want something that harms the minority, if it did, it would justify persecution of minorities, genocide, and ethnic cleansing. The pain or loss of the minority may be much greater than the pleasure or gain of the majority and so outweigh it:

> These claims are often summarized in the slogan that an act is right if and only if it causes "the greatest happiness for the greatest number." This slogan is misleading, however. An act can increase happiness for most (the greatest number of) people but still fail to maximize the net good in the world if the smaller number of people whose happiness is not increased lose much more than the greater number gains. *The principle of utility would not allow that kind of sacrifice of the smaller number to the greater number unless the net good overall is increased more than any alternative.*[40]   [Emphasis ours]

Self-Image

Personalistic ethics (or self-image) ethics are subjective. They reflect the inner values and purpose of each individual. They matter a great deal when people agree to do something which conflicts with their inner values and purpose – violating their values and purpose will discredit them in their own eyes and those of their colleagues and friends. Equally, harmony with their inner values and purpose will reinforce their self-image, reputation, and authenticity, making it easier for them to implement a similar decision in the future.

Ethical and Effective Decision-Making

Making decisions that are both ethical *and* effective decisions requires decision-makers to consider six steps in a cycle:

1. They must establish their own ethical foundations or *virtue*, which should reflect their values (principles) and purpose. Once done, they should move to step 2.
2. The second step is to determine the *effectiveness* of their proposed actions in achieving their purpose, namely whether the "ends justify the means." Only once they have verified that the proposed actions will deliver the desired ends, should they move to step 3.
3. The third step is to make sure actions are acceptably *mutual*, that they represent an equally fair burden on all affected. Only once decision makers are sure their intended actions are generally acceptable, should they move to step 4. (It is most unlikely that unanimous consent can be obtained, but significant dissent should be avoided.)
4. The fourth step is to ensure they pass the *predictability* test and that everybody knows what is expected of them in various circumstances. Without this step, implementing decisions will be ad hoc, often contradictory, and create confusion.

Only once appropriate policies and procedures are in place should decision makers move to step 5.
5. A critical part of evaluation is to determine whether it delivers the maximum benefit for the maximum number of people affected by it – its *utility*. Once decision-makers have a reasonable belief that what they are proposing will deliver the greatest good for the greatest number, should they move to step 6.
6. Finally, decision-makers must decide whether they are personally comfortable with what they are proposing or what they are agreeing to, based on *self-image ethics*.

If at any step in the cycle there is an obstacle to moving to the next step, it is a red flag, warning decision-makers that the decision might be unethical, ineffective, or both. *If such a red flag is detected, decision-makers must re-examine their assumptions, reasoning, and whether the risks are worthwhile.*

Figure 11.1 illustrates the cycle and how it starts all over again.

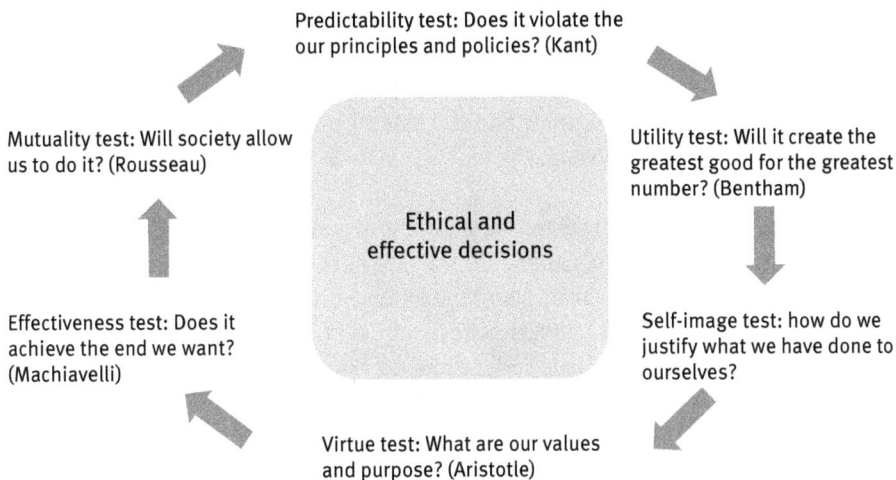

Predictability test: Does it violate the our principles and policies? (Kant)

Mutuality test: Will society allow us to do it? (Rousseau)

Utility test: Will it create the greatest good for the greatest number? (Bentham)

Ethical and effective decisions

Effectiveness test: Does it achieve the end we want? (Machiavelli)

Self-image test: how do we justify what we have done to ourselves?

Virtue test: What are our values and purpose? (Aristotle)

Figure 11.1: Ethical and Effective Decision-Making Cycle.

Covid-19 provides a useful test for this decision-making cycle. For example, if there is a shortage of ventilators during a pandemic (as happened in Northern Italy in 2020 and again at the beginning of 2021 in the US and UK) how should doctors decide which critically ill patient should be put on a ventilator?
1. **Effectiveness:** The first criterion is effectiveness, namely what are the patient's chances of recovery?
2. **Mutuality:** The second is whether the decision can be justified in terms of mutuality – i.e., be seen by all concerned to be fair. This means that society as a whole agrees that this choice makes sense.

3. **Predictability:** The third is that it passes the predictability test, that patient triage is on the basis of universally agreed and acceptable rules.

4. *Utility:* This criterion is harder to apply. How should doctors choose between saving the life of an elderly person with not many years left to live, but who nevertheless is a world recognized authority in epidemiology (for example) and a student who has yet to graduate so that they have no appreciation of the great things she will create throughout her longer expected life? How is a family supposed to decide which of one of three Covid-infected members should get treated when there is only one ventilator available: the husband, the wife, or their child? It does not just depend on the economic value of each of their lives, but also the emotional value and the culture to which the family belongs because that will determine priorities. A difficult balance is required from decision makers between their personal values and beliefs and those of the group or individuals affected. Faced with this type of choice, the UK government chose to roll out scarce vaccines to *all* the most-at-risk elderly after their receiving *only the first of a two-shot vaccine*, even though effectiveness was less than if they had waited until they had all received both shots, arguing that it is better to vaccinate both grandparents once to achieve some protection for both of them, than one grandparent twice, leaving one very well-protected and the other with no protection at all. Fortunately for all concerned, it turned out that delaying the second dose proved to be the correct decision to make.[41]

It is easier for decision makers when values of those making decisions, and the values of those affected by them are shared. The adverse effect of the lack of a shared value system can be seen in the debates about the relative merit of protecting particular at-risk groups from the medical adverse effects of Covid by lockdowns and protecting the economy by reopening schools and businesses. Small countries (e.g., New Zealand, Singapore) and those with more communitarian shared values (e.g., China, Japan, and South Korea) have generally been more able to implement policies that are complied with by their populations and, consequently, have achieved better outcomes than large countries with groups with competing value systems and a focus on the importance of individuals rather than the community (e.g., USA, UK).

The importance of publicly declared values for organizations is highlighted when ethical utility is considered. Making the values explicit means that all know what kinds of decisions are to be expected in particular circumstances. Stakeholders who disagree with the declared value system can disengage from the organization. For example, employees can choose to work elsewhere, investors can decide to stop holding shares, banks can refuse to continue lending, and governments and regulators can make it difficult for such organizations to continue their contentious practices.

Once decision makers have considered ethical utility, they will want to move to the fifth step.

5. ***Self-image:*** Personalistic ethics matter more than many people realize. Doctors and nurses in the Covid pandemic frontline who have had to make choices between who lives and who dies have experienced "moral injury" – incredible levels of personal distress and anguish – because making such choices violates the values that made them enter medicine in the first place.[42]

6. ***Virtue:*** The choices doctors make in the example above will reflect and affect their values and purposes in life. Ethical choices people are comfortable with will reinforce their self-respect and sense of virtue. Decisions that violate their values and purpose will diminish their self-respect and sense of virtue. Compromises people are forced to make that violate their values make it easier for them to behave less ethically the next time they are faced with difficult choices, making them less virtuous. This affects their judgment the next time they follow the six steps of the ethical-effectiveness decision-making cycle.

Applying the Six Steps

It is often said that business ethics are an oxymoron. We do not agree. We believe that the six-step ethical framework can be applied to business by combining the self-image and virtue tests into one test, with "wayfinders" using the "Five Ps" framework (discussed in Chapter 6) as a guide to ensure that business decisions are both ethical and effective, as follows:

1. ***"Purpose"***: Choosing the mission and vision for any organization is both an ethical and commercial decision. Ethics are involved in deciding what kind of business the organization should do and in deciding what products or services are going to be offered. In making such decisions, "wayfinders" must consider the benefits they are proposing – answering the question, "What difference will they make in the lives of our customers?" The ethical answer to this question includes:

   a. *Effectiveness test:* Will the products do what they are supposed to do and allow the organization to make a satisfactory return – the ends (creating and maintaining satisfied customers) must at least justify the means (allocating resources needed to do so).

   b. *Predictability test:* In marketing products, organizations should provide clarity, predictability, and consistency of performance as part of branding. In addition, people in organizations need to know what they can and cannot do in their dealings with internal and external customers. This is the point of codes of conduct and defined procedures internally to complement the externally imposed rules and regulations, with guidance on how to comply and clear penalties for breaking them.

   c. *Mutuality test:* This includes two separate ideas. The first is based on the "Golden Rule" – treating other people as you would expect to be treated. The second builds on this, dealing with implicit and explicit social contracts covering environment, safety, health, and equality, and the damage done by externalities to the environment (pollution, waste, congestion) caused by either legal but harmful behavior (such as the tobacco or junk food business) or illegal behavior, regarded as "the cost of doing business."

d. *Utility test:* At its simplest level, this is stakeholder satisfaction. However, it becomes more complicated if satisfying stakeholders has unintended knock-on effects that harm other people. For example, there seems to be no issue with satisfying customers who want to eat junk food and sweets, or drink sugary drinks and alcohol, or smoke. Surely, if they wish to harm themselves after having been advised of the risks, that is their business? Yet, people who get diabetes and heart disease put a burden on public health systems and increase the taxes for everybody.

e. *Virtue and self-image tests:* This explains why some people do not wish to work for companies whose products are harmful, yet legal. They do not want to be associated with the products they offer, or the way they do business. Others have no qualms, as long as the business is legal. How people see themselves depends on their virtue ethics and whether there is internal conflict between the organization's purpose and values and their own (the virtue test). People who ignore such conflicts risk losing their self-respect and the respect that other people have for them.

2. ***"Principles"***: These define what business the organization is willing to do, with whom, and how. They need to pass the:

a. *Effectiveness test*: Here the question raised by the application of principles is what impact will sticking to declared principles have on the viability of the business? If sticking to principles means that it is impossible to do business (for example, because of corruption in a particular jurisdiction), some organizations violate their principles and justify their actions based on the impact on the bottom line. Others make the tougher decision to not get involved in such markets. What is clear is that declaring one thing, but doing another, leads to a breakdown of trust between the organization and its customers and between the organization and its members. This applies with even greater force when people who violate the declared principles are excused either because of their seniority or because of their importance to the bottom line. In declaring principles of behavior by which the organization will be judged, it is essential that all are held to them, lest they become ineffective.

b. *Predictability test:* Principles pass the predictability test if they are spelled out clearly in codes of conduct and the consequences of failure to abide by them are understood by all. If there are many waivers or exceptions to the rules, they become discredited and a source of cynical disengagement.

c. *Mutuality test:* Society depends on businesses obeying the law and regulations designed to protect the common good, as a minimum. Most organizations declare that they will obey the law and many go beyond that in their declarations of corporate responsibility. Some choose to the break the law and pay the fines on the grounds that this is "the cost of doing business." While this may make sense for the individual organization, the costs to society of "free riding" and lawlessness are high.

d. *Utility test:* When deciding which principles to adopt and adhere to, leaders must recognize that sticking to principles incurs a cost, otherwise they would not be principles. This may mean that sticking to the principles makes it impossible to do certain kinds of business or to do business with certain types of regime or customer. If that is the case, the consequent loss of business must be recognized explicitly and people should not be penalized for losing the business because they adhered to the principles. Equally, if espoused principles are undermined by exceptions being made because certain individuals are senior or too important for the bottom line, the principles cease to have value. Clearly articulated principles help build an organizational personality that allows suppliers, employees, customers, and regulators to know what behavior to expect.

e. *Virtue and self-image tests:* If there is a serious divergence between the espoused values and purpose of the organization and those of individuals working within it, they will be disaffected and disengaged, reflecting the impact of the divergence on their personal values and purpose (the virtue test), and thus how they feel about themselves and are perceived by those who matter to them.

3. **"Power"**: Power is a function of the organizational design. It includes structural relationships between business units, divisions, departments and teams, and reporting relationships within them. Their validity and duration depend on their ability to pass the:

a. *Effectiveness test:* Once strategic objectives and priorities change, organizational designs must reflect the changed context to avoid misallocation of resources, putting people's futures at risk.

b. *Predictability test:* Organization designs change over time. The resulting impact on people in terms of remuneration, job scope, career, and reporting relationships should be understandable.

c. *Mutuality test:* This is particularly important when it comes to appraisals and development plans for individuals. Processes should be fair, transparent, and objective. Evaluations should reflect results achieved and how they were achieved, including cross-departmental collaboration. It also matters when it comes to bullying, sexual harassment, and discrimination of all kinds, as these behaviors are the result of the power structure violating the "Golden Rule."

d. *Utility test:* Engaged employees lead to higher levels of productivity and innovation. Reporting relationships that treat subordinates with respect, allowing people to speak truth to power, help organizations avoid mistakes in execution, maximizing bottom-up, top-down flows of information. Some organizations choose to operate top down and "need to know" styles of management, others choose to grant autonomy to employees, treating them as intelligent contributors capable of solving problems on their own. Such organizations may be more adaptable and have lower levels of employee turnover, depending on operating context.

e. *Virtue and self-image tests:* Here it is a case of whether employees are satisfied with their working conditions and their ability to contribute. It will reflect not just their working conditions but also the impact on their personal values and purpose (the virtue test) The test is: are they good ambassadors for their organizations?

4. **"People"**: Every organization consists of people. It must have the right number of people to meet current and future organizational design needs, with the right skills, attitude, and character. Such people should be able to feel comfortable with the mission, vision, and values of the organization, committing to achieving its goals. To do this, they must pass the:

a. *Effectiveness test:* On all key KPIs, they should perform on average at least up to benchmarked expectations regarding turnover, gross margin, value added, and profit per capita, achieve high employee engagement measures and have lower than industry/sector levels of attrition.

b. *Predictability test:* People are chosen and promoted on merit, not discriminated against on grounds of gender, race, or religion, and evaluated regularly based on objective assessments of their performance and how they have achieved their results in line with the principles of the organization.

c. *Mutuality test:* People understand where they fit in the organization and have a clear "line of sight" between the organization's superordinate goals and their individual role and responsibilities in achieving them. They recognize how their career and personal development plans are built, and regard the process as equitable.

d. *Utility test:* As long as they perform according to the values of the organization and meet their targets, the system is the best for them as individuals and the organization.

e. *Virtue and self-image tests:* They feel proud to be part of their work group and feel that they are respected by their friends and family as a result of working for the organization. The feeling of pride and belonging reflects the level to which their personal values and purpose (the virtue test) are in harmony with those of the organization.

5. **"Processes"**: These ensure alignment with mission and vision. They include all feedback mechanisms, formal and informal, and should provide full, relevant, timely, accurate, and actionable information. They must pass the:

a. *Effectiveness test:* All processes, including financial reports, management information, appraisal, and reward and remuneration systems must be justified.

b. *Predictability test:* All processes and procedures, including standard operating procedures (SOPs) and service level agreements (SLAs) should be evaluated in terms of their ability to eliminate surprises and manage expectations of accurate and on-time/on-cost delivery. It is important that they allow timely progress tracking to allow corrective action to get back to plan.

c. *Mutuality test:* Every activity and department must have proper procedures and processes.

d. *Utility test:* This does not apply.

e. *Self-image test:* This does not apply.

Moral relativists challenge the idea of universal ethics on the grounds that ethical systems are culturally determined and, therefore, subjective. This view presents serious practical problems for leaders. The difficulty often leads to ethics being ignored in books discussing approaches to leadership and management, or being discussed in such convoluted terms that they do not constitute a useful guide for practitioners. Leaders and managers ("wayfinders") shy away from ethical issues or take refuge in oversimplified approaches such as "shareholder value" as the sole ethical obligation. It is not an ethical obligation; it is an economic and legal one.

It seems to us that there are moral laws that are generally accepted regardless of culture, accurately described by C.S. Lewis.[43] He noted the difference between how people feel they *ought* to behave and how they *actually* behave. This distinction between what leaders feel they ought to do and what they actually do enables them to judge in a practical way whether they are behaving ethically or not. No leader, in our experience, says with pride, "I am a thief" or "I am corrupt" or "I damaged the environment," when they do such things, they add another specious justification to themselves and others, "If I didn't do it, someone else would" or "It is the local cultural practice to give gifts." The fact that leaders need to justify their behavior by claiming that "it isn't really what it appears to be" is the giveaway. When people behave ethically, they do not need to spend time justifying to themselves or to others why they have done what they have done.

We can illustrate the concept by imagining "Negative Manifestos." Imagine candidates for political office or people being interviewed to become CEO stating explicitly that they will be more corrupt, steal more, murder more, break the law more often, lie more, abuse human rights, and bully people more ruthlessly than their opponents. How likely do you think they are to be chosen?

We need to be clear here that we do not necessarily take Lewis's position on all matters of morality – but we do find his position that some things are universally recognized as "wrong" persuasive as a practical guide for leaders. We also recognize that this would not satisfy some philosophers, but we are writing for leaders who need practical solutions to the moral dilemmas that they encounter every day.

Without the power to make things happen, there is little point in advocating change. We believe strongly that "wayfinders" can and should be *both* ethical *and* effective.

The ethical elements of decision-making are determined by the purpose and goals of decision-makers and their treatment of others on the journey to achieving desired objectives. We recognize that:

> Making ethical decisions is easy when the facts are clear and the choices black and white. But it is a different story when the situation is clouded by ambiguity, incomplete information, multiple points of view, and conflicting responsibilities. In such situations which ["wayfinders"] experience all the time – *ethical decisions depend on both the decision-making process itself and on the experience, intelligence, and integrity of the decision-maker.*[44]   [Emphasis ours]

> Responsible moral judgment cannot be transferred to decision-makers ready-made. Developing an ethical approach in business turns out to be partly an administrative process involving recognition of a decision's ethical implications, discussion to expose different points of view, and testing the decision's adequacy in balancing self-interest and consideration of others, its import for future policy, and its consonance with the [organization's] traditional values. But after all this, if a clear consensus has not emerged, then the executive in charge must decide – drawing on his or her intuition and conviction. *This being so, the [character] of the decision maker is decisive – especially when an immediate decision must arise from instinct rather than from discussion.*[45]   [Emphases ours]

The best way for people to check whether they are comfortable with a decision and its likely results is to ask themselves if they would be able to sleep at night after making it, using the "newspaper headline test" or "newspaper test" to imagine how they and other people would feel about what happened when they read about the decision in the newspapers or, better yet, to imagine how they would explain/justify what they had done to their eight-year-old child.

Summary

Ethics are difficult because they mean different things to different people and there are six different approaches that need to be combined if decisions taken are to be both ethical and effective.

The six approaches divide into duty-based (deontological) ethics and consequential ethics. The former is black and white, doing right is more important than doing good. The latter recognizes shades of gray, right or wrong, depends on the results of decisions.

We argue that the most effective way to make both ethical and effective decisions is to combine the six ethical approaches of virtue, effectiveness, mutuality, predictability, utility, and self-image.

Virtue establishes the foundation for decision-making through *arête* (personal excellence), moderated by *phronesis* (moral wisdom) in seeking to achieve *eudaimonia* (happiness or flourishing) in Aristotelian thinking. In Confucian thinking, what matters are *ren* (benevolence), *xiao* (filial piety), *xin* (trustworthiness), *zhong* (loyalty), and *yi* (righteousness).

Effectiveness is premised on the "ends justifying the means" and is the first step in evaluating whether to act or not.

Mutuality or "The Golden Rule" comes next, assuming that the action will achieve the intended consequences. It is important to establish whether what is proposed will be acceptable to the community or the society it will affect. Rousseau's "Social Contract" mutuality and its underlying principles determine the sustainability of what is being proposed.

Predictability determines the rules of the game. Kant distinguished between *maxims* and *hypothetical imperatives*. These form the basis of standard operating procedures, generalizable in principle, but customized to suit individual contexts and circumstances, providing predictability as a result. *Categorical imperatives*, however, are a predictable, unconditional set of rules of behavior that define behavior regardless of who people are and of their circumstances.

Utility assumes that Bentham's hedonistic calculus is the best way to determine future behavior. It is a practical approach to most problems but suffers from three drawbacks. The first is that it assumes that all relevant consequences of future actions are knowable and known, often not the case. The second is that it can be used as a justification of the tyranny of the majority over the minority. The third is that we are not just "economic" beings, we are emotional and thymotic as well.

We conclude that decision-makers can reconcile duty-based with consequential ethics to make ethical and effective decisions by adopting the six-step cycle of evaluation in conjunction with the "Five Ps" framework while remembering Lewis's test of the difference between how they feel they *ought* to behave and how they *actually* behave.

References

1 Andrews, K. R. (2003), "Ethics in Practice," *Harvard Business Review on Corporate Ethics* (Boston, MA: Harvard Business School Publishing Corporation), pp. 71–72.

2 Neves, M. P. (2016), "Ethics, as a Philosophical Discipline," Bioethics Research Centre, Bioethics Institute, Catholic University of Portugal, Porto, Portugal, published in *Encyclopedia of Global Bioethics*, January 2016, pp. 2–3.

3 Ibid., p. 16.

4 Hursthouse, R., and Pettigrove, G. (2018), "Virtue Ethics," *Stanford Encyclopedia of Philosophy*, (Winter 2018), https://plato.stanford.edu/archives/win2018/entries/ethics-virtue/, accessed on May 24, 2020.

5 Ibid.

6 Ibid.

7 Ibid.

8 Tan, D., and Snell, R. S. (2002), "The Third Eye: Exploring Guanxi and Relational Morality in the Workplace," *Journal of Business Ethics,* December 2002, p. 362.

9 Csikszentmihalyi, M. (2020), "Confucius," *The Stanford Encyclopedia of Philosophy* (Summer 2020 Edition), https://plato.stanford.edu/archives/sum2020/entries/confucius/, accessed on May 24, 2020.

10 Aristotle, quoted by Russell, B. (1947) *The History of Western Philosophy* (London: George Allen & Unwin), p. 198.

11 Mack, L. (2019), "Filial Piety: An Important Chinese Cultural Value," *ThoughtCo*, August 15, 2019, https://www.thoughtco.com/filial-piety-in-chinese-688386, accessed on May 24, 2020.

12 Confucius, *Analects*, 12, p. 7, quoted in Csikszentmihalyi (2020), op. cit.

13 Confucius, *Analects*, 15, p. 6, quoted in Brown, R. (2015), "Analects of Confucius: On Loyalty," *BrownBeat,* August 30, 2015, https://brownbeat.net/2015/08/analects-of-confucius-on-loyalty/, accessed on May 24, 2020.

14 Confucius, *Analects,* 2, p. 20 quoted in ibid.

15 Confucius, *Analects,* 14, p. 7, quoted in ibid.

16 Csikszentmihalyi (2020), op. cit.

17 Confucius, *The Rites of Record,* quoted in ibid.

18 Nesbitt, R. E. (2003), *The Geography of Thought* (New York: Free Press).

19 Sheikh Zayed bin Sultan Al Nahyan (2003), in Kechichian, J, A., and Dekmejian, R. H. (2003) "Foreword," *The Just Prince: A Manual of Leadership* (Singapore/Kuala Lumpur: Horizon Books), pp. 18–19.

20 Ibid., p. 109.

21 Ibid., pp. 108–109.

22 Ibid., pp. 109–110.

23 Ibid., p. 110.

24 Ibid., p. 111.

25 Machiavelli, N., *Selected Political Writings,* edited and translated by Wootton, D. (1994) (Indianapolis: Hackett Publishing Co.), p. 70.

26 Ibid., p. 70.

27 Ibid., p. 71.

28 Ibid.

29 Ibn Zafar, "Sulwan Al-Muta' Fi 'Udwan Al-Atba'" in Kechichian and Dekmejian (2003), op. cit., p. 162.

30 Ibid., p. 273.

31 Ibid., p. 197.

32 Ibid., p. 273.

33 Kechichian and Dekmejian (2003), op. cit., pp. 111–112.

34 Machiavelli, N. (1994) op. cit., pp. 51–52.

35 Ibn Zafar, "Sulwan Al-Muta' Fi 'Udwan Al-Atba'" in Kechichian and Dekmejian (2003), op. cit., pp. 327–328.

36 "Golden Rule," *Philosophy Terms,* https://philosophyterms.com/golden-rule/, accessed on May 28, 2020.

37 Rousseau, J-J. (1762), *Contrat Social,* quoted in Barry, B. (1964), "The Public Interest" from the Proceedings of the Aristotelian Society, Supp. Vol. 38 (1964), pp. 1–18, in ed. Quinn, A. (1967), *Political Philosophy* (Oxford: Oxford Readings in Political Philosophy), pp. 121–122.

38 Fancourt, D., Steptoe, A., and Wright, L. (2020), "The Cummings effect: politics, trust, and behaviours during the COVID-19 pandemic," *The Lancet,* August 6, 2020, https://www.thelancet.com/journals/lancet/article/PIIS0140-6736(20)31690-1/fulltext, accessed on January 1, 2021.

39 Rohlf, M. (2020), "Immanuel Kant," *The Stanford Encyclopedia of Philosophy* (Spring 2020 Edition), https://plato.stanford.edu/archives/spr2020/entries/kant/, accessed on May 26, 2020.

40 Sinnott-Armstrong, W. (2019), "Consequentialism," *The Stanford Encyclopedia of Philosophy* (Summer 2019 Edition), https://plato.stanford.edu/archives/sum2019/entries/consequentialism/, accessed on May 28, 2020.

41 Associated Press (2021), "UK Says New Study Vindicates Delaying 2nd Virus Shot", *US News*, February 3, 2021, https://www.usnews.com/news/business/articles/2021-02-03/uk-new-study-vindicates-delaying-2nd-virus-vaccine-dose, accessed on February 12, 2021

42 BBC (2020), "Coronavirus: Why healthcare workers are at risk of moral injury," *BBC News*, April 6, 2020, https://www.bbc.com/news/world-us-canada-52144859, accessed on June 25, 2020.

43 Lewis, C. S. (1941), "The Reality of the Moral Law" (BBC Talk 2, *Mere Christianity*, Chapter 2) broadcast on August 13, 1941, *YouTube*, https://www.youtube.com/watch?v=LqsAzlFS91A&list=PL9boiLqIabFhrqabptq3ThGdwNanr65xU, accessed on December 26, 2020.

44 Andrews (2003), op. cit., pp. 71.

45 Ibid., pp. 71–72.

List of Figures

https://doi.org/10.1515/9783110707878-015

List of Tables

https://doi.org/10.1515/9783110707878-016

About the Authors

John Zinkin has written five books on corporate governance (CG): *The Challenge of Sustainability: Corporate Governance in a Complicated World* (2020), *Better Governance Across the Board: Creating Value Through Reputation, People and Processes* (2019), both published by De Gruyter, and *Rebuilding Trust in Banks: The Role of Leadership and Governance* (2014), *Challenges in Implementing Corporate Governance: Whose Business is it Anyway?* (2010), and *Corporate Governance* (2005), published by John Wiley & Sons. He contributed a chapter on "Corporate Governance in Asia Pacific" and another chapter on "Corporate Governance in an Age of Populism" for the *Handbook on Corporate Governance, 2nd edition*, edited by Professor Richard Leblanc, published in 2020 by John Wiley & Sons.

He is a certified training professional. His specialties are "Leading Brand-Based Change," "Reconciling Leadership and Governance" and "Ethics in Business." He has led board effectiveness evaluations in banking, insurance and government entities and has written codes of conduct and board charters for several development banks. Since 2007, he has trained more than 1,700 directors in CG as well as senior managers of public listed companies. He has trained securities regulators from Cambodia, Hong Kong, Laos, Malaysia, Philippines, Singapore, Thailand and Vietnam on behalf of the Australian Government as part of their CG capacity building programs in ASEAN and APEC.

Starting in 1971, John worked in the UK in fast-moving consumer goods (Unilever), insurance broking (Hogg Robinson), management consulting (McKinsey), and office products (Rank Xerox) before moving to Hong Kong in 1985 for Inchcape Pacific. There John ran marketing and distribution companies in a variety of industries across Asia Pacific, before joining Burson-Marsteller in 1997 as the Asia-Pacific Marketing and Change Management Practice Chair. John moved to Malaysia in 2001 and from 2001 to 2006, was Associate Professor of Marketing and Strategy at Nottingham University Business School, Malaysia Campus, responsible for its MBA program. In 2006 he set up the Securities Industry Development Corporation, the training arm of the Securities Commission Malaysia and in 2011 he was appointed Managing Director, Corporate Governance of the Iclif Leadership and Governance Centre under Bank Negara Malaysia, responsible for training directors of banks and insurance companies in CG. Since 2013, he works independently as the Managing Director of Zinkin Ettinger Sendirian Berhad, a boutique consultancy specializing in CG, brand-based change and ethical leadership.

John graduated from Oxford University with a BA in Politics, Philosophy and Economics (1968) and the London Business School with an MSc in Business Administration (1971).

Christopher Bennett has had a wide ranging career as a director, senior executive, researcher, consultant, and teacher/facilitator. His significant international exposure and working experience includes having lived and worked in six countries and held directorships for major British and American companies in 13. Additionally, he has held senior managerial responsibilities in more than 20 countries across Asia, the Middle East, Europe, Australia, NZ, and the Americas. His employers include Bechtel, Honeywell, Burmah Castrol, BP, Towers Perrin, and Watson Wyatt. He has significant experience of directorship, general management, and Senior HR roles across the engineering construction, electronics, oil and gas, and consulting sectors. Much of his board consulting work was in the banking and finance sectors.

https://doi.org/10.1515/9783110707878-017

His functional career has three main episodes: first as a human resources executive and director, second as a chief executive and director, third as consultant at board level. His observations and experiences led him to a deep interest in the ways in which individual and group behavior manifest in decision making and approaches to corporate governance of individual directors and boards of directors in different cultures, situations, and in complex company groups.

He was a faculty member of ICLIF (the International Centre for Leadership in Finance – an arm of Bank Negara Malaysia – now part of the Asia School of Business) and is currently an adjunct member of the faculty. He also serves on the faculty of Australian Institute of Company Directors and has facilitated programs for directors in Australia, Shanghai, Hong Kong, Singapore, Jakarta, and Dubai.

He is a doctoral researcher at Aston University where he explores the cultural and behavioral aspects of board and top management team decision making in multicultural, multinational, and complex company groups.

Chris lives in Kuala Lumpur. His publications (with Professor Mak Yuen Teen, National University of Singapore) include *Guardians of the Capital Markets* (BPA 2016), *Insuring the Future* (The Iclif Leadership and Governance Centre 2015); *The Governance of Company Groups* (CPA Australia & Iclif 2014), *Directors Daze* (BPA 2014), *Corporate Governance of 50 Largest Asian Banks* (BPA 2013), and numerous articles and newsletters (http://www.bpa-australasia.com).

Index

https://doi.org/10.1515/9783110707878-018

www.ingramcontent.com/pod-product-compliance
Lightning Source LLC
Chambersburg PA
CBHW061759210326
41599CB00034B/6812